Understanding Crime Prevention

This book offers a concise and authoritative overview of the full scope of crime prevention, including foundations, theory, application, and techniques. It details how theory sets the groundwork for the practical application of successful crime prevention strategies and illustrates the foundations of and need for crime prevention, the best approaches to implementing crime prevention programs, and the issues that need to be considered when evaluating crime prevention programs. The book is split into three parts, which include:

- Theoretical Foundations. This part includes a brief overview of the history and growth of crime prevention as a field of study, and in practice.
- Crime Patterns and Concentration. This part covers the causes and effects of both large- and small-scale crime concentration, with particular focus on the development of major forms of crime concentration, including hotspots, risky facilities, hot products, repeat offenders, and recurring victims.
- Crime Prevention Application. This part is centered on the practice of crime prevention, focusing on the development and implementation of actual crime prevention programs, including the role of both law enforcement and non-law enforcement agencies.

Understanding Crime Prevention has built-in pedagogical features, including a range of tables, boxed examples, and case studies, as well as discussion questions. This book is essential reading for advanced courses on crime prevention, as well as related courses on policing, crime control, theory, and criminal justice.

Billy Henson is Associate Professor in the Department of Criminal Justice and Social Work at University of Houston-Downtown, USA.

Bradford W. Reyns is Professor in the Department of Criminal Justice at Weber State University, USA.

Jamie A. Snyder is Associate Professor of Criminal Justice at the University of Wyoming, USA.

Heidi Scherer is Professor of Criminal Justice at Kennesaw State University, USA.

Understanding Crime Prevention

From Theory to Practical Application

Billy Henson, Bradford W. Reyns,
Jamie A. Snyder, and Heidi Scherer

Routledge
Taylor & Francis Group
LONDON AND NEW YORK

Designed cover image: © Shutterstock Images / kentoh

First published 2025
by Routledge
4 Park Square, Milton Park, Abingdon, Oxon OX14 4RN

and by Routledge
605 Third Avenue, New York, NY 10158

Routledge is an imprint of the Taylor & Francis Group, an informa business

British Library Cataloguing-in-Publication Data
A catalogue record for this book is available from the British Library

ISBN: 978-1-032-51282-2 (hbk)
ISBN: 978-1-032-51281-5 (pbk)
ISBN: 978-1-003-40155-1 (ebk)

DOI: 10.4324/9781003401551

Typeset in Sabon
by Apex CoVantage, LLC

Dedicated to Drs. John Eck, Bonnie Fisher, and Pamela Wilcox – our professors, mentors, and friends. Your profound influence has not only shaped our understanding of crime prevention but also helped ignite our love for teaching and research.

Contents

CONTENTS

Illustrations

Images

Breakout Boxes

Part 1
Theoretical Foundations

Chapter 1
Introduction to Crime Prevention

ROBERT PEEL

Introduction to Crime Prevention

Billy Henson

Chapter Outline

In this chapter, we will focus on:

Understanding Crime
- Crimes against persons
- Crimes against property
- Statutory crime
- White collar and financial crime
- The need for crime prevention

Defining Crime Prevention
- Crime prevention as an ideology
- Crime prevention as a methodology
- Crime prevention as an outcome
- Measuring crime prevention

Evolution of Crime Prevention
- Early attempts at crime prevention
- Modern crime prevention approaches

Learning Objectives

After reading this chapter, you should be able to:

1.1 Define the term crime prevention
1.2 Describe the goals of crime prevention
1.3 Explain how crime prevention has changed over time
1.4 Identify the key figures in the development of crime prevention
1.5 Hypothesize potential future approaches to crime prevention

DOI: 10.4324/9781003401551-2

Introduction

Criminal justice has grown and evolved over the course of millennia. In that time, there have been significant changes regarding the goals and practices that define the purpose of criminal justice. One of the newer approaches adopted within the criminal justice system is crime prevention. Crime prevention includes philosophies and processes focused on reducing the likelihood of crimes occurring, as well as the risk of their potential harmful effects on both individuals and communities, including harm, social disorder, and fear of crime. In order to more accurately understand how crime prevention operates, however, it is necessary to have a working knowledge of the various concepts that define it, as well as how it has evolved over time. With that in mind, this chapter will introduce the field of crime prevention by providing working definitions of the concept, outlining the overall evolution of the field, and highlighting many of the key figures responsible for its development.

Understanding Crime

To best understand the function of and need for crime prevention, it is beneficial to have a basic comprehension of the common types of crime. Of course, criminal codes will vary across countries, and even across jurisdictions within countries. However, while variation does exist, there are generally four main categories of criminal activity that are relatively universal – crimes against persons, crimes against property, statutory crimes, and white collar/financial crime. It should be kept in mind, though, that while these categories serve as an effective means to help distinguish between crime types, they may not be mutually exclusive, as some types of crime could exist in multiple categories. This fact should also be kept in mind when developing and evaluating crime prevention approaches, as specificity is an important aspect of crime prevention.

Crimes Against Persons

Crimes against persons are criminal acts that directly target an individual or individuals. Often referred to by terms such as violent crime, severe crime, or serious crime, crimes against persons usually involve the use or threat of force and are considered the most egregious forms of criminal behavior, including acts such as homicide, sexual assault, physical assault, robbery, and abuse. In addition, they typically have the highest likelihood of causing someone physical and/or emotional harm and, as a result, frequently carry the harshest legal sanctions and penalties.

Fortunately, crimes against persons are not as common as many people tend to think. In fact, they often make up a relatively small percentage of crimes that occur. For example, in the United States, crimes against persons represented only about 16 percent of serious crimes that occurred in 2022 (Statista, 2023). Further, the incidence of these types of crimes in the United States dropped by about 49 percent between 1994 and 2019 (Gramlich, 2020). While such trends exist, because of the nature of crimes against persons, however, they often receive the most attention from both law enforcement and the public. A simple search of the most popular television shows and podcasts will easily confirm it.

Crimes Against Property

As the term implies, **crimes against property** include criminal acts that target property rather than individuals. Most often, such acts are referred to as property crime or property offenses. Crimes against property are usually divided into two main categories – property theft and property damage. Property theft refers to taking another's property without permission or consent, including behaviors like larceny/theft, burglary, shoplifting, and auto theft. Property damage refers to harming or destroying another's property, including behaviors like vandalism, arson, and destruction of property. Property damage could also include damaging one's own property with the intent of committing fraud, such as burning down one's own home to collect insurance money. Since crimes against property do not typically result in as much physical or emotional harm as crimes against persons, they are seen as not as serious and often carry less harsh legal sanctions and penalties.

Another key difference between crimes against persons and crimes against property is that the latter occur much more frequently. In fact, the majority of serious crimes committed are crimes against property. To illustrate, crimes against property accounted for about 84 percent of all serious crime in the United States in 2022, with larceny making up over 60 percent of all serious crime that year (Statista, 2023). Further, as with crimes against persons, the rate of crimes against property in the United States has declined about 55 percent between 1994 and 2019 (Gramlich, 2020). Finally, certain forms of crimes against property, such as auto theft, tend to be the most commonly reported serious crimes. This is likely due to the necessity of a police report in many situations in order to file an insurance claim.

Statutory Crimes

Statutory crimes are any behaviors specifically prohibited by legal statutes or laws. Technically, all crimes are statutory crimes since they are prohibited by laws; however, statutory crimes in the present sense are minor deviant behaviors designated as dangerous or harmful to society. Additionally, statutory crimes are mainly specified and enforced on localized levels, like cities, counties, or even states. Some of the more common forms of statutory crimes include traffic violations, drug/alcohol violations, and prostitution. While there is a chance these types of behaviors could result in physical harm of another or property damage, the individual committing the act has the greatest chance of harm. As a result, statutory crimes most often carry minor sanctions and penalties, including fines and short periods in jail.

Given the variation and nature of statutory crimes, they are rarely reported on a national level. One caveat to this statement is the Federal Bureau of Investigation's (FBI) National Incident-Based Reporting System (NIBRIS) in the United States, which records information on certain types of statutory crimes on a national level. Instead, statutory crimes are more frequently tracked and analyzed on a local level. Because of this approach, it is much more difficult to examine large-scale statistics on statutory crimes. With that in mind, it should be noted that these types of crimes are seen often as dangerous or harmful to communities and they are often the motivation for many crime prevention programs.

White Collar and Financial Crime

White collar/financial crimes are a special category of crimes against property that are usually committed in conjunction with the offender's job position. Though it does not include every form of white collar/financial crime, the majority of these crimes occur within the business world, including crimes like embezzlement, tax evasion, securities fraud, and money laundering. With white collar/financial crimes, the victim may be an individual, a business or corporation, or even the government. Given the nature of these crimes, they are often investigated and prosecuted by federal or national law enforcement, such as the FBI and other agencies like the Securities and Exchange Commission (SEC).

White collar/financial crimes differ from other forms of crimes against property in that they are not considered street or traditional crime. Instead, they are considered an elevated form of property crime. Further, while individuals may be directly harmed by these types of crimes, it is more likely that white collar/financial crime will damage businesses and corporations, with the main consequence being financial loss. The FBI estimates that the United States loses over 300 billion dollars a year from financial crime (Legal Information Institute, 2023). Further, according to the Association of Certified Fraud Examiners (2020), businesses in the United States lose about 5 percent of their annual gross revenue to fraud. To help control such massive financial losses, crime prevention is extremely important for corporations. As a result, some of the most sophisticated forms of crime prevention, such are fraud detection programs and multilayer forensic accounting, are directly linked to the business world.

The Need for Crime Prevention

As highlighted throughout the previous discussion, criminal behavior is both varied and multifaceted. It is because of that very nature that reactive approaches have been the most common response when attempting to control crime. It can be easy to get overwhelmed when trying to control a seemingly unstoppable wave, and it may seem easier to simply clean up after the fact. Unfortunately, however, simply reacting to behavior after it occurs does little to stop the behavior or prevent individuals from being harmed by it. Fortunately, throughout history, there have been those who believed more could be done to combat crime, and, as a result, crime prevention has evolved.

Defining Crime Prevention

When discussing crime prevention, the actual meaning can be rather murky. It may be seen as a broad philosophy or as a specific approach. Further, understanding exactly where and how crime prevention fits into the larger field of criminal justice may be problematic without a proper understanding of its development over time. It is because of this potential for uncertainty that it is best to start with the basics. The term crime prevention is a multilayered label that has been affixed with several definitions. While each definition is understandably linked, variation exists between them as a direct result of the context and/or framework in which they are applied. Essentially, as with many terms, the meaning can change depending on how it is being used. Crime prevention may be defined as an overarching ideology, a methodology to prevent crime, or an outcome of specific programs and policies. Highlighted below, moving from a broader context to a narrow context, the meaning of crime prevention becomes more concrete and actionable.

Crime Prevention as an Ideology

As is the case with relatively all systems, the criminal justice system is guided largely by several underlying principles or ideologies. Stated simply, an **ideology** is a collection of principles that serve as the foundation for the theories and policies which guide a particular system. For example, within the criminal justice system, many theories and actions are founded on the ideology of crime control. **Crime control** is based on the assumption that the occurrence of crime is a given, meaning it is assumed that it will happen if the opportunity arises. Relatedly, the criminal justice system should then strive to control or limit the amount of crime that occurs. Essentially, "it points to the need for maintenance of a problem, one where crime is kept to a tolerable level" (Chainey & Ratcliffe, 2005, pp. 18–19). It is because of this ideology that the criminal justice system utilizes approaches such as incarceration, and more specifically policies like mandatory minimum sentences, in an effort to reduce or control the level of crime.

As an ideology, crime prevention is both intrinsically linked and diametrically opposed to the ideology of crime control. Crime prevention is grounded in the belief that crime can be prevented from ever occurring by addressing the underlying factors, or problems, that lead to it. While both ideologies focus on crime reduction, crime control tends to be reactive, focusing on crime after it transpires, whereas crime prevention is proactive, focusing on stopping or reducing crime before it happens. The crime prevention ideology is based largely on the public health model, which focuses on strategies to encourage healthy approaches and lifestyles within a community, to help prevent the potential outbreak of illnesses before they occur (CDC, 2022). Consequently, the central focus of both approaches – public health and crime prevention – is to address the root causes or issues that lead to larger problems. Specific theoretical frameworks and practical applications are then designed based on the more general ideology. In the case of crime prevention, theories, programs, and policies all focus on the factors the lead to crime, with the goal of removing or altering those factors in an attempt to prevent the opportunity for crime from ever occurring.

Crime Prevention as a Methodology

From ideologies often come tactics or methodologies. Whereas an ideology is typically a general concept or model, methodologies are more specific. Essentially, they are actions based on ideologies. For example, within the public health model, the general ideology is that if the underlying factors that cause illnesses can be addressed, then it is less likely an outbreak will occur (CDC, 2022). A methodology used to implement that ideology may include providing free vaccinations to the public. We see this approach with the flu. In many communities, flu vaccination shots may be available to the public, or at least specific groups, at no cost. The goal is to reduce the number of individuals who may contract and spread the flu and/or help prevent especially vulnerable individuals from getting ill.

Crime prevention methodologies are typically programs, policies, or practices that directly outline and implement methods of preventing crime. Although they may be instituted by various agencies, governments, or groups, crime prevention programs and tactics are most frequently utilized by law enforcement. Further, they are mainly used to target a specific form of crime. This ensures the tactics used can be tailored specifically to the problems and issues related to that crime. Attempting to develop a single program or tactic to prevent a wide range of crimes can be problematic, as the underlying factors that lead to different crimes can be varied and unique. For example, if a community has an issue with teenagers loitering and committing vandalism, creating a neighborhood recreation center could help prevent crime by giving the teens something to do after school. However, a recreation center would not be useful to help prevent crimes such as speeding or bank robbery.

Crime Prevention as an Outcome

Just as the goal of illness prevention practices is to prevent the growth of sickness, the goal of crime prevention approaches is to prevent the growth of crime. As such, the third and most specific definition of crime prevention is an outcome of a program or strategy designed to reduce crime. It is with this definition that we see the most overlap with crime control and crime reduction, as all three represent the lowering or maintaining of crime. Noted previously, this is also the most concrete definition of crime prevention since it can be measured and evaluated.

The most common application of crime prevention is the development of programs or strategies that target opportunities for crime. These programs or strategies are typically tailored toward specific types of crimes and/or environments because the opportunity structures for crimes are often unique to crime types and environments. To illustrate, while improving lighting is a common, often effective, strategy for preventing auto thefts in parking lots and garages at night, its impact on preventing bomb threats would be relatively low, as bomb threats typically occur during the day in well-lit buildings/areas. To evaluate the effectiveness of such strategies and programs, the level of crime prevented or reduced is often the outcome measure examined. In this case, crime prevention is both the goal and an outcome.

Measuring Crime Prevention

When examining crime prevention programs, strategies, or approaches, it is important to consider how prevention, itself, will be evaluated. Simply, how will it be determined if the approach was effective in preventing crime? To that end, as crime prevention is a relatively broad, and somewhat theoretical, concept, outcomes are usually examined with proxy measures. **Proxy measures** are indirect measures used to represent concepts that may not be directly measurable. For example, with a concept such as crime prevention, it is not really possible to determine how much crime *did not* occur, as you would need to know how much crime was going to occur before the prevention efforts were put into place. As a result, researchers use proxy measures to represent and estimate changes assumed to be caused by the program or initiative.

Depending on the goals of the crime prevention program or strategy, a wide array of proxy measures may be examined. For example, with their analysis of the effectiveness of improved street lighting on crime in public housing areas in the United Kingdom (UK), Painter and Farrington (1999) utilized measures of victimization prevalence and incidence as proxies for crime prevention. **Prevalence** refers to the number or proportion of individuals who have *ever* experienced a crime in their lifetime, while **incidence** refers to individuals who have experienced a crime in a given *period of time*, such as the last month, year, or since the beginning of the year. Additionally, some researchers examine variations in crime rates or recidivism rates as a proxy for crime prevention (Caplan et al., 2011; de Vries et al., 2018). If the crime or recidivism rate decreases, it is then typically assumed that crime was prevented. Others have examined outcomes that are related to crime but that are not necessarily crimes, including changes in community disorder or beliefs, such as fear of crime, feelings of safety, and reduction in social problems (Cho & Park, 2017; Cozens & Sun, 2019). As will be seen throughout this book, crime prevention is often much more than just the prevention of crime.

Evolution of Crime Prevention
It should come as no surprise that crime prevention is intrinsically linked to policing. Not only has crime prevention served as one of the main ideologies of law enforcement since the birth of modern policing, law enforcement officers are also the primary practitioners of crime prevention programs and strategies. While the goals and utilization of crime prevention have evolved over the past 300 years, it has remained ever present as both an ideology and approach for those who have been directly involved in addressing crime and disorder.

Early Attempts at Crime Prevention

Bow Street Runners
An argument could be made that crime prevention has existed in one form or another for most of human history. However, its modern roots, especially with regard to its utilization by law enforcement, can most clearly be traced back to just over 270 years ago, with the birth of the Bow Street Runners. Though not technically an official police force, the Bow Street Runners are often referenced as the first centralized police force in modern history (Brain, 2018). Along with establishing a model for policing, the Bow Street Runners also cemented the ideology and practice of crime prevention as a fundamental approach for law enforcement.

By the mid-1700s, the population of London was growing rapidly, making it one of the largest cities in Europe (Emsley et al., 2022). Understandably, with that population growth came an increase in criminal activity. In an effort to combat the criminal activity in his district, novelist and magistrate of the Bow Street Court, **Henry Fielding**, along with his half-brother

Magistrate John Fielding, developed a police force, consisting of six constables, whose main purpose was to prevent and respond to crime in the Bow Street area (Brain, 2018). Funded by a government grant, the Bow Street Runners became the first professional police force. In addition to investigating criminal activity, a practice performed by numerous groups in London at the time in exchange for payment or rewards, the Bow Street Runners were unique in that they also focused heavily on crime prevention (Brain, 2018). Deterrence and quick responses were the cornerstone of the Runners' approach. As a result, Henry Fielding had his constables patrol the streets, in an effort to prevent crime before it occurred. Later, his brother John also began publishing the *Quarterly Pursuit*, a weekly newspaper containing information about criminals and their acts (Brain, 2018). This allowed citizens to essentially begin a neighborhood watch, keeping an eye out for known criminals and reaching out to the constables if they had any information. Due to his utilization of preventative patrol and his early adoption of community policing, Henry Fielding is often labeled with the moniker, "Father of Crime Prevention."

The London Metropolitan Police Department

The Bow Street Runners continued championing the ideology of crime prevention until 1829, when they were replaced by the first true police force – the London Metropolitan Police Department (Brain, 2018; Britannica, 2022; Crime Prevention Website, 2022). An advocate for both reform and justice, Sir Robert Peel used his influence as Home Secretary of the UK to get the Metropolitan Police Act (1829) passed, which, in part, established the London Metropolitan Police Department. This would be the first large-scale, centralized, government-sanctioned police force and the model for many police forces to follow (Britannica, 2022; Crime Prevention Website, 2022). However, while this development would lead to many changes in law enforcement, one thing that remained constant was the focus on crime prevention.

In helping to establish the Metropolitan Police Department, Sir **Robert Peel** established his nine principles of policing. These have no doubt been echoed in Introduction to Policing classes for decades. With the current discussion, however, two of the principles are key. First, Peel noted that the main reason police should exist is to prevent crime and disorder. Next, he observed that the true test of the efficiency of law enforcement is not their reactive presence, but instead the absence of crime and disorder (Law Enforcement Action Partnership, 2021). Combined, these two principles indicate that Peel felt law enforcement should be about prevention rather than just reaction and that preventing crime alone should not be the sole goal, as reducing disorder and improving the overall well-being of citizens are as equally important. While there were many ups and downs, especially early on, the preventative actions of the Metropolitan Police Department were seemingly successful, as crime and disorder declined for some time in London (Britannica, 2022). As the Metropolitan Police Department's model became the foundation for other police forces throughout Europe and eventually the United States, the inclusion of crime prevention as an overarching ideology for how to deal with crime and disorder also continued.

Clifford Shaw's Chicago Area Project

While crime prevention was most often seen in the actions of law enforcement over the last couple of centuries, it has also been present in the work of sociology and criminology researchers. **Clifford Shaw** and Henry McKay are possibly two of the most well-known sociologists from the early twentieth century. Their work examining juvenile delinquency in Chicago produced one of the most well-known theories of crime causation – **social disorganization theory**. This theory proposes that the presence of three structural factors (low economic status, ethnic heterogeneity, and high residential mobility) leads to the disruption of social organization and cohesion within a community, which accounts for variations in crime and delinquency in that community (Sampson & Groves, 1989; Shaw & McKay, 1929). Almost 100 years later, their theory is still taught and discussed as a means of understanding the geographic distribution of crime. While their theory of juvenile delinquency may be the most well-known contribution of their study, it was not the only outcome of Shaw's work.

After examining juvenile delinquency in Chicago, Shaw wanted to try to do something to help address the issue. His solution was the Chicago Area Project (CAP). CAP is a Chicago-based organization that strives to improve the quality of life within the surrounding neighborhoods, focusing specifically on the issues and problems faced by juveniles and their families, including access to education, social services, and safe environments (CAP, 2022). In the early 1930s, Shaw introduced CAP in three of Chicago's highest crime areas with the goal of developing and evaluating delinquency prevention techniques. The areas selected were highly impoverished, heavily congested, occupied mainly with immigrant workers, and home to several gangs (CAP, 2022).

With CAP, Shaw's main goal was to make delinquency less attractive for juveniles. One of the main approaches he took was to work toward a community-oriented approach to crime prevention. In addition to encouraging families to take on more leadership roles within their community, Shaw also involved some of the problematic residents within the community in neighborhood plans and the decision-making process (CAP, 2022). He understood the power and influence that such people could have in a neighborhood, especially with juveniles. Shaw also worked to develop a delinquency prevention program within the area. He collaborated with local schools and reached out to parolees, as they re-entered the community, in an effort to reduce truancy and juvenile delinquency. He even invited former inmates to participate in the program to help show juveniles how their lives could turn out if they did not change their delinquent behaviors (CAP, 2022). With his efforts, not only did Shaw do much to help his community, but he also led the way in the development of community-oriented crime prevention.

Community-Oriented Policing

The early attempts at crime prevention utilized by law enforcement and researchers, alike, helped to pave the way for new crime prevention strategies during the first half of the twentieth century. In England and the United States, crime prevention developed, in large part, through the adoption of community-oriented policing. **Community-oriented policing** is a "philosophy that promotes organizational strategies that support the systematic use of partnerships and problem-solving techniques to proactively address the immediate conditions that give rise to public safety issues such as crime, social disorder, and fear of crime" (U.S. Department of Justice, 2014, p. 1). This practice encouraged police–citizen collaboration to prevent the opportunity for crimes to occur within a community.

Unfortunately, while popular during the late nineteenth century and early part of the twentieth century, community-oriented policing, and crime prevention more generally, fell somewhat out of favor among practitioners and researchers over the following decades. During that era, more attention was given to the change in crime and clearance rates as a measure of police success (U.S. Department of Justice, 1976). Other measures of success such as the increase or decrease in fear, social disorder, and public satisfaction were considered an afterthought. It would not be until the mid-1900s that government and police officials would come to the realization that crime prevention needed to be more than just arrest and clearance rates (U.S. Department of Justice, 1976). In 1950, a new crime prevention campaign developed by England's Home Secretary, in conjunction with several insurance companies, started in various parts of England. Further, in 1963 a formal training course in crime prevention was initiated for police officers by the Home Office at Stafford (U.S. Department of Justice, 1976). Finally, in 1968, England's Home Office recommended that crime prevention committees be utilized to help develop crime prevention programs in conjunction with local police and community representatives, beginning a resurgence in community-oriented policing (U.S. Department of Justice, 1976).

While the potential benefits of such crime prevention strategies were recognized by officials in the United States, it was not until 1968 that they began to gain momentum. Utilizing a grant from the Ford Foundation, the Dean of the School of Police Administration at the University of Louisville,

John Klotter, and his colleague Robert Cusick Jr., conducted a detailed study of burglary in the United States, describing the benefits of the English crime prevention strategy (Klotter & Cusick, 1968; U.S. Department of Justice, 1976). Based on the results of their study, Klotter and Cusick indicated that burglaries in the United States would continue to increase unless effective crime prevention actions were taken. Further, they recommended that the development and process of such actions involve cooperation between the police, the judicial system, and the public (Klotter & Cusick, 1968). In 1969, the Kentucky Crime Commission recognized the potential importance of such an approach to crime prevention and assisted the University of Louisville in obtaining additional grant funding to develop a pilot crime prevention training program (U.S. Department of Justice, 1976). Other states would soon follow, bringing community-oriented policing back to the forefront of U.S. crime prevention strategies.

Problem-Oriented Policing

Another approach to community-based crime prevention, developed during the 1970s and 1980s, was problem-oriented policing. Championed by **Herman Goldstein,** problem-oriented policing is an approach to crime prevention that focuses on the root causes of problems that lead to crime (Weisburd et al., 2010). Goldstein (1979) felt that the traditional incident-driven reactive tactics police were taking should be replaced with a more holistic problem-based approach, based largely on the assumption that if the basic problems within a community are addressed, then the opportunity for crime to develop can be prevented.

Community-oriented and problem-oriented policing quickly became linked, as both focused on preventing crime within communities by having police and community members work together to address the entire problem, not just the outcome (crime). Whereas community-oriented policing is more akin to an overarching philosophy asserting that the police and community members should work together to prevent crime, problem-oriented policing is a strategy for how the police and community members can work together to address specific crime problems. The two concepts have undergone continued refinement and conceptualization over time. Today, both are still common approaches utilized and championed by police departments. In fact, the Problem-Oriented Policing (POP) Center acknowledges law enforcement agencies' successful applications of problem-oriented policing strategies each year with the Herman Goldstein Award (POP Center, 2022).

Situational Crime Prevention

While problem-oriented policing was quick to gain popularity, many, including Goldstein himself, were worried that the approach would not be used as effectively as it could be (Clarke, 1997). Fortunately, the applicability of problem-oriented policing would receive a boost from the work of **Ronald Clarke**. Building on the theories and practices of environmental criminology, Clarke proposed what many consider to be among the first true crime prevention theories – **situational crime prevention**. Although other criminology theories had/have been utilized to apply and evaluate crime prevention practices, situational crime prevention was one of the first theories developed solely with the intent to expand and refine the application of crime prevention. Incorporating aspects of rational choice theory, routine activity theory, and environmental criminology theories, situational crime prevention focuses on how the environmental setting, and the features within it, may influence the presence or absence of criminal opportunity. More specifically, the theory proposes that managerial and structural changes can be introduced that may reduce opportunities for crimes to occur (Clarke, 1997). An in-depth overview of situational crime prevention is provided in Chapter 4.

The foundation of situational crime prevention is a series of proposed techniques intended to serve as a guide for potential crime prevention strategies. In essence, it provides clear techniques and practices that can be utilized to help address and overcome specific crime problems. Interested parties can then pick and choose which of the proposed techniques they wish to implement, based on the type of crime being targeted and the available resources. Due to its wide-scale applicability and clear organizational design, the theory, and resulting strategies, has proven integral in the continued development of both problem-oriented policing and crime prevention, more generally, over the last few decades. In fact, many researchers and practitioners would argue that it has become a foundational cornerstone of modern crime prevention approaches.

Expand Your Understanding – Who Is Ronald Clarke?

Currently a University Professor at the School of Criminal Justice, Rutgers University, Ronald Clarke is considered a pioneer in the field of crime prevention. With his previous experience heading the British government's criminological research department, Clarke was directly involved in developing both situational crime prevention and the British Crime Survey (now referred to as the Crime Survey for England & Wales). He is also the founding editor of Crime Prevention Studies, which serves as one of the foundational research sources for crime prevention. In addition, he worked alongside Herman Goldstein on problem-oriented policing projects for the Charlotte-Mecklenburg (N.C.) Police Department, and from 1998 to 2004, he served as chair for the selection committee for the annual

Herman Goldstein Award for Excellence in Problem-Oriented Policing. Finally, in 2015, he and his fellow researcher Pat Mayhew were awarded the Stockholm Prize in Criminology (POPCenter.org, 2023).

The Crime Triangle

As problem-oriented policing, and crime prevention more broadly, continued to evolve over the last couple of decades, one of the key developments was the **crime triangle,** advanced by **John Eck** (2003). Building from Cohen and Felson's (1979) routine activity theory, the crime triangle has served to help clarify and illustrate how criminal opportunities arise, as well as which stakeholders may play the biggest role in disrupting that opportunity. The crime triangle (Figure 1.1) outlines the factors associated with community problems by illustrating the links among the victims, offenders, and places, as well as which specific factors may be able to have an impact on each of those components. Specifically, the potential opportunity for a crime involves the intersection of a potential offender and a potential victim in the same place at the same time. While the offender is usually a person, the target/victim could be a person (e.g., an intoxicated person at a bar) or an object/location (e.g., a car or an empty home).

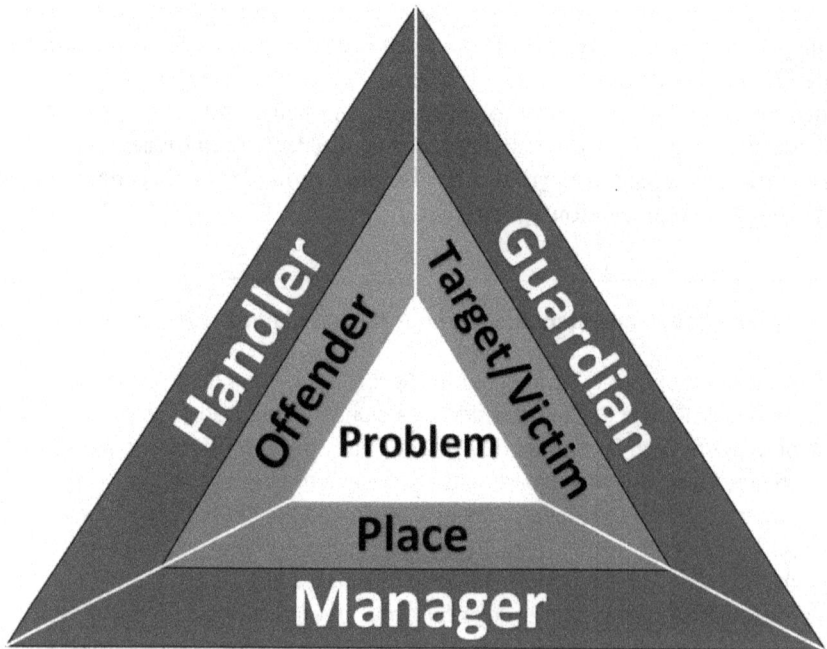

Figure 1.1 The Crime Triangle.

Source: Adapted from Eck, 2003.

The outer level of the triangle represents those individuals, or objects in some cases, that may be able to directly intervene on behalf of the offender, victim, and place. For instance, capable guardians for targets are people, or objects, that could directly protect the target from being victimized (e.g., security guards, night club bouncers, and car alarms). Handlers for offenders are individuals who have the ability to directly influence the offender's behavior, possibly preventing them from acting on their criminal urges (e.g., parents, friends, and probation officers). Finally, place managers are individuals who have a certain amount of control over what happens in a particular place or how the place is structured. Likewise, they can typically control who can access the place and what they are allowed to do (e.g., business owners, bartenders, and hotel clerks). Place managers may be able to help prevent crime by limiting the opportunities for offenders to interact with potential targets. Additional details on controllers will be provided in Chapter 2.

The adoption of the crime triangle provides law enforcement, as well as other community stakeholders, the ability to better understand the options for addressing crime. For example, as noted previously, the underlying problem could be addressed in an effort to prevent potential opportunities for crime. However, stakeholders can also focus on other factors, such as limiting access to potential victims, increasing guardianship, and controlling access to places (U.S. Department of Justice, 2014). With this approach, police and other stakeholders are better able to focus on the strategies within their reach to prevent crime.

Modern Crime Prevention Approaches

Crime Analysis

A major source of progress for the field of crime prevention has been the integration of scientific inquiry into preventative efforts. Specifically, the development of crime analysis has propelled crime prevention efforts forward, while also making them much more effective. **Crime analysis** is the systematic analysis of crime and victimization data to provide timely and useful information on crime patterns and trends (Stiles, 1981). Through crime analysis, law enforcement and researchers can determine where crimes occur the most, when they occur the most, what types of crimes occur the most, and a host of other specific crime patterns. This allows for a better understanding of the needs of and threats to a community, allowing law enforcement to take a more targeted approach to crime prevention.

In one form or another, crime analysis has been a technique utilized by law enforcement for some time. While serving as Chief of Police in Berkeley, California during the early 1900s, **August Vollmer**, often referred to as the "Father of American Policing," adopted crime analysis techniques to improve the efficiency of his officers. In 1906, Vollmer oversaw the creation of a records management system within the department, which helped organize police reports in a more conducive manner (Rheinier et al., 1979). This allowed reports to be better analyzed for trends and patterns. Further, he mapped crime locations using colored pins, to give a visual representation of the crime patterns. Finally, he also used crime analysis to develop patrol districts based on volumes of crime reported (Rheinier et al., 1979).

Unfortunately, the use of crime analysis stalled somewhat during the mid-1900s, as few other police departments felt it had any true utility. However, it would once again be in the spotlight in 1963 thanks to **O.W. Wilson**, one of Vollmer's protégées (Santos, 2017). Wilson served in leadership roles in several police departments, most notably the Chicago Police Department. He was an advocate for crime analysis, even discussing it in several of the police procedural books he wrote. In fact, he was the first person to define the term "crime analysis" (Santos, 2017). Wilson recommended that police departments create a crime analysis unit and focus more on using crime data. Although he did not invent the process, he did champion it.

While crime analysis has been seen as a useful approach for some time, it was during the 1990s that it truly took off. In 1990, Herman Goldstein, who had previously worked as an assistant to O.W. Wilson, published a book focusing on problem-oriented policing. Within the pages of his book, Goldstein highlighted the usefulness of crime analysis as a means of solving community problems. Simply, Goldstein noted that for problems to be solved, it is necessary to first identify and understand the full scope of the problems (Goldstein, 1990). Hence, crime analysis is key in problem solving, and problem-oriented policing. As the popularity of problem-oriented policing increased, so did the popularity of crime analysis.

One of the most useful approaches to crime analysis, developed in the early 1990s by the New York Police Department (NYPD), has been CompStat. Short for Computer Statistics, **CompStat** is a performance management system that is used to track, analyze, and evaluate crime statistics and crime prevention activities. With an emphasis on information-sharing, responsibility, accountability, and improving effectiveness, CompStat serves as a valuable tool for identifying and analyzing problems within a community (Police Executive Research Forum, 2013). Simply, it allows law enforcement to make better decisions based on data.

CompStat was initially developed as a solution to a localized problem. During the early 1990s, crime was a central issue plaguing New York City. Many New Yorkers dreaded leaving their homes for fear of being victimized or accosted (Police Executive Research Forum, 2013). Shortly after his election, Mayor Rudy Giuliani, along with his appointed Police Commissioner

Bill Bratton, began strategizing ideas to improve crime prevention in New York City. They found that one of the central issues to addressing crime and prevention in the city was that there was no concerted effort being made to track and analyze crime data (Police Executive Research Forum, 2013). With a renewed focus on crime prevention, Bratton and his command staff developed and implemented a new data-driven performance measurement system, which would come to be called CompStat. Bratton would explain that this new system would allow the police to track crime statistics and develop more efficient approaches to addressing those statistics (Police Executive Research Forum, 2013). While difficult to attribute solely to CompStat, the crime rate in New York City began dropping during that time and continued to do so for decades. Upon seeing the results in New York, other cities across the United States and around the world began to follow suit, adopting data-driven approaches to crime prevention (Police Executive Research Forum, 2013).

Crime Mapping

Another major boost to the usefulness of crime analysis as a means of crime prevention came in the form of technology, specifically with crime mapping. **Crime mapping** is a process through which crime analysis utilizes maps and/or mapping software to note the locations of crimes, in order to visualize and examine patterns of crime. To be clear, crime mapping is not a new concept, and it existed long before computers. For much of its history, police departments have relied on paper maps and push pins, which was not the most efficient method for examining spatial crime trends. During the 1990s, though, there was a growth in the development of crime-mapping computer programs.

In 1997, the National Institute of Justice (NIJ) established the Crime Mapping Research Center. One of the first tasks of the Center was to survey law enforcement departments to determine how they were using analytic mapping (Hunt, 2019). Based on the feedback, the Center then began creating training programs to improve police departments' ability to use spatial maps and crime data. Over the course of the next several years, the NIJ funded the development of CrimeStat software, which was intended to help practitioners and academics perform spatial analyses (Hunt, 2019). Today, "hotspot" analysis has become a common tactic for police departments to determine where resources can best be used. This approach has led to an increase in the use of "predictive policing," which is a technique that allows law enforcement to create crime forecasting models based on previous crime data (Hunt, 2019). The goal is to be able to determine where crime problems could arise, to better prevent them from occurring. The development and abilities of crime mapping will be discussed in much more detail in Chapters 5 and 6.

Artificial Intelligence

As the field of crime prevention continues to evolve, new approaches are being considered every day. Currently, one of the newest strategies being developed to help expand the scope and effectiveness of crime prevention is the incorporation of artificial intelligence programs. **Artificial intelligence** (AI) refers to computer systems that are designed to simulate human intelligence through data input, analysis, and decision making (SAS, 2023). Unlike humans, however, AI programs have the ability to process extremely large amounts of data, identify patterns from that data, and make predictions based on it, in seconds. Further, the newest form of AI technology, generative AI, can generate new data based on that analysis process. Essentially, based on the volumes of data the programs process, they can develop new content based on simple prompts created by users (SAS, 2023). Today, programs like ChatGPT can be used to create images, music, and even text-based outputs on relatively any topic simply by utilizing user-provided prompts.

The possible applications of AI technology for the field of criminal justice have been a topic of speculation for some time now. Research has already begun examining the potential uses of AI for facial recognition, gunshot detection, crime scene analysis, and behavioral pattern recognition (Rigano, 2019). With regard to crime prevention, there have also been a number of applications proffered. Currently, studies are underway examining the use of AI to predict potential criminal recidivism, to help identify possible victims of physical and financial elder abuse, and to help predict victims of violent crime, based on associations and behavior (Rigano, 2019). In addition, for police departments or communities with fewer resources, generative AI programs can be used, in their current form, to help develop crime prevention strategies for localized issues. For example, with the prompt "What are some effective crime prevention strategies for improving security in parking garages?", ChatGPT produced the suggestions in Table 1.1. While not an exhaustive list, the suggestions provided would be a very beneficial start.

Given the relatively short amount of time AI has been examined for potential crime prevention practices, there is no doubt that the examples described previously are merely scratching the surface of what is to come. The continued growth of technology, and AI specifically, will be able to take crime prevention in whole new directions. As crime prevention continues to evolve, its place in criminal justice will continue to grow.

Summary

Crime prevention is a complex field that has had a long and winding history. It should come as no surprise that developing a proactive approach to reducing crime is no simple task. Cognitive evolutions take time, and formative changes require appropriate evidence. As highlighted throughout this chapter, it has taken centuries to get where we are now. However,

Table 1.1 ChatGPT Output Suggestions for Crime Prevention in Parking Garages

1. *Proper Lighting*
   Ensure that the parking garage is well lit at all times, both inside and outside. Adequate lighting helps deter criminal activity and allows users to navigate the area safely.
2. *Surveillance Cameras*
   Install high-quality surveillance cameras throughout the parking garage, covering all entrances, exits, and key areas. Make sure the cameras are visible to act as a deterrent.
3. *Security Personnel*
   Employ security personnel or hire a professional security service to patrol the parking garage. Having a visible security presence can discourage criminals and provide a rapid response in case of incidents.
4. *Access Control*
   Implement access control systems, such as key cards or electronic passes, to restrict entry to authorized personnel only. This helps prevent unauthorized individuals from entering the garage.
5. *Emergency Call Boxes*
   Install emergency call boxes at various locations within the parking garage. These boxes should be equipped with direct lines to security personnel or law enforcement, providing a quick response in case of emergencies.
6. *Regular Maintenance*
   Keep the parking garage well maintained to eliminate potential hiding spots for criminals. Trim landscaping, repair broken lights promptly, and address any structural issues that may compromise security.
7. *Signage*
   Display clear signage indicating the presence of security measures, such as surveillance cameras, patrols, and restricted access. This can act as a deterrent to potential criminals.
8. *Community Engagement*
   Foster a sense of community among parking garage users. Encourage them to look out for one another and report any suspicious activity promptly.
9. *Technology Solutions*
   Explore technology solutions such as license plate recognition systems, which can enhance the ability to track and monitor vehicles entering and leaving the garage.
10. *Regular Security Audits*
    Conduct regular security audits to identify vulnerabilities and address them promptly. This may include reviewing surveillance footage, testing access controls, and assessing overall security protocols.
11. *Training and Awareness*
    Provide training for parking garage staff and users on security awareness. Educate them on how to recognize and report suspicious behavior.
12. *Collaboration with Law Enforcement*
    Establish a collaborative relationship with local law enforcement. Share information, coordinate security efforts, and request periodic patrols in and around the parking garage.

Source: OpenAI, 2023.

by examining how the field has evolved over time, students, researchers, and practitioners, alike, will be able to see the connections more effectively between the various concepts and approaches used to proactively prevent crime. With that foundation, they will be better able to help move crime prevention into the future.

Keywords

Crime Prevention, Crimes Against Persons, Crimes Against Property, Statutory Crimes, White Collar/Financial Crimes, Ideology, Crime Control, Proxy Measures, Prevalence, Incidence, Henry Fielding, Robert Peel, Clifford Shaw, Social Disorganization Theory, Community-Oriented Policing, Problem-Oriented Policing, Herman Goldstein, Ronald Clarke, Situational Crime Prevention, Crime Triangle, John Eck, Crime Analysis, August Vollmer, O.W. Wilson, CompStat, Crime Mapping, Artificial Intelligence

---

Discussion Questions

1. What are the major categories of crime and how do they differ?
2. How do the three definitions of crime prevention vary?
3. What was the significance of the Bow Street Runners in the development of crime prevention?
4. How are community-oriented and problem-oriented police linked?
5. What is the purpose of the crime triangle?
6. How has technology influenced crime prevention?

References

Association of Certified Fraud Examiners. (2020). *Report to the Nations on Occupational Fraud and Abuse, Association of Certified Fraud Examiners.* Retrieved from https://acfepublic.s3-us-west-2.amazonaws.com/2020-Report-to-the-Nations.pdf

Brain, J. (2018). *Bow Street Runners.* Historic UK. Retrieved from https://www.historic-uk.com/HistoryUK/HistoryofBritain/Bow-Street-Runners/

Britannica. (2022). *The development of professional policing in England.* Retrieved from https://www.britannica.com/topic/police/English-and-American-policing--in-the-late-19th-century

Caplan, J. M., Kennedy, L. W., & Petrossian, G. (2011). Police-monitored CCTV cameras in Newark, NJ: A quasi-experimental test of crime deterrence. *Journal of Experimental Criminology 7*, 255–274.

Center for Disease Control & Prevention (CDC). (2022). *The Public Health Approach to Violence Prevention*. Retrieved from https://www.cdc.gov/violence-prevention/about/publichealthapproach.html

Chainey, S. P., & Ratcliffe, J. H. (2005). *GIS and crime mapping*. London: Wiley.

Chicago Area Project (CAP). (2022). *Chicago Area Project History*. Retrieved from https://www.chicagoareaproject.org/history/

Cho, J. T., & Park J. (2017). Exploring the effects of CCTV upon fear of crime: A multi-level approach in Seoul. *International Journal of Law, Crime, & Justice*, *49*(3), 35–45.

Clarke, R. V. (1997). *Situational crime prevention: Successful case studies* (2nd Ed.). Monsey, NY: Criminal Justice Press.

Cohen, L. E., & Felson, M. (1979). Social change and crime rate trends: A routine activity approach. *American Sociological Review*, *44*(4), 588–608.

Cozens, P., & Sun, M. Y. (2019). Exploring crime prevention through environmental design (CPTED) and students' fear of crime at an Australian university campus using prospect and refuge theory. *Property Management*, *37*(2), 287–306.

Crime Prevention Website. (2022). *Police Crime Prevention Service: A Short History*. Retrieved from https://thecrimepreventionwebsite.com/references-and-library/525/police-crime-prevention-service---a-short-history/

de Vries, S. L. A., Hoeve, M., Asscher, J. J., & Stams, G. J. J. M. (2018). The long-term effects of the youth crime prevention program new perspectives on delinquency and recidivism. *International Journal of Offender Therapy and Comparative Criminology*, *62*(12), 3639–3661.

Eck, J. E. (2003). Police problems: The complexity of problem theory, research, and evaluation. In: J. Knutsson (ed.), *Problem-oriented policing: From innovation to mainstream*. Monsey, NY: Criminal Justice Press, pp. 79–113.

Emsley, C., Hitchcock, T., & Shoemaker, R. (2022). London history: A population history of London. *Old Bailey Proceedings Online*. Retrieved from www.oldbaileyonline.org

Goldstein, H. (1979). Improving policing: A problem-oriented approach. *Crime & Delinquency*, *25*(2), 236–258.

Goldstein, H. (1990). *Problem-oriented policing*. New York, NY: McGraw Hill.

Gramlich, J. (2020). *What the Data Says (and Doesn't Say) about Crime in the United States*. Pew Research Center. Retrieved from https://www.pewresearch.org/fact-tank/2020/11/20/facts-about-crime-in-theu-s/

Hunt, J. (2019). From crime mapping to crime forecasting: The evolution of place-based policing. *National Institute of Justice Journal*, *281*. July 10, 2019, nij.ojp.gov: https://nij.ojp.gov/topics/articles/crime-mapping-crime-forecasting-evolution-place-based-policing

Klotter, J. C., & Cusick, R. I. (1968). *Burglary – Prevention, Investigation, and Prosecution* (NCJ # 73471). Office of Justice Programs. Retrieved from https://www.ojp.gov/ncjrs/virtual-library/abstracts/burglary-prevention-investigation-and-prosecution

Law Enforcement Action Partnership. (2021). *Sir Robert Peel's Policing Principles*. Retrieved from https://lawenforcementactionpartnership.org/peel-policing-principles

Legal Information Institute. (2023). White-collar crime. Cornell University. Retrieved from https://www.law.cornell.edu/wex/white-collar_crime

OpenAI. (2023) ChatGPT (October 2 version) [Large language model]. https://chat.openai.com/chat

Painter, K. A., & Farrington, D. P. (1999). Improved street lighting: Crime reducing effects and cost-benefit analyses. *Security Journal, 12*, 17–32.

Police Executive Research Forum. (2013). *COMPSTAT: Its origins, evolution, and future in law enforcement agencies.* Washington, DC: Police Executive Research Forum.

POP Center. (2022). *Goldstein Award Information.* Retrieved from https://pop-center.asu.edu/content/goldstein-awards

POP Center. (2023). *POP Center Biographies – Ronald Clarke.* Retrieved from https://popcenter.asu.edu/content/biographies-ronald-clarke#:~:text=Clarke%20is%20the%20founding%20editor,(Harrow%20and%20Heston%201997)

Rheinier, B., Greenless, M. R., Gibbens, M. H., & Marshall, S. P. (1979). *Crime Analysis in Support of Patrol.* Law Enforcement Assistance Administration report. Washington, DC: U.S. Government Printing Office.

Rigano, C. (2019). Using Artificial Intelligence to address criminal justice needs. *NIJ Journal, 280.* Retrieved from https:// www.nij.gov/journals/280/Pages/using-artificialintelligence-to-address-criminal-justice-needs.aspx

Sampson, R. J., & Groves, W. B. (1989). Community structure and crime: Testing social disorganization theory. *American Journal of Sociology, 94*, 774–802.

Santos, R. B. (2017). *Crime analysis with crime mapping.* New York: Sage.

SAS. (2023). Artificial intelligence: What it is and why it matters. Retrieved from https://www.sas.com/en_us/insights/analytics/what-is-artificial-intelligence.html#:~:text=Artificial%20intelligence%20(AI)%20makes%20it,learning%20and%20natural%20language%20processing

Shaw, C. R., & McKay, H. D. (1929). *Delinquency areas.* Chicago, IL: University of Chicago Press.

Statista. (2023). Number of committed crimes in the United States in 2022, by type of crime [Infographic]. Statista. https://www.statista.com/statistics/202714/number-of-committed-crimes-in-the-us-by-type-of-crime/

Stiles, S. R. (1981). *Simplified Crime Analysis Techniques.* U.S. Department of Justice, NCJ 80735.

U.S. Department of Justice. (1976). *Establishing A Crime Prevention Bureau.* National Criminal Justice Reference Service (NCJ # 38380). Retrieved from https://www.ojp.gov/pdffiles1/Digitization/38380NCJRS.pdf

U.S. Department of Justice. (2014). *Community Policing Defined.* Community Oriented Policing Services. Retrieved from https://cops.usdoj.gov

Weisburd, D., Telep, C. W., Hinkle, J. C., & Eck, J. E. (2010). Is problem-oriented policing Effective in reducing crime and disorder?: Findings from a Campbell Systematic Review. *Criminology and Public Policy, 9*(1), 139–172.

Chapter 2
Crime Pattern Theory, Rational Choice Theory, and Routine Activities Theory

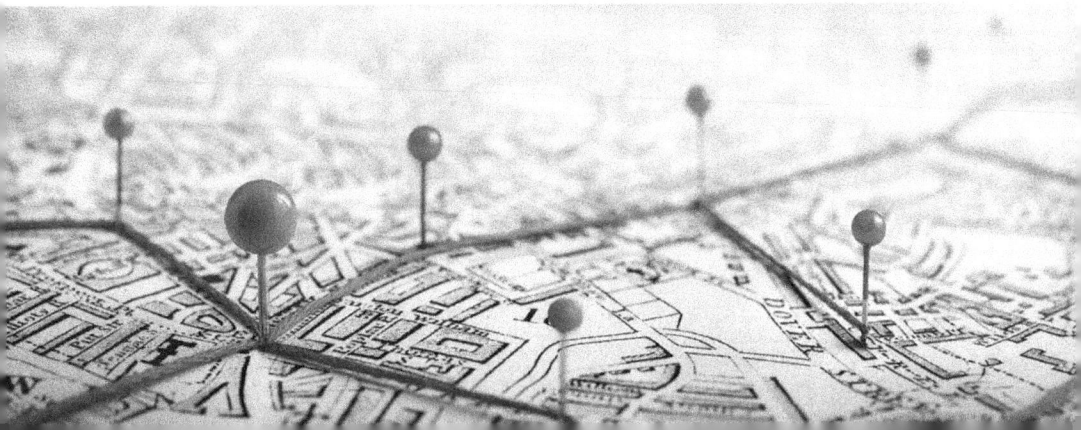

Crime Pattern Theory, Rational Choice Theory, and Routine Activities Theory

Bradford W. Reyns

Chapter Outline

In this chapter, we will focus on:

Studying Crime Patterns
- Guerry and Quetelet
- Human ecology
- Environmental design
- Crime patterns and crime concentration

Crime Pattern Theory
- Nodes, paths, and edges
- Journey to crime
- Environmental backcloth
- Eight key points

Rational Choice Theory
- Assumptions of rational choice
- Involvement decisions
- Event decisions
- Rational choice theory and repeats
- Applications for crime prevention

Routine Activities Theory
- Macro-level routine activities
- Micro-level routine activities
- Applications for crime prevention

Learning Objectives

After reading this chapter, you should be able to:

2.1 Explain how crime is patterned

2.2 Discuss how the study of crime patterns evolved over time

2.3 Describe crime pattern theory, rational choice theory, and routine activities theory

2.4 Explain crime involvement and event decisions from a rational choice perspective

2.5 Explain how crime pattern theory, rational choice theory, and routine activities theory can be used in crime prevention

DOI: 10.4324/9781003401551-3

Introduction

The foundation of crime prevention is identifying and examining patterns in crime, and crime patterns provide the basis for much crime prevention theory. This chapter reviews crime pattern theory, rational choice theory, and routine activities theory, each of which offers a different perspective on understanding the crime event. These three theories also address the utility of crime patterns in developing methods for preventing crime. To this end, the theories feature prominently in the environmental criminology school of thought.

Environmental criminology focuses on criminal events, the role the immediate environment plays in the crime, and on the immediate circumstances under which they occur. Scholars in the field of environmental criminology identify crime patterns and explain how environmental factors contribute to those patterns (Wortley & Mazerolle, 2008). From the perspective of crime prevention, identifying and understanding crime patterns is useful in predicting crime problems and developing solutions to prevent these problems from occurring or reoccurring. If crime patterns are a function of environmental factors, then changes to the environment should be able to reduce criminal events, offending, reoffending, victimization, and repeat victimization.

Crime pattern theory, rational choice theory, and routine activities theory offer theoretical frameworks to guide these solutions. By analyzing crime patterns, strategies can be developed that aid practitioners in the identification, examination, and prevention of crime problems. Environmental criminology is discussed further in Chapter 3.

Studying Crime Patterns

Guerry and Quetelet

Over 200 years of criminological research has been devoted to identifying patterns in crime, at different levels of analysis, to better understand its extent and nature. The first studies examining how crime is patterned were undertaken in the 1820s by French lawyer André-Michel Guerry and Belgian statistician Adolphe Quetelet. Working separately, but arriving at similar conclusions, Guerry and Quetelet analyzed crime data at the macro-level (i.e., city, province) and discovered that crime is not evenly distributed. That is, crime is not random, and instead is patterned in particular ways. Their works suggested that crimes clustered regionally and at certain times. For example, Guerry's early analyses of French crime data suggested that crime was stable over time, but that crimes varied regionally, by type of crime, and seasonally (Friendly, 2022). The pathbreaking work of Guerry and Quetelet sparked subsequent studies of crime patterns in Europe and, eventually, contributed to the development of positivist criminology.

Human Ecology

The next generation of researchers to study crime patterns worked within the field of **human ecology**, which is an interdisciplinary field that emphasizes relationships between humans and their natural, social, and built environments. Although the roots of human ecology and the study of how humans interact with their environments have a long history, it was not until the 1920s that researchers began to view human ecology from a sociological perspective (Park & Burgess, 1925). Park and Burgess' work at the Chicago School examined the development of cities, urbanization, and the social processes that transpire as cities grow and change. They developed a theoretical framework to explain the organization of cities according to concentric zones – known as the **concentric zone model**. A depiction of the concentric zone theory is provided in Figure 2.1. According to the model, crime would be most concentrated in the city center, and gradually dissipate outward.

Two criminologists – Clifford Shaw and Henry McKay (1942) – adopted Park and Burgess' methods to study crime patterns in Chicago, Illinois. As noted in Chapter 1, Shaw and McKay were interested in understanding juvenile delinquency in the city, mapping out patterns in delinquency across neighborhoods, and in identifying the characteristics of delinquency areas. In doing this, they were carrying on the tradition of Guerry and Quetelet, albeit at a smaller until of aggregation. They also supported the concentric zone theory hypothesis, finding that delinquency was concentrated in the city core, and diminished outward with each subsequent city zone (Shaw & McKay, 1942).

Most significantly, Shaw and McKay found that the neighborhoods where crime was concentrated were those that were characterized by **social disorganization** – those in which social institutions (e.g., family, school) had broken down and were not effective at controlling crime. These findings sparked the development of Shaw and McKay's **social disorganization**

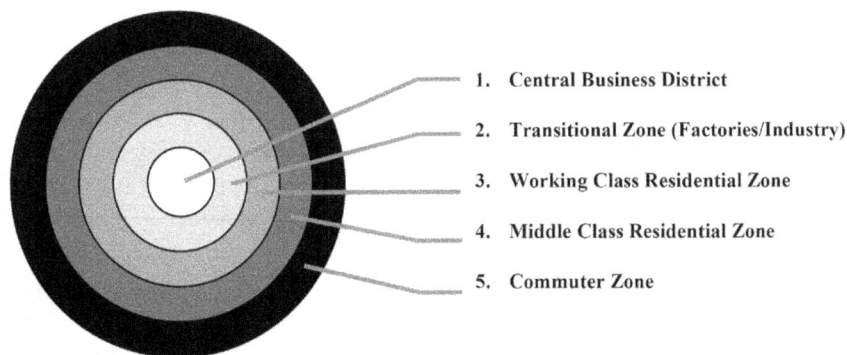

1. **Central Business District**
2. **Transitional Zone (Factories/Industry)**
3. **Working Class Residential Zone**
4. **Middle Class Residential Zone**
5. **Commuter Zone**

Figure 2.1 Concentric Zones.

theory, which was one of the most prolific theories in twentieth-century criminology. Briefly, social disorganization theory posits that neighborhoods become socially disorganized as a result of three factors: poverty, residential mobility, and ethnic heterogeneity. Without effective mechanisms to control crime as a result of neighborhood social disorganization, crime and delinquency rates increase, and these neighborhoods become "delinquency areas." Thus, although not a theory of crime patterns per se, social disorganization theory is relevant to the discussion of the study of crime patterns, both in terms of the evolution of the field and in explaining crime and delinquency concentrations in neighborhoods.

Environmental Design

The next leap forward in studying crime patterns came with the works of C. Ray Jeffery (1971) and Oscar Newman (1972). Both wrote influential books about how crime is patterned in the immediate environment, suggesting strategies for designing crime out of physical/built environments. Their theories provided the modern-day groundwork for crime prevention theory and feature prominently in environmental criminology. These theories are more fully explained in Chapter 3 but are also relevant to the discussion of crime patterns.

Crime prevention through environmental design, or CPTED, is a crime prevention strategy focused on altering the built environment to make it less conducive for crime or to at least make individuals perceive that it is less conducive. CPTED is based on the idea that there are six main factors associated with the built environment that could be altered to reduce crime: (1) natural surveillance, (2) territorial reinforcement, (3) access control, (4) target hardening, (5) activity support, and (6) image and space management (Jeffery, 1971). Likewise, Newman's (1972) concept of **defensible space** suggests that characteristics of the built environment can be designed or altered to create stronger community responses to problems such as crime and disorder. Effectively, Newman discussed the ways in which environmental design could produce social action. The three pillars of his theory were territoriality, surveillance, and image and milieu (see Chapter 3 for a full discussion of these concepts). In a way, Newman (1972) was describing how to counter social disorganization through architectural design.

Theoretically, both CPTED and defensible space focus on ways that the environment produces signals to those within it. By understanding how these signals are interpreted – or how our perceptions of our physical environment are patterned – the environment can be designed or changed to either discourage offenders from committing crimes (i.e., CPTED) or encourage others (e.g., neighborhood residents) to intervene to prevent crime (i.e., defensible space). For example, the CPTED principle of *access control* involves restricting access to only authorized individuals. As an illustration, only ticketed passengers can pass through airport security to access the terminals and gates. Thus, environmental design is used to prevent crime in actuality, and also to signal to would-be offenders that crime is not possible. CPTED and defensible space are central to crime prevention theory and practice and rely on environmental design to disrupt crime patterns.

Crime Patterns and Crime Concentrations

In the 1980s, Patricia and Paul Brantingham (1984) began their work in environmental criminology, developing crime pattern theory, which is one of the premier theories of environmental criminology and of the field of crime prevention. The theory addresses situational and environmental contributors to crimes and is grounded in understanding crime patterns and crime concentrations. Consequently, crime is patterned in many interesting ways. It is useful to think of crime patterns in terms of crime concentrations. Crime concentrations represent the distribution and clustering of crime, which can take several forms, including geographic, temporal, or clustering among a particular group of individuals or targets. For example, the "delinquency areas" identified by Shaw and McKay represent a geographic clustering of juvenile delinquency in Chicago. Similarly, Guerry's analysis of French crime data revealed that personal crimes occurred with the greatest frequency in the summer and the lowest frequency in the winter – an example of a temporal crime pattern (Friendly, 2022). While crime concentrations are addressed throughout the book in greater depth, the different forms of crime concentration are provided in Table 2.1.

Crime Pattern Theory

Crime pattern theory was developed by Brantingham and Brantingham (1984, 1993a) to explain patterns in criminal events by focusing on the ways that offenders use time and space. According to the theory, crimes occur with regularity around the times and places of normal activity and awareness for offenders. To explain the nature of offender activity and

Table 2.1 Crime Patterns as Crime Concentration

Form of Crime Concentration	*Type of Crime Concentration*
Geographic	Hotspots
Temporal	Hot Times
Specific Locations	Risky Facilities
Offenders	Repeat Offending
Victims	Recurring Victimization
Products/Items	Hot Products

awareness of their environment, the theory also addresses how all human activity (not just that of offenders) is patterned as a result of the physical environment. The theory states that for most individuals – offenders included – routine activities, such as those at home, school, work, and recreation provide anchor points, around which we develop awareness spaces and paths to connect those points. As we travel between these points we develop a familiarity with the places, routes, and immediate surrounding areas. Figure 2.2 provides a visual example of routine activity and awareness spaces for a fictitious offender, and the places where they may encounter crime opportunities.

Our **awareness spaces** extend to a limited degree around these key locations, as we become familiar with the geographic layout of an area and the activities that occur therein during familiar times. The time spent at these locations is a function of the normal pace and rhythm of daily life, which is structured around business hours, morning and evening commutes, school schedules, weekdays, weekends, holidays, and so forth (Brantingham, 2010). For example, a college student may be familiar with campus, the nearby amenities, grocery stores, gas stations, and so on, but will not know all locations in the neighborhood or city. If the student lives on campus, they will recognize the times of the day, week, or month when activities occur there, but probably will not know what the campus is like during the summer – when they leave for break.

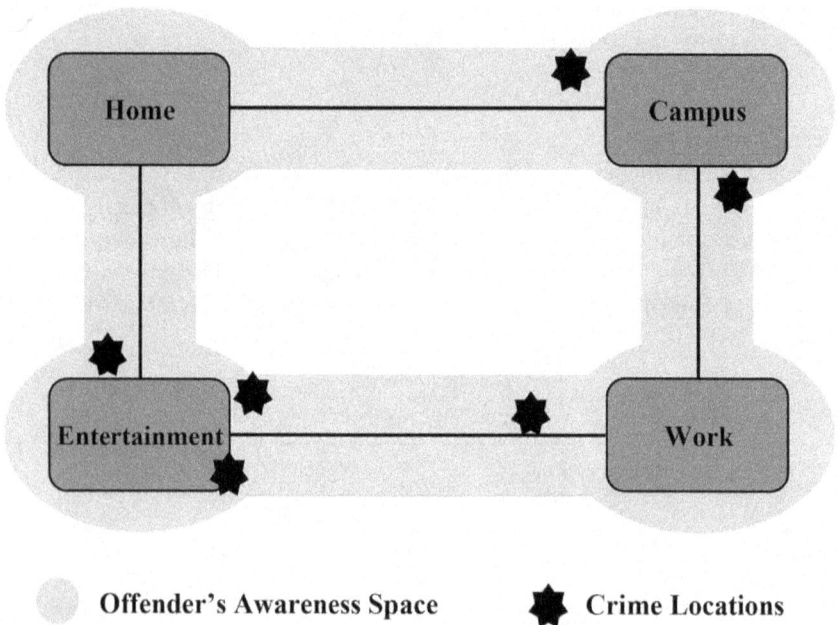

Offender's Awareness Space   Crime Locations

Figure 2.2 Offender Awareness Space and High Activity Areas.

Nodes, Paths, and Edges

In addition to an individual's routines and awareness spaces, activity patterns are shaped on a large scale by the layout of the physical environment, which possesses three characteristics that can influence crime patterns: nodes, paths, and edges. **Nodes** are centers for activities. At the aggregate level, they are places where large numbers of people concentrate, such as business districts, mass transit stations, or shopping centers. At the individual level, nodes are places that individuals regularly go, such as home, work, and school. The concept of nodes is useful for understanding crime patterns because offenders and potential victims share these same nodes, potentially bringing them into proximity with each other. **Paths** are the ways or channels that connect nodes to each other. In other words, paths are the routes that people use to get from place to place, such as road networks, mass transit stations, or walkways. Offenders will be familiar with nodes and paths that they regularly use and will look to these areas for crime opportunities. Therefore, we would expect crimes to concentrate in these areas. Finally, **edges** are the spaces or boundaries surrounding nodes and paths. They act as physical, social, or economic boundaries that delineate one area from the next. Offenders will often commit crimes along edges because strangers overlap in these areas and an offender's presence is less likely to be noticed, and crimes less likely to be reported (Brantingham, 2010).

Journey to Crime

In examining how offenders choose their targets, researchers and practitioners study the offender's **journey to crime**. This refers to the specific travels an offender takes leading up to a specific crime. Concepts from crime pattern theory tell us that offenders tend to travel between nodes, paths, and edges, and if they are going to commit crimes, they are likely to occur within their activity and awareness spaces. In addition, the likelihood of an offender committing a crime decreases with the distance from their home – an observation called **distance decay**. Exploring the journey to crime illustrates how offenders make decisions about committing crimes and enables law enforcement to make predictions about the probable locations of offenders. Journey to crime research concentrates on three particular features of the offender's travels: (1) the starting point, (2) the direction of the trip, and (3) the distance traveled. Research into the offender's journey to crime suggests that offenders typically choose crime targets near their home bases, and certainly within their awareness spaces. For example, researchers analyzed crime data from the city of Sheffield, UK and found that the average journey from the offender's home to the site of the crime was 1.88 miles for burglary and 2.36 miles for auto theft (Wiles & Costello, 2000). Supplementing these data with offender interviews, the authors (2000, p. 2) concluded that "most travel associated with crime was not primarily driven by plans to offend. Offending appeared to be much more dependent upon opportunities presenting themselves during normal routines, rather than as a result of instrumental, long-range search patterns."

Offenders make rational (to them) decisions about exploiting criminal opportunities during their journey to crime. These decisions are based on whether the situation aligns with the offender's mental template or **script** for suitable criminal opportunities. These templates will differ by crime type and the context in which the crime will be committed but provide offenders with a means of making quick decisions about whether to act upon available criminal opportunities. Templates consist of mental images of criminal opportunities and successfully committed crimes based on past experiences and decisions that have become regularized, such as the ideal target or ideal situation for committing a crime. When, during an offender's journey to crime, they encounter a situation that matches this mental script for committing a crime, they will decide to exploit the criminal opportunity. This decision is often triggered by some situational factor or event that signals to the offender that the situation, environment, or context is presenting an available opportunity. The script provides offenders with the steps and actions required to complete the crime.

Environmental Backcloth

The journey to crime occurs against the **environmental backcloth**, which represents the physical, structural, social, economic, legal, and cultural conditions that exist in the environment, and within which individuals operate. Brantingham and Brantingham (1993b, p. 7) described the backcloth as "the uncountable elements that surround and are part of an individual and that may be influenced by or influence his or her criminal behavior." In short, the backcloth is the larger context within which crimes occur and within which decisions are made. It represents a broader focus on the environment, which is dynamic, always changing, and provides a nearly infinite number of cues to those within the environment, which individuals perceive, interpret, and react to. For example, someone who wants to commit a crime will look for a place and time that fit their mental template or script for a successful crime using the cues provided by the environmental backcloth. Figure 2.3 depicts the environmental backcloth, which includes a number of characteristics of the environment and the climate within which decisions are made.

Eight Key Points

Identifying nodes, paths, and edges, and understanding the offender's journey to crime, help us to understand the formation of hotspots of crime. Based on the tenets of crime pattern theory, hotspots should be expected to form at the locations where offender awareness spaces overlap with

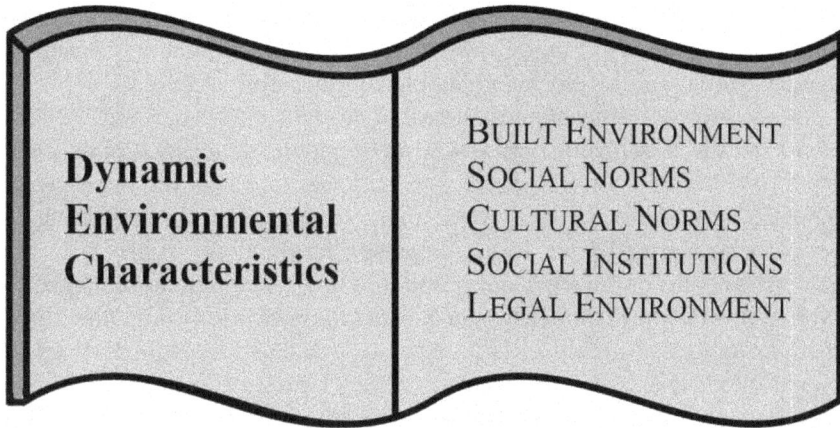

| Dynamic Environmental Characteristics | BUILT ENVIRONMENT SOCIAL NORMS CULTURAL NORMS SOCIAL INSTITUTIONS LEGAL ENVIRONMENT |

Figure 2.3 The Environmental Backcloth.

potential crime targets in the absence of willing and capable guardianship. The convergence of offenders and victims can be understood in terms of the movement of people from place to place. As Brantingham and Brantingham (2008, p. 79) put it: "What shapes non-criminal activities helps shape criminal activities." They also explained that the formation of crime hotspots can be predicted by considering eight key points from crime pattern theory:

1. The locations of motivated offender populations (home, work, and recreation).
2. The locations of vulnerable populations (home, work, and recreation).
3. The distribution of other types of crime targets in space and time.
4. The distribution of different forms of security or guardianship in space and time.
5. The broad activity structures of the city.
6. The mix of activity types and land uses.
7. The methods of transportation and the structure of transportation networks.
8. The spatial and temporal movements of people through the city.

The body of research investigating crime patterns and crime pattern theory is quite voluminous, but a few representative examples of research studies will provide readers a sense of empirical support for the theory. As an example, research by Felson and Boivin (2015) used survey data from a Canadian municipal transport agency to test a "funnel hypothesis" suggesting that daily flows of people explain crime concentrations within a city. They found that flows of daily visitors for work, shopping, recreation, and school had a major impact on the distributions of property and violent crimes in the city.

These findings support points 7 and 8 above (and perhaps others), highlighting the roles of transportation, transportation networks, and movement of people throughout the city in explaining concentration of crime.

In a study of crime pattern theory in Malmö, Sweden, Gerell (2021) examined the relationship between flows of people in the city and different types of crime hotspots. To do so, various types of crimes in the city were mapped, and then crime levels were analyzed in relation to the number of people who boarded a local bus – representing the flows of people in the area. The results of the study suggested that flows of people were related to every type of crime hotspot examined, including robbery, assault, bike theft, theft from a car, vandalism, and arson. In other words, high densities of people were predictive of the locations of very high levels of crime in the city (i.e., hotspots). Gerell noted that the association between flows of people and violence and theft was particularly strong. The results are open to interpretation, but these findings are potentially supportive of all of the points listed above related to crime pattern theory (1–8). Gerell also suggested that the results were supportive of both crime pattern theory and routine activities theory – a crime prevention theory that is discussed later in this chapter.

As a final example of a study of crime pattern theory, Song and colleagues (2019) examined the locations of personal thefts in a large city in China, and considered the daily movement patterns of people in the city using tracked mobile phone data as well as the presence of crime generators. Their results suggested that certain facilities act as crime generators, increasing the likelihood of personal theft. They noted that subway stations, movie theaters, and hospitals have the largest effects, increasing the odds of targets being chosen by 57 percent, 15 percent, and 13 percent respectively. Other facilities with significant crime-generating effects included stores, markets, supermarkets, restaurants, banks, and bus stops. In terms of the offender's journey to crime, they found that the closer the offender's home, the more likely an area was to be chosen as a crime site. Thus, this study supported three of the key propositions of crime pattern theory – crime generators, journey to crime, and distance decay.

Rational Choice Theory

The field of crime prevention is heavily invested in the assumption that criminal behavior is a purposeful and rational choice, and as a paradigm, rational choice underlies many of the primary theories of environmental criminology (e.g., crime pattern theory, routine activities theory, situational crime prevention) (Brantingham & Brantingham, 1984; Clarke & Cornish, 1985; Felson & Clarke, 1998). This approach challenges some of the assumptions of other criminological perspectives, which take a more deterministic view of criminal behavior or focus on criminal motivations or predispositions. **Rational choice theory** was developed for crime prevention by

Ronald Clarke and Derek Cornish, starting in the 1970s (Clarke & Cornish, 1985; Cornish & Clarke, 2003). The proliferation of rational choice within criminal justice and criminology in the 1970s may, in some ways, be seen as a response to mixed results about the effectiveness of correctional rehabilitation programs and the desire to find more immediate ways of preventing or responding to crime (Cornish & Clarke, 2008).

Rational choice theory provides a framework for assessing the conditions that give rise to crime. It suggests that individuals make offending decisions based on the many pieces of information that they have about the crime, much of which will come from signals provided in the immediate environment. Simply put, with this information, a decision to offend (or not) is made. The practical implication of this theory is that discouraging criminal decision making may be a matter of targeting criminal opportunities within the environment and manipulating environmental circumstances in ways that make criminal behavior unappealing to a rational offender. Thus, rational choice theory focuses on the offender's decision-making process and offender decision making is viewed as a *purposeful decision*, in which the would-be offender assesses the costs and benefits of criminal behavior. Theoretically, based on a consideration of the information that is available, the individual makes a decision that will maximize benefits while minimizing the costs. These ideas are not original or unique to criminology and instead speak to philosophical perspectives on human nature spanning both time and many fields of study.

Assumptions of Rational Choice

These decision-making processes are essentially the same as those undertaken by offenders and non-offenders alike when faced with a decision, and rational choice theory views offenders as fundamentally the same in their thinking and decision making as non-offenders. That is, our decisions are the product of opportunities and constraints – whether the circumstances are favorable to whatever we are considering doing. This calculus applies to buying a house, making a date, or committing a crime. In the case of criminal behavior, these considerations will include a number of factors, such as the potential payoff, how guarded or protected the target may be, the likelihood of getting caught, the potential punishments, and so on. Cornish and Clarke (2008, p. 24) explained that modern-day rational choice theory, as it applies to crime, consists of the following six core concepts:

1. Criminal behavior is purposive.
2. Criminal behavior is rational.
3. Criminal decision making is crime specific.
4. Criminal choices fall into two broad groups: involvement and event decisions.

5. There are separate stages of involvement.

6. Criminal events unfold in a sequence of stages and decisions.

To elaborate on Cornish and Clarke's (2008) points, criminal behavior is both purposeful and rational (points 1 and 2). Decisions are made with intention in ways that maximize pleasure and minimize pain. Yet, our decisions are imperfect, and often poorly thought out. Criminal decisions are frequently made casually, without much planning. These points apply to instrumental offenses (i.e., for tangible gains) as well as violence (i.e., intangible gains) (Felson & Eckert, 2018). In instrumental offenses, the offender might rob a convenience store, and be rewarded with money, while in a violent offense, they could get revenge on someone or restore their self-image (other types of rewards).

Criminal offending decisions are situational and depend on the type of crime and the conditions under which the crime may be committed. For instance, the costs and benefits associated with robbery are different from those for burglary, larceny, or theft. From crime to crime, there are different opportunity structures and different situational dynamics that must be considered by the potential offender in making an offending decision (point 3 above). In the case of robbery, the offender may consider whether the target is alone, whether they are likely to resist, how they are dressed, the time of day, and the level of nearby foot traffic; whereas for a crime such as pickpocketing, factors such as crowding, pace of activity, and environmental distractions will work to the offender's advantage.

Involvement Decisions

As stated above, rational choice theory explains involvement and event decisions (point 4 above). Involvement decisions are those in which an offender considers whether they are ready and/or willing to engage in criminal behavior, while event decisions are those related to the nuts and bolts of committing the crime, such as target selection or the tools that will be used. As point 5 indicates, there are different stages of involvement: (1) initial decisions to become involved in criminal behavior, (2) criminal event actions, and (3) continuing involvement or desistance decisions. Clarke and Cornish (1985) developed decision-making models for each of these three stages, emphasizing the role of different factors in the rational choice calculation at each stage.

In what they called the initiation model, offenders are weighing aspects such as background factors (e.g., values, attitudes), their experiences (e.g., skills), current circumstances (e.g., marital status, employment), needs and motives (e.g., family crisis, need cash), opportunities for meeting their needs (i.e., legitimate and illegitimate), perceived solutions to their needs or situation (i.e., legitimate and illegitimate), and finally, a rational calculation of

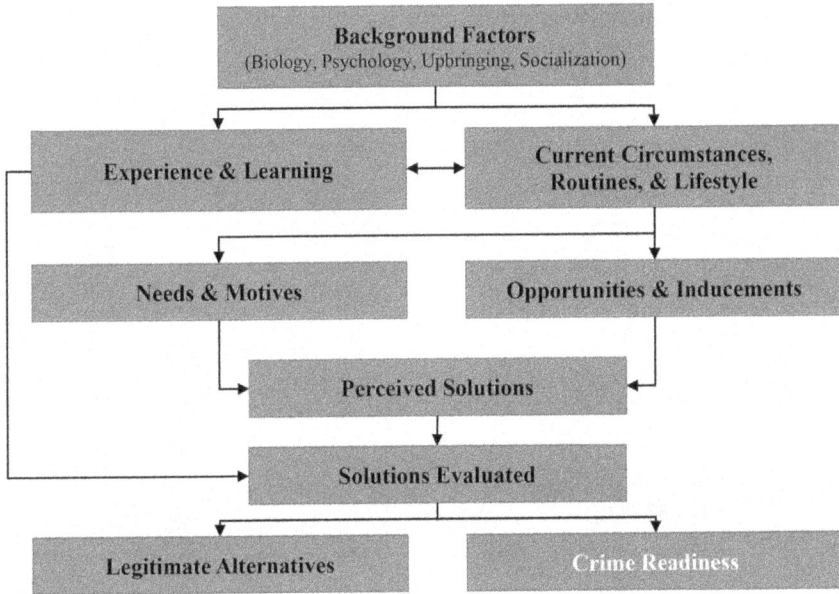

Figure 2.4 Initiation Stage of Crime of Rational Choice Theory.

the risks and rewards of crime as a solution. If the rewards outweigh the risks, the individual will decide to commit the crime. Each of these elements is presented in Figure 2.4.

Upon deciding to commit a crime, the offender then enters the criminal event stage. It is during this stage that the offender actually chooses a target. The first step in choosing a target is to choose the area to search for a potential target. Again, during this stage the offender weighs the risks and rewards of various locations, taking into account factors such as the number of potential targets, the perceived quality of potential targets, the presence of law enforcement, and the ability to escape easily. Once a location is chosen, the same process is then utilized to choose a suitable target, while considering factors such as perceived vulnerability, presence of security features, and level of effort needed to victimize the target. As presented in Figure 2.5, after a target is chosen, the offender then commits the crime.

Finally, the offender must decide whether to continue to or desist from committing further criminal acts. In the decision to continue perpetrating crimes, or what Clarke and Cornish (1985) called habituation, different factors influence decision making. According to Clarke and Cornish (1985), these would be more contemporary factors, including changes in peer group (e.g., making friends with other offenders), increased professionalism (e.g., getting better at crime), and changes in lifestyles and values (e.g., getting used to the rewards of crime). Lastly, the decision-making model for quitting, or desistance, emphasizes success in crime as a major factor, with other considerations such as changes in life circumstances (e.g., getting married, getting injured), or new legitimate alternatives to crime (e.g., new job) playing a role.

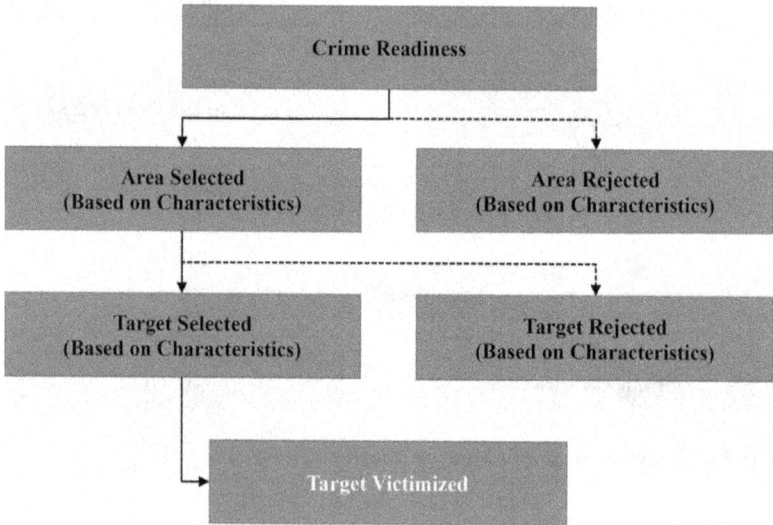

Figure 2.5 Event Stage of Crime of Rational Choice Theory.

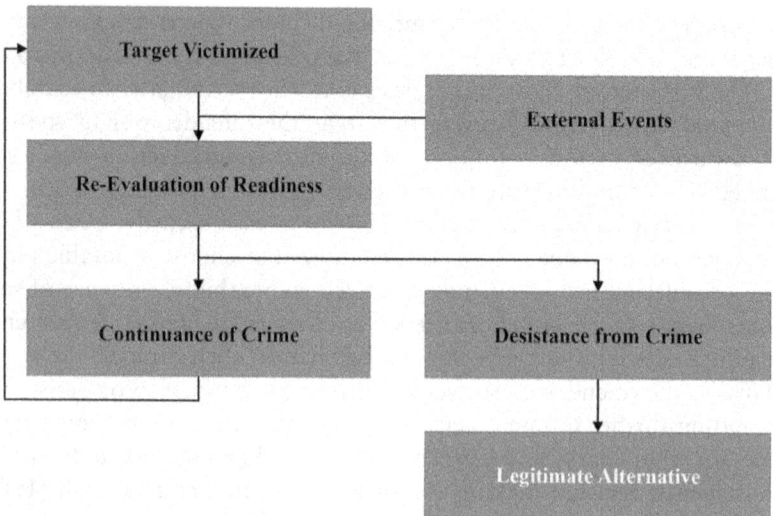

Figure 2.6 Continuance or Desistance Stage of Rational Choice Theory.

While offending can be understood in terms of rational choice decision making by motivated offenders, involvement and event decisions are never made with complete information. Rather, they are made with the information that is available to offenders at the time, so while decisions may be based on rational thinking, they may still be bad decisions. It may also be that the information available to offenders is inaccurate and that offenders interpret costs and benefits incorrectly. This phenomenon is known as **bounded rationality** (or limited rationality), and suggests that offenders make rational (to them) decisions with the information that is available and based on their interpretation of the situation. For instance, an offender might judge the likelihood they will be caught and/or punished to be lower than it actually is, leading them to make the wrong choice and perpetrate the crime. After all, offenders regularly misjudge their situation and get caught and punished for their crimes.

Event Decisions

Most practical crime prevention is concerned with offender *event decisions*, as these decision points suggest means of deterring rational offenders. Cornish and Clarke (2008, p. 38) explained that in event decisions experienced offenders "will tend to concentrate solely on those situational factors that hinder or advance instrumental action in fulfillment of the criminal goal." In other words, offender event decisions revolve around factors that increase or decrease their chances of successfully perpetrating the crime – or the rational calculation of risks versus rewards. Situational factors impacting the offender's perception of risk and reward are varied, and depend on the type of crime, the environment, and the offender's motives.

To illustrate, consider a residential burglar. The first event decisions that a burglar will make relate to his choice of target. Here, experienced offenders may follow a script and base decisions on what has worked for them when they have committed previous crimes. He might choose a home in an area where he previously committed a burglary and pick a house that has similar characteristics to previous crime targets (e.g., no one is home, no lights). Other event decisions in this scenario will include how to approach the home, how to enter, how to select items to steal, how to load up the stolen goods, and how to leave without being caught. Each of these will be driven by a consideration of the situational factors impacting the likelihood of success or failure. These event decisions illustrate point 6 above – criminal events unfold in a sequence of stages and decisions. For instance, a burglar may enter the home with the intention to steal one thing, but find something better, or, they may find that someone is home after all, resulting in a violent encounter that requires decisions to be made.

A research study by Lasky and colleagues (2017) about shoplifting decisions is illustrative here. They used a combination of eye-tracking technology and interviews to understand how shoplifters make their offending decisions. In particular, the study focused on specific security measures and whether shoplifters are deterred by them. The security measures included: mirrors, closed-circuit television (CCTV), public viewing monitors, electronic article surveillance, product packaging, and product placement. They reported that shoplifters viewed mirrors and CCTV as ineffective and not as a deterrent to their shoplifting decisions. However, the shoplifters said that public viewing monitors, electronic article surveillance, product packaging, and product placement were factors in their decisions. For instance, several shoplifters explained that they avoid items that are locked in cases because they see them as being too risky. One participant said that they avoided stealing a cellphone because it was "right up by the registers . . . And I'm pretty sure those are strategically placed so they're hard to steal" (Lasky et al., 2017, p. 785).

Rational Choice Theory and Repeats

Farrell and colleagues (1995) discussed the dynamics of repeat offending as a rational choice, reviewing several crimes (e.g., burglary, car crimes, robbery, intimate partner violence) for which continuing criminal involvement (i.e., repeating a crime) is the rational choice for the offender to make. In particular, the authors were interested in explaining why offenders target the same victims or other entities repeatedly – a phenomenon known as repeat victimization. Farrell and colleagues explained that repeat victimization occurs because the characteristics that made the target suitable in the first place continue to make the target suitable, and therefore, define the choice as rational. They explained that "a case can be advanced that repetitions involve less effort, lower risk, and equivalent reward when compared to first victimizations" (Farrell et al., 1995, p. 390). In other words, the constellation of risks, rewards, and so on will continue to make a once-victimized target a rational choice for crime unless, and until, these characteristics change. These choices and experiences begin to create a script, or shorthand, for the offender to follow for future criminal events. Overall, it is rational for the offender to not only repeat the crime, but often to repeat the crime against the same target.

Applications for Crime Prevention

Within the field of crime prevention, rational choice theory was developed to suggest immediate solutions to crime. Knowing how offenders approach their decisions, especially criminal event decisions, has practical applications, as the shoplifting study by Lasky and colleagues (2017) suggests.

A particular focus is upon changing the environmental factors that signal to potential offenders the attractiveness of criminal opportunities. This is an effective approach to designing crime prevention strategies and programs. Rational choice theory informs this process by emphasizing five key methods to reduce criminal opportunities (Cornish & Clarke, 2003):

1. Increase the perceived effort of crime.
2. Increase the perceived risks of crime.
3. Reduce the expected rewards of crime.
4. Remove excuses for crime.
5. Reduce the provocations for crime.

These five methods for altering criminal opportunity structures form the basis for situational crime prevention. **Situational crime prevention** (SCP) is described further in Chapter 6, but is briefly addressed here, because it is so closely connected to the rational choice perspective. As Cornish and Clarke (2008) note, rational choice theory was conceived as a means of assisting in the development of situational crime prevention. SCP provides a framework for designing crime prevention strategies catered to the crime and to the specific situation. SCP is designed to take advantage of an offender's rational decision-making process by manipulating the perceived effort, risks, rewards, excuses, and provocations for crime, thereby guiding them toward a non-criminal decision when faced with an opportunity (Cornish & Clarke, 2003). For example, in the burglary scenario described above, a motivated burglary may decide that a target is too risky if the home is occupied, the lights are on, the street is busy, or neighborhood watch signs are posted.

Routine Activities Theory

Routine activities theory provides a compatible perspective to rational choice and crime pattern theories that explains how criminal opportunities are formed within the environment. Together, these theoretical frameworks are especially useful because routine activities theory explains how criminal opportunities are formed, rational choice theory explains the decision-making processes of offenders when they encounter such opportunities, and crime pattern theory identifies how and why crime concentrates as a result. Routine activities theory is one of the most popular theoretical perspectives in the field of criminology. Originally introduced by Cohen and Felson in 1979, it has since been repurposed a number of times to explain many different outcomes related to crime (e.g., criminal behavior, deviance, victimization, fear of crime).

Routine activities theory focuses on the immediate circumstances surrounding criminal events. The circumstances favorable to crime are those that provide opportunities for crimes to occur, and according to routine activities theory, there are three essential components to criminal opportunities. First, criminal opportunities require a **motivated offender** – someone who is inclined to offend if the conditions are right. The theory largely assumes that a sufficient pool of motivated offenders exists in society, and does not explain why people are driven to commit crime. Instead, it approaches motivated offenders in relation to potential crime targets. That is, the motivated offender concept of the theory refers to the exposure and/or proximity of motivated offenders to crime targets.

Second, criminal opportunities require a **suitable target**. The characteristics that make a target suitable vary according to the type of crime and the offender's motivations, but may include attributes such as monetary value or portability of goods. In the original routine activities research article, Cohen and Felson (1979) described suitable targets as having value, visibility, accessibility, and inertia. At the time, they were mostly describing consumer goods that might be the targets of theft. Later, in describing hot products, or products that are perpetually targeted by thieves, Clarke and Webb (1999) explained target suitability in terms of the acronym CRAVED. CRAVED products are concealable, removable, available, valuable, enjoyable, and disposable. Of course, the ultimate hot product is cash as it has all of these characteristics.

Third, opportunities require an absence of capable guardianship. "**Guardians**" are those individuals capable of preventing crimes from occurring (Cohen & Felson, 1979, p. 590). Offenders are often discouraged from committing crimes if there are others around who may witness the crime or intervene to stop them, so guardians may be anyone from passersby to police officers. From an opportunity perspective, the presence of **capable guardianship** disrupts the criminal opportunity structure and makes the criminal event less likely. According to Marcus Felson (1995), there are four degrees of responsibility for guardianship to prevent victimization, including personal (protecting oneself), assigned (specific people), diffuse (multiple people), and general (amongst those present). This concept of degree of responsibility is discussed further in Chapter 6.

In short, routine activities theory explains crimes as a function of **criminal opportunities**. Criminal opportunities form when motivated offenders, suitable targets, and an absence of capable guardians meet in the same place at the same time. These three elements of criminal opportunities are often depicted as a "crime triangle," as discussed in Chapter 1, with each routine activity concept representing a separate side of the triangle (Eck, 2003; see Figure 2.7). When these three elements converge, criminal opportunities are created, and when rational offenders decide that the benefits of crime outweigh the costs, they exploit these opportunities and crimes occur. From a crime prevention standpoint, removing one of the sides of this triangle should theoretically disrupt the opportunity structure, thereby making the

Figure 2.7 The Crime Triangle.
Source: Adapted from Eck, 2003.

crime less likely to occur. This could be accomplished by increasing capable guardianship, minimizing target suitability, or decreasing exposure or proximity to motivated offenders.

Macro-Level Routine Activities

In their classic research study, Cohen and Felson were interested in addressing why crime rates had increased so significantly in the United States following the Second World War. Between 1960 and 1975, robbery rates had increased by 263 percent, aggravated assault rates by 164 percent, and homicide rates by 188 percent; property offenses had similarly increased by over 200 percent (Cohen & Felson, 1979). Yet, traditional correlates of crime, such as economic conditions, were not proving to be useful explanations because economic conditions in the United States were good at the time. In contrast to many other criminological theories, routine activities theory does not attempt to explain criminal motivation, but rather, seeks to "examine the manner in which the spatio-temporal organization of social activities helps people to translate their criminal inclinations into action," (Cohen & Felson, 1979, p. 589). In other words, Cohen and Felson explained that crime rates could be understood as a function of societal routines. These societal routines facilitate circumstances under which already criminally motivated people find favorable conditions for crime.

The results from Cohen and Felson's (1979) research suggested that crime rates had increased in the United States because post-war societal routines resulted in greater criminal opportunities, and hence, higher crime rates. Put differently, something had changed in society that resulted in more frequent convergence of motivated offenders, suitable targets, and a lack of guardianship. This original formulation of the routine activity perspective was intended to explain increases in crime rates in the United States as a function of changes to societal routine activities. This was a macro-level approach to studying crime. **Macro-level** refers to large-scale, broad, wide-angle, or group-based analyses of the phenomenon under study. This contrasts with **micro-level**, or individual-level, approaches, which would instead focus on individual patterns or behaviors. In both cases, the goal is to identify patterns related to an outcome of interest.

Cohen and Felson (1979) suggested that changes to routine activities within U.S. society at the macro-level corresponded with how crime was patterned, particularly the percentage of women who entered the workforce, the percentage of the population enrolled in higher education, and the availability of suitable crime targets (i.e., durable goods). They called this a "household activity ratio," which represented the proportion of U.S. households most exposed to risk for personal and property victimization (Cohen & Felson, 1979, p. 600). They argued that these changes to society's routines also changed the nature of criminal opportunities in the country – with more homes unoccupied during the day and more people outside their homes that could be targeted by motivated offenders. They reported significant relationships between their household activity ratio and each crime rate change (non-negligent homicide, forcible rape, aggravated assault, robbery, and burglary).

Macro-level routine activities have remained an important area of study for researchers and crime prevention practitioners. Aside from the significant changes that occurred in the United States following the Second World War that Cohen and Felson examined, society has undergone at least two large shifts in its routine activities – the advent of the Internet and the COVID-19 pandemic. Researchers have begun to examine how these changes to societal routines may have affected crime rates. To address the former, Brady and colleagues (2016) developed a new activity ratio that reflected the shift to online activities and the corresponding increases in monetary losses to cybervictimization. They calculated an "online activity ratio" based on total annual e-commerce sales divided by the total number of U.S. Internet users per year – indicating a degree of exposure to online risk and/or opportunity. Their results indicated a linear relationship between increases in online opportunities for crime and increases in financial cybervictimization, suggesting strong support for the theoretical premise that macro-level routines are related to crime rates, even online.

Similarly, Stickle and Felson (2020) have argued that the COVID-19 pandemic and the consequent stay-at-home orders have offered a unique opportunity to test whether these changes to the world's routine activities affected crime rates. Research by Nivette and colleagues (2021) addressed this question by analyzing crime data from 27 cities across 23 countries in the Americas, Europe, the Middle East, and Asia. They reported that stay-at-home policies were associated with significant drops in crime, although the effects varied by crime type and across cities.

Micro-Level Routine Activities

As discussed, routine activities theory was initially a macro-level theoretical explanation of crime. However, it did not take long for criminologists to adapt the theory to also explain micro-level patterns in crime. Recall that a micro-level explanation focuses on individual behaviors rather than group-level dynamics. At the micro-level, the theory retains its emphasis on criminal opportunities, but views the three concepts of motivated offenders, suitable targets, and guardianship individually and behaviorally rather than societally. Here, the focus is on how *individuals* might engage in routine behaviors that increase or decrease their likelihood of becoming a crime victim. In 1978, Michael Hindelang and his colleagues published results of the first national victimization survey in the United States. As part of their analyses, they proposed a theory of personal victimization very similar to this idea. Their theory, lifestyle-exposure theory, highlights lifestyle behaviors that might increase individuals' exposure to victimization risk. For example, they stressed going out at night and spending more time in public as lifestyle behaviors that increase victimization risk (Hindelang et al., 1978).

Over time, micro-level routine activities and lifestyle-exposure theory have commingled and are now often referred to as **lifestyle-routine activities theory**. Lifestyle-routine activities theory is discussed further in Chapter 8, but briefly, it explains victimization in terms of risk factors grounded in the three essentials of the theory – motivated offenders, suitable targets, and a lack of capable guardianship. In this context, risk factors are those routines that make individuals more susceptible to being targets of criminal behavior. So routine behaviors that expose would-be crime victims to motivated offenders would be considered risk factors for victimization, such as the example provided by Hindelang and colleagues (1978) involving spending time in public. Other risky routine activities may be those that increase target suitability or that decrease guardianship. For example, someone who posts pictures of themselves to their online social network may increase their target suitability for motivated offenders, or a person who walks home alone from work would be better off walking with someone thereby increasing guardianship.

Countless studies have utilized routine activities to better understand crime and victimization. Generally, research studies have supported the theory, and the premise that individuals' routine activities may foster opportunities for criminal victimization and increase their victimization risk (e.g., McNeeley, 2015). All four authors of this textbook have been involved in research studies of micro-level routine activities, and our research can provide examples to illustrate these points. A research study by Snyder and colleagues (2021), for instance, investigated risk factors for personal victimization against U.S. college students using lifestyle-routine activities theory. Among their findings were that binge drinking, number of sexual partners, and Greek membership (networks of student social clubs present mainly in U.S. colleges and universities) were significant predictors of victimization. In another study, Henson and colleagues (2010) analyzed data from high school students to identify routine activity-based risk factors for violent victimization. They found that certain routines, such as driving around, increased risks for serious violent victimization, while participating in family activities decreased victimization risks. They also reported that having a delinquent lifestyle was one of the strongest predictors of victimization risk. In a final example, Reyns and Scherer (2019) identified risk factors for sexual and stalking victimization against college students with, and without, disabilities. They found that alcohol use, illicit drug use, and number of sexual partners significantly increased one's odds of experiencing sexual victimization and stalking victimization, although some of the effects also varied by one's type of disability (i.e., no disability, physical disability, learning disability, mental disability).

Applications for Crime Prevention

The routine activities perspective is one of the theoretical pillars of crime prevention theory. Like the other theories of environmental criminology discussed in this chapter, it provides a useful framework for thinking about criminal opportunities and how to disrupt them. Felson and Clarke (1998) note that this can be accomplished through problem-oriented policing, defensible space architecture, crime prevention through environmental design, and situational crime prevention. Each of these strategies is discussed throughout the book. The crime triangle provided in Figure 2.7 is also helpful in this way because it visually represents the conditions under which criminal opportunities are formed. It follows, then, that eliminating or altering one of more of these conditions will disrupt opportunities for crime or victimization to occur. This principle applies to both the macro-level and the micro-level. In both cases, the inference is that decreasing exposure or proximity to motivated offenders, decreasing target suitability, and increasing guardianship will diminish criminal opportunities.

At the macro-level, for example, environmental design might be used to change flows of people into an area, decreasing the numbers of motivated offenders coming into contact with suitable targets. Or, perhaps instituting a neighborhood watch to provide more eyes on the street would increase aggregate levels of guardianship, making homes more protected and discouraging offenders.

At the micro-level, these same principles apply, but to individual behavior. For example, a pedestrian might avoid high-crime areas of a city to decrease their exposure or proximity to motivated offenders, or, a driver might place any valuable items (e.g., backpacks, purses, shopping bags) in their trunk when they park their car, decreasing target attractiveness to motivated offenders. Most micro-level research has focused on identifying risk factors for victimization – a concept discussed further in Chapter 8 – with the implication being that avoiding these risk factors will reduce victimization risk. From a research perspective, evaluating whether this is the case is a challenge because it requires longitudinal data. However, a research study Turanovic and Pratt (2014) utilized longitudinal data from the Gang Resistance Education and Training program to determine whether changes to risky lifestyle behaviors reduce victimization risk. They found that changes in risky lifestyles reduced individuals' risks for repeat victimization, but they also noted that one's level of self-control influences whether these changes are made. In a somewhat similar study, Butler and colleagues (2022) used longitudinal data to identify risk factors for sexual assault victimization against college women, and assess whether changing risk factors between the first and second time they were examined reduced victimization risk. Their results indicated that binge drinking was a significant risk factor for sexual assault victimization. Importantly, those students who only experienced an alcohol- or drug-related sexual assault at time one (but not time two) had reduced the number of days they binge drank from time one and time two, which was significantly different from repeat victims.

Summary

The three theoretical perspectives reviewed in this chapter belong within the environmental criminology school of thought. While they each have distinct characteristics and foci, they have a shared emphasis on criminal opportunities as the root cause of crime. Environmental criminology explores the relationship between the environment and crime, with a focus on how environmental factors (e.g., urban design, situational factors) contribute to opportunities for crimes to occur. By understanding these complex relationships, crime prevention practitioners can develop more effectives strategies for crime control and prevention.

> ### 🔍 Keywords
>
> Environmental Criminology, Human Ecology, Concentric Zone Model, Social Disorganization, Social Disorganization Theory, Crime Prevention through Environmental Design, Defensible Space, Crime Pattern Theory, Awareness Spaces, Nodes, Paths, Edges, Journey to Crime, Distance Decay, Script, Environmental Backcloth, Rational Choice Theory, Bounded Rationality, Situational Crime Prevention, Routine Activities Theory, Motivated Offender, Suitable Target, Guardians, Capable Guardianship, Criminal Opportunities, Macro-Level, Micro-Level, Lifestyle-Routine Activities Theory

Discussion Questions

1. Write a list of the crime patterns that exist in your campus, city, or town. In what places or times do you think crime concentrates, and why?
2. Are offenders rational? What bounds their rationality? Apply your answer to both involvement and event decisions.
3. Henson's study found that for high school students, activities such as driving around increased risks for serious violent victimization, while participating in family activities decreased victimization risks. What lifestyle-routine activities theoretical concepts do these two activities represent and why?
4. How did macro- and micro-level routine activities change as a result of the COVID-19 pandemic?
5. How do the theoretical explanations for crime patterns provided by crime pattern theory, rational choice theory, and routine activities theory overlap?

References

Brady, P. Q., Randa, R., & Reyns, B. W. (2016). From WWII to the World Wide Web: A research note on social changes, online "places," and a new online activity ratio for routine activity theory. *Journal of Contemporary Criminal Justice, 32*(2), 129–147.

Brantingham, P. (2010). Crime pattern theory. In B. S. Fisher & S. P. Lab (Eds), *Encyclopedia of victimology and crime prevention* (pp. 192–198). Thousand Oaks, CA: Sage.

Brantingham, P. L., & Brantingham, P. J. (1984). *Patterns in crime.* New York: Macmillan.

Brantingham, P. L., & Brantingham, P. J. (1993a). Environment, routine and situation: Toward a pattern theory of crime. *Advances in Criminological Theory, 5,* 259–294.

Brantingham, P. L., & Brantingham, P. J. (1993b). Nodes, paths and edges: Considerations on the complexity of crime and the physical environment. *Journal of Environmental Psychology, 3*, 3–28.

Brantingham, P. L., & Brantingham, P. J. (2008). The rules of crime pattern theory. In: R. Wortley, L. Mazerolle, & S. Rombouts (Eds.), *Environmental criminology and crime analysis*. Devon, UK: Willan Publishing.

Butler, L. C., Fisher, B. S., & Reyns, B. W. (2022). Does change in binge drinking reduce risk of repeat sexual assault victimization? Evidence from three cohorts of freshman undergraduate women. *Crime & Delinquency, 68*(3), 357–380.

Clarke, R. V., & Cornish, D. B. (1985). Modeling offenders' decisions: A framework for research and policy. *Crime and Justice, 6*, 147–185.

Clarke, R. V. G., & Webb, B. (1999). *Hot products: Understanding, anticipating and reducing demand for stolen goods* (Vol. 112). London: Home Office, Policing and Reducing Crime Unit, Research, Development and Statistics Directorate.

Cohen, L. E., & Felson, M. (1979). Social change and crime rate trends: A routine activity approach. *American Sociological Review, 44*(4), 588–608.

Cornish, D. B., & Clarke, R. V. (2003). Opportunities, precipitators and criminal decisions: A reply to Wortley's critique of situational crime prevention. *Crime Prevention Studies, 16*, 41–96.

Cornish, D. B., & Clarke, R. V. (2008). The rational choice perspective. In R. Wortley & L. Mazerolle (Eds), *Environmental criminology and crime analysis* (pp. 21–47). Portland, OR: Willan Publishing.

Eck, J. E. (2003). Police problems: The complexity of problem theory, research and evaluation. *Crime prevention studies*, vol. 15 (pp. 79–113). Monsey, NY: Criminal Justice Press.

Farrell, G., Phillips, C., & Pease, K. (1995). Like taking candy: Why does repeat victimization occur? *British Journal of Criminology, 35*(3), 384–399.

Felson, M. (1995). Those who discourage crime. In J. E. Eck & D. Weisburd (Eds), *Crime and place: Crime prevention studies* (pp. 53–66). Monsey, NY: Criminal Justice Press.

Felson, M., & Boivin, R. (2015). Daily crime flows within a city. *Crime Science, 4*(1), 1–10.

Felson, M., & Clarke, R. V. (1998). Opportunity makes the thief. *Police Research Series, Paper, 98*. London: Home Office.

Felson, M., & Eckert, M. A. (2018). *Crime and everyday life* (6th ed.). Thousand Oaks, CA: Sage Publications.

Friendly, M. (2022). The life and works of André-Michel Guerry, revisited. *Sociological Spectrum, 42*(4–6), 233–259.

Gerell, M. (2021). Does the association between flows of people and crime differ across crime types in Sweden? *European Journal on Criminal Policy and Research, 27*(3), 433–449.

Henson, B., Wilcox, P., Reyns, B. W., & Cullen, F. T. (2010). Gender, adolescent lifestyles, and violent victimization: Implications for routine activity theory. *Victims & Offenders, 5*(4), 303–328.

Hindelang, M. J., Gottfredson, M. R., & Garofalo, J. (1978). *Victims of personal crime: An empirical foundation for a theory of personal victimization*. Cambridge, MA: Ballinger.

Jeffery, C. R. (1971). *Crime prevention through environmental design*. Beverly Hills, CA: Sage.

Lasky, N. V., Fisher, B. S., & Jacques, S. (2017). "Thinking thief" in the crime prevention arms race: Lessons learned from shoplifters. *Security Journal, 30,* 772–792.

McNeeley, S. (2015). Lifestyle-routine activities and crime events. *Journal of Contemporary Criminal Justice, 31*(1), 30–52.

Newman, O. (1972). *Defensible space: Crime prevention through urban design.* New York: Macmillan.

Nivette, A. E., Zahnow, R., Aguilar, R., Ahven, A., Amram, S., Ariel, B., . . . & Eisner, M. P. (2021). A global analysis of the impact of COVID-19 stay-at-home restrictions on crime. *Nature Human Behaviour, 5*(7), 868–877.

Park, R. E., & Burgess, E. W. (1925). *The city.* Chicago, IL: University of Chicago Press.

Reyns, B. W., & Scherer, H. (2019). Disability type and risk of sexual and stalking victimization in a national sample: A lifestyle–routine activity approach. *Criminal Justice and Behavior, 46*(4), 628–647.

Shaw, C. R., & McKay, H. D. (1942). *Juvenile delinquency and urban areas.* Chicago, IL: University of Chicago Press.

Snyder, J. A., Scherer, H. L., & Fisher, B. S. (2021). Poly-victimization among female college students: Are the risk factors the same as those who experience one type of victimization? *Violence Against Women, 27*(10), 1716–1735.

Song, G., Bernasco, W., Liu, L., Xiao, L., Zhou, S., & Liao, W. (2019). Crime feeds on legal activities: Daily mobility flows help to explain thieves' target location choices. *Journal of Quantitative Criminology, 35,* 831–854.

Stickle, B., & Felson, M. (2020). Crime rates in a pandemic: The largest criminological experiment in history. *American Journal of Criminal Justice, 45*(4), 525–536.

Turanovic, J. J., & Pratt, T. C. (2014). "Can't stop, won't stop": Self-control, risky lifestyles, and repeat victimization. *Journal of Quantitative Criminology, 30,* 29–56.

Wiles, P., & Costello, A. (2000). *The road to nowhere: The evidence for travelling criminals.* London: Home Office (Home Office Research Study No. 207).

Wortley, R., & Mazerolle, L. (Eds) (2008). *Environmental criminology and crime analysis* (pp. 21–47). Portland, OR: Willan Publishing.

Chapter 3
Environmental Criminology Theories

Environmental Criminology Theories

Jamie A. Snyder

Chapter Outline

In this chapter, we will focus on:

Environmental Theories of Crime

- Definition and major assumptions of environmental theories
- The history of CPTED

Defensible Space Theory and CPTED

- Elements of defensible space
- Additional elements of CPTED

Applying the Elements of Defensible Space and CPTED

- Clason Point and CPTED
- Summary of CPTED research
- Criticisms of CPTED
- Second and third generation CPTED

Learning Objectives

After reading this chapter, you should be able to:

3.1 Define defensible space and CPTED

3.2 Describe the key elements of defensible space and CPTED

3.3 Discuss the evolution of CPTED

3.4 Apply the concepts of defensible space and CPTED

3.5 Evaluate research on defensible space and CPTED

DOI: 10.4324/9781003401551-4

Introduction

As discussed in Chapter 2, opportunity theories, such as routine activity, rational choice, and crime pattern theories, allow us to use what we know about routines, decision-making patterns, and crime concentration to alter the opportunity structure for crime, hopefully resulting in crime prevention. In a similar vein, environmental theories attempt to alter environments with the same goal, blocking opportunities for crime. This chapter will focus on environmental theories and how these approaches can be applied to prevent crime and influence levels of fear. The chapter begins with an overview of defensible space theory and its main elements of territoriality, natural surveillance, image, and juxtaposition or milieu. Examples of each of these elements and how they may or may not influence an area's defensible space will be presented. Next, empirical applications of defensible space will be examined to highlight its effectiveness. Building upon the discussion of defensible space, the focus will then center on specific individual elements categorized under crime prevention through environmental design, such as lighting, locks, alarms, and access control. Studies examining the effectiveness of these strategies will be discussed along with examples of specific applications. This chapter will close with a summary of the empirical evidence for CPTED and future directions such as second and third generation CPTED.

Environmental Theories of Crime

Definition and Major Assumptions of Environmental Theories

Environmental theories are those which consider how the environment, including objects such as buildings in these spaces, can shape opportunities for crime and impact fear of crime. Specifically, the environment may help or hinder these opportunities, providing intervention points for crime prevention. For example, a potential offender may see one area as more advantageous for crime over another based on its physical features. Further, the physical design of an area can impact levels of fear. Environmental theories have similar assumptions; that opportunity reduction can result in the prevention of crime and that environments can be manipulated in multiple ways, including physical design, to reduce crime opportunities and fear while improving overall community health. These theories tend to focus on *how* a criminal act is possible rather than trying to understand motivations of a potential offender (Gooren, 2023). In this sense, environmental theories are often different in their strategies for crime prevention from more traditional criminological theories that attempt to understand offender motivations.

The History of CPTED

The most common framework utilized to describe how physical design and opportunities for crime may be related is **Crime Prevention Through**

Environment Design (CPTED). This environmental design framework was proposed in the early 1970s by C. Ray Jeffery, a criminologist, in the book aptly titled, *Crime Prevention Through Environmental Design* (1971). However, ideas related to CPTED can also be traced further back to Jane Jacobs, a writer who was interested in sociology and urban development, asserting in *The Life and Death of Great American Cities* (1961) that cities could increase safety through three strategies; having clear demarcation of space, having more "eyes on the street" for surveillance, and increased public use of spaces such as sidewalks (Jacobs, 1961). In addition, defensible space theory, coined around the same time as CPTED by Oscar Newman (1972) provides the foundational elements for describing ways in which environmental design can influence crime and fear of crime. While these two frameworks were originally proposed primarily for neighborhood design, they have now been integrated and utilized for a variety of spaces including schools, public transit stations, stadiums, hospitals, bars and restaurants, shopping centers, parks, and parking garages. Below, the elements of defensible space theory will be described, along with additional individual design factors that combine to form the CPTED framework.

Defensible Space Theory and CPTED

Defensible space theory, first proposed by architect Oscar Newman, as outlined in his book *Defensible Space*, and subsequent works, is defined as "the range of mechanisms – real and symbolic barriers, strongly defined areas of influence and improved opportunities for surveillance – that combine to bring an environment under the control of its residents" (1972, p. 3). Often focused on the neighborhood setting, including areas both inside and outside of residences, defensible space seeks to use physical design to reduce opportunities for crime through control and deterrence. The physical design of a community includes interior common spaces, such as hallways and lobbies, as well as outside grounds and surrounding streets. Spaces where the elements of defensible space are used would, therefore, be more in control of the residents and would deter crime, reduce fear, and overall have less disorder. On the other hand, places that exhibit low levels of defensible space would provide greater opportunities for crime, fear, and disorder.

Elements of Defensible Space

Newman outlined four major elements to consider when examining the level of defensible space in an environment – 1) Territoriality, 2) Natural Surveillance, 3) Image, and 4) Juxtaposition or Milieu. He argued that the four major elements act together to create a secure environment. Elements can influence one another in a positive manner, such as territoriality resulting in an improved image, while they can also hinder one another, such as a poor image resulting in lower territoriality. Thus, areas that were high in these elements would be more under control of its residents and therefore have lower levels of crime and fear. Each of these elements is described below.

Expand Your Understanding – The Case of Pruitt–Igoe

Pruitt–Igoe was a multi-rise apartment complex with 2,740 units built in St. Louis, Missouri in the 1960s. It was designed by a famous architect at the time and was lauded as a model for low-income housing. By 1972, less than 20 years after it was built, it was declared an utter failure and ultimately destroyed at the loss of millions (Newman, 1996). So, what happened? As Newman mused from his then nearby job as a professor, "It was impossible to feel or exert proprietary feelings, impossible to tell resident from intruder" (1996, p. 12). In other words, the physical design of the building and grounds prevented residents from being able to control who was in most of the public space, how public spaces were used, or even identify neighbors. The high-rise design prevented any real natural surveillance and the common nature of the third floor, which had been idealized as a place for residents to do laundry and socialize, had become overrun with litter, graffiti, and other forms of disorder. Staircases were blocked, broken windows remained unfixed, and crime overtook most public spaces in the buildings. Interestingly, most private spaces inside of apartments were well maintained, and some spaces remained clean and well taken care of. Newman argued that the "residents maintained and controlled those areas that were clearly defined as their own" (1996, p. 11).

Territoriality

Territoriality considers how well a space is demarcated or designated. In other words, how clear it is what the space is intended for, where the boundaries are for that space, and who "owns" the space. The design of both private and public spaces factor into an area's overall territoriality. Spaces that have high territoriality are those in which the space is clearly defined, such as having a clear beginning and end, and clearly convey what that space is to be used for. There are several ways to create territoriality, including the use of fences, bushes, sidewalks, other landscaping, or any aspect that creates a sense of ownership or clear boundaries. Newman (1972) asserted that barriers such as shrubs and fences, both real and symbolic, reinforced the notion of ownership over a space. He further argued that territoriality was important because residents were more likely to take action over spaces, especially private ones, they felt ownership of or investment in. In other words, if a person feels a space belongs to them, such as a front yard, and something suspicious is happening in that space, they may be more likely to intervene by calling the police or reporting their concern. Thus, the creation of even the illusion of a space as private and owned by certain residents is important for establishing territoriality and can translate into effective crime deterrence.

On the other hand, spaces that are poorly designated and lack boundaries or features that denote what the space should be used for may be less likely to be watched over. For instance, spaces that are used by multiple individuals, entirely public spaces, such as overlapping outdoor spaces in an apartment complex or some recreation spaces, may lack territoriality. Individuals in these spaces may feel less ownership over them and, therefore, may be less likely to intervene when they see something concerning or may feel like it's someone else's responsibility to take care of that space. Newman also identified shared spaces inside apartment buildings, such as lobbies, hallways, and other multi-user spaces as those that could have low territoriality. Overall, the concept of territoriality relies on the perception of who owns a space and how likely individuals are to defend it.

Natural Surveillance

The second element of defensible space, **natural surveillance**, refers to the ability of people in a space to see around them without the use of technology. This could include the placement of doors, windows, landscaping, or other environmental design elements that allow for surveillance by people using or near a space. Examples of things that may block natural surveillance include the positioning of doors and or lack of windows, overall building layout and design, bushes or other landscaping, and other objects that may hinder the ability of individuals to see others in that space. To illustrate, the more floors a building has, the less likely residents on higher levels of the building will be able to easily surveil what is going on outside on the street level. Improving overall surveillance not only adds what is often called, "eyes on the street," increasing the risk of identifying potential offenders, but it can change perceptions, attitudes, and behaviors of both residents and potential offenders (Farrington & Welsh, 2002).

Newman considered good natural surveillance as buildings with street-facing doors, numerous windows, and open lobbies, so that individuals passing by could see into these public spaces, as well as out of these spaces. Ideally the windows would be large, allowing people to easily see into the lobby of, for example, an apartment building. Even if active surveillance is not occurring, simply having these elements can provide the illusion of surveillance, suggesting that anyone in the space could easily be watched at any time. This illusion could prevent potential criminal activity from taking place in that space and provide residents with a sense of safety, knowing they can easily be seen from the outside. Fear is an important element to natural surveillance according to Newman, serving to encourage residents to actively surveille areas and increase the chances of intervention. Newman further argues that natural surveillance is closely related to territoriality, with both serving to increase the ability of residents to distinguish between strangers, including potential offenders, and those that live there. Natural surveillance can be further encouraged by residents through design elements like parks, benches, and well-designed paths that encourage the use of spaces and increase deterrence, as well as the likelihood of detection of potential crimes.

Image

The third major element of defensible space is **image**. Image can be determined by the appearance of an area, commonly in terms of how an area looks and if the area is well kept. This includes the maintenance of an area, such as the appearance of the outside of an apartment building and the surrounding grounds. The image of an area is typically broken into two concepts, physical and social, and is often examined in terms of disorder. **Physical disorder** refers to features that suggest an area may be in disrepair, including abandoned, boarded-up, or run-down buildings, graffiti, trash, peeling paint, broken windows, overgrown landscaping, unkept common spaces such as parks or recreation areas, and other evidence of damage in an environment. Physical disorder is often associated with higher levels of fear, which could keep residents out of certain spaces, resulting in the undermining of territorially.

The second concept of image, **social disorder**, considers the people in a space and in what types of activities they are engaging. For instance, if individuals are openly participating in drug dealing on the street, this would be a sign of high social disorder. Other examples of social disorder include evidence of gang activity, excessive noise, groups of unsupervised teens, or overt criminal behavior taking place in public areas. The level of physical and social disorder in a space is important for defensible space. First, if an area has high levels of physical disorder, it suggests that the area is not well taken care of, meaning little ownership or control is exerted over the area. If residents are not able to keep buildings from falling into disrepair or remove graffiti, there is less chance they are able to stop or deter crime. Similarly, if high social disorder is present, this suggests that residents have little control over what people are doing in the space and that offenders have little fear of being caught, presenting the overall image that the space is undefendable. This perception of low control, coupled with increased fear that potentially impacts resident behavior, makes it difficult to create defensible space.

Several studies have examined the relationship between disorder and fear, finding that the physical appearance of an area is related to perceptions of fear of crime (Gainey et al., 2011; Franklin et al., 2008; Perkins & Taylor, 1996) and that as neighborhood physical condition improves, so do perceptions of an area, including reductions in fear of crime (Hur & Nasar, 2014). The physical condition of an area is also related to resident satisfaction (Hur & Nasar, 2014), which could then translate into higher feelings of territoriality, linking image with this element of defensible space. Disorder has also been examined within the context of crime, again, often finding that areas with higher levels of physical and social disorder, subsequently, also have higher levels of crime (Chen & Rafail, 2022). Although not as robust as research linking fear of crime and disorder, this relationship has been found for several types of crime including burglary's association with vacant homes as a source of disorder (Jones & Pridemore, 2016) and violence more generally (Wilcox et al., 2004).

Expand Your Understanding – Fear of Crime in University Spaces

Fisher and Nasar (1992) had students at Ohio State University rate spaces based on fear levels. Students were provided several different pictures of spaces on campus and then asked to rate their fear level in these spaces. The results suggested that the physical design of the space was directly related to levels of fear. Specifically, areas that had high levels of refuge (spaces where people could hide), low escape (meaning the person felt it would be difficult to leave the space quickly), and low prospect (meaning it was difficult to surveille the space) had the highest levels of fear. On the other hand, areas with low refuge, high escape, and high prospect had the lowest levels of fear. This study demonstrates how important simple design features can be in influencing levels of fear.

Taken together, defensible space theory would argue that areas with high social and physical disorder cannot be defended as well, allowing more opportunities for crime and fear of crime to flourish. On the other hand, Newman asserted that a positive image could provide an area with a sense of uniqueness and pride, further building territoriality and a sense of control over an area. This would be especially true for design elements that provide an image that the area is well cared for, such as new paint or different colors of paint for each apartment building, well-kept landscaping, and elements that further demarcate a space as "owned" by specific residents. These image elements could then work in conjunction with territoriality to create not only the image that the area is under the watch of its residents, but that the area is under the ownership and care of those that live there.

Juxtaposition or Milieu

The final element of defensible space is **juxtaposition** or **milieu**, which refers to what is physically around, or next to, a space. What is adjacent to an area can influence the ability of those in the area to provide security (Cozens & Love, 2015). In the context of a neighborhood, it often consists of what is nearby, including land use. **Land use** is described as what types of buildings are in the area, or what purpose an area is supposed to serve, such as commercial, residential, industrial, or mixed-use purposes. Land use is an important consideration because it determines *who* will be in a space. If the space is all residential, it would be natural to assume people coming to the space would be mostly residents and visitors to residential properties in the area. On the other hand, if the space is mixed-use with some of the land being residential zoned and some being commercial or industrial zoned, this increases the variety of people that may be in an area. For example, an area that contains an apartment complex, a gas station, a restaurant, and a bar would attract a much different mix of people compared with an area that only has an apartment complex.

Defensible space theory asserts that areas with more mixed land use provide more opportunities for crime, since the types of people using the area would increase. Newman argued that residential areas should be more defendable since, hypothetically, the users of these areas should mostly be residents or people known to residents. This also increases the chances of being able to differentiate legitimate users of an area from those who may have illegitimate purposes, such as committing crimes. This would also act as a deterrent, increasing the perception that those who do not live in the area or have legitimate business would be easier to identify. In contrast, an area that contains both commercial and residential land use would attract both residents and non-residents alike, making it nearly impossible for residents of the area to discern between those there for legitimate purposes compared with those there looking for opportunities to commit crime.

In addition to how the land is utilized, what is beside, or adjacent to, an area also matters. Defensible space considers the meeting of public with private spaces and how the lines between these spaces can sometimes be blurred. For instance, consider a primarily residential area that has a school within the neighborhood. While the land may be zoned residential, the inclusion of a school in the area adds opportunities for potential offenders. This would again make it more difficult to know the intention of people near the school, since they could be simply dropping off their children, but could also be using the presence of the school to conceal their criminal intentions for burglarizing houses nearby. Further, specific places like schools, parks, or certain businesses in an area can act as crime generators or attractors, as referenced in Chapter 2, and as will be discussed in more detail in Chapter 5. Overall, understanding how the land is utilized and what types of opportunities may be presented by nearby businesses, schools, places of recreation, and other public gathering spaces is important to the understanding of defensible space.

Additional Elements of CPTED

Aside from the four major components of defensible space proposed by Newman, several other individual design elements fall under the framework of CPTED and can be utilized to further decrease opportunities for crime. These elements include additional types of surveillance using technology (e.g., cameras), forms of access control, and activity or motivation reinforcement. Each of these elements will be discussed below.

Surveillance

When discussed within the context of defensible space, **surveillance** is typically thought of as design elements that can improve *natural* surveillance, or surveillance that does not rely on some form of technology. However, CPTED can also utilize surveillance through the use of technology to decrease opportunities for crime and reduce fear. One common way to do this is with the use of lighting. It has long been proposed that lighting is related to both crime and fear of crime. Areas that are well lit tend to exert less fear among residents and encourage both resident and public use, while areas that are poorly lit may exert more fear and be avoided and remain largely unused (Cozens et al., 2003). This occurs because the more well lit an area is, the easier it is for those in the space to see their surroundings, including any potential criminal or suspicious activity. Being able to adequately see in an area also increases the sense of safety, indicating there is less chance that anyone could conceal themselves in a space or approach a person without them noticing. Consider how you would feel in a dark alley at night with no lighting. Now, consider the same alley with the addition of bright lighting. While the level of fear of being in an alley at night may still be higher than in the day, there is no doubt it would likely be less than if there were no lighting.

Overall, the research on lighting, crime, and fear of crime has been mixed, but mostly positive. Research on lighting and fear of crime more consistently finds a positive impact, while research on lighting and crime is also mostly positive. Several studies conducted in the early 1990s in the United Kingdom found some impact of lighting and reductions in crime (Pease, 1999), while others found little impact, mostly using samples in the United States (Quinet & Nunn, 1998). Similarly, the research on fear of crime and lighting has also been mixed, albeit a little more positive overall. Some research even suggests residents would be willing to pay for brighter lighting to improve overall use of an area (Kaplan & Chalfin, 2022). On the other hand, it has been argued that lighting may only be impactful in certain situations and at certain crimes. For example, Pease (1998) asserted that only high crime areas should be targeted for lighting interventions and that very specific locations should be chosen based on opportunity for crime. This relies on the assumption that the greatest impact can be felt in areas that need it the most, something that is echoed in other crime prevention efforts and research (Eck & Guerette, 2012). Pease (1998) also emphasized the utility of multiple crime prevention strategies, not just relying on lighting, suggesting that the effect of lighting may be most prominent in conjunction with other changes, such as the addition of cameras or locks.

In a systematic review of more than 20 studies across multiple countries on lighting and crime, Welsh and colleagues (2022) found that lighting was consistently associated with reductions in property crime. This impact was again most consistent in studies conducted in the United Kingdom and was less consistent for studies in the United States. These differences across countries suggest that different opportunity structures for crime may exist, highlighting the importance of understanding the nature of a crime before designing an intervention. Another review of studies, focusing on fear, also concluded that most lighting interventions had a positive impact, with 84 percent of studies having some impact on fear of crime out of the 53 studies examined (Ceccato, 2020). Overall, research suggests that some impact exists, for at least property crimes, and that lighting typically makes people feel safer, reducing fear.

While lighting acts as an enhancement to natural surveillance, the addition of cameras, or closed-circuit television (CCTV), provides another opportunity to increase surveillance of an area through the use of technology. Built on the notion of deterrence, cameras seek to provide the impression that one is always being watched, capturing both regular and irregular activities. If a potential offender sees a camera, this should act as a deterrent, as it increases the chances they will be identified and caught. On the other hand, people engaged in regular routine activities should see cameras as a safety mechanism, providing a sense of security. Research on cameras suggests they can be effective in deterring or reducing crime. However, cameras may be most useful in deterring street crimes, or crimes occurring in public, and may not be as effective for crimes occurring within homes or private spaces. Additionally, little research has found a deterrent effect on violent crimes (Circo & McGarrell, 2021).

In a systematic review by Piza and colleagues (2019) of 76 studies utilizing CCTV, an overall modest impact on crime was found. Most of the positive effects were driven by studies on the use of CCTV in parking lots, or car parks; however, effects were also positive for residential areas. CCTV was most effective at reducing property and drug crimes, with no effects found for violent crimes. Further, efforts that utilized more than one type of crime prevention strategy, such as CCTV and lighting, were more effective at reducing crime than interventions that only changed lighting (Piza et al., 2019)

Research also suggests that cameras can influence fear, with some evidence that the presence of cameras makes people feel safer in spaces, especially when used in conjunction with other CPTED elements such as lighting. For instance, studies have examined how CCTV can influence perceptions of fear, typically finding weaker effects than lighting, but also some impact. When additional strategies are employed with CCTV, the impact on fear reduction typically increases. Overall, CCTV appears to have an impact on crime, but displays weaker impacts on fear when examined alone and may vary by gender (Ceccato, 2020; Cozens & Davies, 2013; Yavuz & Welch, 2010). On the other hand, some research suggests that CCTV may actually increase fear in some areas. It may be that people perceive that the cameras are there because the area is "unsafe," and this may actually trigger fear that would otherwise not be present. This is in contrast to lighting, which could appear more natural or expected in a space, rather than the artificiality of adding a camera. Perceptions of CCTV may also be demographic dependent, with some research finding that older people may feel less fear when a camera is present compared with younger individuals (Chatterton & Frenz, 1994).

Access Control

Another element that can impact opportunities for crime under CPTED is **access control**. Access control seeks to make it more difficult for a potential offender to come into contact with a potential crime target, increasing the risk of detection and providing deterrence (Cozens et al., 2005). Simply put, the easier an area, item, or person is to access, the more opportunities for crime that exist. Access control can also serve to define a space in terms of use. Neighborhoods with several entry and exit points, for instance, are not only convenient for the residents that live in the area, but also for potential criminals. The ease of entry and exit provides ample ability for escape after a crime has been committed. Further, it makes it more difficult to discern between who lives in an area and who is using the street to pass through, or potentially commit a crime. On the other hand, if a neighborhood only has one access point that serves as both the entry and exit, this allows for not only increased surveillance of who is entering and exiting a space, but it also discourages non-residents from using the space since everyone would have to turn around, rather than simply entering at one entrance and leaving through another.

Newman discussed how access control can be enhanced through proper street layouts, suggesting that cul-de-sacs were the most ideal street type. In particular, Newman asserted that street design could be used to create territoriality and natural surveillance, elements of defensible space discussed earlier. The use of a cul-de-sac could create a feeling of community and then translate to greater feelings of ownership over the street, increasing the overall defensible space of an area through the ability to surveille. Additionally, cul-de-sacs are seen as more private, suggesting to potential offenders that they are entering a space where only the residents would be expected, creating a deterrent effect (Armitage, 2011). This contrasts with a street design that allows for through traffic, with many arteries and options for those passing through an area.

A study conducted by Johnson and Bowers (2010) examined this notion using the concept of permeability, or the amount of access to an area. Overall, they found that cul-de-sacs had lower levels of crime, supporting the notion that street layout is related to opportunity. Additionally, burglary was higher on major roads and lower on the roads that were connected to fewer other streets (Johnson & Bowers, 2010). Another study on the decision making of burglars also found support for permeability of an area. Specifically, burglars preferred areas that had more non-local foot traffic than areas that were mostly dominated by locals, citing the increased risk of being detected by locals as a deterrent to these areas (Frith et al., 2017).

While most studies have focused on property crimes, there is some evidence that street design may also be able to influence violent crime (MacDonald, 2015). Research in this area is limited, but the use of cul-de-sacs created through the application of physical barriers to curb specific types of violence, such as gang violence, has been attempted with some success. However, once the barriers were removed, crime rebounded to levels that were similar to before the intervention (Lasley, 1996). Finally, in a study by Haberman and Kelsay (2021) that examined robberies in Cincinnati Ohio, the slope of the street along with the number of street connections was connected to robbery opportunity, suggesting that some types of violence may be influenced by street layout.

In addition to street layout, access control can also be created through the use of technology or formal surveillance such as key card entry to an apartment building, having a door person or security guard stationed in a lobby, or locking a building during certain times of the day. Other examples of access control include gates to enter and exit a parking garage or lot and fencing or gates around buildings or parking structures. Defining parking spaces in residential areas to those who live there and limiting parking can also be utilized as a form of access control. Finally, the use of locks and alarms can be utilized to limit access to locations, such as residences or businesses. Sometimes referred to as **target hardening**, this approach seeks to increase the effort a potential offender must make to access a crime target, such as a building, person, or item (Cozens et al., 2005). Target hardening is used across crime prevention approaches and is also applicable here in terms of design features, specifically focused on making targets less desirable such as gates, locks, and alarms.

Research on the relationship between the use of access controls and crime has been positive, mostly for property crimes, such as burglary. Case in point, a review of 14 studies that utilized CPTED elements found that 93 percent of the studies that used access controls, typically through locks and alarms, in a residential setting were effective, with only one inconclusive finding (Eck & Guerette, 2012). Another study in which alley-gates were installed to restrict access to the rear of homes found a 54 percent decline in burglaries after their installation (Ekblom, 2002). The vast majority of these studies focused on burglary, reinforcing the notion that the type of crime being examined matters in terms of potential success and that different strategies likely work better for some crimes than others. However, research examining access controls through the use of parking gates or security attendants has found reductions of theft from vehicles or vehicle theft, particularly for parking lots or car parks (Poyner, 1991), suggesting access control effectiveness exits beyond burglary reduction.

Activity Support/Motivation Reinforcement

A final element that is often discussed in terms of CPTED is **activity support or motivation reinforcement**. This concept includes tactics that increase a sense of community in an area and encourage community members to engage in the use of public spaces, for instance, a park or walking path. This could include the design of public spaces that support certain activities such as exercise, walking, or dog or children's play areas that result in increased interaction between residents. This increased interaction could then allow residents to better know one another and translate into increased territoriality and feelings of ownership, leading to them exercising more control over spaces. It also allows residents to better distinguish neighbor from stranger, increasing possible surveillance in the area.

The overall idea behind this element is that residents who know one another and develop a sense of community will be more likely to exert control over an area and this control provides fewer opportunities for crime. Knowing and caring for other residents can also decrease fear, further contributing to overall community health and the ability to prevent crime in an area. Finally, it can increase perceptions of the area's safety by residents, encouraging additional legitimate residents to use the area. For example, a renovated park space in a residential area that now includes a playground, benches, clearly defined walking paths, and lighting may increase the level of resident traffic to the area, influencing territorially, surveillance, and the overall image of the area. This, in turn, may promote pro-social behaviors and deter anti-social behaviors, suggesting activity support can be an influential addition to physical design (Gooren, 2023).

Applying the Elements of Defensible Space and CPTED

Taken together, the four major elements of defensible space and the additional elements (e.g., lighting, access control, etc.) discussed above, combine to encompass CPTED and provide a blueprint for how to alter an environment to prevent and deter potential opportunities for crime. Newman outlined what he perceived as "defensible spaces." In terms of residential areas, the ideal situation would be single family homes with clearly defined front and backyard spaces. Backyards would have fencing or other clear boundary markers, while sidewalks and other landscaping could be utilized to clearly delineate front yard spaces.

For apartments, two-story walk-ups or row housing is ideal according to Newman, instead of high-rise apartments. These spaces again would have private backyard spaces that were only shared by the residents that lived there and semi-private front yards. The residences could be uniquely painted or include features to distinguish them, such as flower beds or bushes, to improve their image. Windows would be large and street-facing, including windows to lobbies and other shared spaces. Cameras and lighting could be added to further improve surveillance, along with access controls to the buildings and the parking lots. Access controls could include a desk attendant in the lobby of an apartment building or keycard access to the building or parking lot. Ideally, the street design would be one-way or in the most optimal situation, a cul-de-sac.

While this is the ideal situation, it is also understood that many factors including space, money, and other restrictions may hinder the ability to design the "ideal" space. Additionally, utilizing CPTED requires a balance. As Gooren notes, "The installation of high fences and barbed wire might be good for access control and territoriality, but it is bad for surveillance and activity support" (2023, p. 429). This assertion shows the importance of considering all elements of CPTED and how one might help or hinder the other, highlighting the significance of planning when implementing CPTED elements. As shown in Figure 3.1, certain residence designs would provide greater opportunities for defensible space. Which of the two locations do you think would be easier to modify with CPTED techniques?

Clason Point and CPTED

The case of Clason Point provides an example of how CPTED principles can be applied to a residential area. Clason Point was a public housing development in the Bronx, New York that contained 46 buildings set up as

Figure 3.1 Comparison of Housing Designs.

row housing (Newman, 1996). While the buildings themselves had many features of defensible space, such as only containing two or three floors, the outside grounds were unkept, lacked any territoriality, and were not often used by residents. Residents stated they were fearful of being victimized and often confined themselves to the interior of their homes (Newman, 1996). Efforts to create defensible space focused on the lack of territoriality and poor image of the outside grounds. Specifically, the outside of each building was resurfaced and painted different colors chosen by the residents, providing uniqueness to the buildings to create a sense of territoriality. Next, fencing was installed to provide clear boundaries for backyard spaces, giving residents ownership over outside spaces. Pavers and other landscaping were used in the front of the building to delineate that space as semi-private, and benches were installed along major walking paths, along with new lighting, to encourage resident interaction and natural surveillance (Newman, 1996). Finally, the central area of the housing development was transformed into a multi-use recreation center. This included the addition of new seating, lighting, and separate play areas for children, as well as congregating areas for adults (Newman, 1996). The transformation was an overall success. After the first year, crime decreased overall by 54 percent on the grounds of the housing development, with a 50 percent decrease in serious crimes at night, coupled with residents taking caring of their individual yard spaces, demonstrating a change in perception on ownership and territoriality. Further, fear of crime decreased dramatically, and the development achieved full occupancy with a waiting list (Newman, 1996).

Summary of CPTED Research

Overall, the research on CPTED to date has been relatively positive. Table 3.1 provides a summary of major CPTED elements and the level of evidence that exists related to their effectiveness. As noted in the table, CPTED has been found to be most effective against property crimes – mainly burglary – although there is some research to support it being effective for other property crimes as well, such as auto theft and theft from vehicles. The evidence of effectiveness overall for violent crimes is limited, with few studies examining these types of crime and limited evidence of effectiveness when they are studied. Evidence for the connection between fear of crime and CPTED is very optimistic, with most design features being positively related to reductions in fear. This highlights the notion that perception of crime is also important when considering the impact of crime prevention. Given that fear can drive use of spaces, reducing fear could translate into opportunity reduction over time with the increased use of a space and the deterrent effect that could arise from this increased use. For instance, if a park is getting little use during the evening hours due to fear of dark spaces in the park, adding lighting and other features may encourage more use during this time. Not only could this decrease fear, but it could also increase use of the space, increasing surveillance, potentially resulting in decreases in criminal opportunity.

Table 3.1 Major Findings of Relationship Between CPTED Elements and Crime Outcomes

CPTED Element	Outcome Measures		
	Fear of Crime	*Property Crime*	*Violent Crime*
Locks/Alarms	Positive	Mostly positive	No evidence
Lighting	Positive	Mostly positive	Limited evidence
Street Design	Positive	Positive	Limited evidence
CCTV	Mostly positive	Positive	No evidence
Gates/Access Control	Mostly positive	Positive	Limited evidence

Criticisms of CPTED

While much of the research on CPTED and defensible space has been positive, concerns have also arisen. The most commonly cited concern is that of action, which defensible space hinges on. As you may recall from the discussion above, defensible space creates the ability for residents to "defend" an area through intervention, but what happens when an area is designed well in terms of CPTED, yet still has higher levels of crime? This criticism was discussed by Merry, in her 1981 article. Merry examined a low-income housing complex, finding that even though the area was well designed in terms of defensible space and contained CPTED features, the residents still failed to act, a problem that Merry asserted was related to social relationships between the residents. Specifically, this highlights the importance of not just having good environmental design, but also encouraging residents to act upon situations where they see concerns.

A second criticism of CPTED is the lack of evidence for its impact on violent crimes. Most of the research discussed above has focused on property crime, mainly burglary. Research on CPTED's impact on violent crime remains understudied, with few studies specifically focusing on violent crimes. Additional studies examining very specific types of violence, such as robbery, are needed. This ties into the notion that CPTED should be utilized with a very specific crime type in mind, not generally (Eck & Guerette, 2012). Finally, it has been noted that certain types of offenders may not respond to CPTED strategies. Specifically, those who are under the influence of drugs or are incapacitated may not be affected by CPTED strategies (Cozens et al., 2005), limiting the ability of CPTED for some crime types.

Second and Third Generation CPTED

CPTED in its original form primarily focuses on specific physical design changes to the environment, which has been criticized for ignoring the social aspect of crime prevention as noted by Merry (1981). While some of these changes might result in increased social interaction, other than the element of activity support and recognizing that disorder is part of image, little attention was paid by original CPTED, or first generation CPTED, interventions to specifically develop relationships among residents. This criticism, along with others, has led to proposed modifications to CPTED, resulting in second and third generations for the framework. The second generation of CPTED includes both neighborhood conditions and social relationships, recognizing the importance of these elements to overall neighborhood health and how these can contribute to crime. Thus, the focus of many **Second Generation CPTED** efforts includes the element of social cohesion or the relationships between the residents that live in an area (Mihinjac & Saville, 2019). This evolution of CPTED to reintegrate social cohesion is demonstrated through research that includes elements of disorder and activity support leading some researchers to blend first and second generation CPTED together, not completely separating the two. For example, second generation CPTED would suggest that natural surveillance of an area is still important, but that social cohesion should be encouraged to increase the ability for residents to act on natural surveillance opportunities (Cozens et al., 2005).

On the other hand, **Third Generation CPTED** may be differentiated from its predecessors through the inclusion of green crime prevention, or the idea that urban planning and sustainability should be an integral part of CPTED. Third generation CPTED relies on building sustainability with previous forms of CPTED in four main ways: environmentally, socially, economically, and through public health (Mihinjac & Saville, 2019). While still relatively unstudied compared with other generations of CPTED, several ways to incorporate these notions into design have been suggested. Examples for environmental sustainability include expanding green spaces, and reducing vacant spaces, while examples of social sustainability include the incorporation of residents in design decision and planning. Public health sustainability could be achieved through expanding public and school programming availability, while economic stability could be achieved through the availability of programs that focus on job creation at the local level (Mihinjac & Saville, 2019). A study by Skudder and colleagues (2018) provides an example of third generation CPTED with burglary. This study paired traditional techniques of CPTED using locks, alarms, CCTV, and lighting with environmental considerations in the form of carbon output. The authors concluded that window and door locks, paired with lighting, are both effective and environmentally friendly in terms of carbon output compared with alarms and CCTV, suggesting that environmental impacts can be taken into consideration when designing crime prevention efforts (Skudder et al., 2018).

Summary

The environmental crime theory frameworks of CPTED and defensible space were outlined in this chapter. Crime prevention relies on the notion that opportunity must be present for crime to occur. CPTED provides a framework for how environmental design can enhance or reduce opportunities for crime. The four major elements of defensible space, natural surveillance territorially, image, and milieu/juxtaposition were discussed. In addition, individual design elements such as access control, surveillance, and motivation/activity support in the context of CPTED were discussed along with examples of application. Research evidence for CPTED was presented along with criticisms and future directions for the framework.

Keywords

Environmental theories, Crime Prevention Through Environment Design (CPTED), Defensible Space Theory, Territoriality, Natural Surveillance, Image, Physical Disorder, Social Disorder, Juxtaposition, Milieu, Land Use, Surveillance, Access Control, Target Hardening, Activity Support/Motivation Reinforcement, Second Generation CPTED, Third Generation CPTED

Discussion Questions

1. Which of the four elements of defensible space do you think is most important for reducing opportunities for crime? Why?
2. Discuss why you think it is important for CPTED strategies to target specific types of crimes, rather than all crimes in general.
3. Why is reducing fear of crime through CPTED as important as reducing actual crime?
4. Why do you think that CPTED has typically been found to be more effective for property crimes than violent crimes?
5. What might influence residents' ability to defend spaces that are already designed with CPTED in mind? Is there anything we can do to counteract this?

References

Armitage, R. (2011). *The impact of connectivity and through-movement within residential developments on levels of crime and anti-social behaviour.* Huddersfield: University of Huddersfield. https://eprints.hud.ac.uk/id/eprint/13592/

Ceccato, V. (2020). The architecture of crime and fear of crime: Research evidence on lighting, CCTV and CPTED features. In V. Ceccato & M.K. Nalla (Eds), *Crime and fear in public places* (pp. 38–72). London and New York: Routledge.

Chatterton, M. R., & Frenz, S.J. (1994). Closed circuit television: Its role in reducing burglaries and the rear of crime in sheltered accommodation for the elderly. *Security Journal, 5*(3), 133–139.

Chen, X., & Rafail, P. (2022). Physical disorder and crime revisited: New evidence from intensive longitudinal data. *Social Science Research, 102*, 102637.

Circo, G., & McGarrell, E. (2021). Estimating the impact of an integrated CCTV program on crime. *Journal of Experimental Criminology, 17*, 129–150.

Cozens, P., & Davies, T. (2013). Crime and residential security shutters in an Australian suburb: Exploring perceptions of "Eyes on the Street", social interaction and personal safety. *Crime Prevention and Community Safety, 15*, 175–191.

Cozens, P., & Love, T. (2015). A review and current status of crime prevention through environmental design (CPTED). *Journal of Planning Literature, 30*(4), 393–412.

Cozens, P. M., Neale, R. H., Whitaker, J., Hillier, D., & Graham, M. (2003). A critical review of street lighting, crime and fear of crime in the British city. *Crime Prevention and Community Safety, 5*, 7–24.

Cozens, P., Saville, G., & Hillier, D. (2005). Crime prevention through environmental design (CPTED): A review and modern bibliography. *Journal of Property Management, 23*(5), 328–356.

Eck, J. E., & Guerette, R. T. (2012). Place-based crime prevention: Theory, evidence, and policy. In B. C. Welsh & D. P. Farrington (Eds), *The Oxford handbook of crime prevention* (pp. 354–383). Oxford: Oxford University Press.

Ekblom, P. (2002). From the source to the mainstream is uphill: The challenge of transferring knowledge of crime prevention through replication, innovation and anticipation. In N. Tilley (Ed.), *Analysis for crime prevention* (pp. 131–203). London: Willan Publishing.

Farrington, D. P., & Welsh, C. (2002). *Effects of improved street lighting on crime: A systematic review. Home Office research study 251.* Development and Statistics Directorate, Crown Copyright, London.

Frith, M. J., Johnson, S. D., & Fry, H. M. (2017). Role of the street network in burglars' spatial decision-making. *Criminology, 55*(2), 344–376.

Fisher, B., & Nasar, J. (1992). Fear of crime in relation to three exterior site features: Prospect, refuge, and escape. *Environment and Behavior, 24*, 35–65.

Franklin, T. W., Franklin, C. A., & Fearn, N. E. (2008). A multilevel analysis of the vulnerability, disorder, and social integration models of fear of crime. *Social Justice Research, 21*, 204–227.

Gainey, R., Alper, M., & Chappell, A. T. (2011). Fear of crime revisited: Examining the direct and indirect effects of disorder, risk perception, and social capital. *American Journal of Criminal Justice, 36*, 120–137.

Gooren, J. (2023). The logic of CPTED for public space or the social potential of physical security. *Crime, Law and Social Change, 79*(4), 417–436.

Haberman, C. P., & Kelsay, J. D. (2021). The topography of robbery: Does slope matter? *Journal of Quantitative Criminology, 37*, 625–645.

Hur, M., & Nasar, J. L. (2014). Physical upkeep, perceived upkeep, fear of crime and neighborhood satisfaction. *Journal of Environmental Psychology, 38*, 186–194.

Jacobs, J. (1961). *Death and life of great American cities.* New York: Random House.

Jeffery, C. (1971). *Crime prevention through environmental design*. Beverly Hills, CA: Sage.

Johnson, S. D., & Bowers, K. J. (2010). Permeability and burglary risk: Are cul-de-sacs safer? *Journal of Quantitative Criminology*, 26, 89–111.

Jones, R. W., & Pridemore, W. A. (2016). A longitudinal study of the impact of home vacancy on robbery and burglary rates during the US housing crisis, 2005–2009. *Crime & Delinquency*, 62(9), 1159–1179.

Kaplan, J., & Chalfin, A. (2022). Ambient lighting, use of outdoor spaces and perceptions of public safety: Evidence from a survey experiment. *Security Journal*, 35, 694–724.

Lasley, J. (1996). *Using traffic barriers to "design out" crime: A program evaluation of LAPD's operation cul-de-sac*. Washington, DC: National Institute of Justice, US Department of Justice.

MacDonald, J. (2015). Community design and crime: the impact of housing and the built environment. *Crime and Justice*, 44(1), 333–383.

Merry, S. E. (1981). Defensible space undefended: Social factors in crime control through environmental design. *Urban Affairs Quarterly*, 16(4), 397–422.

Mihinjac, M., & Saville, G. (2019). Third-generation crime prevention through environmental design (CPTED). *Social Sciences*, 8(6), 182.

Newman, O. (1972). *Defensible space: Crime prevention through urban design*. New York: Macmillan.

Newman, O. (1996). *Creating defensible space*. Collingdale, PA: Diane Publishing.

Pease, K. (1998). Lighting and crime: Summary. www.ile.co.uk/documents/Lighting_and_crime_summary.htm

Pease, K. A. (1999). A review of street lighting evaluation: Crime reduction effects. In K. A. Painter & N. Tilley (Eds), *Surveillance of public space: CCTV street lighting and crime prevention* (pp. 47–76). Monsey, NY: Criminal Justice Press.

Perkins, D. D., & Taylor, R. B. (1996). Ecological assessments of community disorder: Their relationship to fear of crime and theoretical implications. *American Journal of Community Psychology*, 24(1), 63–107.

Piza, E. L., Welsh, B. C., Farrington, D. P., & Thomas, A. L. (2019). CCTV surveillance for crime prevention: A 40-year systematic review with meta-analysis. *Criminology & Public Policy*, 18(1), 135–159.

Poyner, B. (1991). Situational crime prevention in two parking facilities. *Security Journal*, 2(1), 96–101.

Quinet, K. D., & Nunn, S. (1998). Illuminating crime: The impact of street lighting on calls for police service. *Evaluation Review*, 22, 751–779.

Skudder, H., Brunton-Smith, I., Tseloni, A., McInnes, A., Cole, J., Thompson, R., & Druckman, A. (2018). Can burglary prevention be low-carbon and effective? Investigating the environmental performance of burglary prevention measures. *Security Journal*, 31, 111–138.

Welsh, B. C., Farrington, D. P., & Douglas, S. (2022). The impact and policy relevance of street lighting for crime prevention: A systematic review based on a half-century of evaluation research. *Criminology & Public Policy*, 21(3), 739–765.

Wilcox, P., Quisenberry, N., Cabrera, D. T., & Jones, S. (2004). Busy places and broken windows? Toward defining the role of physical structure and process in community crime models. *Sociological Quarterly*, 45(2), 185–207.

Yavuz, N., & Welch, E. W. (2010). Addressing fear of crime in public space: Gender differences in reaction to safety measures in train transit. *Urban Studies*, 47(12), 2491–2515.

Chapter 4
The Role of Situational Crime Prevention

The Role of Situational Crime Prevention

Jamie A. Snyder

Chapter Outline

In this chapter, we will focus on:

Defining Situational Crime Prevention
- History and evolution of situational crime prevention
- Major assumptions of situational crime prevention

Elements of Situational Crime Prevention
- Increasing the effort
- Increasing the risk
- Reducing the reward
- Reducing provocations
- Removing excuses

Applying Situational Crime Prevention
- Redesigning Hell
- Burglary prevention
- SCP use by owners of pill mills
- Theft at a retail market

Empirical Evidence for SCP and Future Evaluation
- Misconceptions of situational crime prevention

Learning Objectives

After reading this chapter, you should be able to:

4.1 Define situational crime prevention

4.2 Identify and describe the 25 key elements of situation crime prevention

4.3 Discuss specific applications of situational crime prevention

4.4 Evaluate situational crime prevention research

4.5 Describe criticisms of situational crime prevention

DOI: 10.4324/9781003401551-5

Introduction

Crime prevention strategies can be broad or focused. In the previous chapters, some of the broader crime prevention theories that attempt to limit crime opportunities more generally have been discussed. This chapter will focus on a specific crime prevention approach that examines each situation, seeking to limit opportunities for specific crimes. Aptly called Situational Crime Prevention (SCP), this set of techniques will be examined in detail, along with examples. This chapter starts by presenting the history and evolution of SCP, along with its major assumptions. Next, each of the 25 techniques will be discussed followed by applications. This chapter will end with some criticisms of SCP, along with recommendations and potential future directions for the approach.

Defining Situational Crime Prevention

History and Evolution of Situational Crime Prevention

As has been noted in previous chapters, many criminological theories seek to understand *why* people may commit criminal acts. These theories often focus on motivations, rationales, and characteristics that may predispose or increase the chances of offending. **Situational Crime Prevention** (SCP), on the other hand, takes a different approach, that "is unlike other criminological approaches to crime control. It focuses on the *settings* in which crimes occur, rather than on those committing criminal acts." (Eck & Clarke, 2019, p. 355). This is not to say that SCP does not share any of the assumptions of crime prevention theories; indeed, SCP combines many of the notions from Crime Prevention through Environmental Design (CPTED) and defensible space, as described in Chapter 3, and also embraces the assertions of rational choice theory, which was discussed in Chapter 2. Specifically, SCP assumes that potential offenders have some level of rationality and that they weigh costs and benefits of a potential crime. This calculation of costs and benefits can be altered through techniques of SCP, which includes utilizing methods of both CPTED and defensible space, among other tactics. Thus, SCP can be seen as complementary to other crime prevention theories, rather than conflicting with them. Eck and Clarke (2019) assert that SCP is one of the four major foundations of environmental theory, with routine activities theory, crime pattern theory, and rational choice theory (Chapter 2) encompassing the other three.

Major Assumptions of Situational Crime Prevention

SCP is built upon four main assumptions, according to Eck and Clarke (2019). First, "crime is the result of an interaction between disposition and situation" (Eck & Clarke, 2019, p. 359). In other words, when situational factors that are favorable for opportunities for crime encounter an offender who is motivated, crime is more likely to occur. SCP seeks to manipulate these situational factors for specific crimes, reducing opportunities (Clarke, 1983). Second, people make the choice to commit crime, which is in line with rational choice theory. Third, opportunity is a key component of whether a crime occurs or not. Without opportunity, a highly motivated potential offender is just that, a potential offender. Finally, the fourth major assumption is that situational factors can act as a catalyst for crime to occur. Meaning, some potential offenders can be provoked by a situation into committing a crime (Eck & Clarke, 2019).

Originally proposed as 12, then later 16, techniques by Ronald Clarke in 1995 and 1997 respectively, SCP is a set of tactics intended to reduce or remove opportunities for crime altogether (Clarke, 1997a; Clarke, 1995). This can be accomplished by altering the potential offender's sense of risk, reward, or effort (Cornish & Clarke, 2003). It is important to note that this can mean altering the actual *or* perceived risk, reward, and effort since the potential offender's perceptions matter when considering costs and benefits of a criminal offense. These original techniques were criticized by Wortley (2001) for not considering "situational precipitators" such as factors that provoke or excuse offender behavior. As a reply, Cornish and Clarke (2003) proposed 25 techniques of SCP organized under five major headings: 1) increasing effort, 2) increasing risk, 3) reducing rewards, 4) reducing provocations, and 5) removing excuses. The addition of a new category "removing excuses," and some altering of the language of other techniques, sought to address the concerns that were discussed by Wortley. Today, these 25 techniques represent modern-day SCP. Table 4.1 contains all 25 techniques of SCP, which will be discussed below. It may be helpful to refer back to this table as you read through the chapter to identify which techniques fall under which categories.

Elements of Situational Crime Prevention

Increasing the Effort

The first major category of techniques in situational crime prevention includes strategies that seek to increase the actual or perceived effort needed to commit a crime. **Increasing the effort** consists of any action or change to a situation to make it more difficult for an offender to victimize a target. This could be the addition of extra steps needed to carry out a crime or simply altering the perception of the effort needed. Research suggests that potential offenders often look for the easiest, lowest effort targets, so increasing the effort needed to complete a crime can drastically reduce the chances of it occurring (Brantingham et al., 2005). The first technique in this category is *target hardening*, discussed briefly in Chapter 3,

Table 4.1 Twenty-Five Techniques for Situational Crime Prevention

Increase Effort	Increase Risk	Reduce Rewards	Reduce Provocations	Remove Excuses
Target Hardening	Extend Guardianship	Conceal Targets	Reduce Frustrations & Stress	Set Rules
Control Access	Assist Natural Surveillance	Remove Targets	Avoid Disputes	Post Instructions
Screen Exits	Reduce Anonymity	Identify Property	Reduce Emotional Arousal	Alert Conscience
Deflect Offenders	Utilize Place Mangers	Disrupt Markets	Neutralize Peer Pressure	Assist Compliance
Control Tools/Weapons	Strengthen Formal Surveillance	Deny Benefits	Discourage Imitation	Control Drugs & Alcohol

Source: Adapted from Cornish & Clarke, 2003.

which seeks to provide protection over potential targets. Specifically, **target hardening** seeks to, "obstruct the vandal or the thief by physical barriers through the use of locks, safes, screens or reinforced materials" (Clarke, 1997b, p. 17). An example of this provided by Cornish and Clarke (2003) is tamper-proof packaging. The hard plastic packaging that is utilized on some electronics, such as prepaid cell phones, or high-value items such as makeup and perfume, makes it more difficult for a potential offender to simply open the package and take the item.

The second technique under increasing the effort is *access control*, sometimes worded as controlling access to facilities (Clarke & Eck, 2003), a core element of defensible space discussed in Chapter 3, that is also utilized in SCP. This technique focuses on blocking potential offenders' entry to specific places such as apartment buildings, schools, businesses, and other locations where they may find opportunities to commit crimes (Clarke, 1997b). Examples of access control provided by Cornish and Clarke (2003) include the use of technology such as key cards to enter buildings or other systems that people must use such as phones, buzzers, or keypads to enter into a specific space. This type of access control has become routine in most apartment buildings, many businesses, and dorms on college campuses. Other barriers such as fences, gates, and landscaping may provide additional opportunities for access control and are commonly utilized in creating defensible space. Public spaces, such as parks, that close at certain times of day may use gates to control access at nighttime, while parking lots may use arm barriers or attendants to oversee points of entry. Another example of this is requiring occupational licensing and certification, making it more difficult for offenders to run illegitimate businesses (Benson & Madensen, 2007).

The third technique under increasing the effort is the *screening of exits*. This technique focuses on detection of potential offenders and is similar to access control, but instead of blocking entry, it seeks to identify and remove potential offenders (Clarke, 1997b). This technique can be particularly useful to deter shoplifting from stores and can include alarms or sensors at the exits of stores to detect merchandise that has not been paid for. The most commonly used example of this technique provided by Cornish and Clarke (2003) is the screening of baggage that is now routine at airports and other transportation hubs such as bus stations and railways. This screening acts as both deterrence and detection for the transport of dangerous materials and weapons. Another example of this is to require passengers on transit systems to show their ticket at both entry and exit (Cornish & Clarke, 2003), something that is now common in many train and other types of transit stations. This helps to curb fare avoidance or loitering, which may occur in public transit stations. This additional screening makes it more difficult for potential offenders to linger, potentially looking for targets, and provides an extra level of surveillance, increasing the perception of risk.

Expand Your Understanding – Terrorism and Situational Crime Prevention

While SCP might be thought of mostly as techniques to deter property crimes, it has been applied to a wide range of offenses. One such effort is to examine opportunities for terrorism from a SCP lens. Clarke and Newman (2007) suggest that SCP can be applied to terrorism because terrorists are "rational," do not randomly select targets, are opportunistic, and rely on certain tools and weapons to carry out an offense. Therefore, SCP can be utilized in several ways to help prevent these types of crimes. For example, increasing the effort by making it more difficult for terrorists to access targets is one specific tactic that can be used (Clarke & Newman, 2007). Further, controlling tools and weapons to limit access to bank accounts and necessary funding makes it more difficult for terrorists to obtain the money needed to carry out offenses. Finally, using defensible space and other environmental design features to target harden buildings and other target locations can reduce potential rewards for terrorists (Clarke & Newman, 2007). This example highlights the potential applicability of SCP across a wide range of crimes outside of traditional street and property crimes.

The fourth technique in this category is the *deflection of offenders*. This technique seeks to decrease the chances that a potential offender will encounter a potential target. One example of this is the separation of rival fans at sporting events, including separate entry and exit points and access barriers (Clarke & Eck, 2016; Madensen & Eck, 2008). This way the rival fans never come into direct contact with one another, decreasing the chances of violence stemming from conflicts that may arise. Another example could be the use of street closures and the dispersion of bars to reduce the chances of large groups of people, who might be potential offenders or victims, from encountering one another (Cornish & Clarke, 2003).

The fifth and final technique under the category of increasing the effort is *controlling tools and weapons*. This technique tries to manage the access that potential offenders have to items they need to carry out a particular criminal offense. Tools can be conceptualized as things like spray paint needed for graffiti or items used for lock picking. Cornish and Clarke (2003) suggest restricting spray paint sales to those over 18 as one way to accomplish this control. The use of plastic rather than glass beer mugs has become more common at bars and sports venues to reduce the chances of glass being shattered or used as a weapon (Clarke & Eck, 2016). Additionally, many concert venues now also use plastic instead of glass for beverages and may remove the cap from the bottle at the time of sale to reduce the chances of the bottle being used as a filled projectile. Another example of this is the selling of certain medications behind the pharmacy counter such as anything that contains pseudoephedrine that can be used to make methamphetamine. This control on access makes it more difficult for a potential offender to manufacture this drug.

Increasing the Risk

The second major category of techniques seeks to increase the actual or perceived risk related to a specific crime. **Increasing the risk** focuses on actions that either increase the perception or actual risk of the potential offender being caught committing a crime or arrested at a later date. In other words, these are strategies that make it riskier for the offender, potentially altering the cost–benefit balance. Cornish and Clarke (2003) provide five specific techniques, as listed in Table 4.1, designed to increase risk, with the first being *extending guardianship*. This could entail any effort that provides surveillance or protection over a target such as walking in groups at night, carrying a cell phone, or neighborhood watches that take place during certain times of day. Another example would be to make it appear as if someone is occupying a residence even when they are not home by leaving lights on or other signs of occupancy (Cornish & Clarke, 2003). Requiring multiple employees to be present to deposit funds at a bank, especially at night, is another example of providing extra guardianship. Finally, providing improved and regular training for auditors to identify healthcare fraud is an example of how this could be applied in the white-collar crime area (Benson & Madensen, 2007). These examples could then signal to a potential offender that a space or target is being watched or guarded, altering the perception of risk attached to the crime.

The second technique for increasing risk is expanding opportunities for *natural surveillance*. This could include utilizing strategies from defensible space, discussed in Chapter 3, such as physical design changes including lighting and landscaping that improve the ability of residents to observe the area around them (Clarke, 1997b). This type of surveillance goes beyond physical design changes though and can also include any opportunity for people to naturally detect and report potential issues. An example of this type of natural surveillance, called *supporting whistleblowers* is provided by Cornish and Clarke (2003). This could include providing incentives and anonymity for employees to be on the lookout for workplace violations or potential criminal offenses as they go about their daily activities. For example, a reward system could be put into place for employees that report internal theft or safety violations such as the improper disposal of chemicals.

The third technique in this category is *reducing anonymity*, which seeks to make it more difficult for a potential offender to blend in with legitimate users of a space. Examples of this include the use of school uniforms and ID badges by both staff and students at schools (Cornish & Clarke, 2003). For ride-sharing companies, requiring the use of identifiers such as name plates, license plates, and other company markings on the vehicles helps passengers to ensure they are entering not only the correct, but a legitimate, vehicle. Another example of this is uniforms for employees, clearly identified security, and other techniques that make it clear who is a legitimate user of a space. Trucks and other commercial vehicles could include decals with a phone number to report driving violations, making it more difficult for these drivers to engage in speeding or other illegal and dangerous behaviors on the road (Cornish & Clarke, 2003).

The fourth technique is to *utilize place managers*, a strategy that attempts to leverage the ability of those who own, manage, or are employed in specific places to provide surveillance. A **place manager** is a person who can exercise control over a space, typically as part of their employment. These individuals include "parking lot attendants, bus drivers, train conductors, and others who perform a surveillance function by virtue of their position of employment" (Douglas & Welsh, 2022, p. 68), but is typically a secondary role to their primary job. Vital to this technique is the willingness and ability for these place managers to intervene when potential criminal situations arise. Clarke and Cornish (2003) asserted that reward structures which provide incentives to employees that act as place managers, similar to supporting whistleblowing discussed above, is one way to assist in this technique. For example, bonuses could be provided for bus drivers who do not have any incidents on their buses each month or parking lot attendants could be rewarded for reporting concerns in the lot.

Place managers' compliance can also be assisted with technology to enhance surveillance opportunities. For example, the use of security cameras on public transit such as trains and buses makes it easier for employees to detect and report potential issues (Cornish & Clarke, 2003). The effectiveness of these types of surveillance for some crimes was discussed in Chapter 3, suggesting this can be a low-cost way to increase perceptions of risk among potential offenders. Additionally, not allowing employees to work alone at night, especially in businesses like gas stations and convenience stores that may be targeted for robbery, is another method to utilize place managers (Cornish & Clarke, 2003). The utility of place managers and their role in SCP have been the focus of several empirical studies, with positive outcomes. An example of this is provided later in this chapter.

The final technique under the category of increasing risk is to *strengthen formal surveillance*. This is different from the prior technique in this category which focused on natural surveillance. This type of surveillance is carried out by law enforcement, security guards, or other individuals whose main function is to deter potential offenders from carrying out offenses (Clarke, 1997b). Unlike place managers, surveillance is a primary role of these individuals. Formal surveillance can also include security cameras, alarms, or other forms of technology that seek to identify or deter criminal behavior. For example, red-light cameras can be installed at intersections where significant amounts of traffic violations occur to serve as a deterrent or as detection for those engaging in speeding or running the light (Clarke & Eck, 2003). The research evidence for these techniques was discussed in Chapter 3, again suggesting that these methods can be effective for certain crimes.

Reducing the Rewards

The third major category of situational crime prevention is **reducing the rewards**, which refers to actions that decrease the actual or perceived benefits of a crime. This set of techniques is based on the notion that if a potential offender sees little benefit or reward for a crime, then they are less likely to engage in that offense. The first technique in this category is the *concealing of targets*. Quite simply, an offender cannot steal something they cannot see. Thus, hiding or concealing targets from the view of an offender reduces the potential rewards an offender may perceive. An example of this would be off-street parking for cars (Cornish & Clarke, 2003). Dozens of vehicles parked on a street present opportunity for theft from vehicle or theft of the entire vehicle. If perceived as highly rewarding by a potential offender, this could lead to an increase in crime. Concealing the targets off the street, behind properties or in alleys, could lower the number of vehicles an offender sees at one time, reducing the overall benefits of the crime while also increasing the risk of detection. Another example of this is the use of unmarked armored vehicles to transport valuables such as money (Clarke & Eck, 2016). If unmarked, it makes it more difficult for a potential offender to identify the vehicle as a high-value target, altering the perception of reward. In other words, they may not know what is in the vehicle and therefore do not see it as beneficial to attempt to break into it or steal from it.

The second technique in this category is the *removal of targets*. This technique takes reducing rewards a step further than the previous one with the complete removal of a target from an offender. Examples of this include the removal of valuables in a vehicle, such as purses, shopping bags, phones, or other items that may be in plain sight of a potential offender. Expensive items like gaming systems, TVs, and other electronics could be removed from boxes and displayed empty, adding the step of getting an employee to gain access to these items. Another example of this provided by Clarke and Eck (2016) is the utilization of shelters for domestic violence victims. Research suggests that domestic violence revictimization can occur quickly after the first offense, so removing the victim and placing them in a shelter is one option that can reduce the opportunity for this revictimization (Mele, 2009).

The third technique utilized to reduce rewards is the *identification of property*, which commonly focuses on property marking. This makes it more difficult for potential offenders to resell items they may have stolen and also makes it easier to track items that are lost. Many cell phones today now have tracking devices or identifiers that make them difficult to sell to a pawn shop or other resale stores. Similar identifiers exist on vehicles with VIN numbers (vehicle identification numbers) and GPS (Global Positioning System). Cornish and Clarke (2003) provide the example of branding or tagging cattle to make them more difficult to steal. Electronics such as gaming consoles, TVs, stereo systems, car parts, and other high-value items could also be marked or tagged for easy identification when an offender attempts to resell them.

The fourth technique in this category is the *disruption of markets*. These tactics attempt to make it more difficult for an offender to dispose of or resell an item through the identification of specific markets where opportunities may exist. One example of this is to regulate pawn and other resale shops through encouraging their assistance in reporting suspicious transactions (Cornish & Clarke, 2003). Additionally, many pawn and resale shops now require identification, such as a driver's license, which is kept on file with a picture to complete a transaction. They keep records of all transactions that can be supplied to law enforcement if the item is suspected to be stolen. This is also commonplace in businesses that concentrate on the resale of gaming consoles, accessories, and computer or video games. In the realm of white-collar crime, the FBI's Health CareFraud Unit was established to identify businesses and individuals defrauding Medicare and Medicaid, effectively disrupting these markets (Benson & Madensen, 2007). Another example of disruption of markets is to require all street vendors to have a license to sell their goods (Cornish & Clarke, 2003). This helps to ensure that goods sold at these vendors are not stolen or counterfeit, making it more difficult for these items to reach legitimate customers. This can be particularly effective in large cities where street vendors are common.

Outside of targets that are items such as property, this technique could also include individuals as targets. One way this could be applied to individuals is the disruption of human trafficking markets. Examples of this could include additional security and surveillance around events that are known attractors for human trafficking such as large sporting events, multi-day festivals, and concerts.

Expand Your Understanding – Human Trafficking at Large-Scale Public Events

Recently, the connection between large-scale events and opportunities for human trafficking has been a focus for crime prevention research. These events, such as the World Cup, Super Bowl, and the Olympics can provide increased or new opportunities for traffickers. Specifically, the substantial increase of visitors can result in surges in the demand on the sex industry, encouraging potential illegal trafficking to fulfill these needs (Bowersox, 2016). When demand outpaces the current supply, traffickers may seize on this opportunity to use illegal means, especially when large amounts of profit are involved. Additionally, depending on the location, new infrastructure including venues, lodging, and other services may be needed, providing opportunities for trafficking in labor (Bowersox, 2016). SCP can be utilized in these situations, especially the techniques of disrupting markets; in this case, large-scale sporting events and target hardening. Widespread media campaigns like the one conducted for Super Bowl LIV in Miami can also increase risks and decrease benefits perceived by potential offenders (Sant et al., 2023).

The final technique under the category of reducing rewards is to *deny the benefits* of an offense to a potential offender. Some offenses may have motivations driven by the perceived benefit the person gains from completing the offense; removing this can alter the perception of rewards. Like property marking ideas to reduce the chances of pawning or selling a stolen item, this technique may involve rendering items inoperable if missing. This could include cell phones that become non-functional or vehicles that can be remotely shut down so they cannot be driven. This type of technology is now commonly available on cell phones and can be added to many vehicles through GPS tracking and additional security systems.

Cornish and Clarke (2003) provide the example that graffiti should be cleaned off as soon as possible to deny the benefit of the offender "showing off" their work, discouraging the future vandalism of these spaces. Another example of this is to render items such as clothing unusable so they cannot be worn or sold. Security ink tags that explode all over the garment when tampered with, ruining the fabric, are an example of this tactic (Cornish & Clarke, 2003). Ensuring that fraudulent healthcare claims are denied quickly, so the money is never distributed, is an example of this technique for white-collar crime (Benson & Madensen, 2007). Benefits can also be derived from engaging in a certain behavior in a certain area. For example, if speeding or street racing is commonplace on a certain street, potentially because the street design allows for a thrilling ride, speed bumps could be added to deny the benefit of the thrill (Cornish & Clarke, 2003).

Reducing Provocations

The fourth category of situational crime prevention is the reduction of provocations, which seeks to mitigate circumstances or situations that may provoke or induce criminal behavior from an individual. This includes situations where a person who was unmotivated becomes a motivated offender based on situational factors. Cornish and Clarke (2003, p. 77) asserted that certain types of situations were more likely to provoke or incite action among offenders including when they were perceived threats to the individual's life, when they threatened the individual's ability to maintain core aspects of their lifestyle, when the provocation is repeated, or when the individual is already motivated and situational factors provide a catalyst to "tip" the individual into action. For example, the repeated exposure to intoxicated individuals who are perceived as bothersome in a bar setting may provoke an otherwise unmotivated offender to assault another person.

The first techniques under the category of **reducing provocations** is to *reduce frustrations and stress*. This technique is based on the assertion that exposing an individual to large amounts of frustration or stress can then provoke them into actions they may not have engaged in otherwise. Consider your feelings when waiting in a large line such as baggage screening at an airport. Are there things that can be done to reduce annoyance in this situation? Cornish and Clarke (2003) argue that lines that are perceived as efficient and organized can reduce irritation and anger on the part of those in the line, reducing chances of arguments and other problems that may arise. Ensuring there are clear signs for where the line begins, not allowing people to cut in line, and having enough people to manage the line are all ways to potentially reduce frustration attached to this situation. This can be further mitigated by polite employees (Cornish & Clarke, 2003) who help to move the line along and provide conflict resolution should it arise. Another example of this technique is to ensure that spaces have enough seating, such as airports, waiting rooms, DMVs (department of motor vehicles), and other locations that attract large amounts of people who may have to wait for services. This reduces the chances of conflicts over seating that could result in potential arguments and subsequent violence (Cornish & Clarke, 2003).

The second technique in this category is *avoiding disputes*. Similar to the previous technique, this approach attempts to manipulate situations so that conflicts can be avoided that may result in criminal offenses. For example, the separation of rival soccer fans, provided as an example to deflect offenders, also serves to avoid disputes (Cornish & Clarke, 2003). If they cannot encounter one another, it makes it very difficult for conflict to occur that may result in violence. Another example is to control crowding, specifically in areas where large amounts of people may come into contact with one another in situations where alcohol is often used. Limiting the amount of people in a bar or club reduces the chances of potentially intoxicated people bumping into one another or fighting for space on a dance floor or seating at the bar (Cornish & Clarke, 2003). Research suggests that bar density is linked to violence, so efforts to reduce crowding can translate into fewer disputes (Macintyre & Homel, 1997).

This technique can also be applied in situations where money is exchanged. Historically, calling a cab meant you typically did not know how much it would cost until you reached your destination. Having a "fixed" price for certain cab routes is one way to avoid potential disputes that may arise over fares (Cornish & Clarke, 2003). The system that most ride-sharing companies utilize today eliminates most of this, showing customers up front the exact amount they will pay for a certain ride. This way there are no surprises that could cause disputes later. This also eliminates rides that could increase dramatically in price because of traffic or other factors that could result in conflict.

The third technique utilized to reduce provocations is tactics that *reduce temptation and arousal* among potential offenders. This technique focuses on altering the environment to reduce stimuli that may entice a potential offender. For example, Cornish and Clarke (2003) suggest one way to achieve this is to enforce good behavior in sports. Ensuring that poor behaviors such as yelling at officials, dangerous plays, and other bad behaviors are not tolerated sends a message that can reduce the temptation to engage in these behaviors by other individuals. Players and fans who engage in these behaviors could be immediately ejected, suspended, or fined, depending on the situation, making it clear that other players and fans should not engage in these behaviors. Another example of this would be controls on violence or the prohibiting of discriminatory or hate speech or other derogatory language (Cornish & Clarke, 2003). Again, the zero tolerance of these behaviors sends a message and reduces the temptation among others to participate in similar actions.

The fourth technique in this category is the *naturalization of peer pressure*. This tactic seeks to remove the influence of others that may translate into criminal behaviors. Often, individuals engage in behaviors that are praised by their peers and refrain from those that are rebuked. For example, many individuals may feel pressured to drink or take illegal drugs based on their friends' behaviors. If this is neutralized through tactics such as it's okay to "say no" or that drinking and driving is not acceptable, this could remove the peer pressure to engage in these activities (Cornish & Clarke, 2003). For healthcare fraud, the use of professionalism standards and ethics can help dispel the myth that "all physicians do it" (Benson & Madensen, 2007, p. 622). Another example of this neutralization is to identify and separate deviant peers. This could be done in a school setting by dispersing students who cause trouble, decreasing the influence they may have over one another's behaviors (Cornish & Clarke, 2003). Students may "feed" off one another's bad behaviors, so reducing contact among them may reduce provocations.

The final technique in the category of reducing provocations is *discouraging imitation*. This strategy attempts to make it more difficult for possible imitation or "copy-cat" offenders to see the successes of another offender.

For example, if an area sees a lot of vandalism that is not repaired quickly, this may encourage other offenders to commit vandalism in the same area. On the other hand, if vandalism is repaired quickly so it is not seen by others it may reduce the chance of other offenders seeing it as an easy target (Cornish & Clarke, 2003). Another example of this is to provide less information in the media about crimes that have been committed. This can discourage "copy-cats" who may use information about modus operandi to commit their own crimes (Cornish & Clarke, 2003). **Modus operandi** can be defined as the collection of actions, techniques, and steps needed to commit a crime. They are typically specific to a type of crime, such as the steps that an offender completes to commit a burglary. If information about certain crimes is not made public, this can make it more difficult for other potential offenders to copy techniques.

Removing Excuses

The last major category of SCP is the removal of excuses. This category of techniques focuses on "reducing permissibility" (Clarke & Cornish, 2003, p. 88.) In other words, these tactics attempt to remove rationalizations or things that may be used as justifications for certain behaviors. The first technique under the category **removing excuses** is the *setting of rules*. This tactic attempts to ensure potential offenders know what behaviors are acceptable and what are not. For example, rental agreements (Cornish & Clarke, 2003) from property managers provide their tenants with guidelines on what they are allowed to do in a space such as keeping pets, painting walls, and the number of occupants they may have. If the individual then breaks the rules of the agreement, the property manager has a clear path forward, holding them accountable, removing any excuses or reasons they may have had for their behavior. This is similar to the use of hotel registration agreements (Cornish & Clarke, 2003) where guests agree to things like not smoking in rooms or bringing pets without permission. Signing agreements like this is relatively standard when staying in a hotel or leasing a property and seeks to reduce any justification individuals might have for breaking rules. Another example of this is having anyone who submits healthcare claims sign that they understand the rules of how to submit and what is allowed, removing the excuse they did not know a claim was fraudulent later (Benson & Madensen, 2007).

The second way SCP attempts to remove excuses is through the *posting of instructions*, which focuses on using signage to indicate what is allowed in a space. For example, the posting of "no parking" and other traffic signs signal to individuals that they could get a ticket if they park in areas that are signed otherwise. This could also include signage not allowing loitering, drug use, or other deviant or illegal behaviors in a specific location. Cornish and Clarke (2003) assert this technique also extends to other behaviors such as telling people to put out campfires to avoid start-ing a forest fire and altering them to private property that could result in trespassing if ignored.

The third technique in the category of removal of excuses is to *alert conscience*. This tactic acknowledges that some individuals may not be fully aware that they are engaging in illegal activity or need to be reminded that their actions are illegal. An example of this is speeding. It is easy to see how people may be lost in thought while driving, potentially not realizing they have gone over the speed limit. A sign on the side of the road that flashes red and blue and alerts them to their speed (Cornish & Clarke, 2003) is a good way to get attention and remind people of their behavior, resulting in the person slowing down. Additionally, it seeks to remind them of the morality of certain actions, playing on the notion that illegal behaviors are unethical. An example of this is to remind people that behaviors that may not seem that serious are still illegal. Shoplifting is a behavior that people may think is harmless and they may need to be reminded of the consequences for it. Posting signs which state that shop-lifting is in fact illegal, and people will be prosecuted if caught is one way to engage their conscience (Cornish & Clarke, 2003). Similarly, reminding physicians that submitting fraudulent healthcare claims is not only illegal, but a federal crime, may alert them to the consequences or induce guilt (Benson & Madensen, 2007).

The fourth technique in this category is to *assist compliance* among individuals. This could include changes to the physical design of a space that make it easier for individuals to comply and eliminate reasons they may have for breaking rules. For example, providing ample trash cans reduces the chances of litter, and having public restrooms available avoids issues with public urination or other deviant behaviors (Cornish & Clarke, 2003). Another example of this would be to ensure large venues such as concert spaces have enough services to assist concertgoers, making it more difficult for them to rationalize potentially illegal behavior.

The final technique in the category of removing excuses is to *control drugs and alcohol* access. This tactic is based on the notion that individu-als under the influence of illegal drugs and alcohol could behave in ways that they normally would not, providing a justification for their behaviors. Removing this through limiting these substances is one way to remove these possible neutralizations or excuses. This could include the promo-tion of "drug free" events targeting teenagers, demonstrating that enjoy-ment can be found without partaking in substance use, including alcohol (Cornish & Clarke, 2003). Another way this tactic could be utilized is to have limits on alcoholic drinks at bars and restaurants. Many restaurants now have limits on the amounts of drinks you can order within a certain time frame, often no more than one drink per hour. Empowering servers to intervene and limit alcohol is another way to accomplish this (Cornish

& Clarke, 2003). Servers could be allowed to cut off customers and limit the number of drinks they can order over a short period of time. Many entertainment venues also have a "one ID, one drink" rule, reducing the chances of one person buying either themselves or others a large number of alcoholic drinks at one time.

Applying Situational Crime Prevention

Now that each of the 25 techniques of SCP has been outlined, some specific applications of this type of crime prevention will be presented. As discussed above, SCP has been applied to a wide variety of situations, including terrorism and human trafficking, provided as examples earlier. It should be noted that the five major categories do share overlap, as targeting one category, such as increasing risk, may impact others. As Clarke noted, "measures that increase the effort demanded for crime and delay the offender will also increase the risks of apprehension." (1997b, p. 17). Thus, Clarke states that some techniques may fit into more than one category, and they should not be seen as mutually exclusive or as competing. Since its inception, SCP has been utilized across multiple crimes, places, targets, and situations, including both traditional street- and cybercrimes. Here we will focus on some selected examples of interventions that specifically employed SCP and their outcomes.

Redesigning Hell

Project description and main problem: As described by Felson and colleagues (1996), this project centered around the Port Authority bus terminal in New York City. This extremely busy bus terminal was suffering from several problems, including heavy levels of disorder, loitering, begging, drug dealing, and robbery. The sheer number of people who traveled through the terminal every day, coupled with low levels of surveillance, a high transient population, and several design flaws, created abundant opportunities for crime and disorder. These problems led to declining use among the public due to fear and levels of crime.

Solutions and results: In 1991 and 1992, 62 different changes borrowed from situational crime prevention and CPTED were implemented in the bus terminal. Examples of some of the changes included new lighting and security throughout the bus terminal, placing locks and bars on crawlspaces, the removal of dark spaces and hiding spots, and the complete redesign of restrooms. An operations control center was placed in a central location to increase overall security and efforts were made to improve customer service with more efficient lines and ticket sales. Maintenance and upkeep were made a major priority along with information centers utilizing place managers so that surveillance and assistance were provided to customers. Overall, crime and disorder declined significantly and there were large increases in perceptions of safety, suggesting the changes had notable positive impacts on the bus terminal.

Burglary Prevention

Project description and main problem: According to Sturgeon-Adams et al. (2005), this project focused on burglary reduction through the identification of hotspots. Specifically, two neighborhoods in the town of Hartlepool, England were identified as having high levels of burglary. Preliminary analysis indicated that a large proportion of these burglaries were committed through entering the rear of the house, suggesting that access through alleys was the main mode of entry to these properties. There were also a number of properties that experienced repeat victimization, which were identified as candidates for target hardening. Young people were identified as the most likely offenders in these areas.

Solutions and results: The project used several SCP techniques, including hardening targets through the addition of alley gates, the use of property marking, and additional surveillance. Fourteen alley gates were installed, over 800 homes used property marking, and repeat victims were identified and provided further target hardening through new locks on windows and doors and security lighting. The alley gate main function was to limit access to alley ways behind homes to only residents, increasing the overall effort offenders would need to access these areas. Diversionary programming such as climbing, mountain biking, and other activities was conducted to not only provide youth with information about the negative consequences of criminal behavior but also to involve them in community activities. Overall, burglary was reduced by 25 percent in the targeted areas, with reductions seen around the target area as well. Repeat burglary victimization was also significantly impacted with an overall reduction of 26 percent (Sturgeon-Adams et al., 2005).

SCP Use By Owners of Pill Mills

Project description and main problem: With their study, Moreto and colleagues (2020) took a unique approach to SCP through the lens of an offender, in this case a pill mill operator. Specifically, this study identified SCP techniques used by offenders to circumvent detection of illegal pill mill businesses in Florida by law enforcement. **Pill mills** are illegal businesses that provide "patients" for a fee with legal prescriptions for non-medical purposes, often for opioids, which can then be filled at a pharmacy. Typically, a person pays to see a "doctor" or medical professional who provides them with a legal prescription. Driven by large increases in recreational opioid use, pill mills have become an increasing problem in the United States. Detection and closure of these facilities have become a focal point for law enforcement in states like Florida where they have thrived. Through a series of interviews conducted with law enforcement, several SCP techniques were identified as being used by pill mill operators, putting a twist on the approach.

Solutions and results: Techniques used by offenders operating pill mills included increasing the effort of law enforcement through registration under different clinic types, making it more difficult for police to investigate, and drug testing potential clients to ensure they are opioid users and not undercover law enforcement. Pill mill clinics also utilized place managers to screen for law enforcement and concealed targets (in this case the desired non-medical prescriptions such as OxyContin) through prescribing a variety of drugs including opioids. Thus, it gave the pill mill the appearance of a legitimate pain clinic. Finally, provocations were reduced through having no parking lots or spaces in which drug users could loiter and requiring that all "customers" be dropped off and picked up promptly after visits. This reduced issues with neighboring businesses such as needles being left on the ground and drug users hanging out around their properties, potentially causing problems that could result in nearby businesses calling the police (Moreto et al., 2020).

Theft at a Retail Market

Project description and main problem: Finally, this application of SCP examined by Poyner and Webb (1992) was utilized to combat theft, mostly of purses from the top of open shopping bags, in a large retail market in England composed of four major sections, the Rag Market, the Flea Market, the Bull Ring Market Hall, and the Bull Ring Open Market. This market held thousands of stalls that sold various goods such as fresh fruit, vegetables, eggs, and other types of food. A preliminary analysis of theft in the area found that thefts were almost all accounted for in the market and followed a particular pattern. There were particular days, times, and locations at which the thefts were most likely to occur, specifically during the summer months and in the densest portion of the market, suggesting that crowding was related to the opportunity for theft.

Solutions and results: Considering the preliminary analysis of the problem showed that the level of crowding was related to opportunities for theft, it was proposed that the solution was to reduce crowding.

The easiest way to reduce high-density areas was to increase the space between stalls. Specifically, the distance between stalls in certain high-density areas was increased by about three feet. The distance behind the stalls and the aisle also saw an increase in space. One market, the Rag Market, also received improved lighting. Overall, these changes were meant to increase the risk of offenders being detected and also increase the effort through better surveillance. Data demonstrated that in the areas these changes had been made, theft declined significantly, with a 40 percent reduction in theft after the first year of the intervention and a 70 percent reduction over a two-year period (Poyner & Webb, 1992).

Empirical Evidence for SCP and Future Evaluation

The examples provided above are only a small number of applications that have been attempted using SCP. Numerous studies exist that have applied SCP to burglary, theft, terrorism, crime in general, fear of crime, white-collar crimes, and even environmental crime. Overall, the results are often positive, with most studies showing reductions in crime. Perhaps Guerette and Bowers (2009) provide one of the most comprehensive reviews of SCP to date, examining hundreds of SCP interventions over decades of time. They found that 75 percent of SCP interventions led to reductions in crime, while only 8 percent had inconclusive results, suggesting that most SCP programs have some impact on crime (Guerette & Bowers, 2009). Similar results were reported by Eck and Guerette (2012), when SCP interventions were grouped by place, finding that 60 percent of interventions were effective. It should be noted that evaluation of many crime prevention initiatives is difficult, and SCP is no exception. A few of these difficulties are outlined by Shariati and Guerette (2017), including the difficulty of establishing randomized controlled experiments, the use of multiple tactics in the same intervention, the ex-post facto evaluation of interventions, concerns over displacement measurement, and the use of some tactics that may not be appropriate for the situation. These methodological concerns, while not unique to SCP, are an important consideration for future SCP initiatives and interventions. In addition, as will be discussed in the next section, SCP has been the subject of other criticisms.

Misconceptions of Situational Crime Prevention

While much positive empirical evidence exists for SCP, as was discussed above, it has also been criticized. These criticisms typically center around what Clarke and Bowers (2017) refer to as "misconceptions" about the techniques. They present seven of these misconceptions, as summarized in Table 4.2, and their responses to them. The first misconception is that SCP does not rely on any theory for its basis. This is rebutted by Clarke and Bowers who pointed out that SCP is rooted in several theories, including routine activities theory, crime pattern theory, and rational choice theory. It shares fundamental assumptions of these theories, as was discussed earlier in this chapter. Second, a large body of research now supports that SCP can be very effective in many situations, dispelling the second myth in Table 4.2 that it is ineffective. Further, research does not support the idea that it simply displaces crime, with no studies to date finding full displacement and very few studies finding displacement in substantial amounts (Guerette & Bowers, 2009).

The third criticism is addressed by Clarke and Bowers by noting that SCP can result in immediate reductions in crime; something that has been supported in the literature, suggesting that this benefit may outweigh concerns over its lack of attention to root causes of crime. The fourth criticism of SCP being managerial, or conservative, is addressed by Clarke and Bowers as an advantage, since it allows for techniques that are less expensive and easier to implement than other forms of prevention. The fifth criticism focuses on SCP as potentially being exclusionary or

Table 4.2 Criticisms of SCP and Rebuttals

Criticism	Rebuttal
It is simplistic and atheoretical.	It is based on three crime opportunity theories: routine activity, crime pattern, and rational choice. It also draws on social psychology.
It has not been shown to work; it displaces crime and often makes it worse.	Many dozens of case studies show that it can reduce crime, usually with little displacement.
It diverts attention from the root causes of crime.	It benefits society by achieving immediate reductions in crime.
It is a conservative, managerial approach to crime.	It promises no more than it can deliver. It requires that solutions be economic and socially acceptable.
It promotes a selfish, exclusionary society.	It provides as much protection to the poor as the rich.
It promotes "big brother" and restricts personal freedom.	The democratic process protects society from these dangers. People are willing to endure inconvenience and small infringements of liberty when these protect them from crime.
It blames the victim.	It empowers victims by providing them with information about crime risks and how to avoid them.

Source: Adapted from Clarke & Bowers, 2017.

only available to certain members of society. Clarke and Bowers rebuke this idea through asserting the SCP is accessible and can be used by any member of society. Several SCP techniques require little to no monetary investment and can be carried out by everyday citizens. The sixth criticism suggests that SCP promotes "big brother," with the response by Clarke and Bowers focusing on the idea that most people are willing to accept some level of surveillance in exchange for safety. Consider baggage and security screenings now present at all airports as an example of this acceptance. The final criticism that has been levied against SCP suggests that it engages in victim blaming. **Victim blaming** is defined as placing some level of responsibility on the victim of the crime for their own victimization, such as saying the victim "asked for it" or "drank too much," resulting in the victimization. Clarke and Bowers (2017) note that SCP provides victims with information about how to potentially protect themselves from crime and do not suggest victims who do not take precautions are at fault for their victimizations.

Summary

The main goal of this chapter was to examine the crime prevention approach of situational crime prevention. This history of SCP, along with its assumptions, were discussed, then all 25 techniques of situational crime prevention were outlined with examples. SCP is most effective when tailored to the specific crime and relies on opportunity perspectives. All of these techniques seek to influence the offender's perceptions of crime and hope to alter the cost–benefit analysis from a rational choice and routine activities perspective. Specifically, the tactics across the five major categories of SCP were discussed, including increasing the effort, increasing the risk, reducing the rewards, reducing provocations, and removing excuses. This chapter also outlined some specific applications of SCP, discussed the empirical evidence for SCP, and considered criticisms of the techniques and the possible responses to these criticisms.

Keywords

Situational Crime Prevention (SCP), Increasing the Effort, Target Hardening, Increasing the Risk, Place Manager, Reducing the Rewards, Reducing Provocations, Modus Operandi, Removing Excuses, Pill Mills, Victim Blaming

Discussion Questions

1. What are the four major assumptions of Situational Crime Prevention? How do these assumptions move away from traditional criminological theories?

2. How does situational crime prevention utilize the ideas from rational choice theory and routine activities? Why are they complementary and not conflicting?

3. What are the five major categories of situational crime prevention and how do they work together to reduce opportunities for crime?

4. Discuss whether situational crime prevention can be applied to the crime of identity theft. Give at least two examples of techniques that could be utilized.

5. Are there elements or techniques of situational crime prevention that may work for some crimes better than others? Discuss two examples of this.

References

Benson, M. L., & Madensen, T. D. (2007). Situational crime prevention and white-collar crime. In H. N. Pontell & G. Geis (Eds), *International handbook of white-collar and corporate crime* (pp. 609–626). Boston, MA: Springer US.

Bowersox, Z. (2016). International sporting events and human trafficking: Effects of mega-events on a state's capacity to address human trafficking. *Journal of Human Trafficking, 2*(3), 201–220.

Brantingham, P., Brantingham, P., & Taylor, W. (2005). Situational crime prevention as a key component in embedded crime prevention. *Canadian Journal of Criminology and Criminal Justice, 47*(2), 271–292.

Clarke, R. V. (1983). Situational crime prevention: Its theoretical basis and practical scope. *Crime and Justice: An Annual Review of Research, 4*, 225–256.

Clarke, R. V. (1995). Situational crime prevention. *Crime and Justice: Review of the Research, 19*, 91–150.

Clarke, R. V. (1997a). A revised classification of situational crime prevention techniques. *Crime Prevention at a Crossroads*. Cincinnati, OH: Anderson.

Clarke, R. V. (1997b). *Situational crime prevention: Successful case studies* (2nd ed.). Monsey, NY: Criminal Justice Press.

Clarke, R. V., & Bowers, K. (2017). Seven misconceptions of situational crime prevention. In N. Tilley & A. Sidebottom (Eds), *Handbook of crime prevention and community safety* (pp. 109–142). London: Routledge.

Clarke, R. V., & Eck, J. E. (2003). *Become a problem-solving crime analyst: In 55 small steps*. London: Jill Dando Institute of Crime Science.

Clarke, R. V., & Eck, J. (2016). *Crime analysis for problem solvers in 60 small steps*. Washington, DC: Office of Community Oriented Policing Services. https://portal. cops.usdoj.gov/resourcecenter/content.ashx/cops-w0047-pub.pdf

Clarke, R. V., & Newman, G. R. (2007). Situational crime prevention and the control of terrorism. In O. Nikbay, & S. Hancerli (Eds), *Understanding and responding to the terrorism phenomenon* (pp. 285–297). Amsterdam: IOS Press.

Cornish, D. B., & Clarke, R. V. (2003). Opportunities, precipitators and criminal decisions: A reply to Wortley's critique of situational crime prevention. *Crime Prevention Studies, 16*, 41–96.

Douglas, S., & Welsh, B. C. (2022). There has to be a better way: Place managers for crime prevention in a surveillance society. *International Journal of Comparative and Applied Criminal Justice, 46*(1), 67–80.

Eck, J. E., & Clarke, R. V. (2019). Situational crime prevention: Theory, practice and evidence. In M. Krohn, N. Hendrix, G. Penly Hall, & A. Lizotte (Eds), *Handbook on crime and deviance* (pp. 355–376). Cham: Springer, doi:10.1007/978-3-030-20779-3_18

Eck, J. E., & Guerette, R. T. (2012). "Own the place, own the crime" prevention: How evidence about place-based crime shifts the burden of prevention. In R. Loeber & B. C. Welsh (Eds), *The future of criminology* (pp. 166–171). Oxford: Oxford University Press.

Felson, M., Belanger, M. E., Bichler, G. M., Bruzinski, C. D., Campbell, G. S., Fried, C. L., . . . & Williams, L. M. (1996). Redesigning hell: Preventing crime and disorder at the port authority bus terminal. *Preventing Mass Transit Crime, 6*, 5–92.

Guerette, R. T., & Bowers, K. J. (2009). Assessing the extent of crime displacement and diffusion of benefits: A review of situational crime prevention evaluations. *Criminology, 47*(4), 1331.

Macintyre, S., & Homel, R. (1997). Danger on the dance floor: A study of interior design, crowding and aggression in nightclubs. *Policing for Prevention: Reducing Crime, Public Intoxication and Injury, 7*(1), 91–113.

Madensen, T. D., & Eck, J. E. (2008). Violence in bars: Exploring the impact of place manager decision-making. *Crime Prevention and Community Safety, 10*(2), 111–125.

Mele, M. (2009). The time course of repeat intimate partner violence. *Journal of Family Violence, 24*, 619–624.

Moreto, W. D., Gau, J. M., & Brooke, E. J. (2020). Pill mills, occupational offending, and situational crime prevention: a framework for analyzing offender behavior and adaptation. *Security Journal, 33*, 161–178.

Poyner, B., & Webb, B. (1992). Reducing theft from shopping bags in city center markets. In R. V. Clarke (Ed.), *Situational crime prevention: Successful case studies* (pp. 99–107). New York: Harrow and Heston.

Sant, S. L., Maleske, C., Wang, W., & King, E. J. (2023). Leveraging sport events for the promotion of human rights in host communities: Diffusion of anti-trafficking campaigns at Super Bowl LIV. *Sport Management Review, 26*(2), 203–223.

Shariati, A., & Guerette, R. T. (2017). Situational crime prevention. In B. Teasdale & M. Bradley (Eds), *Preventing crime and violence* (pp. 261–268). Cham: Springer.

Sturgeon-Adams, L., Adamson, S., & Davidson, N. (2005). *Hartlepool: A case study in burglary reduction.* Hull, UK: Centre for Criminology and Criminal Justice. https://popcenter.asu.edu/sites/default/files/177-SturgeonAdams.pdf

Wortley, R. (2001). A classification of techniques for controlling situational precipitators of crime. *Security Journal, 14*, 63–82.

Part 2
Crime Patterns and Concentration

Chapter 5
Crime Concentration and Hotspots

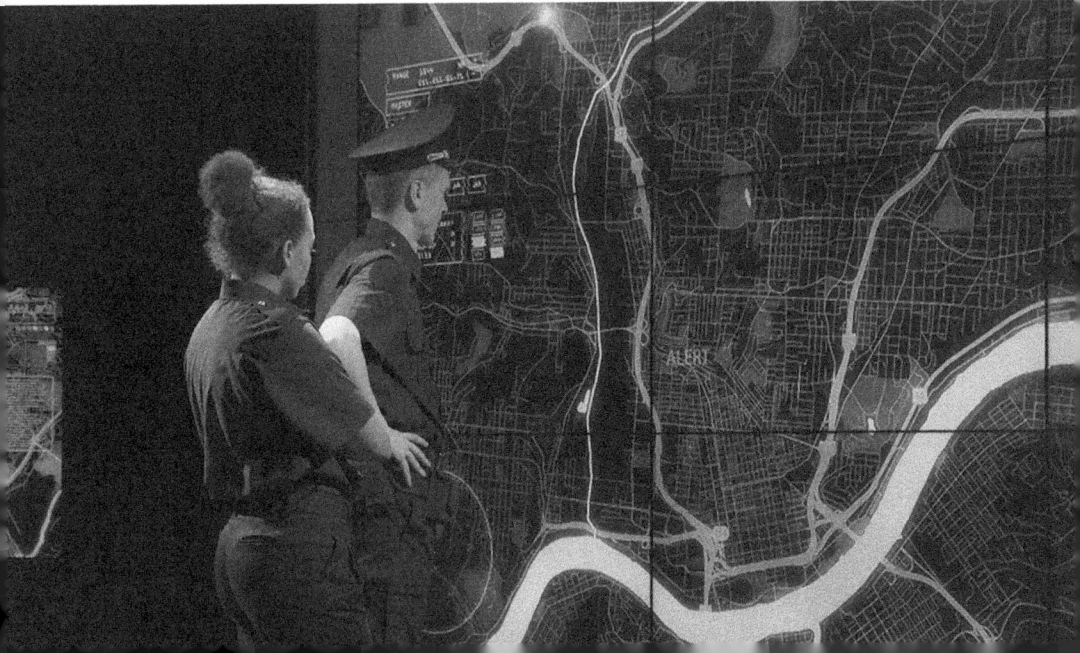

Crime Concentration and Hotspots

Billy Henson

DOI: 10.4324/9781003401551-7

Introduction

As discussed in Chapter 2, the cornerstone of crime prevention is the presence (and resulting examination) of patterned behavior. Whether we realize it or not, almost all human activities, at both the aggregate and individual levels, are patterned. As highlighted by both rational choice and routine activity theories, people tend to go to the same places, take the same routes, and interact with the same people repeatedly. In fact, some research has shown that as much as 93 percent of human behavior is predictable, largely due to our patterned behavior (Song et al., 2010). When given some thought, it can be easy to see just how patterned our behaviors are. Think about how often you go to the same grocery store, gym, bar, or movie theater. Next, think about how often you take the same routes to get to those locations. Patterns emerge because human beings are creatures of habit.

Now, when the repeated actions of large numbers of individuals overlap in time and space, a phenomenon known as behavioral concentration occurs. Such areas of behavioral concentration may be specific geographic locations (e.g., a large department store, a popular restaurant) or virtual locations (e.g., popular social media websites, gaming forums). Moreover, examining areas of behavioral concentration can provide significant information about the movement and activities of large groups. Because of the wealth of knowledge that can be obtained through such analysis, this process is a central component of effective crime prevention strategies.

Understanding Crime Concentration

One of the foundational aspects of crime prevention is the understanding that crime is actually a relatively common behavior. To illustrate, each year the FBI produces what it refers to as a "crime clock," which indicates how many crimes were reported to the police that year, across the United States, presented in a fixed time ratio. As indicated by the **"crime clock,"** there is a murder about every half an hour, a rape about every 4 minutes, a robbery every 2 minutes, and an aggravated assault every 38 seconds. Further, there is a burglary about every 28 seconds, a larceny-theft about every 6 seconds, and an auto theft about every 44 seconds (FBI, 2019). While these figures should not be taken literally (they represent averages, not specific times crimes actually occur), they are a good indication that crime is just as common as many legal behaviors. Further, as with legal behavior, criminal behavior is often patterned, resulting in some areas of higher crime concentration and some areas of lower crime concentration. Those areas where criminal behavior does tend to concentrate are typically referred to as crime hotspots.

Defining and Distinguishing Categories of Hotspots

Crime hotspots are places where numerous crimes tend to occur in relative proximity to each other. Essentially, these are areas where criminal behavior tends to concentrate. In many cases, hotspots will be designated by pre-established geographical or social boundaries. For example, a hotspot may be defined by a physical boundary, such as a street or river, or it may be defined by a social boundary, such as the understood perimeter of a neighborhood. Further, while hotspots are most often evaluated in terms of physical geography, in the case of technological or cybercrime, they may be examined in terms of virtual locations, such as websites or social media platforms, where online crime tends to occur most often. In that case, boundaries will be virtual rather than physical, producing what may be referred to as a **cybercrime hotspot**. While research on cybercrime hotspots is currently sparse, it has been found that certain online platforms and apps are often linked with cybercrime more than others. For example, crimes such as cyberbullying and cyberstalking are often linked to social media platforms (e.g., Snapchat, Instagram, Twitter), making them hotspots for those types of cybercrimes (Alim, 2016; Giumetti & Kowalski, 2022; Henson et al., 2011).

In addition to the general forms of hotspots (physical or virtual), it also should be noted that hotspots of crime may differ depending on the component of the criminal event to which they refer. Simply, there are both hotspots of offending and hotspots of victimization. On the surface, it may seem as though these hotspots would be the same, as both offenders and victims are needed for crime to occur. However, while they are undoubtedly linked, there is a key difference between the two. To help understand this difference, it is better to think of offending and victimization hotspots as two sides of the same coin. **Offending hotspots** are those locations where a large number of criminal offenders commit crime, while **victimization hotspots** are locations where a large number of victims experience crime. Though it is reasonable that one's first instinct may be to think of these areas as the same, there is, in fact, a major difference between them, which is necessary to understand in order to develop more effective crime-prevention strategies.

Offending hotspots may have a large number of criminal offenders, but few victims. Likewise, victimization hotspots may have many victims but few offenders. Highlighted in detail in Chapters 7 and 8, these phenomena may result from repeat offending and/or repeat victimization. Briefly, repeat offending occurs when one or a few offenders commit multiple, and in some cases large numbers of, crimes. As a result, an area with a high concentration of crime may have a few offenders who have targeted a large number of victims. This is considered a victimization hotspot. To illustrate, imagine a subdivision in which a single offender burgles several homes. That area may have a lot of victims, but only one offender. Comparatively, repeat victimization occurs when one or more victims experience multiple crimes. Such areas of high crime concentration may then have many offenders but few actual victims. These areas are considered offending hotspots. Again, to illustrate, picture a secluded convenience store that has very little security.

That store may get robbed multiple times by different robbers. As a result, the area may have many offenders, but only one victim. Finally, there may also be general hotspots, which are those locations with both high numbers of offenders and victims, as well as unique hotspots, including high crime areas with both a few repeat offenders and repeat victims.

As noted, it is important to determine which specific type of crime hotspot is being examined, in order to ensure the most effective crime prevention approaches are being implemented. In offending hotspots, it may be more effective to utilize strategies and techniques that focus specifically on offenders and their actions, such as better securing entry points (e.g., placing bars on windows), improving formal surveillance (e.g., installing closed-circuit television (CCTV) cameras), or restricting access to the tools needed for particular crimes (e.g., spray paint for graffiti). For example, Eric Piza and his colleagues (2019) performed a systematic review of 40 years of studies focusing on the use of CCTV as a crime prevention strategy. They reported that by reducing the opportunities and increasing the potential risk for offenders, CCTV cameras appear to have significant, although modest, impact on reducing crime, especially in parking areas.

On the other hand, when focusing on victimization hotspots, the more effective strategy may be to apply techniques that directly serve to protect victims, such as concealing potential targets (e.g., making phone directories gender neutral), improving guardianship (e.g., having more bouncers at bars), or providing victim-specific educational programs (e.g., self-defense classes). For example, several research studies have indicated that self-defense behaviors help reduce the likelihood of sexual victimization of women (McCaughey & Cermele, 2015; Ullman, 1997, 2007). As a result, providing self-defense classes in a community may help reduce the number of sexual assault victims in that community.

Other Forms of Hotspots

While crime hotspots are typically the most common form of behavioral concentration examined within the field of crime prevention, there are also other, closely related, forms of concentration that warrant attention, including hotspots of fear and disorder. Fear of crime typically refers to how fearful someone is of being victimized. That fear may be influenced by past experiences (direct or indirect), general perceptions, or even personal expectations (Farrall et al., 2009; Lane et al., 2014; Pain, 2000). A **fear hotspot** (or fear spot), then, is an area in which many individuals are afraid they may be victimized. As such, fear and crime hotspots often overlap, as people tend to be more fearful of areas where crime tends to concentrate. Of course, this is not always the case, as there are certain types of locations where crime may frequently occur, yet most people are not afraid to go there. As will be discussed in more detail in Chapter 6, there are certain types of facilities where the risk of being victimized may be relatively high, due to their location, management, layout, or other factors. However, potential victims will still often patronize those locations. For example, bars tend to be hotspots for crimes such as sexual assault, physical assault, and theft. Nevertheless, many people still go to bars with little fear of being victimized. In this case, a bar may be in a crime hotspot, but not necessarily part of a fear hotspot.

Often associated with crime, disorder typically refers to levels of physical and social incivilities within a specific area. In this context, physical incivilities refer to issues such as litter, graffiti, and abandoned buildings or cars, while social incivilities refer to things such as yelling and fighting, poor relationships between neighbors, and a lack of collective efficacy. With that in mind, a **disorder hotspot** would be an area with higher levels of physical and social incivilities. Further, hotspots of disorder often overlap with fear and crime hotspots. People are often afraid of areas with lots of disorder. This link can be better understood with a simple exercise. Take a moment and think about a neighborhood that you may be afraid to visit, one that you may consider bad. Now, what does that neighborhood look like? Is it clean, with lots of grass and nice-looking buildings? It is more likely that you pictured a neighborhood with lots of property damage, graffiti, and litter. Likewise, areas with more disorder often have higher rates of crime. There are many theories as to why areas with higher disorder tend to have higher concentrations of crime, including the idea that the issues that lead to disorder (e.g., lack of social bonds, territoriality, and collective efficacy among the residents of the area) are the same factors that lead to crime. Many theories outlining these ideas are highlighted in other chapters in this book. Simply, one form of behavioral concentration may lead to other forms of behavioral concentration.

Levels of Hotspot Analysis

In addition to the type of behavioral pattern, it is also important to consider the **level of analysis** when examining and/or evaluating hotspots. Simply, hotspots may be very large or very small, the size of which often depends on the purpose of the analysis. Case in point, if researchers or practitioners wanted to examine which parts of the world have the highest crime rates, the level of analysis used to highlight hotspots of crime could be the nation-level. By examining and comparing the crime rates of various countries, it could be determined which countries have the higher crime rates, for general or specific types of crimes. In doing so, undoubtedly, some countries would have much higher rates of crime than others, essentially appearing as a hotspot of crime, at the nation-level. Of course, you may be asking yourself, why would anyone want to perform an analysis at such a large level? In actuality, this level of analysis is quite common for certain types of phenomena, like disease. The World Health Organization, as well as individual nations' departments of health, often performs this type of analysis to determine hotspots, potential origins, and the spread of diseases and illnesses. With regard to crime, this level of analysis may be performed in order to issue travel warnings to people who are planning to visit other locations around the world. For example, in the United States, the State Department issues such warnings, providing information about high crime alerts for specific countries and indicating the relative level of danger that individuals visiting those countries may experience.

Of course, hotspots may also be examined at much smaller levels of analysis. For instance, utilizing data reported by law enforcement agencies across the United States, crime hotspots may be analyzed using information from the Uniform Crime Report (UCR) and/or the National Incident-Based Reporting System (NIBRS). This data could be used to analyze crime hotspots at multiple levels, including states, standard metropolitan statistical areas (SMSAs), and cities. These types of analyses may be useful with federal funding decisions regarding support for law enforcement agencies, prisons, victim programs, or other criminal justice organizations. Finally, the level of analysis used may also be as small as city districts (e.g., entertainment districts, residential areas), streets, blocks, and even specific facilities. As noted by John Eck and his colleagues (2005), the level of analysis used for hotspot examination depends mainly on the question one wants to answer.

With that said, the most common level of analysis for hotspot examination tends to be the street level. Street-level hotspot analysis may involve examining multiple streets, single streets, or even sections of streets (i.e., intersections, blocks). In many cases, the smaller the level of analysis, the more detailed the information gained may be because the location is more precise and external factors can be more easily controlled. This is why street-level analysis is frequently preferred over analysis of larger aggregate levels. When trying to review behavioral patterns on a couple of streets, there are far fewer factors to consider than when trying to review behavioral patterns for a larger area, such as an entire city. As will be discussed later in this chapter, smaller levels of analysis are also more beneficial when pinpointing and evaluating hotspots of crime.

Explaining the Formation of Hotspots of Crime

The Role of Opportunity in Hotspot Formation

In order to better understand the concept of hotspots, it is important to have a solid grasp on how they are formed. As previously detailed, hotspots typically form in areas of higher behavioral concentration. This occurs because such areas produce increased levels of opportunity for crime to take place. The role of opportunity was discussed in great detail in Chapter 2. However, as a reminder, opportunity refers to the likelihood of a crime occurring when a motivated offender and potential target are in the same place at the same time. This concept was further highlighted with the discussion of opportunity and environmental criminology theories throughout Chapters 2 and 3. In those chapters, it was noted that there are several related theoretical perspectives that directly influence the development and presence of crime opportunities, including rational choice theory (Cornish & Clarke, 1986), routine activity theory (Cohen & Felson, 1979), and environmental criminology (Brantingham & Brantingham, 1981).

Rational choice theory was described as the assumption that offenders focus mainly on their own interests, often weighing the costs and benefits of a crime before choosing to act. With routine activity theory, it was suggested that crime is the result of the convergence in time and space of a motivated offender, a suitable target, and a lack of capable guardianship. Finally, it was explained that environmental criminology, which includes concepts like crime pattern theory, focuses more specifically on the role and importance of the characteristics of places where crime happens, including both the **built environment** and **social environment**. Combined, these three theoretical perspectives indicate that criminal opportunities are created when offenders and potential victims are in the same place at the same time and the perceived benefits of committing a crime outweigh the potential costs for the offender, all of which is typically influenced by the structure and common use of their environment. The more frequently such interactions occur, or the more behaviors concentrate, the greater the opportunity for crime, and thus, the greater the likelihood that a hotspot will form.

Types of Hotspot Places

While the presence or absence of opportunities directly influences the presence or absence of hotspots of crime, the link between the two phenomena is not necessarily a straight line. In fact, the development of hotspots of crime often depends on the primary use of an area, the types and number of people drawn there, and the reason they are drawn to it. With that in mind, while it may appear as though hotspots simply form wherever opportunities for crime exist, the mechanism actually leading to the creation of that hotspot could vary greatly. This variation is probably best understood by discussing types of hotspot places. When discussing crime hotspots, there are a number of specific types of places that should be considered.

Crime Generators

One of the main types of places associated with crime hotspots is known as a crime generator. A **crime generator** is a location where people go with no initial intention to commit crime (Brantingham & Brantingham, 1993). In fact, these types of places generally have no direct association with crime and are typically places people simply enjoy going. However, once there, opportunities for crime may arise due to the nature of the environment, the behavior of those in the environment, and the management of that environment. For example, many people enjoy going to bars, pubs, and/or clubs as a social activity, including potential criminal offenders. While there, however, an offender may notice the bar has poor lighting, the patrons are very intoxicated and not being very observant, and there are few staff members with the bar. As a result, the ability to steal another patron's possessions (e.g., phone, purse, wallet), with little chance of getting caught, may present itself. Subsequently, opportunities for theft are created. If these types of opportunities continue to occur, and motivated offenders are there to take advantage of them, a hotspot for theft may develop in that area.

Crime Attractors

Another major type of place that warrants attention when discussing hotspots is a crime attractor. A **crime attractor** is a location that attracts individuals who are intending to commit a crime (Brantingham & Brantingham 1993). Unlike crime generator locations, potential offenders go to crime attractor locations specifically because they know there will be opportunities to offend there. Whether due to past experiences or simply word of mouth, offenders are aware that certain locations routinely present easy targets and/or lower levels of guardianship. Typically, offenders go to these types of areas to commit a specific type of crime. For example, a drug dealer may go to a specific park at night, that is known as a high-activity drug market, to sell drugs. Simply, if someone wants to sell drugs, they go to a place where drugs are sold. On the other hand, an offender who is interested in stealing a car may choose a location based on environmental and security factors, rather than it being known as a place to steal cars. For example, they may choose a specific parking lot without too many people and/or where the lighting and security may be poor. They are attracted to that location because of the opportunities created by the physical and social environments.

Crime Generators and Attractors

While crime generator and attractor locations may develop based on differing factors, the two do not exist in a vacuum. Instead, it is very possible that a place may be both a crime generator and a crime attractor. The factors that create opportunities that make the location a crime generator could also be the same factors that create the opportunities that make it a crime attractor. In this situation, the only difference is the motivation of the potential offenders. For example, with a sporting event, such as an NFL game, there are often large crowds of potentially intoxicated individuals who are distracted by the game. A situation like that is a perfect storm for a thief. As a result, there may be numerous offenders who go to the game specifically because they think there will be many opportunities to steal various items, making the stadium and/or surrounding area a crime attractor location. However, there may also be individuals who go to the game simply because they love football. But, while there, they may notice several opportunities to steal items from other fans. Although they did not go to the game with the initial purpose of offending, they may still do so because an opportunity arose, making the stadium and/or surrounding area a crime generator location. A similar pattern can be seen with other locations as well, such as malls, bars, or laundromats.

Crime Neutral Areas

In addition to places where crime tends to occur more frequently, there are also places that experience very little, if any, crime, often referred to as crime neutral areas. Sometimes called cool spots of crime (Eck et al., 2005), **crime neutral areas** neither generate many opportunities for crime nor attract criminal offenders (Brantingham & Brantingham, 1993). It should be noted that while these areas may not have high rates of crime concentration, crimes may still occasionally happen there. When they do, it is most often at the hands of insiders. Insiders are individuals who live, work, or frequently socialize in an area, which makes their presence in that area seem legitimate. Further, crime neutral areas are often those places with little behavioral concentration. Moreover, crime neutral areas may be neutral only for specific crimes or for relatively all crimes, for example an industrial park is an area zoned for industrial facilities (i.e., warehouses, refineries, factories). While those types of facilities may experience a crime, such as burglary, they will most likely be neutral for crimes such as rape, homicide, or robbery. However, there are other areas, such as places with large rural farms, that may not generate or attract any type of crime. Turns out, there are not a lot of corn thieves.

Upon initial inspection, it may seem as though crime neutral areas are unimportant when examining crime hotspots. If one is examining areas where crime concentrates, what is the point of considering areas with relatively no crime? As it turns out, crime neutral areas can actually be very important for hotspot analysis. As will be discussed in more detail later in this chapter, examining cool spots of crime can provide a lot of insight into crime patterns, especially when compared with hotspots of crime. By comparing the two, police, practitioners, and researchers may be better able to identify what environmental factors in the hotspot area are key precursors for crime, by determining which of those factors are not present in cool spots. Comparing the two also allows for a better understanding of behavior patterns and community problems, which can help with the development of more effective crime prevention programs and strategies.

CHAPTER 5   **117**

Fear Generators

The final main type of hotspot place is known as a **fear generator**. As discussed previously, in addition to crime, there are also areas of other types of concentration, such as fear of crime. While fear hotspots could be areas with high crime rates, in many instances, there is actually very little crime in places that generate fear (Brantingham & Brantingham, 1995). As a result, there is often overlap between crime neutral areas and fear generator areas. In fact, being a fear generator area may actually lead to lower crime rates in that location. For example, people often assume they have a higher risk of being victimized in areas that are dark and secluded. Because of that belief, they then avoid those types of areas. The more people who avoid those areas, the fewer opportunities for victimization there are. Likewise, areas that are disorder hotspots also tend to be fear generators. Places with graffiti, vandalism, and litter often make people feel uncomfortable and more fearful of going there, even if the actual crime rates in that area are low.

Although fear generator areas may not initially have much crime, they are still important to consider. From a community development perspective, having areas where people are afraid to go could hurt businesses, negatively affect property values, and even isolate the individuals who live in the area. These effects could lead to increased disorder, which could then influence the generation of crime in that area. By addressing the areas early, it may be possible to avoid the development of criminogenic behavior. Further, people who live in locations that generate fear may also have a lower quality of life. In those areas, it may be difficult to find a job, obtain quality housing, or get access to necessary services, such as hospitals or schools. With that in mind, focusing on fear generator locations could not only help with potential crime growth, it could also help solve other problems in the area.

Overview of Hotspot Analysis

As mentioned throughout this chapter, the analysis of hotspots can prove vital for the development and implementation of effective crime prevention strategies. In order to understand how best to address a crime issue, it is important to know where that issue is most problematic. For much of the modern history of crime prevention, the most common approach to examining and evaluating hotspots has been with the use of crime mapping. **Crime mapping** is a tool used by police and researchers to analyze the locations of criminal activity, in order to better recognize crime patterns and develop strategies for crime prevention. Crime mapping can help police departments and communities analyze problems, develop crime prevention initiatives, determine which stakeholders are important to include in the process, and evaluate the outcomes of those initiatives. This allows for more appropriate allocation of police manpower and resources, while also addressing the needs of the community.

History of Crime Mapping

While crime mapping has become extremely popular among law enforcement agencies today, it is far from a new concept. In fact, crime mapping has existed in some form or another for well over a century (Harries, 1999). In that time, the most common approach to crime mapping has been to use maps to pinpoint and examine the geographic locations of crimes and/or related issues. This approach has been well documented throughout the history of crime prevention. For example, with their seminal work, which led to the development of social disorganization theory, Shaw and McKay (1942) utilized a version of crime mapping to examine juvenile delinquency in Chicago. They mapped thousands of incidents of juvenile delinquency, in order to analyze relationships between delinquency and various social and structural conditions, such as socioeconomic disadvantage, residential turnover, and population heterogeneity. The popularity of crime mapping grew even more in the 1970s, as criminologists began to emphasize the importance of place in the perpetration and prevention of crime. Lawrence Cohen and Marcus Felson's (1979) routine activities theory described how and why criminal behaviors concentrate in specific places. A decade and a half later, Paul and Patricia Brantingham proposed their crime pattern theory, positing that crime is a complex event that can be linked to discrete locations that directly influence how, where, and why people decide to commit crimes (1993; 1995). As these theories of crime concentration grew, so did the use of crime mapping to test them.

In the early days of crime mapping, the process was rather rudimentary. Crime analysts would use push pins to mark the location of crimes on a physical map. Typically, the analysis would focus on a single type of crime, utilizing a specific color pin to represent the crime. The areas with the most pins would be considered hotspots of that crime. This approach did have some benefits, such as allowing police to see where crime problems were located in their jurisdiction and which areas may need additional patrol units. However, it also had several limitations. For example, the maps were often very static, because it was difficult to examine crime trends over time, as the pins for different dates could be hard to distinguish. Further, examining multiple types of crimes at the same time was problematic, with the various colored pins being mixed together. Finally, it was difficult to effectively archive the data, especially if the maps had to be moved (Harries, 1999).

Crime mapping would undergo a major evolution with the development of computer mapping programs. While such programs existed as early as the 1960s, they did not become widely used until the early 1990s, when the capacity of computers and quality of printers was greatly improved (Harries, 1999). These programs allow users to create, manipulate, save, and share maps highlighting the locations and concentrations of various crimes, which could not typically be done with paper maps. They also make it much easier to examine crime hotspots in relation to other behavioral phenomena, such as gang or drug activity. Today, electronic crime mapping has become a common practice of law enforcement, especially as a tool for problem-oriented policing and crime prevention. In addition, it is regularly used by city officials and academic researchers who study crime patterns.

Geographic Information Systems

Crime mapping programs are a form of **Geographic Information Systems** (GIS). Originally developed by geographers and cartographers examining phenomena such as land use, wildlife populations, and even mortality rates, GIS are computer programs used to store, visualize, analyze, and interpret geographic data (also commonly referred to as spatial or geospatial data). As the name implies, geographic data identify the location of specific geographic features or points. This data can also be used, in many instances, to highlight temporal features as well, such as changes in geographic features over time. For example, a GIS program could be used to describe and examine changes in wildlife migration patterns, the spread of disease, and, of course, changes in crime hotspot locations.

Today, the most widely used GIS software is a program called ArcGIS. Originally available only as physical software (i.e., disks and CDs), ArcGIS has been transitioned into an online software format as well. This has allowed for easier access, an improvement in software updates, and better customer support (ESRI, 2023). As a result, law enforcement agencies, agricultural managers, and others more readily utilize the software to analyze patterns of behavior. Programs like ArcGIS work by layering maps, representing different features, on top of each other. For example, picture a basic street map of a city. Then, imagine another map file indicating the locations of reported crimes being placed on top of the street map. Once combined, this would produce a map pinpointing the locations of all reported crimes based on their street addresses. A sample illustration is presented with Image 5.1.

Crime and Hotspot Mapping

While GIS programs are used by numerous agencies, organizations, and governments, they have become especially important tools for law enforcement. Within law enforcement, GIS programs have been employed for numerous applications. For example, law enforcement agencies have utilized geospatial data to help show offenders' movements over time; it is frequently used to track cell phones and vehicles of both offenders and victims; and it has been used to determine the likely area of residence for serial killers based on the location of their crimes (a process known as geographic profiling) (Wang, 2012). Without a doubt, however, one of the main uses of GIS programs by law enforcement is to examine patterns and hotspots of crime, a process often referred to as hotspot mapping.

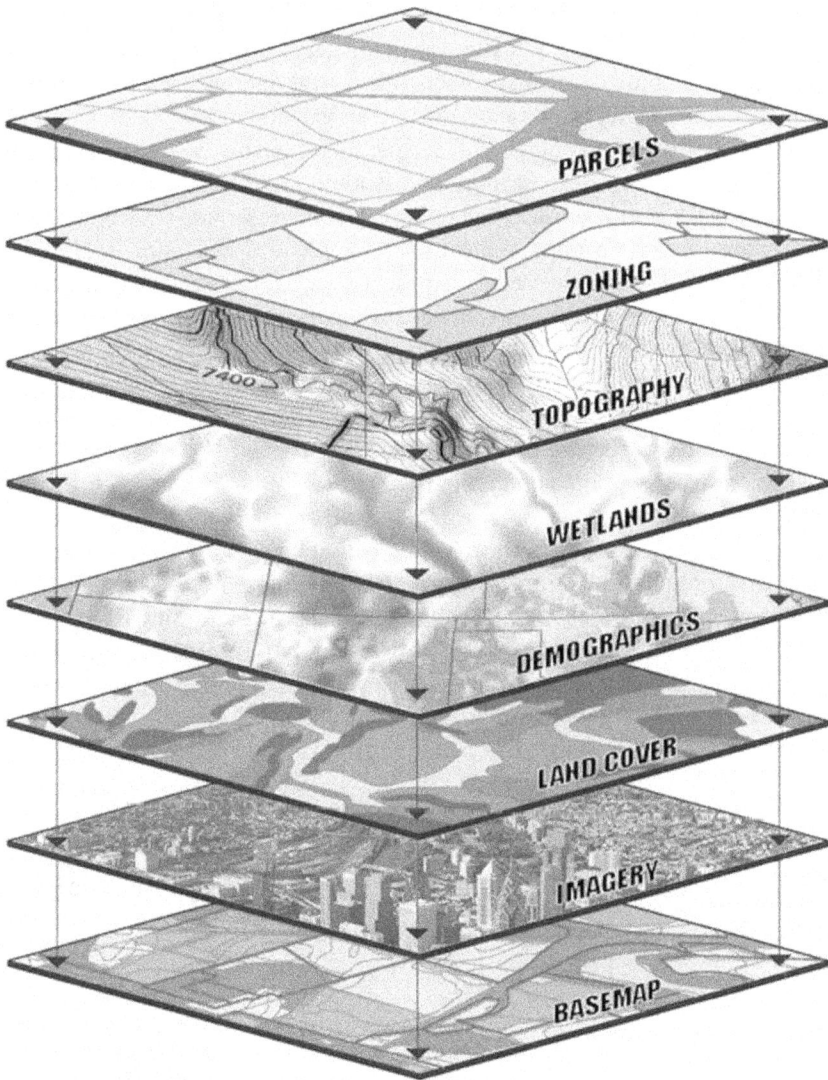

Image 5.1 GIS Map Layering.

Hotspot mapping is the process of identifying and examining specific locations within an area where there is clustering of particular spatial and temporal phenomena. As indicated previously, these phenomena may include crime, fear of crime, and/or disorder. Although police may focus on all of these, the central focus for hotspot mapping is typically crime. With GIS programs, many law enforcement agencies in the United States utilize GPS and other geospatial data to develop maps that show 2- and 3-D representations of the locations and distribution of crimes within a specific area. These maps can then be used to determine if and where crimes geographically concentrate, indicating the location of crime hotspots.

When developing crime maps, there are several options for how to display the information being examined. One of the most commonly used methods is referred to as point mapping. This technique essentially replicates the traditional pin mapping of the past by placing a point (e.g., a circle or other geometric symbol) at the location where a crime occurred. Although somewhat basic, this method is still an improvement over the physical pin maps, as different symbols and colors can be used to represent various crimes, points can be hidden and revealed as needed, and changes or movement in crime can be viewed. Further, size gradience can be employed with the points to indicate repeat offending or victimization. For example, a small dot could be used to represent a bank robbery location on a map. However, if some banks have experienced multiple robberies, the size of the dot could be increased to designate repeated victimization. An example of a point map can be seen in Image 5.2.

Another common method to display information for crime mapping is line mapping. As the name implies, this method involves the use of lines to highlight the desired information. In most cases, the lines will represent specific streets, or street subsections; although they may also be used to note features such as railroad tracks, walkways, or other pathways. Line mapping is especially useful when examining crime that may not have a precise geospatial marker or address. For example, if a law enforcement agency wanted to analyze drug dealing activity in a specific

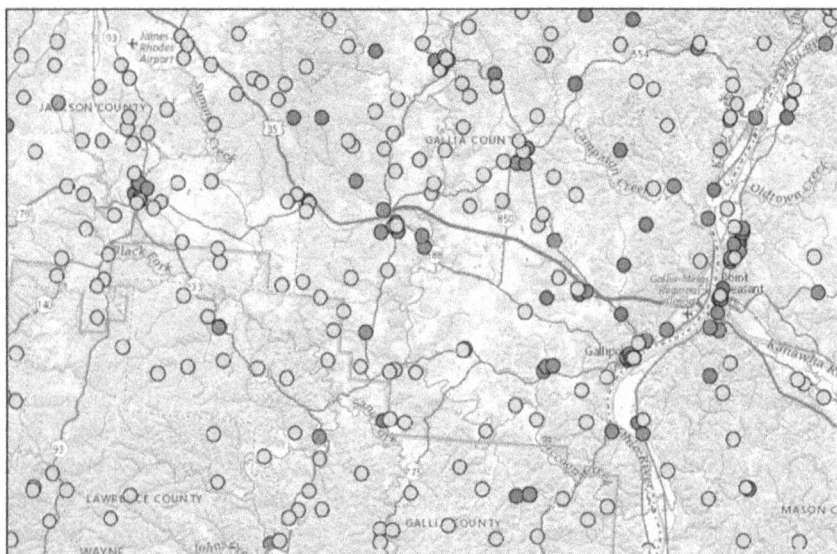

Image 5.2 Sample Point Map.

neighborhood, they could use line mapping to signify which streets had drug arrests. With these types of crimes, the location reported may not be exactly right, so examining the entire street, or a portion of it, could be more useful in identifying drug markets. An example of a line map can be seen in Image 5.3.

If a law enforcement agency wants to examine a larger area, they can utilize polygon mapping. This involves the use of various shapes to outline specific areas of interest. The type of shape depends on the area being examined, and it could be a square, rectangle, or nearly any other multisided figure. The user draws the shape around the area being examined. Polygon mapping could be used to examine crime within police beats, neighborhoods, or even just a few blocks. This type of crime mapping is especially useful when analyzing large areas. To illustrate, if a police department wanted to examine crime within the territory of a street gang, a polygon could be drawn around the known "turf," or geographic location, of the gang. Then, all crimes that occurred within that polygon can be examined. An example of such a map is shown in Image 5.4.

Finally, when it comes to hotspot mapping, one of the most typical approaches is the use of a density map. A density map utilizes gradient color schemes to denote the relative concentration of crime points. Usually, the areas with the highest concentration of points are assigned a darker color, most often red. The areas with lower concentrations of points are

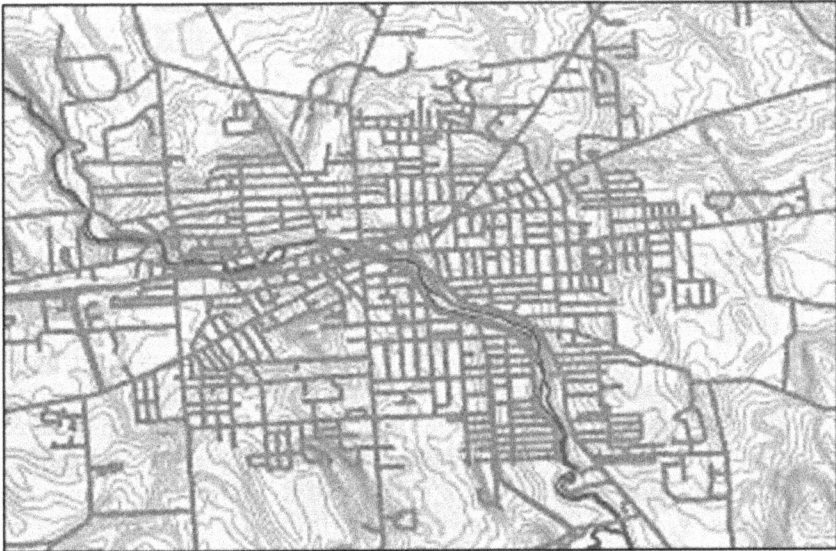

Image 5.3 Sample Line Map.

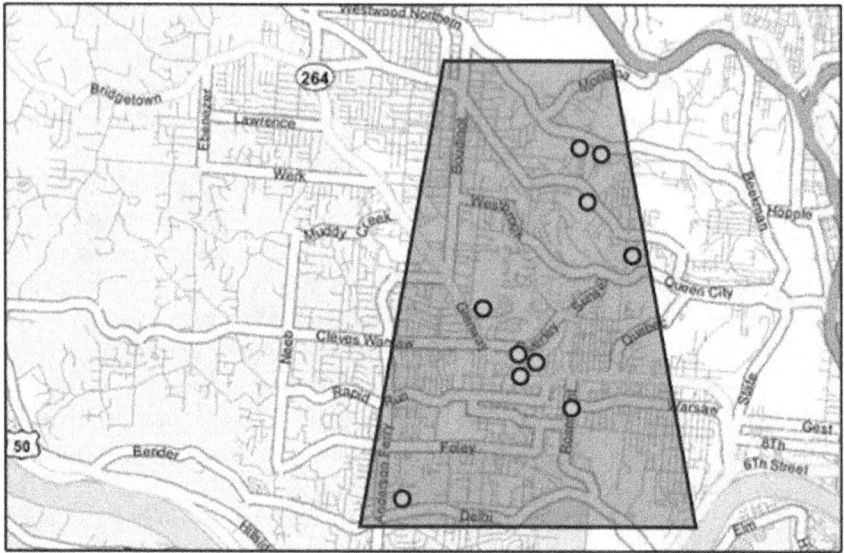

Image 5.4 Sample Polygon Map.

then given lighter colors. This coloration helps to highlight where crime is the most concentrated (i.e., more or less density of crime). The size, or dispersion, of the colored areas can be adjusted larger or smaller to make the hotspot zones more precise. For example, if law enforcement wanted to see more precisely where the epicenter of a hotspot is located, they could decrease the size of the color radiance. An example of a density map can be seen in Image 5.5.

Hotspot Policing

Today, hotspot analysis, also known as **hotspot policing,** is an approach taken by police departments across the United States and the world. The growth of technology has continued to allow law enforcement to evaluate and even predict the growth of crime. Further, as alluded to previously, hotspot policing is being utilized to help develop a variety of strategies to control crime-adjacent issues, such as public disorder matters, including social disorder, prostitution and drug activity, juvenile delinquency, and problems associated with homelessness. In fact, hotspot policing has become a common component of problem-oriented policing. **Problem-oriented policing** is an approach involving police-led efforts to identify and address the underlying problems at hotspots that lead to the growth of crime in those areas. With the growth of problem-oriented policing, a number of strategies have been developed to help target the main problems within a community, including the SARA model. Both problem-oriented policing

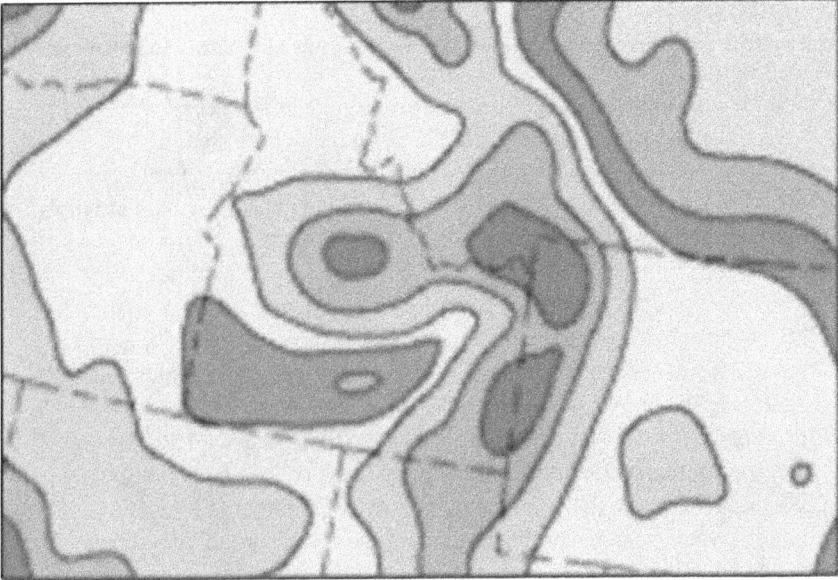

Image 5.5 Sample Density Map.

and the SARA model will be discussed in much more detail in Chapters 9 and 10. Because of the growth in the use of hotspot policing, law enforcement and criminology researchers have been better able to evaluate its effectiveness, while also better tailoring crime prevention strategies to meet the needs of communities they serve.

Benefits of Hotspot Policing

Hotspot policing has been shown to have several key benefits for both crime prevention and law enforcement. First, and foremost, evidence has been found that hotspot policing does, in fact, reduce crime and disorder. As described in Breakout Box 5.1, a targeted approached to hotspot policing was utilized during the late 1980s by the Minneapolis Police Department. At the end of the year-long experiment, researchers reported that police calls for service dropped in high crime areas. Further, hotspot policing allows law enforcement to focus more attention on those areas with the highest crime rates. Given the limits of both budgetary allocations and manpower within police departments, hotspot policing allows agencies to use their resources more effectively to deal with the worst crime problems. In doing so, law enforcement can essentially get a bigger bang for their buck. Finally, as hotspot policing is frequently used in conjunction with problem-oriented and community-oriented policing, its usage can help with the development of positive relationships between police and the general public.

Expand Your Understanding – The Minneapolis Hot Spots Experiment

The Minneapolis Hot Spots Experiment was a directed policing approach focused on preventing and reducing crime in high-crime areas of Minneapolis, Minnesota by modifying police patrol patterns. Primarily taking place in the late 1980s, the experiment was one of the first attempts to utilize and evaluate the practice of hotspot policing as a form of crime prevention.

   In order to determine the impact of police patrol on crime prevention, the Minneapolis Police Department pinpointed "hotspots" of crime throughout the city, by identifying addresses with frequent calls for service, and alternated the presence of patrol officers in those areas. In total, 110 hotspots of crime were identified. Those locations were then divided into two groups, an experimental group and a control group, each containing 55 hotspots. For the locations within the experimental group, police presence, in the form of patrols, was increased. For the locations in the control group, police presence remained the same. The overall goal was to determine if increased police patrol reduced calls for service in high-crime areas.

   Over the course of a year, officers within the department worked with researchers to track and evaluate calls to the police within the areas in both the control and experimental groups. Analysis of police calls for service data, along with observations made in the hotspot areas, showed that increased patrolling may have a positive and significant impact on crime in hotspot areas. Specifically, it was found that the hotspots with increased levels of police patrol reported fewer calls for service, compared to the control areas (Sherman & Weisburd, 1995). While the change was modest, it still provided important evidence for the benefits of hotspot policing.

Limitations of Hotspot Policing

While hotspot policing has many benefits, it is not without limitations. A central issue with hotspot policing is its reliance on data and statistical analyses. Although the utilization of such practices is becoming much more common among law enforcement agencies, there are some, especially veteran officers, who are still reluctant to rely on them. Instead, they may be more inclined to rely on their experience and personal "hunches." Simply, they dislike academic researchers telling them the best way to do their jobs. Related, new crime prevention strategies are being proposed on a somewhat regular basis. Some may see hotspot policing as just another crime prevention "fad," with no real long-term benefits. As a result, it may not be used in good faith, which could directly limit its effectiveness. Finally, a more certain limitation to the use of hotspot policing is the lack of long-term studies. Unfortunately, many experiments examining the effect of hotspot policing are limited to focusing on short-term outcomes. This limits the ability to show hotspot policing as a permanent approach to crime prevention.

Summary

The purpose of this chapter was to introduce readers to the idea of crime concentration and hotspots, concepts that serve as the foundation for much of crime prevention. Throughout the chapter, it was explained how the analyses of hotspots of crime, victimization, and other analogous behaviors are key for better understanding crime problems and how to address them. As a result, hotspot analysis has become a common approach for law enforcement, especially with the birth of crime mapping. Readers were familiarized with the different types of crime mapping, as well as the growth of hotspot policing. In the next chapter, the focus on crime concentration will continue with the discussion of risky facilities and hot products.

Keywords

Crime Clock, Crime Hotspots, Cybercrime Hotspot, Offending Hotspots, Victimization Hotspots, Fear Hotspot, Disorder Hotspot, Level of Analysis, Built Environment, Social Environment, Crime Generator, Crime Attractor, Crime Neutral Areas, Fear Generator, Crime Mapping, Geographic Information Systems, Hotspot Mapping, Hotspot Policing, Problem-Oriented Policing

Discussion Questions

1. Why is the concept of crime concentration important for crime prevention?
2. Choose one type of hotspot and explain why a researcher may want to focus on that type.
3. What is the fundamental difference between crime generators and crime attractors?
4. How has the development of computer programs benefited the growth of crime mapping?
5. How do you think hotspot policing may continue to impact crime prevention?

References

Alim, S. (2016). Cyberbullying in the world of teenagers and social media: A literature review. *International Journal of Cyber Behavior, Psychology and Learning*, 6(2), 68–95.

Brantingham, P. J., & Brantingham, P. L. (1981). *Environmental criminology*. Sage Publications.

Brantingham, P. L., & Brantingham, P. J. (1993). Nodes, paths, and edges: Considerations on the complexity of crime and the physical environment. *Journal of Environmental Psychology*, 13(1), 3–28.

Brantingham, P. L., & Brantingham, P J. (1995). Criminality of place: Crime generators and crime attractors. *European Journal on Criminal Policy & Research*, 13(3), 5–26.

Cohen, L. E., & Felson, M. (1979). Social change and crime rate trends: A routine activity approach. *American Sociological Review*, 44(4), 588–608.

Cornish D. B., & Clarke, R. V. (1986). *The reasoning criminal*. New York: Springer-Verlag.

Eck, J. E., Chainey, S. Cameron, J. G., Leitner, M., & Wilson, R. E. (2005). *Mapping crime: Understanding hot spots*. National Institute of Justice. Retrieved from http://discovery.ucl.ac.uk/11291/1/11291.pdf

ESRI. (2023). ArcGIS Online. Retrieved from https://www.esri.com/en-us/arcgis/products/arcgis-online/overview

Farrall, S., Jackson, J., & Gray, E. (2009). *Social order and the fear of crime in contemporary times*. Oxford: Oxford University Press.

FBI. (2019, June 1). *2019 crime clock: Crime in the United States*. Department of Justice. https://ucr.fbi.gov/crime-in-the-u.s/2019/crime-in-the-u.s.-2019/topic-pages/crime-clock

Giumetti, G. W., & Kowalski, R. M. (2022). Cyberbullying via social media and well-being. *Current Opinion in Psychology*, 45, 101314.

Harries, K. (1999). *Mapping crime: Principle and practice*. National Institute of Justice. Retrieved from www.ojp.usdoj.gov/nij/maps/pubs.html

Henson, B., Reyns, B. W., & Fisher, B. S. (2011). Security in the 21st century: Examining the link between online social network activity, privacy, and interpersonal victimization. *Criminal Justice Review*, 36(3), 253–268.

Lane, J., Rader, N. E., Henson, B., Fisher, B. S., & May, D. C. (2014). *Fear of crime in the United States: Causes, consequences, and contradictions*. Durham, NC: Carolina Academic Press.

McCaughey, M., & Cermele, J. (2015). Changing the hidden curriculum of campus rape prevention and education: Women's self-defense as a key protective factor for a public health model of prevention. *Trauma, Violence and Abuse*, 18(3), 287–302.

Pain, R. (2000). Place, social relations, and the fear of crime. *Progress in Human Geography*, 24(3), 365–387.

Piza, E. L., Welsh, B. C., Farrington, D. P., & Thomas, A. L. (2019). CCTV surveillance for crime prevention: A 40-year systematic review with meta-analysis. *Criminology & Public Policy*, 18(1), 135–159.

Shaw, C. R., & McKay, H. D. (1942). *Juvenile delinquency and urban areas*. Chicago, IL: University of Chicago Press.

Sherman, L. W. & Weisburd, D. A. (1995). General deterrent effects of police patrol in crime "hot spots": A randomized, controlled trial. *Justice Quarterly*, 12(4), 625–648.

Song, C., Qu, Z., Blumm, N., & Barabasi A. L. (2010). Limits of predictability in human mobility. *Science, 327*(5968), 1018–1021.

Ullman, S. E. (1997). Review and critique of empirical studies of rape avoidance. *Criminal Justice and Behavior, 24*(2), 177–204.

Ullman, S. E. (2007). A 10-year update of "review and critique of empirical studies of rape avoidance." *Criminal Justice and Behavior, 34*(3), 411–429.

United States Geological Survey. (2023). *USGS: Science for Changing the World.* Retrieved from https://www.usgs.gov/

Wang, F. (2012). Why police and policing need GIS: An overview. *Annals of GIS, 18*(3), 159–171.

Chapter 6
Crime Concentration Among Places and Things

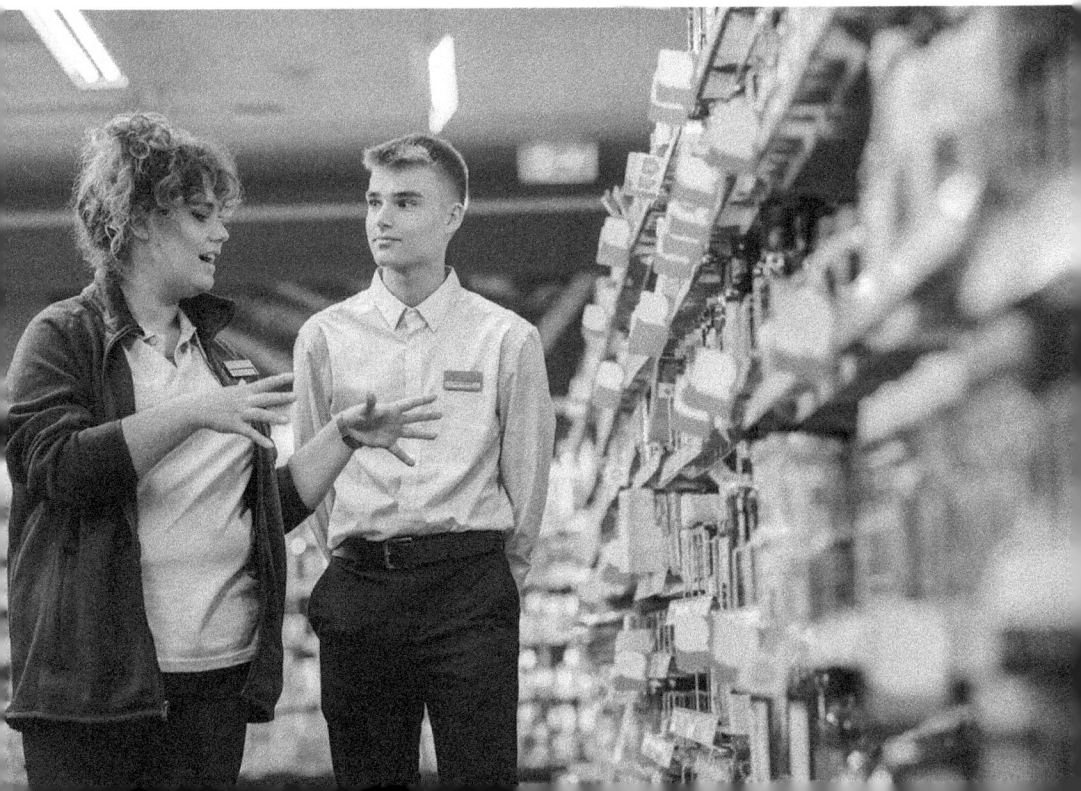

Crime Concentration Among Places and Things

Billy Henson

Chapter Outline

In this chapter, we will focus on:

Examining Risky Facilities

- Defining risky facilities
- Development of risky facilities
- Identifying risky facilities
- Risky facilities as hotspots of crime

Examining Hot Products

- Defining hot products
- Identifying hot products
- Hot products and hotspots

Understanding the Role of Place Management

- Defining place management
- Forms of place management responsibility
- Place management as crime prevention

Learning Objectives

After reading this chapter, you should be able to:

6.1 Explain what is meant by the term risky facility

6.2 Describe how theory may be helpful in identifying risky facilities

6.3 Define the term hot product

6.4 Explain how the CRAVED model can be used to identify hot products

6.5 Justify how effective place management may improve crime prevention

DOI: 10.4324/9781003401551-8

Introduction

Highlighted throughout Chapter 5, crime concentration, and more specifically hotspots of crime, can appear in many forms. However, while the focus thus far has been mainly on forms of geographic hotspots, there are also several types of crime hotspots that are not necessarily defined only by geography, with two of the more common types being risky facilities and hot products. With these forms of hotspots, although geographic location may play a role in their development, other factors tend to be more important, including the structural layout and management of places. As a result, these forms of hotspots tend to be much more specific than geographic hotspots, with very unique crime opportunity structures. Throughout this chapter, you will be introduced to the concepts of risky facilities and hot products. In addition, the ability of each phenomenon to develop into a hotspot of crime, and even influence the development of larger geographic hotspots, will be described. The chapter will conclude with a discussion of the role of place management in preventing or reducing the growth of these types of hotspots.

Examining Risky Facilities

Defining Risky Facilities

The first step in discussing the development and impact of risky facilities is understanding what exactly the term means, as it is not a common phrase in many individuals' vernacular. To do so, the easiest approach is to first define its parts. Let us begin with the word *risky*. It is a common enough word that, no doubt, brings certain images and thoughts to mind when heard. Most often thought of as synonymous with danger, hazardousness, and even fear, the term risky is usually used to describe situations where potential harm could result. In the present context, while risky could mean all those things, it also refers to the potential presence of criminal opportunity. Essentially, a risky location is one where there is an increased likelihood of factors converging in a manner that escalates the possibility for crime to take place.

Next, let us focus on the word *facility*. While not an uncommon word, it is not necessarily one that many people use in everyday conversation. Typically, the term facility refers to a place created or structured to serve a specific purpose. In most cases, the purpose of the facility is unique to that location, as well. For instance, hospitals are medical facilities. They are designed and operated in a manner specific to the needs of medical services. Attempting to provide medical services in a warehouse would not be nearly as safe or effective, as that facility was not created with such purposes in mind. Further, although facilities are most typically thought of as buildings, that is not a requirement. Instead, a facility is any *area* created for a specific purpose. To illustrate, a bus stop is an area designed to allow passengers to wait and enter/exit buses. However, it is generally an open area, along a street or thoroughfare, as opposed to being an enclosed building. In this case, facility refers to a general location. Finally, as mentioned, the purpose of a facility is frequently very specific. This is an important factor to keep in mind, as facilities with similar purposes could still be designed very differently. For example, hospitals and dentist offices could both be considered health or medical facilities. But, because of the specific functions and purposes of each field, the facilities typically vary drastically in both appearance and use.

As will be discussed more in Chapter 11, different types of facilities may experience different types of crime. For instance, convenience stores frequently experience robberies (Altizio & York, 2007), while hospitals often experience assaults (Rock, 2021). Additionally, certain types of facilities tend to experience more crime than others. For example, bars, and other alcohol-serving establishments, are often the scene of a large number of violent offenses, when compared with other types of facilities (Eck et al., 2007; Eck et al., 2009; Franquez et al., 2013). However, while bars, in general, may have high rates of crime, not every bar will have a lot of crime. Instead, some bars may have really high rates of crime, while others have relatively no crime. With that in mind, the bars with higher crime rates would be referred to as risky facilities, as compared with those with low crime rates. To clarify, a **risky facility** is a specific facility that produces high levels of criminal opportunity, when compared with other similar types of facilities. As a result, those specific facilities often have higher crimes rates than their counterparts.

As with neighborhoods, blocks, intersections, and other locations, risky facilities may exist as areas of high crime concentration. For instance, one study found that about 50 percent of all violent crimes that occurred in higher level schools in Stockholm, Sweden was reported by only 8 percent of schools (Lindstrom, 1997), while another study examining crime reported on buses in Merseyside, England found that about 80 percent of all reported crime on bus routes occurred along only 4 percent of bus routes (Newton, 2004). Still, another study performed in the United States found that 6.5 percent of convenience stores experience about 65 percent of all convenience store robberies (National Association of Convenience Stores, 1991). Other studies have reported similar results. It simply seems that, with any type of facility, there will be specific ones that generate and/or attract more crime than others.

Development of Risky Facilities
Upon learning about the presence of risky facilities, the first question that usually comes to mind is *why do they exist*? *Why do some facilities experience much more crime than other similar facilities of the same type?* Unfortunately, the answer to that question is not straightforward, as there are

a multitude of factors that could influence the development of risky facilities. To illustrate this phenomenon, let us discuss a few examples. First, larger facilities typically contain more potential targets for offenders. For example, larger department stores have more items that could be shoplifted, and larger bars often have more patrons that could be assaulted or robbed (Clarke & Eck, 2016). Further, the location of a facility may influence how frequently it is targeted. For instance, if a bank is located near a major highway, offenders may see that as a good means of escaping the scene and may choose to rob that bank over one located downtown. Finally, whether due to location, type, or some other factor, some facilities may attract individuals who are more vulnerable to victimization; therefore, serving as a crime attractor for potential offenders (Clarke & Eck, 2016). For example, there may be a specific gym that offers classes to elderly people. Potential offenders may be attracted to that facility thinking elderly people are easier to rob. If that were the case, then that particular gym could have much higher rates of crime than other gyms in the area.

Theoretical Perspectives

In an effort to better explain the development and growth of risky facilities, a number of theoretical perspectives have also been proffered. As highlighted by Madensen and Eck (2008), there are at least four separate theories that have been used to explain the presence of risky facilities: 1) neighborhood theory, 2) patron theory, 3) management theory, and 4) behavior setting theory. These theories include both macro- and individual-level explanations for the presence of risky facilities, with one theory offering a multi-level explanation. In addition, some of the theories could be considered in unison, as the causal factors discussed among them appear to have clear overlap.

Table 6.1 Theories Explaining Causes of Risky Facilities

Theory	Key Factor	Characteristics of Risky Facility
Neighborhood	Neighborhood Characteristics	In Neighborhood with High Crime
Patron	Patron/Customer Characteristics	High Number of Motivated Offenders as Patrons
Management	Owner/Manager Actions	Poor Management
Behavior Setting	Neighborhood Characteristics, Patron/Customer Characteristics, & Owner/Manager Actions	Combination of Factors Creates an Overall Environment that Encourages Crime

First, there is the **neighborhood theory**. With this theory, it is suggested that facilities in more problematic neighborhoods will experience higher rates of crime (Skogan, 1986; Madensen & Eck, 2008). Essentially, if there is a lot of crime around a specific place, criminal behavior will most likely occur within or at least just outside of that place. As a result, facilities located within existing crime hotspots may have a greater likelihood of being a risky facility, as compared with similar facilities located outside of hotspot areas. Of course, with this theory, the specific types of crime being committed both within the neighborhood and the facility need to be considered. For example, if the neighborhood is a hotspot of violent crime, yet a business within that neighborhood mainly experiences only theft, it may be more difficult to link the two phenomena.

The second theory commonly associated with the explanation of risky facilities is the **patron theory** (Madensen & Eck, 2008). This theory highlights the role of customers or patrons that enter and use a specific facility. As noted in Chapter 2, with the discussion of routine activity theory, exposure to motivated offenders increases the opportunity for crime to occur. The more offenders a potential victim may come into contact with at a location, the higher that opportunity increases. The patron theory suggests that risky facilities are patronized by a higher number of motivated offenders than non-risky facilities, therefore increasing the opportunity for crime at those locations (Fishbine & Joelson, 1978). Further, if nothing is done to prevent offenders from frequenting the facility, it may then become a crime attractor location, drawing in additional offenders (Brantingham & Brantingham, 1995).

Third, quite possibly the theory most often applied to the development and continuation of risky facilities is the **management theory**. With this theory, emphasis is placed on the role and behavior of the individual or individual(s) who manage a facility. This could be the owner of the facility or someone who has been hired to serve as the manager. According to the theory, the driving factor behind whether or not a particular facility becomes risky is how well it is managed, regardless of whether it is located in a crime hotspot area or if many offenders patronize it (Marsh, 1980; Eck, 1994). The general assumption is that if a place is managed effectively, the opportunities for criminal behavior within or just outside it can be tempered. On the other hand, if a facility is mismanaged, the opportunity for criminal behavior may increase at that location. For instance, if drug dealing occurs in the courtyard of an apartment complex, the apartment manager's willingness to report it to the police could determine if the behavior continues or not.

Finally, the fourth theory utilized to help explain the presence of risky facilities is the **behavior setting theory**. The easiest way to describe this theory is that it is like a combination of the previous three theories. According to the behavior setting theory, risky facilities develop as a result of the combination of neighborhood, patron, and management characteristics, which creates an overall environment that either encourages or discourages criminal behavior (Cavan, 1966; Barker, 1968; Wicker, 1979; Madensen & Eck, 2008; Caplan et al., 2017). In actuality, the behavior setting theory is probably the most complete explanation of risky facilities. This theory provides a multi-level explanation for how risky facilities emerge; however, it is more difficult to test as doing so would require multi-level analyses of data from multiple sources (e.g., patrons, neighborhoods).

Identifying Risky Facilities

Armed with basic knowledge of what risky facilities are and why they may exist, it becomes much easier to understand how it is determined which facilities are actually risky. Determining this can be a complex process, as it is necessary to go beyond simply examining which facilities experience crime. Of course, crime analysis is an essential component of pinpointing risky facilities, but there are several factors that must be considered when doing such an analysis. By considering each of these factors, researchers and practitioners will be better able to determine exactly which facilities warrant attention and which do not. This process essentially includes three steps.

The first step in identifying risky facilities is to decide the unit of analysis being examined. While the obvious choice would be crime, one must consider how crime will actually be measured. Researchers have examined a number of different outcomes to measure crime at risky facilities. For example, crime could be measured as the number of times the police are called to a location (i.e., calls for service), the number of incidents at a location actually reported to the police (when called or otherwise), the number of individuals arrested at a location, or even the number of individuals prosecuted/convicted of crime that occurred at a location. For the purposes of the current discussion, calls for service will be used.

Once the unit of analysis is chosen, the next step is to collect data on that behavior for all of the same types of facilities in a given area, for a specific time period. While this may seem like a simple task, this too can be somewhat complex, and it is necessary to be as specific as possible. For example, if choosing to examine calls for service at bars, would it be prudent to also include other types of facilities that serve alcohol, such as dance clubs, taverns, beer gardens, and restaurants? Regardless of what is decided, effort should be made to ensure the facilities being compared are as similar as possible. Relatedly, the time period being analyzed must be chosen carefully. When doing so, it is necessary to consider factors that may alter behavior at different times. Case in point, during the COVID-19 pandemic, more people stayed home. As a result, crime at many locations outside the home dropped during that period. In addition, it is also important to choose a long enough timeline in order to capture an adequate number of incidents. One year is a common length of time used by researchers; however, using a longer time-line is also suitable.

The last step in determining which facilities are riskiest is to calculate the number of incidents that occur at each facility. This process typically begins with a raw count of incidents. While it is up to the researcher to determine what crime types will be analyzed, it is usually best to be very specific, at least in the beginning. For instance, comparing violent crime among bars could be very informative; however, comparing specific types of violent crime, such as sexual assault, may be more even more informative, especially if developing a crime prevention strategy to address the crime. Once the data have been collected, it is often beneficial to convert them into a more user-friendly format, especially if presenting the information to a large audience. A common approach is to calculate the percentage of crime that occurs at each examined facility, relative to the total amount of crime across the facilities. This will allow for a comparison across facilities. An example of this process can be seen in Table 6.2.

In examining Table 6.2, it can be seen that crime data is presented for three fictional bars. Across the three bars, the number and percentage of calls for service are indicated for several types of crime. The crime types are divided into broad categories – violent and property crime – and specific categories – homicide, assault, robbery, theft, and property damage. This allows for both general and specific comparisons. There are statistical anal-yses that can be utilized to determine if the differences between the three bars are statistically significant, but for the sake of this discussion we will merely make simple comparisons. Based on the data presented in Table 6.2, it seems that Bar 1 has made the highest percentage of calls to the police for service. In fact, with certain crimes, such as overall violent crime, homicide, assault and theft, Bar 1 is responsible for over half of all calls to the police.

Table 6.2 Calculating Crime at Risky Facilities

Crime Types	Bar 1 (no. and % of calls for service)	Bar 2 (no. and % of calls for service)	Bar 3 (no. and % of calls for service)	Total
Violent Crime	12 (55%)	6 (27%)	4 (18%)	22
Homicide	1 (100%)	0 (0%)	0 (0%)	1
Assault	9 (56%)	4 (25%)	3 (19%)	16
Robbery	2 (40%)	2 (40%)	1 (20%)	5
Property Crime	16 (46%)	10 (29%)	9 (26%)	35
Theft	12 (55%)	6 (27%)	4 (18%)	22
Property Damage	4 (31%)	4 (31%)	5 (38%)	13

CRIME PATTERNS AND CONCENTRATION

As a result, it seems as though there is something unique about Bar 1 that is creating more opportunity for crime to occur, when compared with the other bars, making it a risky facility.

Potential Problems Identifying Risky Facilities

Given that identifying risky facilities is mostly data driven, the process is not immune from issues, much like most other forms of crime data analysis. According to Clarke and Eck (2007), there are eight major issues that can be problematic for risky facility analysis. First, an issue that is prevalent throughout all forms of crime analysis, the underreporting of crime makes it especially problematic to obtain reliable data. In addition to reducing the amount of data available to identify risky facilities, under-reporting could also lead to statistical distortion (Clarke & Eck, 2007). For example, if Bar 1 reports every crime that occurs there, but other bars only report a small percentage of crimes, the high-reporting bar may appear as a risk facility, since it has many more calls for service than other bars. In reality, however, the other bars could experience much more crime that simply is not reported.

The second major issue comes in the form of incomplete or incorrect address information. When calls for service are made and/or police reports are completed, there is a chance that the address of the facility may not be recorded correctly. The facility may have multiple addresses; there may be multiple facilities at a single address; and/or key information, such as unit numbers, may simply be left off the report (Clarke & Eck, 2007). Given that most crime analyses utilize police data, these errors may prevent the exact matching of addresses. As a result, the number of calls for service made from a specific facility may not be calculated correctly.

Next, another central issue that could affect the ability to accurately evaluate risky facilities is the presence of mixed-use locations (Clarke & Eck, 2007). Simply, some locations, especially large buildings, may contain multiple facilities. For example, many hotels also contain bars. As the hotel and the bar will typically have the same address, it can be difficult to determine where the crime occurred, if it is not clearly noted in the report or call log. In some cases, crimes that occurred in a hotel room may be attributed to the bar and vice versa. When comparing facilities, it would then be more difficult to make an accurate comparison.

Further, the frequency with which particular crimes occur could also be problematic when identifying risky facilities, especially in the case of infrequent crimes (Clarke & Eck, 2007). For some crimes, such as homicide, the relatively low number of incidents could lead to inappropriate identification of risky facilities. Case in point, with Table 6.2, it can be seen that 100 percent of homicides were reported by Bar 1. On the surface, this may make Bar 1 seem to be a very risky facility when it comes to homicide. However, when drilling down on the data, it becomes evident that there was only a single homicide at that bar, compared with zero homicides at the other bars. While an argument can be made that any number of homicides is too many, it is much more difficult to claim that a single incident is indicative of a persistent problem.

Related to the previous issue, it can also be problematic if some facilities report no criminal activity. This issue is most challenging if one is relying solely on police data to identify risky and non-risky facilities (Clarke & Eck, 2007). If a particular facility reports no criminal activity, it may not even appear in the police data. To that end, not only would a researcher not be able to get the full picture when identifying risky facilities, but by also not examining facilities with no crime, valuable crime prevention information could be overlooked. Perhaps the facility with no crime is doing something that riskier facilities could adopt.

A sixth issue that could create problems when identifying risky facilities is the presence of only a few types of specific facilities in a given area (Clarke & Eck, 2007). For example, a city may have only one (or no) airports, a couple of hospitals, or only a few hotels. The fewer facilities there are to compare, the less meaningful the difference between them becomes. Of course, that is not to say that a small number of facilities, or even a single facility, should not be examined for potential application of crime prevention strategies, but it would be more prudent to examine each facility individually, rather than attempting to make comparisons.

In addition to the number of facilities and reported crimes, the length of time being examined could also result in a problematic analysis (Clarke & Eck, 2007). As noted previously, many such analyses focus on one year's worth of data. However, it is perfectly reasonable to examine a longer period of time. In doing so, though, one must consider the possibility that the occupant, function, and even layout of a facility may have changed. It is not unusual for businesses to come and go in a single location during a year's time. Think about the last time you saw a real estate company in a building that clearly used to be a Burger King. As a result, crime reported at a specific location could actually have occurred in different facilities. This must be considered if you want to make an effective comparison of facilities.

Finally, as with any type of crime analysis, there exists the possibility of random variation (Clarke & Eck, 2007). Sometimes things simply do not make sense based on the data being analyzed. Perhaps it is a data reporting or collection error. Or, perhaps there was just a random event that cannot be explained with the observable characteristics of the data. In any case, there's always the possibility of error or unexplainable variation.

Risky Facilities as Hotspots of Crime

As discussed in Chapters 2 and 5, criminal opportunity is often more prevalent at high-activity nodes (places frequently utilized by both potential victims and offenders). Where there is greater opportunity, there also tends to be more crime, and, with enough crime, we see the formation of hotspots. In many cases, risky facilities may be high-activity nodes themselves, which could then account for a sizable amount of crime concentration. For example, retail stores are often popular locations, visited by many people on a regular basis. Relatedly, they also experience a high number of shoplifting incidents, in addition to being the location for other crimes such as assault and drug activity. Because of the frequency with which such locations experience crime, compared with the surrounding areas, it often appears that crime concentrates at those locations. This was the case in Springfield, Missouri, when police began examining areas of high crime within the city in 2014. After mapping the locations of calls to the police, Springfield police noticed Walmart Supercenters at the center of five different areas of high-crime concentration (Gounley, 2016). Upon examining the data, police found that of the 1,441 shoplifting calls in 2014, 56 percent came from one of the five Walmart stores. Further, almost 18 percent of all theft calls and about 13 percent of all robbery calls within the city also originated from one of the five stores (Gounley, 2016). Compared with other retail stores, and even other Walmarts, in the area, these five Walmarts are risky facilities.

Expand Your Understanding – The Dollar Store Hotspot

As of late, one particular type of department store, the dollar store, has received a fair amount of attention due to criminal activity on their premises. Dollar stores are department stores that sell items at extremely low prices, typically one dollar or less. To help keep the prices so low, many such stores keep staffing to a minimum, often with no security personnel and only a single employee working the checkout (Picchi, 2023). This leads many potential offenders to see the stores as easy targets. In addition to a very high rate of theft, dollar stores also experience elevated levels of other types of crimes. For example, from 2014 to 2021, more than 150 people were killed with guns at dollar stores, while another 329 people were injured (Picchi, 2023). Compared with the surrounding facilities and locations, this makes dollar stores stand out as a hotspot for crime.

Covered in detail in Chapter 5, areas where crime is found to concentrate at high rates are often labeled as crime hotspots. To that end, if enough crime is concentrated at a risky facility, compared with the surrounding area, it could be designed as a crime hotspot itself. Further, depending on the circumstances, the hotspot may include only the facility, or it may also encompass some of the surrounding area. This could occur because of the ability of risky facilities to act as crime attractors and/or generators. The characteristics that make a particular facility risky could be generating criminal opportunities. For instance, a particular sports arena may report a lot of assaults occurring in the parking lot. The assaults may be occurring because fans noticed a lack of security and took the opportunity to commit violence. Likewise, criminal offenders may also be attracted to that particular arena parking lot because they think there will be a lot of opportunity for crime due to the lack of security. As a result, that area may appear as a hotspot of crime. Additionally, however, crime could spread from that location into the surrounding area. Motivated by the apparent lack of security (low risk) and potential number of targets (high reward) at the stadium, potential offenders may begin robbing fans outside and/or on their way to the stadium, expanding the scope of the hotspot.

While on the surface a risky facility may appear similar to other forms of crime hotspots, it can actually be very different. With that in mind, simply comparing risky facility hotspots with other types of hotspots would not be an effective means of understanding them. Comparing a risky bank with a high-crime block or neighborhood would be problematic, as one is a single building and the other is a large geographic area. There are simply too many factors to consider. Instead, it would be more appropriate to compare risky facilities with similar, non-risky facilities; for example, comparing a high-crime gas station with low-crime gas stations. This approach would allow researchers and practitioners to gain a better understanding of what is different or unique about that specific facility which could be resulting in more opportunity for crime to occur. Through this process, it can also be determined what, if any, crime prevention strategies are being utilized by the less risky facilities. With that information in hand, potentially effective crime prevention tactics could then be applied to the risky facility.

Examining Hot Products

Defining Hot Products

Thus far, we have examined crime concentration only among places, whether large geographical areas (as discussed in Chapter 5) or specific facilities. However, there is another form of crime concentration that is not geographically defined. Instead, the focus is on specific items, referred to as hot products. As explained by Ronald Clarke (1999), **hot products** are items that are frequently targeted by thieves, more so than other items. These may include common manufactured goods, such as smart phones, jewelry, or cars, or they may include items such as food, animals, or even lumber. Of course, one of the most commonly sought after items, by far, is money. Further, as indicated by the definition, in terms of crime concentration, hot products are unique in that they are mainly associated with the specific forms of crime that involve taking something, including robbery, burglary, theft (of all types), and auto theft. Fortunately, however, this specificity allows for more effective crime prevention strategy development.

Identifying Hot Products

When discussing hot products, one of the first thoughts that is usually brought up is *which products are hot products?* The simple answer to that question is *whatever items are stolen the most.* We realize that is not a very satisfying response, but that is the most direct way to determine which products are hot. Of course, it is a little more complex than that, as you must consider the location, time of year, type of community, and a number of other factors to get the full picture. For example, it is doubtful that thick coats and jackets are oft stolen items in July, just as bathing suits are probably not frequently stolen in December. However, while such factors may create some variation in making products hot, we generally see the same categories of items stolen more often. Examples of those items are highlighted in Table 6.3. Although there is some variation from year to year, most of the items in the table remain hot products.

While an analysis of police data and/or consumer retail data can provide insight into which items are hot products, it still does not explain why those items are hot products. No doubt, your first thought is that hot products are simply the most expensive or valuable items. However, while many hot products may hold significant financial value, that cannot be said for all of them. For example, as indicated in Table 6.3, one of the most frequently shoplifted items is laundry detergent. Although there are some expensive detergents, most are priced relatively low. With that in mind, there must be other factors to consider when determining why some products are hot and others are not. Fortunately, crime prevention researchers have proposed some theoretical frameworks over the years to help identify why some items are more in demand than others among thieves.

As discussed in detail in Chapter 2, a cornerstone of Cohen and Felson's (1979) routine activity theory is the assumption that some potential targets

Table 6.3 Top Ten Most Frequently Stolen Items in the United States (2022/23)

Residential Burglary+	*Shoplifting++*
Bicycles	Alcoholic Beverages
Cars/Car Parts	Clothing
Cash/Wallets	Cosmetic/Hygiene Items
Clothing	Electronics
Electronics	Food
Firearms	Infant Formula
Furniture	Intimate Items (e.g., condoms)
Jewelry/Watches	Laundry Detergent
Personal Documents (e.g., passport)	Office Supplies
Prescription Drugs	Toys

Source: +Rivelli, 2022; ++Latham, 2022; Tobin, 2023.

of crime are more attractive than others. For instance, a home with a single occupant and no alarm would be much more attractive to burglars than one with a large family, dog, and alarm system. As part of their theoretical explanation for the development of criminal opportunity, Cohen and Felson proposed a model, referred to as VIVA, to help evaluate the attractiveness targets. **VIVA** is an acronym representing the four central factors used to explain why some potential targets are more attractive than others. VIVA stands for value, inertia, visibility, and access. The meaning of each concept is detailed in Table 6.4.

When proposed by Cohen and Felson (1979), the VIVA model did not focus solely on targets of theft. Instead, they intended for it to be an explanation for the suitability of any type of target (e.g., item, person, location). Further, it is not necessary for a target to meet all the criteria of VIVA in order to be considered attractive by an offender. For instance, if a burglary offender were evaluating a home to rob, the fact that they can easily see within the home and can access it may be enough for them to consider it an attractive target. In fact, Cohen and Felson proposed VIVA as more of a general guide rather than a definitive model (Clarke, 1999). Regardless of its initial purpose, however, the VIVA model has served as the foundation for the development of many crime prevention strategies.

Although useful in identifying hot products, VIVA was not proposed for that specific purpose. To that end, because of this, many researchers

Table 6.4 The VIVA Model for Target Attractiveness

Factor	Meaning
Value	The desirability of the target. May refer to either monetary or symbolic value.
	The higher the monetary or symbolic value of a target, the more attractive it is to potential offenders.
Inertia	The ability to physically take and/or move the item. Characteristics considered include size, weight, etc.
	The lower the inertia of a target, the more attractive it is to potential offenders.
Visibility	The ability to see and evaluate the target. This may include visibility with the naked eye or an electronic device.
	The better the visibility of a target, the more attractive it is to potential offenders.
Access	The ability to physically approach and take the target. Often also refers to ability to escape with the target.
	The easier the access to a target, the more attractive it is to potential offenders.

Source: Based on Cohen & Felson, 1979.

and practitioners have found it somewhat lacking in its ability to detect specific items that may be more targeted by thieves. With that in mind, Clarke (1999) proposed a revised model that could more effectively identify hot products. Also an acronym, Clarke's model is called **CRAVED**. This new model "was designed to overcome some of the limitations of the VIVA model, such as taking into account the motivation, as well as the characteristics that are important to consider when contemplating theft (e.g., concealing and disposing of the goods)" (Beauregard & Martineau, 2015, p. 2). With the CRAVED model, Clarke built upon the existing components of VIVA by adding in additional factors that should be considered when examining potential hot products. CRAVED stands for concealable, removable, available, valuable, enjoyable, and disposable. A description of the components of the CRAVED model can be seen in Table 6.5.

Similar to the VIVA model, it is not necessary for an item to meet all the criteria of the CRAVED model in order to be a hot product. However, the more criteria from the model the item meets, the greater the likelihood of it

Table 6.5 The CRAVED Model for Hot Products

Factor	Meaning
Concealable	How easily an item can be hidden. This may mean hidden from view or more difficult to identify.
	Items that are more concealable are more likely to be stolen.
Removable	How easily an item can be taken. This includes both the initial theft and the following transport of the item.
	Items that are more easily removed are more likely to be stolen.
Available	How abundant an item is. This may refer to both the number of individual items and the availability of the items across geographic areas.
	The more of an item that is available, the more likely it is to be stolen.
Valuable	How desirable an item is. This includes both monetary and symbolic value.
	The higher the monetary or symbolic value of an item, the more likely it is to be stolen.
Enjoyable	How much joy an item brings to the owner. This may include joy from the ownership or use of the item.
	All else being equal, items that are more enjoyable are more likely to be stolen.
Disposable	How easy an item can be gotten rid of. This includes both consuming an item (e.g., food, drugs) or selling/giving away the item.
	The easier an item is to dispose of, the more likely it will be stolen.

Source: Based on Clarke, 1999.

becoming a hot product. CRAVED has proven very useful in explaining why certain items are more frequently stolen, including items such as cellphones, bags, and even parrots (Whitehead et al., 2008; Smith et al., 2006; Pires & Clarke, 2012). Take a moment to revisit the lists outlined in Table 6.3. How many items in the lists meet at least a few of the criteria of the CRAVED model? We are sure you noticed that everything on those lists meets multiple criteria from the model. Today, this model is widely used by researchers, practitioners, and even law enforcement to help better understand the growth of hot products, as well as how to prevent their theft.

Hot Products and Hotspots

Like risky facilities, the presence of hot products has the ability to contribute to the development of crime hotspots. The concentration of a large amount of a single hot product (e.g., numerous smart phones at a store) or a mass of different types of hot products at a specific location (e.g., items in a department store) could produce more opportunities for theft. Unless the opportunities for theft are prevented or reduced, that location could become both a crime generator and crime attractor. With an increase in offender activity at the place where the hot products are located, crime will begin to concentrate in that area, producing a hotspot of theft. For example, as was discussed previously, certain department stores limit the number of security and employees present in the store at any given time, while also offering a wide range of products. These factors create a perfect storm where potential thieves may attempt to access, conceal, and remove items from the stores. The more frequently this occurs, the more crime is associated with that store. With enough incidents, that store may become a risky facility, which could then develop into a hotspot of crime.

Understanding the Role of Place Management

Defining Place Management

When compared with more general areas of crime concentration, risky facilities and hot products are somewhat unique for a number of reasons. First, rather than being spread across a larger geographic area, crime concentration resulting from risky facilities and hot products tends to be more localized, as the criminal opportunity originates often from a single point (e.g., a specific business or other high-activity node). Second, given the nature of the location, risky facilities and hot products are often controlled by an additional level of supervision. Although streets, sidewalks, parks, and other public use areas are monitored by law enforcement, most facilities are also monitored and controlled by another party – place managers. As indicated in the crime triangle presented in previous chapters, a **place manager** is an individual or individual(s) who have ownership over or authority within a specific facility or place. Typically, place managers have the power to control the layout and function of a facility, as well as to determine what is and is not appropriate behavior for individuals working in or visiting that facility. To that end, they are also responsible for helping to discourage or deter crime in that place.

Forms of Place Management Responsibility

So, who exactly is responsible for managing and deterring crime in a specific place? While the obvious answer would be the owner of the place, there are actually multiple levels of responsibility. In fact, **place management theory** suggests there are four levels of individual responsibility for a place (Felson, 1995). The first, and highest, level of responsibility is **personal responsibility**. This is the level of responsibility assigned to owners of places, or others who are intimately associated with them (Felson, 1995). For example, individuals who own or live in a home have a personal responsibility to manage and secure that home. Likewise, the owner of an apartment complex is directly responsible for managing and taking care of the complex. With this level of responsibility, individuals are effectively the primary managers of the place and carry the majority of the responsibility for ensuring the place is safe and secure.

The second level of responsibility is **assigned responsibility**. This level is specified for individuals who are hired to manage a specific facility (Felson, 1995). In many cases, their specific job will be as a manager. For instance, someone could work as the manager of a convenience store or restaurant. However, it could also include other managerial-types roles, such as a bar tender, who is responsible for managing the bar area. While individuals at this level do not have as much responsibility for the safeguarding of a facility as the owner, they are still expected to contribute to that process by ensuring all relevant policies and rules are followed, as well as by reporting any issues to the owner.

The third level of responsibility is **diffuse job responsibility**. This level of responsibility is assigned to non-managerial employees who work at a specific facility (Felson, 1995). Essentially, this will apply to the majority of employees at the facility. Depending on their position, they may be responsible for regulating behavior at the facility. At the very least, though, employees are expected to remain observant and report any potentially dangerous or suspicious behavior to their managers. For example, a bank teller would be responsible for ensuring patrons, and even employees in some cases, are following the rules and not causing problems; however, they would not be responsible for deterring bank robberies.

Finally, the lowest level of responsibility for a place is allocated for individuals who are visiting the place. **General responsibility** is the expectation that customers, patrons, and/or bystanders at a place will play a basic role in making sure crime is prevented or controlled at that facility (Felson, 1995). Obviously, visitors cannot be expected to be hyper-vigilant for suspicious or criminal activity, nor can they be expected to actively stop an offender. However, it is not unreasonable to assume that they should report any potentially criminal behavior they witness to an employee or manager of a facility. For instance, if someone were to notice a person attempting to break into a car as they were leaving a parking garage, it is rational to assume they would at least notify the parking garage attendant.

Place Management as Crime Prevention

Over the last few decades, research has shown that targeted, or hotspot, policing has proven effective in reducing or preventing crime at specific locations (Braga, 2001; 2005), even if only for a short time (Koper, 1995; Sherman, 1990). By allocating more attention to places where crime is the highest, it becomes easier to identify the central factors that may be increasing the growth of criminal opportunities in that location, which then allows for the development of more appropriate crime prevention strategies. This **place-based crime prevention** approach can also be adopted and adapted to address criminal opportunities at specific facilities (risky and non-risky alike). Further, if utilized, place-based crime prevention can actually work to reduce criminal activity at facilities (Eck & Guerette, 2012).

Understandably, the main individual(s) responsible for place-based crime prevention within a facility is the place manager. However, a place manager's primary concern is rarely to prevent crime. Instead, it is to make sure everything functions smoothly at the facility by managing its social and physical characteristics (Madensen, 2007). With than in mind, though, the same characteristics and approaches that help a facility run smoothly are also effective for the prevention of crime (Douglas & Welsh, 2020). Place managers' actions may directly reduce the opportunity for crime in that facility by ensuring the employees of the facility are doing their assigned tasks appropriately, visitors are following the rules and guidelines of the facility, the facility is clean and all equipment is functioning correctly, the space is well-organized and set up, and access to the facility is closely monitored (Madensen, 2007; Madensen & Eck, 2013). Opposingly, though, ineffective management could fuel the growth of criminal opportunity in a place.

The utilization of place management as a crime prevention strategy has many benefits. First, it does not require as much input or participation by law enforcement. As will be discussed in detail in Chapter 10, place management approaches, such as third-party policing, allow police departments to use fewer resources and manpower, which can then be used to address larger crime prevention programs and strategies. Second, since place managers have intimate knowledge of the facility in which they work, they are better equipped to understand the intricacies of the design of the facility, as well as the habits of the employees and patrons. Third, and related to the previous point, unlike law enforcement (in most situations), place managers actually have the authority to develop policies, improve security features, and even redesign the layout of a facility. Finally, they may also have the ability to make quick changes to polices, designs, or other factors if they find them to be unbeneficial to the function and security of the facility. Taken as a whole, the benefits of place management could lead to many effective approaches to reducing the opportunity for crime within a facility.

Summary

The purpose of this chapter was to expand upon the concept of crime concentration by describing two key forms of more localized hotspots – risky facilities and hot products. Both of these concepts are important to understand in order to fully identify crime problems and develop effective crime prevention strategies to address those problems. The presence of both risky facilities and hot products could serve as the catalyst for the growth of a crime hotspot. Often, to address these issues, we must go beyond police-based crime prevention and, instead, utilize all the tools at our disposal, including place-based strategies, led by place managers. Examples of this approach will be described in more detail in later chapters.

Keywords

Risky Facility, Neighborhood Theory, Patron Theory, Management Theory, Behavior Setting Theory, Hot Products, VIVA, CRAVED, Place Manager, Place Management Theory, Personal Responsibility, Assigned Responsibility, Diffuse Job Responsibility, General Responsibility, Place-Based Crime Prevention

Discussion Questions

1. How is it determined which facilities in a given area may be risky facilities?
2. What factors should be considered when evaluating the presence of risky facilities?
3. How did the CRAVED model advance the VIVA model of identifying hot products?

4. Select one of the levels of responsibility for deterring crime in a facility and explain how someone at that level could help prevent crime in that facility.
5. Describe an example of something a place manager could do to help prevent or reduce crime in their facility.

References

Altizio, A., & York, D. (2007). Robbery of convenience stores. In Problem-specific guides series no. 49, Problem-oriented guides for police. U.S. Department of Justice.

Barker, R. (1968). *Ecological psychology*. Stanford, CA: Stanford University Press.

Beauregard, E., & Martineau, M. (2015). An application of CRAVED to the choice of victim in sexual homicide: A routine activity approach. *Crime Science*, 4(24), 1–11.

Braga, A. A. (2001). The effects of hot spots policing on crime. *Annals of the American Academy of Political and Social Science*, 578, 104–125.

Braga, A. A. (2005). Hot spots policing and crime prevention: A systematic review of randomized controlled trials. *Journal of Experimental Criminology*, 1(3), 317–342.

Brantingham, P., & Brantingham, P. (1995). Criminality of place: Crime generators and crime attractors. *European Journal on Criminal Policy & Research*, 3(3), 1–26.

Caplan, J. M., Kennedy, L. W., Barnum, J. D., & Piza, E. L. (2017). Crime in context: Utilizing risk terrain modeling and conjunctive analysis of case configurations to explore the dynamics of criminogenic behavior settings. *Journal of Contemporary Criminal Justice*, 33(2), 133–151.

Cavan, S. (1966). *Liquor license: An ethnography of bar behavior*. Piscataway, NJ: Aldine.

Clarke, R. V. (1999). *Hot products: Understanding, anticipating and reducing demand for stolen goods*. Police Research Series, Paper 112. Policing and Reducing Crime Unit, Research Development and Statistics Directorate. London: Home Office.

Clarke, R. V., & Eck, J. E. (2007). *Understanding risky facilities. Tool guide No. 6*. Retrieved from https://popcenter.asu.edu/content/understanding-risky-facilities.

Clarke, R. V., & Eck, J. E. (2016). *Crime analysis for problem solvers in 60 small steps*. Office of Community Oriented Policing Services.

Cohen, L. E., & Felson, M. (1979). Social change and crime rate trends: A routine activity approach. *American Sociological Review*, 44(4), 588–608.

Douglas, S., & Welsh, B. C. (2020). Place managers for crime prevention: The theoretical and empirical status of a neglected situational crime prevention technique. *Crime Prevention & Community Safety*, 22(2), 99–109.

Eck, J. E. (1994). *Drug markets and drug places: A case-control study of the spatial structure of illicit drug dealing*. Baltimore, MD: University Press of Maryland.

Eck, J. E., & Guerette, R. T. (2012). "Own the place, own the crime" prevention: How evidence about place-based crime shifts the burden of prevention. In R. Loeber & B. C. Welsh (Eds), *The future of criminology* (pp. 166–171). Oxford: Oxford University Press.

Eck, J. E., Clarke, R. V., & Guerette, R. T. (2007). Risky facilities: Crime concentration in homogeneous sets of establishments and facilities. In G. Farrell, K. Bowers, S. D. Johnson, & M. Townsley (Eds), *Imagination for crime prevention* (pp. 255–264), vol. 21. Monsey, NY: Criminal Justice Press.

Eck, J. E., Madensen, T. D., Payne, T., Wilcox, P., Fisher, B. S., & Scherer, H. (2009). *Situational crime prevention at specific locations in community context: place and neighborhood effects*. Final Research Report: U.S. Department of Justice. Retrieved from ncjrs.gov/pdffiles1/nij/grants/229364.pdf

Felson, M. (1995). Those who discourage crime. In J. E. Eck & D. Weisburd (Eds), *Crime and place: Crime prevention studies*, vol. 4. (pp. 53–66). Monsey, NY: Criminal Justice Press.

Fishbine, G. M., & Joelson, M. R. (1978). *Crime impact statements: A strategy suggested from the study of crime around bars*. Minnesota Crime Prevention Center.

Franquez, J. J., Hagala, J., Lim, S., & Bichler, G. (2013). "We be drinkin": A study of place management and premise notoriety among risky bars and nightclubs. *Western Criminology Review*, 14, 34–52.

Gounley, T. (2016, October 25). Walmarts are still hotspots of crime, but Springfield police see progress. *Springfield News-Leader*. Retrieved from https://www.news-leader.com/story/news/crime/2016/10/25/walmarts-still-hotspots-crime-but-springfield-police-see-progress/91603296/

Koper, C. S. (1995). Just enough police presence: Reducing crime and disorderly behavior by optimizing patrol time in crime hot spots. *Justice Quarterly*, 12(4), 649–672.

Latham, S. (2022, December 8). These are stores' most-stolen items. Cheapism. Retrieved from https://blog.cheapism.com/these-are-stores-most-stolen-items/

Lindstrom, P. (1997). Patterns of school crime: A replication and empirical extension. British *Journal of Criminology*, 37(1), 121–130.

Madensen, T. D. (2007). *Bar management and crime*. PhD dissertation. Cincinnati, OH: University of Cincinnati.

Madensen, T. D., & Eck, J. E. (2008). Violence in bars: Exploring the impact of place manager decision-making. *Crime Prevention and Community Safety*, 10(2), 111–125.

Madensen, T. D., & Eck, J. E. (2013). Crime places and place management. In F.T. Cullen and P. Wilcox (Eds), *The Oxford handbook of criminological theory* (pp. 554–578). New York: Oxford University Press.

Marsh, P. (1980). Violence at the pub. *New Society*, 52, 210–212.

National Association of Convenience Stores. (1991). *Convenience store security report and recommendations*. National Association of Convenience Stores.

Newton, A. (2004). *Crime and disorder on busses: Toward an evidence base for effective crime prevention*. PhD dissertation, University of Liverpool.

Picchi, A. (2023, September 6). As dollar stores spread across the nation, crime and safety concerns follow. *CBS News*. Retrieved from https://www.cbsnews.com/news/dollar-general-dollar-stores-safety-crime-worker-pay/

Pires, S. F., & Clarke, R. V. (2012). Are parrots CRAVED? An analysis of parrot poaching in Mexico. *Journal of Research in Crime and Delinquency*, 49, 122–146.

Rivelli, E. (2022, October 6). Most common items stolen in home burglaries. *Homeowners Insurance: Bankrate*. Retrieved from https://www.bankrate.com/insurance/homeowners-insurance/common-items-stolen/.

Rock, A. (2021). *Hospital assaults hit all-time high in 2020, IAHSS survey finds.* Hospital, School, University Campus Safety. Retrieved from https://www.cam pussafetymagazine.com/hospital/iahss-2021-healthcare-crime-survey-results/

Sherman, L. W. (1990). Police crackdowns: Initial and residual deterrence. In M. Tonry & N. Morris (Eds), *Crime and Justice: A Review of Research*, vol. 12. Chicago, IL: University of Chicago Press.

Skogan, W. (1986). Fear of crime and neighborhood change. In A. J. Reiss & M. Tonry (Eds), *Communities and Crime*, vol. 8. Chicago, IL: University of Chicago Press.

Smith, C., Bowers, K. J., & Johnson, S. D. (2006). Understanding bag theft within licensed premises in Westminster: Identifying initial steps toward prevention. *Security Journal, 19*, 3–21.

Tobin, B. (2023, January 21). Organized retail thieves' most-wanted list: Survey reveals which items are most likely to be stolen from stores. *Business Insider.* Retrieved from https://www.businessinsider.com/most-stolen-items-list-what-organized-retail-criminals-want-nrf-2023-1

Whitehead, S., Mailley, J., Storer, I., McCardle, J., Torrens, G., & Farrell, G. (2008). In safe hands: A review of mobile phone anti-theft designs. *European Journal on Criminal Policy and Research, 14*, 39–60.

Wicker, A. W. (1979). *An introduction to ecological psychology.* Pacific Grove, CA: Brooks-Cole.

Chapter 7
Criminology and Crime Prevention

Criminology and Crime Prevention

Bradford W. Reyns

<table>
<tr><td>

Chapter Outline

In this chapter, we will focus on:

Understanding Criminal Behavior
- Brief history of criminology
- Identifying patterns in crime
- Criminological risk factors, theories, and causation

Perspectives on Offending
- Biological and biosocial factors
- Psychological factors
- Sociological theories

Repeat Offending as Crime Concentration
- The extent and nature of repeat offending
- Recidivism and crime rates

Offending, Recidivism, and Crime Prevention
- Crime prevention from a life course perspective
- Justice system responses to preventing criminal behavior

</td><td>

Learning Objectives

After reading this chapter, you should be able to:

7.1 Discuss crime prevention from a criminology perspective

7.2 Review the different theories of criminal behavior

7.3 Explain the importance of recidivism and desistance to preventing crime

7.4 Apply the principles of crime prevention to offending, reoffending, and recidivism

7.5 Describe crime prevention from a life course perspective

7.6 Describe justice system responses to preventing criminal behavior

</td></tr>
</table>

DOI: 10.4324/9781003401551-9

Introduction

Criminology is the scientific study of crime and criminal behavior. Criminologists utilize a variety of social science research methods (e.g., interviews, surveys) to develop and test theories that explain why people commit crimes. This research produces findings that can inform policy decisions related to crime. Criminologists are also interested in other aspects of crime, including how society responds to crime, such as the operations of the criminal justice system, as well as how crime prevention programs or policies might be developed. These crime prevention strategies are discussed throughout the book, but this chapter focuses on two particular ways that studying crime from a criminological perspective can be useful in crime prevention. First, this chapter reviews how criminological theories about the root causes of criminal behavior might inform crime prevention strategies. Second, the chapter emphasizes how preventing repeat offending, which represents a sizable portion of all crime, could have a significant impact on the overall crime picture.

Understanding Criminal Behavior

Criminology has a long history. Discussions of modern criminology usually begin with the works of Enlightenment scholars, such as Cesare Beccaria, who talked and wrote about rational responses to crime in society. Indeed, contemporary criminal justice systems are at least partially based on their writings about deterrence and punishments commensurate with the offense. Current approaches to understanding and explaining criminal behavior have developed over the course of hundreds of years and are for the most part rooted in social science research methods. These methods involve identifying relationships between individual or structural characteristics, and different dimensions of crime. This requires researchers to identify patterns in crime, and establish statistically that particular variables, such as poverty or urbanization, correspond with changes in certain other variables, such as crime rates. Based on research findings, criminologists can identify those factors that place individuals at risk for criminal behavior. From a crime prevention perspective, the goal is to minimize these risk factors to reduce the likelihood of crime or criminal behavior.

Brief History of Criminology

Humans have always been interested in aberrant behavior. Even before laws were codified, societies across the globe historically identified certain behaviors as unacceptable and punishable by some means. The earliest explanations of the causes of criminal behavior centered on the spiritual or supernatural, and over time developed into more natural and scientific theories. The first ideas about crimes and punishments can be traced back to ancient civilizations such as Mesopotamia and Babylon where legal codes were established. Philosophies about the causes of criminal behavior and ideas about justice can be traced back to at least ancient Greece and the works of Plato and Aristotle.

In the Middle Ages, criminal justice was based on religious principles and therefore criminality was viewed as a sin or spiritual offense calling for spiritual punishments. During this time, trial by combat and trial by ordeal were common tests to determine the guilt or innocence of the accused. During the Inquisition, the lines between criminal justice and religion were blurred, and offenses such as heresy and witchcraft were punished with torture, imprisonment, and execution. Later, Enlightenment thinkers such as Cesare Beccaria and Jeremy Bentham suggested the need for rationalization in criminal justice. More recognizable theories about the causes of criminal behavior arose in the early nineteenth century with the emergence of positivism and the suggestion that people could be born to be criminals, and that this criminality could be manifested in individuals' physical characteristics.

In the late nineteenth and early twentieth centuries, criminological thinking shifted toward sociological explanations of criminal behavior. In particular, Emile Durkheim suggested that there was a relationship between social factors within society and crime, although Durkheim's primary focus was upon suicide. Scholars associated with the Chicago School of Sociology at the University of Chicago, notably Robert Park and Ernest Burgess, studied the relationship between the environment and facets of urban life, including crime. The Chicago School is also discussed in Chapter 2. Criminology continued to develop into the twentieth century and into the present, with a focus on developing sociological theories of crime.

Today, criminological explanations of criminal behavior span several fields and subfields and are informed by many social science disciplines, such as sociology, psychology, and economics. Sociological approaches were particularly influential to the development of modern-day criminology with the publication of Merton's (1938) strain theory, Shaw and McKay's (1942) social disorganization theory, Sutherland's (1947) differential association theory, and Hirschi's (1969) control theory. Other notable contemporary perspectives on explaining criminal behavior can be found in personality, developmental, and life-course approaches.

Initially, many of these theories were generated inductively, wherein a pattern in criminal behavior was identified, and a corresponding theoretical explanation developed. Conversely, theories can be developed deductively, in which case an idea is offered and then tested. In either case, criminologists rely on data and evidence to validate theories. With crime data, it is possible to identify patterns in crime and develop policies and programs to prevent it from happening.

Identifying Patterns in Crime
Over 200 years of criminological research has been devoted to identifying patterns in crime, at different levels of analysis, to better understand its

Rate of Violent Crime Offenses by Population

-O- United States Violent Crime

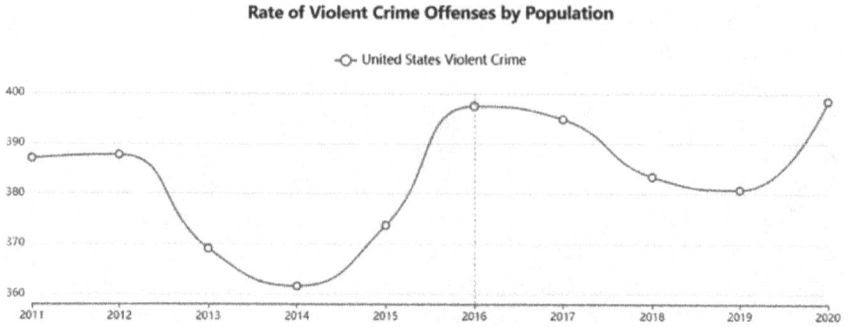

Figure 7.1 Rate of Violent Crime in the United States, 2011–2020.

extent and *nature*. In this context, **extent** refers to the degree, scope, or magnitude of crime, or more simply put, how much crime exists. There are a number of sources of crime data in the United States and in countries throughout the world. For instance, the Federal Bureau of Investigation's (FBI) Uniform Crime Reporting (UCR) Program has been estimating crime rates in the United States since 1930. The crime statistics provided by the UCR, as well as other data sources on crime, aid law enforcement by making it possible to identify patterns in crime.

Figure 7.1 illustrates the extent of violent crime in the United States from 2011 to 2020, expressed as a rate per 100,000 people. According to the figure, the violent crime rate in 2020 was about 400 per 100,000 people, meaning that for every 100,000 persons in the United States, there are 400 violent crimes annually. These estimates of the extent of crime in the United States were provided by the FBI's Crime Data Explorer. Overall, an understanding of the extent of crime is useful for identifying patterns in crime and developing explanations for those patterns. For example, Figure 7.1 suggests that crime was at a ten-year low point in 2014 – a criminologist may want to explain why the decrease happened. Alternatively, they may focus on why crime appears to be on the rise.

Expand Your Understanding – Examining Crime Data in the United States

Interested readers can investigate other crime trends by visiting the FBI's Crime Data Explorer website. A wealth of information on crime in the United States is available for easy access for different crime types, different years, and other criminal justice topics.

Just visit https://cde.ucr.cjis.gov/LATEST/webapp/#/pages/home

---

The **nature** of crime refers to the characteristics, qualities, or aspects that characterize crime, such as the circumstances under which it occurs. Questions such as who is involved in criminal activity, who it affects, whether a weapon is involved, and where it occurs relate to the nature of crime. Among the major discoveries from studies of individual offending is the finding that not everyone is equally at risk of committing crime. That is, crime is patterned according to certain characteristics. For instance, research consistently finds that males commit more crimes than females; younger people commit more crimes than older people; and single people commit more crimes than married people. As an illustration, Figure 7.2 demonstrates offender sex patterns in homicide in the United States in 2021.

Although identifying offender characteristics such as those in Figure 7.2 is necessary to understand crime, explaining criminal behavior is more complex than simply identifying demographic patterns in offending. Crime prevention specialists are interested in the extent and nature of crime, so that they can craft effective responses to undercut or respond to the factors driving the crime problem. Thus, much of the current focus is upon risk, and those characteristics, experiences, or factors that can be avoided or minimized through policy or programs to lessen that risk.

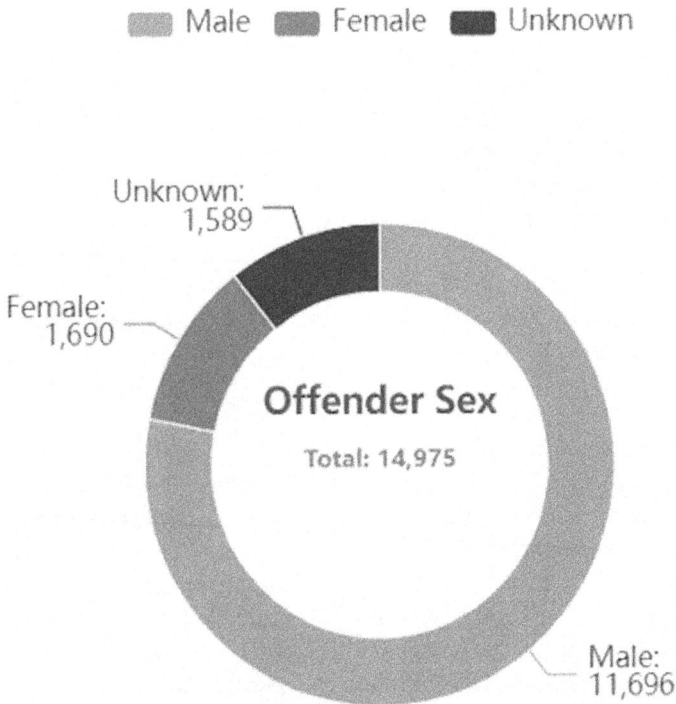

Figure 7.2 Sex of Homicide Offenders.

Criminological Risk Factors, Theories, and Causation

Over the years, criminologists have worked toward better understanding why certain individuals commit crimes, and seeking to identify the factors that are related to a greater or lesser likelihood of criminal behavior. These factors are known as **risk factors** or **protective factors**, depending on whether they are said to increase or decrease the probability that individuals will engage in criminal conduct. Yet, because criminology is a social science, these relationships are probabilistic, meaning that a given characteristic or risk factor may increase one's likelihood of criminal behavior, but it does not guarantee it.

Decades of research and thousands of published research studies indicate that criminal behavior is patterned and that there are risk factors for criminal behavior. Understanding how crime is patterned is an essential step in developing theoretical perspectives on offending, and further, creating methods for reducing its impact or preventing its occurrence. A **theory** is a systematic and logical explanation for why something happens the way that it does. Thus, criminologists have devoted significant research attention to developing and testing theories of crime to explain how and why crime is patterned the way that it is. Part of this process involves establishing causal relationships between observable variables, which requires correlation, time order, and non-spuriousness between the variables (Babbie, 2021).

Criminological theories generally fall into one of two categories – those based on individual differences and those based on structure or process arguments. These criminological theories focus on such influences as personality traits, structural factors, cultural explanations, and poverty, to name only a few. Identifying causal relationships between these factors and crime advances the field of criminology toward better understanding the nature of criminal behavior. With an understanding of the "causes" of crime, the implications for crime prevention are clear – addressing the factors that lead to criminality can reduce the incidence of criminal behavior, thereby preventing crime.

Perspectives on Offending

As was previously stated, criminological theories have been developing for hundreds of years and there are thousands of published research articles that examine the causes of crime. Consequently, it is not possible to comprehensively review all the theories in criminology, but rather, this chapter provides a broad overview of some the leading contemporary perspectives that may have applicability to crime prevention. First, theories focused on individual differences, specifically biological, biosocial, and psychological perspectives, are addressed, followed by sociological theories, which make structural or social process arguments about the causes of crime.

Biological and Biosocial Factors

Some of the first theories of crime focused on biological characteristics that were hypothesized to increase individuals' risk for committing crimes. While contemporary criminology does not suggest that biological factors cause criminal behavior, it does support the hypothesis that there are biological factors that increase one's risks for engaging in violent or antisocial behaviors – behaviors which are criminalized. A number of these perspectives also highlight the interaction between biological characteristics and the social or physical environment.

Early research into biological sources of criminal behavior investigated factors such as physical appearance, physical characteristics, and heredity. Heredity studies have taken different approaches to investigating whether there are relationships between parental characteristics and the behaviors of offspring, including family studies, twin studies, and adoption studies. In short, these types of studies examine whether criminal tendencies might be inherited. While some of these results have suggested that there is a link, thus supporting an argument for genetic sources of violent, antisocial, or criminal tendencies, the challenge with these approaches is separating the effects of heredity from the effects of environmental factors.

Biological Factors

Biological factors that may affect criminal behaviors are those rooted in human physiology. Hormones, neurotransmitters, and the central and autonomic nervous systems have been examined for their effects on human behavior. Hormones are chemical messengers within the body that help maintain its internal balance. It appears that hormonal changes can be correlated with aggression and violence in men and women, but establishing direct relationships is difficult and conclusions have been mixed. Neurotransmitters are chemical compounds that play an essential role in the transmission of signals within the nervous system. In short, they are critical to the brain in processing information. Two of these – serotonin and dopamine – have been found to influence aggression and violent behavior when serotonin is low, dopamine is high, or when both occur. Finally, dysfunction in the nervous system has been linked to behavioral change, including antisocial and violent behavior. The central nervous system (CNS) is responsible for

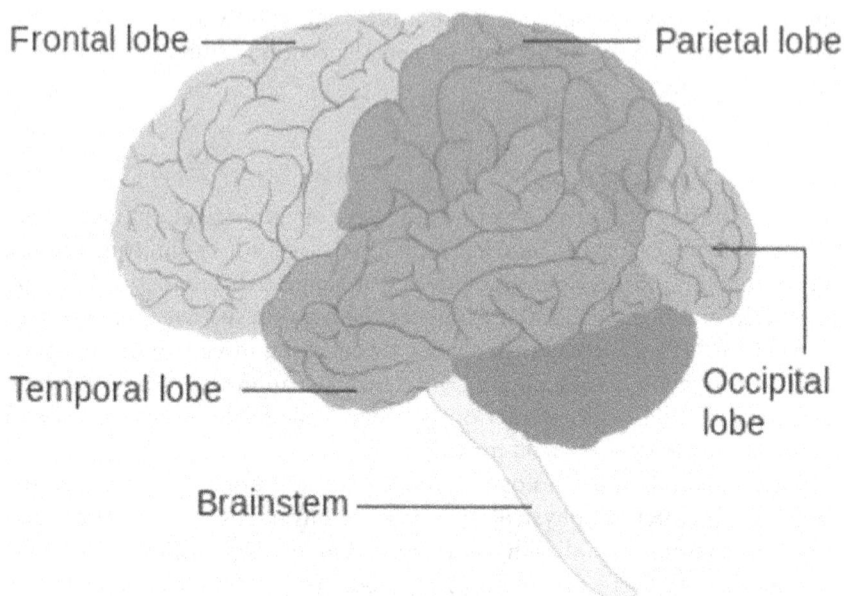

Figure 7.3 The Lobes of the Brain.

controlling the body's activities and consists of the brain and spinal cord. Brain irregularities or damage can influence behavior, but the CNS itself is not solely responsible for criminal behavior. The four lobes of the brain are illustrated in Figure 7.3.

Environmental Factors

The environment can also influence biological factors that, in turn, affect criminal behavior. These include factors such as head injuries, drugs and alcohol, and diet or toxin intake. For each of these it should be noted that while research finds apparent relationships between these factors and behavior, it is not clear whether the relationships are causal, or how precisely the relationships operate. Similar to the discussion about the CNS, head injuries can result in brain damage, affecting social skills, cognition, or, depending on the area affected, feelings of anxiety, hostility, irritability, or anger. For example, trauma to the frontal lobe (Figure 7.3) is linked with changes to one's personality, impulsivity, and aggression (Raine, 1993).

Drugs and alcohol are among the most consistent correlates of crime with, particularly, alcohol use being a known contributor to criminal behavior. However, the basis for this relationship is uncertain, and may be due to impaired judgment or diminished ability to make rational decisions, but its effects also depend on individual factors, consumption patterns, and the social environment. In addition, particular drugs, such as stimulants (e.g., methamphetamine), phencyclidine, synthetic cathinones ("bath salts"), and steroids are associated with violence because of their effects on the CNS but, once again, this can depend on a host of factors, such as the drug, the dosage, the frequency of use, and polydrug use. Finally, nutritional factors and toxin intake can affect behavior by impacting physical and mental health. For example, nutritional deficiencies can influence brain development and function. Similarly, exposure to toxins such as lead can lead to neurological effects and impairment of executive functions (e.g., decision making, planning).

Biosocial Criminology

Criminal behavior is complex and none of the above is the sole cause of criminal behavior. Instead, it is most likely that a combination of factors best explains criminality. This is the approach taken with **biosocial criminology**, which suggests that biological factors increase the likelihood of a person's participation in crime, but that these factors also interact with psychological factors, social forces, and facets of the environment. An example of this can be found in gene–environment interactions. For instance, some individuals may carry a genetic predisposition that affects how they respond to alcohol or drugs. We also know that individuals with this genetic susceptibility are at higher risk of developing substance abuse disorders when they are exposed to environments that promote substance use (e.g., high availability). Thus, an interaction between the genetic predisposition and the availability in the environment can lead to substance abuse, which is related to a range of criminal behaviors, such as violence or theft to support a drug habit. Overall, biosocial criminology focuses on the interplay of biological factors with other determinants of crime to explain the development of criminal behavior.

Psychological Factors

Biological and biosocial factors explain criminal behavior in terms of individual characteristics that increase individuals' risks for committing crimes. Psychological factors likewise explain criminal behavior by identifying individual characteristics that may increase one's likelihood of committing crime. Among the psychological factors studied by criminologists in relation to criminal behavior are personality, impulsivity, and psychological disorders, notably Antisocial Personality Disorder.

Personality

Our personalities define us as individuals and distinguish us from other people. They represent our emotional, social, and cognitive makeup, and are relatively stable over time. There are different theories and models that explain the various dimensions of personality. For instance, the Big Five Model is a trait-based theory and focuses on five traits: openness, conscientiousness, extraversion, agreeableness, and neuroticism (McCrae & Costa, 2003). While the Big Five Model is a trait-based approach, there are also psychodynamic theories, such as those proposed by Sigmund Freud; behavioral theories, which address personality in terms of environment, conditioning, and reinforcement; cognitive theories, as evinced in the work of Albert Bandura; and humanistic theories, which are focused on personal growth in shaping personality. These theories are not crime theories, per se, and so while they offer insights into the causes of criminal behavior, they do not provide a "profile" of a criminal personality. That said, there are two consistent correlates of criminal activity addressed within the personality theories literature: impulsivity and Antisocial Personality Disorder.

Impulsivity

Impulsivity is a psychological trait that is often associated with criminal behavior, or more broadly, antisocial behavior. **Impulsivity** is a tendency to act spontaneously without considering the consequences of one's actions. Being impulsive means thinking in the short term about risks and rewards and behaving accordingly. For example, an impulsive individual might decide to behave in ways that are immediately rewarding, such as stealing something that they want, rather than deferring gratification and waiting to buy what they want. In this scenario, the rewards are immediate, and the risks or punishments, if they come at all, will be later. Impulsivity is not a theory of criminal behavior, but it has been acknowledged by psychologists and criminologists as an important correlate of criminal behavior and has been integrated into different theories. The general theory of crime, for instance, which is discussed below, orients impulsivity within the larger construct of low self-control, and argues that low self-control is the primary explanation for criminal behavior across one's life course. Impulsivity is hypothesized to be learned through socialization, although biosocial criminologists have also argued for biological roots to having an impulsive personality. As a stand-alone concept, impulsivity does not explain all criminal behavior, because not all impulsive individuals will commit crimes, nor will all offenders have the impulsivity personality trait. Yet, the propensity toward short-term thinking is consistently associated with undesirable or antisocial behaviors, which include criminal behavior. Impulsivity is also a key component of Antisocial Personality Disorder and other psychological disorders.

Antisocial Personality Disorder

Diagnostic criteria for mental health disorders are published in a handbook by the American Psychiatric Association (2013) called the *Diagnostic and Statistical Manual of Mental Disorders* (DSM). The DSM-5 is the current iteration of the manual and includes the criteria used by mental health professionals for diagnosing Antisocial Personality Disorder (ASPD). According to the manual, ASPD can be diagnosed if the individual shows a pattern of behavior that disregards the rights of others that includes three of these criteria: 1) perpetrating unlawful behaviors that are grounds for arrest; 2) deceitfulness, including lying, using aliases, or conning others; 3) impulsivity; 4) aggressiveness, including physical fights or assaults; 5) reckless disregard for the safety of others; 6) consistent irresponsibility with respect to work or financial obligations; and 7) lack of remorse. ASPD is not diagnosed in persons under 18 years old. Interestingly, while readers may be familiar with the terms "psychopath" or "sociopath," the DSM-5 does not diagnose these disorders or differentiate them from ASPD (American Psychiatric Association, 2013).

It is clear that individuals with ASPD have an increased risk of engaging in criminal behavior and why this would be the case. For example, a person who lacks remorse will have few qualms in criminally victimizing another person. Indeed, some of the criteria used to diagnose the disorder are criminal by definition. Yet, ASPD is not necessarily a cause of criminal behavior, because, like impulsivity, not all persons with ASPD will commit crimes, nor will all persons who commit crimes have ASPD. The relationship between ASPD and criminal behavior will be influenced by various other factors discussed in this chapter, such as biological and sociological factors. Further, from a crime prevention perspective, treating those with ASPD is difficult as individuals with the disorder may not recognize they need treatment or seek help.

Sociological Theories

Sociology is concerned with human behavior, which includes criminal behavior. Primarily, sociologists study the effects of society on behavior, and there are many sociological approaches to explaining criminal behavior. Here, three of the leading approaches will be briefly reviewed to provide background for sociological influences on crime prevention strategies: learning theories, control theories, and neighborhood theories.

Learning Theories

According to learning theories, criminal behavior is learned, but the role of learning in criminal behavior differs across learning theories. Learning theories basically take three approaches to understanding the role of learning in criminal behavior. First, these theories explain that learning attitudes or beliefs that are favorable to crime can increase criminal behavior. Second, these theories address the process by which criminality is learned, but recognize that it is essentially a normal learning process. Third, theories of cultures and subcultures are considered learning theories, because different groups have crime-supportive values that are disseminated (learned) throughout the group. As an example of a learning theory, Edwin Sutherland's (1947) differential association theory addresses both the content that is learned and the process by which it is learned. The theory contends that through a learning process within intimate personal groups, individuals develop definitions of conduct as either favorable or unfavorable toward crime. Those who develop more criminal than non-criminal definitions learn that criminal behavior is acceptable and are more likely to commit crime. If criminal behavior is learned, then crime prevention programs could be designed to counter the adoption of criminal definitions.

Control Theories

Control theories propose that there are many factors that cause criminal behavior, but the reason that most of us do not break the law is because there are counter forces "controlling" our behavior and preventing us from doing so. Control theories have been quite popular within criminology and have received a great deal of research attention and theoretical refinement. Impulsivity was previously identified as a personality trait that is related to criminal behavior. It is also a primary concept within the general theory of crime – a control theory. According to the general theory of crime, individuals with low self-control are more likely to engage in delinquency and crime (Gottfredson & Hirschi, 1990); impulsivity being one of the characteristics of low self-control. Another prominent control theory is Travis Hirschi's (1969) social bond theory. Whereas the general theory of crime identifies self-control as the controlling force on individuals' behavior preventing them from offending, social bond theory argues that control comes from four social bonds: attachment, commitment, involvement, and belief. Attachment refers to attachments to others, such as parents or loved ones. Commitment is an investment in society and its conventions, such as doing well in school. Involvement addresses conventional activities, including working or volunteering. Finally, belief refers to one's acceptance of the values and morals of society. The theory explains that individuals with weak bonds are more likely to engage in delinquent and criminal behaviors. It is interesting that control theories ascribe obeying the law to an internal force, rather than external forces such as the presence of police officers.

Neighborhood Theories

The theory of human ecology, which was discussed in Chapter 2, is where much of the research into the study of neighborhoods is rooted. As a reminder, human ecology emphasizes relationships between humans and their natural, social, and built environments. In the case of neighborhood theories, the environment is the neighborhood. A neighborhood can be geographically defined or defined by its residents as part of a larger community or area within a city. Although there are a number of approaches to explaining crime at the neighborhood level, our focus is upon two: social disorganization theory and collective efficacy.

Working within the field of human ecology, Clifford Shaw and Henry McKay (1942) developed social disorganization theory to explain patterns in juvenile delinquency across Chicago neighborhoods. As noted in Chapter 1, social disorganization theory was the result of extensive research and study of the characteristics of neighborhoods that had the most juvenile delinquents according to police and court records. Shaw and McKay concluded that the neighborhoods with the highest concentrations of juvenile delinquents were those that were socially disorganized. Here, social disorganization refers to the breakdown of social institutions to the point that the community is unable to enforce common values and norms, such as the ability to prevent juveniles from engaging in delinquent behaviors. Several factors contribute to neighborhood social disorganization, but Shaw

Figure 7.4 Pilsen Neighborhood – Chicago, Illinois.

and McKay pointed to low economic conditions, high residential mobility or population turnover, and population composition with respect to ethnic heterogeneity, as the primary factors creating social disorganization. Social disorganization theory has received considerable research attention and refinement since Shaw and McKay's time, and it remains a popular perspective within criminology.

Collective efficacy can be viewed as the inverse of social disorganization, meaning while social disorganization theory argues delinquency areas are those that are disorganized and cannot effectively enforce norms and values against crime and delinquency, collective efficacy suggests that communities with the collective ability to maintain order have less crime. The concept of collective efficacy was developed by Robert Sampson, who argued that social relationships between community residents are important in mustering the collective ability to keep crime out of communities (Sampson & Raudenbush, 1999). Collective efficacy, then, could be reflected in community activities and organizations, as well as the social ties between residents. In one famous study, 196 Chicago neighborhoods were videotaped from a moving car, and the video later analyzed; the videos were supplemented with interview data from residents. Findings indicated that the usual correlates of neighborhood crime (e.g., physical disorder, social disorder) were present in neighborhoods with crime problems, but that there was less crime in more socially cohesive neighborhoods that could be characterized as having collective efficacy (Sampson & Raudenbush, 1999). This suggests that fostering that sense of community cohesion and collective efficacy could be an effective approach to crime prevention.

Repeat Offending as Crime Concentration

Just as crime concentrates on a large scale within geographic hotspots, and on a smaller scale within certain facilities or products – as discussed in other chapters – it also concentrates at the individual level among offenders. In other words, a substantial proportion of all crimes are committed by repeat offenders (e.g., Moffitt, 1993). A focus on repeat offending is essential for crime prevention because if repeat offenders were to desist from committing any further crimes, a significant amount of all crime would be prevented. The criminal justice system punishes offenders in order to provide a deterrent against reoffending, or recidivism. Recidivism is a core concern within the criminal justice system, and is the focus of policies related to law, sentencing, and corrections. Although each of the theoretical perspectives previously outlined (e.g., psychological factors, sociological theories) speak to the causes of offending and reoffending, research involving repeat offending specifically has often been grounded in developmental and life-course explanations.

The Extent and Nature of Repeat Offending

Patterns in criminal behavior indicate that not everyone is equally likely to commit crime due to a number of factors (e.g., presence of risk factors, protective factors). However, regardless of the factors that influence initial offending decisions, criminologists have found that repeat offending is also patterned, and that crime concentrates within a small number of offenders. Put differently, a small group of offenders is responsible for the majority of crimes that are committed (Tilley, 2013). **Reoffending** occurs when an individual commits more than one criminal offense. For instance, a burglar may break into a home, and reoffend a week later by breaking into a different home. **Recidivism**, a related concept, occurs when an individual has previously been sanctioned for committing a crime and reoffends, nevertheless. As an example, perhaps this repeat burglar is arrested, charged, convicted of burglary, and sentenced to six months in jail. If he reoffends after being released from jail, he is a recidivist. According to a report from the U.S. Department of Justice, about 4 in 9 (44 percent) state prisoners released in 2005 across 30 states were arrested at least once during their first year after release (Alper & Durose, 2018).

Recidivism and Crime Rates

Research into recidivism is quite extensive, and based on this research, a few conclusions about offending and repeat offending can be reached. First, most people commit crimes or analogous behaviors at some point in their lives, especially young males. Second, this criminal behavior usually peaks in adolescence – around 14 to 17 years – and is short lived. Most of us grow out of participation in crime and delinquency around this time (Farrington, 1992). Third, there is a group of offenders who not only continue to commit crimes into adulthood but are responsible for a substantial and disproportionate amount of all crime that is committed (Budd et al., 2005; Moffitt, 1993). It has been estimated that this group of prolific offenders is responsible for half of all crimes that are committed (Tilley, 2013). From a prevention perspective, focusing resources on this group should theoretically yield considerable crime prevention benefits.

Extent of Recidivism

Most world governments do not regularly publish statistics concerning reoffending or recidivism rates, in part because establishing whether another crime has occurred is difficult. Criminal justice records, such as subsequent arrests, are one method for doing so, but this is an imperfect method because not all of those who reoffend will be rearrested. With this in mind, there are estimates of the extent of recidivism from the United Kingdom and the United States that are illustrative.

Data from the Ministry of Justice for the United Kingdom indicate that the proven reoffending rate from January to March 2019 was just over 26 percent, with an adult reoffending rate of 26 percent and a juvenile reoffending rate of 36 percent. Further, adults released from custody or starting court orders had a reoffending rate of nearly 34 percent, and adults released from custodial sentences of less than 12 months had a reoffending rate of nearly 60 percent (Ministry of Justice, 2021). In calculating these statistics, a proven reoffence is one in which an offense is committed during a one-year follow-up period that results in some type of reprimand such as a court conviction. Considering this, the true reoffending rate is likely higher than this, because not all subsequent offenses will come to the attention of the criminal justice system. These trends are generally representative of reoffending and recidivism statistics from other countries, as well. In the United States, 5 in 6 (83 percent) state prisoners released across 30 states in 2005 were arrested at least one time during a 9-year follow-up period succeeding their release from prison (Alper & Durose, 2018).

Statistics on the extent of recidivism are also available from individual states. For instance, the Florida Department of Corrections (2021) reports a recidivism rate of 25 percent, based on the fact that 25 percent of those released from custody in 2016 were released from prison, rearrested, convicted, and reincarcerated within three years. Using similar measures, the Montana Department of Corrections (2021) reported a recidivism rate in 2017 of 39 percent among men and 32 percent among women. Among the states with the highest recidivism rates, the Alaska Department of Corrections (2021) reported a 60 percent recidivism rate in 2017. Thus, these three states provide examples of states in the United States with low, mid-range, and high recidivism rates, with other states having rates along this spectrum. These figures suggest that, overall, those who commit crimes are likely to reoffend, and those who come to the attention of the criminal justice system and receive some form of punishment, such as incarceration, are very likely to reoffend upon being released.

The counterpart concept to recidivism is desistance. **Desistance** represents an offender's exit from crime. As previously noted, most people cease committing crime or analogous behaviors when they are young, emphasizing the idea that criminal behavior is not a static behavior, and that we can change. For repeat offenders, the desistance from crime can take longer, wherein individuals commit crimes into their adult years. For these offenders, desistance is a process, and can occur as a result of different factors or events in the offender's life. These processes can be imposed upon the individual, such as legal interventions within the criminal justice system (e.g., rehabilitation programs, counseling). Change can also happen as the individual ages and matures, and loses motivation to offend. For others, desistance might be because of social (e.g., support from others), environmental (e.g., employment), or individual factors (e.g., personal decision, change in values or attitudes). Data from the Bureau of Justice Statistics found that only 17 percent of prisoners released in the nine years following their release did not have a new arrest, providing some indication of the extent of desistance (Alper & Durose, 2018). Understanding recidivism and desistance is important to crime prevention practitioners and is the focus of many crime prevention strategies within the criminal justice system.

Offending, Recidivism, and Crime Prevention

The implications for understanding and reducing recidivism and encouraging desistance are consequential. In particular, if policies could be crafted that effectively reduce recidivism rates, the impact on crime rates would be substantial. For this reason, an extensive body of research has been devoted to understanding why individuals recidivate, and to developing policy recommendations and programs within the criminal justice system to reduce recidivism. This approach is known as **tertiary crime prevention** because the focus is on recidivism and preventing future offending. Another approach is to try to predict who is at risk of offending and intervening early to prevent criminality in the first place. This is known as **secondary crime prevention**. Although there are myriad approaches to intervening in individuals' lives to prevent offending and reoffending, our focus is upon early intervention and developmental crime prevention, and justice system responses to preventing criminal behavior.

Crime Prevention from a Life Course Perspective

In thinking about how crime prevention could be accomplished by early interventions into individuals' lives – before they ever enter the criminal justice system – it is useful to consider some of the basic concepts from life-course criminology. Broadly speaking, the **life course perspective** is an interdisciplinary movement informed by biology, psychology, and sociology that is interested in studying patterns and variations in experiences throughout the stages of life (Benson, 2002). In general, the life course can be viewed as comprising phases spanning infancy, early childhood, middle childhood, adolescence, early adulthood, middle adulthood, and late adulthood.

Life-course criminology takes a developmental approach to studying criminal behavior. In doing so, criminologists study trajectories and transitions in criminal behavior. A **trajectory** is a series of linked pathways or states that we move through during our lives (Elder, 1985). For example, most of us have trajectories for our education, work life, and family life, among other paths. **Transitions** are related to trajectories and represent the change points across stages within a trajectory. An example of these concepts can be found in our educational trajectory and our transitions from elementary school, to junior high, to high school, and so on (Benson, 2002).

Life events can also spark transitions or turning points in the life course. From the perspective of crime prevention, the goal is to change criminal trajectories by fostering transitions or turning points toward prosocial behavior and away from crime.

Terrie Moffitt (1993) identified two main types of criminal offender trajectories: adolescent-limited and life course-persistent. These trajectories each have unique characteristics and factors that help to explain them. **Adolescent-limited (AL) offenders** essentially only engage in delinquency during the adolescence stage of the life course. This is a normal part of adolescence, and the offending behaviors tend to be relatively minor, lasting for only a few years. Most of us are AL offenders. **Life course-persistent (LCP) offenders** do not restrict their criminality to adolescence and instead continue reoffending through their adult lives. This group of offenders is relatively small, shows stability over time in their offending, and commits more serious offenses. This group represents the recidivists. These AL and LCP designations may be useful in thinking about the crime prevention strategies reviewed below.

Early Intervention and Developmental Crime Prevention

Early intervention can be viewed as an attempt at avoiding criminal behavior or making a delinquent or criminal trajectory a short one. Early intervention targets people who are early in the life course, because the goal is to prevent this group from becoming LCP offenders. Approaches to early intervention are diverse, and we will briefly consider two main groups: prenatal and postnatal. Prenatal interventions focus on health care for pregnant women and infants. Fetal development and prenatal care are especially important during the first eight weeks because this is when major body systems are developing. Pregnant women should receive prenatal care to ensure there are no problems during pregnancy, which would include getting proper nutrition and vitamins, and also avoiding stress. At the same time, a developing fetus can be harmed by exposure to alcohol, drugs, nicotine, or other chemicals. While it may not be obvious that these are crime prevention-related, prenatal development has implications for the offspring's physical health and has been linked to later problem behaviors, including offending.

Postnatal interventions are those that involve crime prevention efforts after the child has been born. This developmental approach to crime prevention targets early risk factors that are related to later offending. The focus is upon identifying the factors that place individuals at risk for offending and developing crime prevention strategies to avoid them, and/or identifying protective factors against offending and finding ways to support them. Research has identified many factors that are related to risks for criminal behavior, spanning individual, family, community, and school characteristics. Developmental crime prevention can be directed toward individuals and their families, or more broadly directed at the school and community (Welsh & Farrington, 2010).

Individual- and Family-Based Programs. Successful interventions oriented around individuals and their families have involved home visiting, parenting classes, day care, and skills training. One well-known program is the Nurse–Family Partnership (formerly called Elmira Prenatal/ Early Infancy Project), in which specialized nurses visit first-time mothers beginning early in the pregnancy and continuing until the child is two. The Nurse–Family Partnership has been evaluated by David Olds and colleagues (e.g., Olds et al., 1998), including a 15-year follow-up study. The majority of participants in Olds' evaluations were low-income, married, first-time mothers who received visits by nurses during their pregnancies with an emphasis on prenatal and postnatal health of the mother and child, infant development and childcare, and advice about nutrition. Olds' evaluations found that, among participants, child abuse and neglect were reduced, that fewer mothers had alcohol or drug problems, and that participants – both mothers and children – had fewer arrests compared with those who did not receive the home visits. The evaluation findings have been replicated elsewhere and cost–benefit analyses suggest that the program benefits outweigh the costs. The Nurse–Family Partnership is still in operation and helping families today, but it is not the only program of its kind. Readers may be interested to investigate other programs including Parents Anonymous, Healthy Families America, The Parent–Child Home Program, and The Incredible Years.

Expand Your Understanding – Nurse–Family Partnership

Readers can learn more about Nurse–Family Partnership by visiting the link below. The website includes a wealth of information for first-time mothers and nurses, as well as providing public policy and advocacy information that may be of interest to crime prevention practitioners.

https://www.nursefamilypartnership.org/

School- and Community-Based Programs. Developmental crime prevention also can be school- or community-based. These programs typically target children from disadvantaged backgrounds, or those who may be at high risk. At the school level, there are several notable programs, including the Perry Preschool Program and Head Start. In general, preschool programs work toward getting these kids ready to start school at the same level as other kids who do not have disadvantaged

CRIME PATTERNS AND CONCENTRATION

backgrounds. The Perry Preschool lasted two years and was provided to African American children living in poverty in Ypsilanti, Michigan. The program included a daily preschool as well as weekly home visits and was designed to help children with thinking and reasoning and increase school achievement. The program has been evaluated over the years using an experimental design, with results suggesting that the program had a lifelong positive impact on participants. By age 27, preschool participants had attained a higher level of schooling, had lower lifetime criminal arrests, and had higher monthly earnings, in comparison with the control group that did not attend the Perry Preschool (Schweinhart et al., 1993). Head Start is a program that is similar in philosophy and design to the Perry Preschool, but much wider in scope having reached millions of children across the United States since starting in 1965. In addition to early education, Head Start also emphasizes parent involvement, health, and nutrition. Contemporary evaluations of Head Start highlight its crime prevention benefits, specifically finding that participants are less likely to be charged or convicted of a crime (Garces et al., 2002).

School-based programs for older children are quite varied, but largely focus on the school environment or the individual students. For the school environment, prevention programs might emphasize establishing norms or expectations, classroom or instructional management, or school discipline. Those programs aimed at the individual students include components that work on self-control or social competency, methods involving cognitive-behavioral, behavioral modeling or behavior modification, or supplemental instruction or counseling (Wilson et al., 2001). Even though there is an abundance of school-based programs, most have not been scientifically evaluated. However, a meta-analysis by Wilson and colleagues (2001) assessed 165 evaluations and concluded that school-based programs are effective in reducing conduct problems, dropping out or non-attendance, and alcohol and drug use – particularly those focused on the school environment. Numerous programs also address bullying, as bullying is a risk factor for delinquency and offending for both bullies and victims. Overall, these programs have been found to reduce bullying perpetration by as much as 20 percent and bullying victimization by as much as 16 percent (Gaffney et al., 2019), but their effects on delinquency and offending are less clear.

One noteworthy approach to developmental crime prevention at the community-level is mentoring programs. These programs differ in approach, but typically involve providing a mentor for at-risk youth or offenders with the goal of helping them avoid further offending and providing assistance to that end, such as help with job applications. A meta-analysis of the effects of mentoring programs in the United States and United Kingdom found that they are associated with reduced subsequent offending, but that not all programs are effective (Jolliffe & Farrington, 2007). As an example of a specific mentoring program, Big Brothers Big Sisters (BBBS) matches youths from single-parent households with adult volunteers, who then meet two to four times a month for a year or more. By providing at-risk youth with an adult friend and mentor, the program is designed to help youth see and reach their full potential. Research suggests that children in the BBBS program are more likely to do better in school and have improved relationships with family and friends, and be less likely to commit crimes, use illegal drugs or alcohol, or drop out of school (Grossman & Tierney, 1998).

Adulthood and Change in Offending Behaviors

The goal of early interventions and individual, family, school, and community crime prevention programs is to reduce offending, but also to prevent adolescent offenders from becoming LCP offenders. A developmental approach to crime prevention also suggests that a focus on those later in the life course, especially LCP offenders, is important. Ultimately, this can be viewed as an attempt to encourage desistance from crime. Robert Sampson and John Laub's (1993) **age-graded theory of informal social control** explains stability and change in offending throughout the life course, with implications for crime prevention. Stability refers to continuance of criminal behavior and a sustained criminal career trajectory, whereas change refers to a turning point away from crime. The theory explains that stability is the result of cumulative continuity, which means that there is a cumulative effect of sustained delinquent behavior. Continued delinquent behavior in adolescence damages one's social bonds, school performance, and adult prospects such as employment. This accumulation of bad experiences closes doors on future opportunities and sustains the criminal career trajectory.

In thinking about crime prevention, the utility of the theory is in provoking change and creating instability in criminal trajectories. The theory draws on Hirschi's (1969) social bond theory, discussed earlier, to illustrate how change can happen. The primary source of change in offending trajectories is stronger social bonds in adulthood, especially getting married or getting a job. According to the theory, and supported by research, marriage and employment can alter offender trajectories toward a law-abiding life. This is because these life events lead to **social capital**, which is investment in social relationships that help people accomplish their goals legitimately, not criminally. For instance, a former repeat offender with a new wife and family would compromise their new life and jeopardize the well-being of the family if they were to return to a life of crime. The former offender's strong social bonds and social capital are strong forces against a return to crime. For example, a study of London males reported that married men were less likely to engage in crime, and that marriage was the strongest predictor of desistance from crime (Farrington & West, 1995). Sampson and Laub's

(1993) own research reinforces the importance of marriage and employment. Their research reported that those with stable jobs were less likely to engage in crime, while job instability was related to adult crime. They further found that having strong attachments to one's spouse was related to a lower likelihood of criminal behavior.

Of course, because of the cumulative continuity of years of criminal behavior, it may be difficult for LCP offenders to find "good" spouses or good jobs that will have a positive influence and create strong social bonds resulting in social capital. Therefore, crime prevention programs directed at adulthood that focus on families and marriages may be promising. Doing so would also theoretically have the effect of producing healthier families, with children more likely to avoid criminal behavior and be law abiding citizens.

Justice System Responses to Preventing Criminal Behavior

AL and LCP offenders often come to the attention of the juvenile justice or criminal justice systems. By this time, the goal is to correct and prevent future criminal behavior, rather than preventing its initial occurrence, as would be the case for early intervention. Although there are numerous approaches to tertiary prevention, the remainder of this chapter reviews three: incapacitation, deterrence, and rehabilitation.

Incapacitation

The purpose of **incapacitation** is to deny an offender the ability to commit further crimes. In this way it is prospective, or looking forward to what is likely to happen in the future. Imprisonment is the primary method used by the correctional system to incapacitate offenders by placing them in jail or prison, although capital punishment is also a form of incapacitation. Historically, banishment was also used as a method of incapacitating offenders. The philosophical purpose of incapacitation may not always be purely to prevent future offending, but may also be to accomplish retributive, deterrent, or rehabilitative goals.

Incapacitation takes two forms: collective incapacitation and selective incapacitation. **Collective incapacitation** means that conviction for a given crime results in a given punishment, regardless of the future offending potential of the convicted. Mandatory sentences are an example of collective incapacitation. For instance, maybe all jaywalkers are sentenced to two weeks in jail to reduce the amount of overall jaywalking in the city. With collective incapacitation, then, there is no consideration of the likelihood of future jaywalking potential and offenders are treated equally. In contrast to collective incapacitation, **selective incapacitation** does not take a blanket approach to sentencing, but rather sentences offenders based on identifying those who are at high risk for future offending. To continue the jaywalking example, not all jaywalkers are treated equally. Instead, serial jaywalkers and those judged to be the most likely to reoffend will be given longer sentences, while others will be given lighter sentences or alternative forms of punishment.

Assessing whether incapacitation is effective from the perspective of crime prevention depends on how inefficient society is willing to be. That is, the crime prevention benefits of collective incapacitation do not appear to be worth the costs. Cohen (1978) examined the issue and concluded that substantial increases in prison populations would be required to attain modest decreases in index crime rates. He assessed a number of states, but using New York as an example, he found that New York would have to increase its prison population by 263 percent to see a 10 percent reduction in its index crime rate. A more efficient approach would be selective incapacitation, wherein those most likely to commit future offenses are incapacitated. Here, LCP and serious repeat offenders would be sentenced to longer periods of incarceration. This would be consistent with the previous discussion of recidivism, which suggests that a small number of offenders commit a large number of serious crimes. This would prevent a larger share of future offenses from taking place, but it would also require the justice system to be able to predict who is most likely to reoffend.

Deterrence
Deterrence is a foundational principle of modern criminal justice systems. The concept is usually discussed in the context of Cesare Beccaria's work and the publication of his 1764 essay "On Crimes and Punishments." This essay proposed that criminal justice needed to be more rational, logical, and just, especially with respect to punishments for crime (Beccaria, 1986). His ideas were quite revolutionary for their time, but in our time are easily recognizable as features of criminal justice systems around the world. Of particular interest here is his argument that the purpose of punishment is to deter crime, which means that the threat of punishment should be sufficient to prevent would-be offenders from committing crimes. This assumes that would-be offenders are rational and consider the risks and rewards of crime before acting.

There are two types of deterrence – general deterrence and specific deterrence. With **general deterrence**, offenders are punished for their crimes, but the utility of the punishment is to convince others that the crime is not worth the pain of punishment. In other words, punishment exists as a warning against future criminal behavior by members of society. In this way, general deterrence attempts to prevent future crimes from happening. For example, if a law is violated, and an offender is punished, the value of the punishment is not in retribution against that offender, but in the crimes not committed by others who want to avoid punishment. Contrary to this, with **specific deterrence**, the purpose of punishment is to punish an individual offender to prevent their future criminal behavior. Here, a college student who gets a parking ticket on campus will remember that negative experience and be sure to park only in their designated lot next time they are on campus. Again, the utility of this is to prevent future offending, but this time, repeat offending by a particular offender.

Beccaria also addressed the conditions under which deterrence is effective, specifying that punishments should be certain, swift, and severe to produce maximum deterrent effects. Certainty refers to the likelihood that a law breaker will be apprehended and punished for their criminal behavior. Swift punishments are those that follow soon after the crime has been committed. Lastly, severe punishments negate whatever benefits the offender was to gain from their criminal behavior. Collectively, punishments that negate the benefits of the crime, are certain to be realized, and occur soon after the crime was committed should be those that produce the greatest deterrent effects. Conversely, an offender might judge a crime with a weak punishment, that the criminal justice system is unlikely to discover, or for which the punishment is far removed to be worth the risk – therefore giving the law little deterrent effect.

Deterrence research is not conclusive, or particularly supportive, of the effectiveness of deterrence on crime or the importance of the three concepts themselves. A meta-analysis of 40 deterrence studies suggested that the effects of deterrence concepts on crime are "modest to negligible" but that certainty of punishment appears to be the most consistently significant of these (Pratt et al., 2008, p. 383). These findings are consistent with those of other reviews of the body of deterrence research (e.g., Nagin, 2013). Research by Daniel Nagin (2013) examined different perspectives on deterrence research (e.g., imprisonment, police presence, capital punishment), for differing study methodologies, and across deterrence concepts. He concluded that certainty in the form of changes in police presence appear to affect the crime rate via deterrence; severity in the form of long prison sentences does not deter crime, but incapacitation itself may have some crime prevention benefits; and that it is difficult to reach conclusions because individuals' perceptions of certainty, swiftness, and severity are probably inaccurate, affecting their ability to actually be deterred (Nagin, 2013).

Correctional Rehabilitation

The purpose of **correctional rehabilitation** is to treat criminal behavior and provide convicted offenders with the opportunity to become productive members of society through therapy, vocational training, education, substance abuse treatment, or mental health services. There are a variety of programs and techniques that have been utilized in the name of rehabilitating offenders but they generally aim to address the causes of criminal behavior and reduce recidivism by providing individuals with skills and abilities that will lead to successful reintegration into society.

Andrews and colleagues (1990) described the influences on adult recidivism in terms of static and dynamic risk factors – or factors that increase the likelihood of recidivism. Static risk factors are those that increase the likelihood of recidivism, but that cannot be changed. Examples of static risk factors are age, sex, and prior criminal history. Dynamic risk factors also increase the likelihood of recidivism, but are changeable and, therefore, are the focus of prevention efforts and policies to reduce recidivism. Gendreau and colleagues (1996) conducted a meta-analysis of studies that have examined static and dynamic risk factors, summarizing findings from across 131 published studies. Based on their analysis, they concluded that research finds both static and dynamic risk factors to be statistically significant predictors of recidivism. For static risk factors, they identified age/gender/race, criminal history, family factors, intellectual functioning, and socioeconomic status as significant predictors of recidivism. For dynamic risk factors, they found that criminogenic needs, personal distress, and social achievement predicted recidivism. These dynamic risk factors, therefore, can be targeted by policies and rehabilitation programs designed to help individuals develop prosocial changes and reduce the likelihood of reoffending. Effective rehabilitation programs are designed around three principles: risk, need, and responsivity (Andrews et al., 1990).

The risk principle refers to dynamic risk factors and holds that treatment should match the individual's level of risk. Following an evaluation of their risks, an individual can be assigned to a treatment program that aligns with their assigned risk. The need principle maintains that effective offender rehabilitation programs should meet the needs of the offender, and these needs can be classified as either non-criminogenic (e.g., mental health) or criminogenic (e.g., antisocial attitudes), both of which are important to successfully reducing reoffending. Finally, the responsivity principle suggests that an effective program should be catered to the individual offender and the environment. For instance, programs should be responsive to factors such as the individual's learning style, ability, and motivations in order to maximize their chances for success. Approaches to offender rehabilitation are continually evolving and have thus far seen four generations of offender assessment approaches, ranging from discretionary professional judgments about an offender's likelihood of reoffending to more sophisticated assessments that are theoretically informed and empirically validated (Andrews et al., 2006).

There exist a number of offender-based programs based on the three principles for effective offender-based rehabilitation programs. Cognitive-behavioral approaches, for example, focus on changing the ways offenders think about problems, with an expected corresponding change in behavior as a result. There are also community models that emphasize resocialization with principles and practices grounded in social learning theory. As discussed earlier in this chapter, social learning theory explains that criminal behavior is learned, and can thus be unlearned. Still, there are programs oriented toward specific types of offenders or particular situations, such as programs focused on sex offender treatment. There are also specialized courts, which concentrate on offenders in specific circumstances, such as drug courts, mental health courts, and teen/youth courts. Each of these offers an alternative to traditional criminal courts and generally emphasizes rehabilitation/treatment.

Overall, policy makers are invested in identifying and implementing evidence-based programs that may reduce recidivism. Not only are there possible crime prevention benefits to offering rehabilitation and treatment programs to offenders, but offender-based rehabilitation programs are often less costly than more punishment-oriented approaches such as incarceration. Still, research is not unanimous on the effectiveness of offender-based rehabilitation programs as a method of crime prevention. Researchers continue to investigate which programs and treatments offer the most promising results. There is also the question of how best to measure success. Many programs target recidivism, but recidivism can be difficult to measure (e.g., reincarceration, parole violation). Other programs focus on helping individuals find employment or educational opportunities. Still others address psychological well-being, such as self-esteem and attitudes toward crime. Generally speaking, not all offender-based programs are equally effective, and those that are most successful are ones that follow the principles of risk, need, and responsivity.

Summary

The purpose of this chapter was to cover some of the ways that criminology can be useful to crime prevention practitioners. Primarily, this was undertaken by reviewing some of the root causes of criminal behavior according to criminological research and also by focusing on repeat offending. From here, crime prevention was discussed in terms of concentrating on initial offending, repeat offending, and recidivism. Our approach was to discuss these crime prevention approaches in terms of the life course perspective and also from the perspective of the criminal justice system. Still, this chapter provides only a starting point, as criminology is an expansive field and crime prevention programming is itself varied and extensive.

Discussion Questions

1. If criminal behavior is learned, what sorts of crime prevention strategies might be effective at preventing offending and reoffending?
2. If criminal behavior is caused by biological or biosocial factors, is it fair to hold individuals accountable for their criminal behaviors? Explain.
3. Think of someone you know who has been involved in juvenile delinquency or adult crime. Identify some possible life events or turning points that you think may have contributed to this behavior. What factors contributed to their desistance?
4. Did your school (elementary, junior high, high school) have a crime prevention program? If so, describe the program: was it focused on the school environment or on the students themselves? What were the goals of the program? Do you think it was successful?
5. The criminal justice system responds to crime by incapacitating offenders, providing deterrence, and offering rehabilitation. Which of these approaches seems to have the most crime prevention benefits? How could the criminal justice system better respond to crime from a prevention perspective?

References

Alaska Department of Corrections. (2021). *Key performance indicators.* https://omb.alaska.gov/html/performance/program-indicators.html?p=24&r=0

Alper, M., & Durose, M. R. (2018). *2018 update on prisoner recidivism: A 9-year follow-up period (2005–2014).* Washington, DC: Bureau of Justice Statistics.

American Psychiatric Association. (2013). *Diagnostic and statistical manual of mental disorders* (5th ed.). doi:10.1176/appi.books.9780890425596

Andrews, D. A., Bonta, J., & Wormith, J. S. (2006). The recent past and near future of risk and/or need assessment. *Crime & Delinquency, 52*(1), 7–27.

Andrews, D. A., Zinger, I., Hoge, R. D., Bonta, J., Gendreau, P., & Cullen, F. T. (1990). Does correctional treatment work? A clinically relevant and psychologically informed meta-analysis. *Criminology, 28*(3), 369–404.

Babbie, E. R. (2021). *The practice of social research* (15th ed.). Belmont, CA: Wadsworth, Cengage Learning.

Beccaria, C. (1986). *On crimes and punishments.* Translated by Henry Paolucci. New York: Macmillan. (Originally published 1764.)

Benson, M. L. (2002). *Crime and the life course: An introduction.* Los Angeles, CA: Roxbury Publishing Company.

Budd, T., Collier, P., Mhlanga, B., Sharp, C., & Weir, G. (2005). *Levels of self-report offending and drug use among offenders: Findings from the Criminality Surveys.* London: Home Office.

Cohen, J. (1978). The incapacitative effect of imprisonment: A critical review of the literature. In A. Blumstein, J. Cohen, & D. Nagin (Eds.), *Deterrence and incapacitation: Estimating the effects of criminal sanctions on crime rates.* Washington, DC: National Academy Press.

Elder, G. H. (1985). Perspectives on the life course. In G. H. Elder (Ed.), *Life course dynamics: Trajectories and transitions, 1968–1980* (pp. 23–49). Ithaca, NY: Cornell University Press.

Farrington, D. P. (1992). Criminal career research: Lessons for crime prevention. *Studies on Crime & Crime Prevention, 1*(1), 7–29.

Farrington, D. P., & West, D. J. (1995). Effects of marriage, separation, and children on offending by adult males. *Current Perspectives on Aging and the Life Cycle, 4,* 249–281.

Florida Department of Corrections. (2021). Quarterly recidivism report. www.dc.state.fl.us/index.html

Gaffney, H., Ttofi, M. M., & Farrington, D. P. (2019). Evaluating the effectiveness of school-bullying prevention programs: An updated meta-analytical review. *Aggression and Violent Behavior, 45,* 111–133.

Garces, E., Thomas, D., & Currie, J. (2002). Longer term effects of Head Start. *The American Economic Review, 92*(4), 999–1012.

Gendreau, P., Little, T., & Goggin, C. (1996). A meta-analysis of the predictors of adult offender recidivism: What works! *Criminology, 34*(4), 575–608.

Gottfredson, M. R., & Hirschi, T. (1990). *A general theory of crime.* Stanford, CA: Stanford University Press.

Grossman, J. B., & Tierney, J. P. (1998). Does mentoring work? An impact study of the Big Brothers Big Sisters program. *Evaluation Review, 22*(3), 403–426.

Hirschi, T. (1969). *Causes of delinquency.* Berkeley, CA: University of California Press.

Jolliffe, D., & Farrington, D. P. (2007). *A rapid evidence assessment of the impact of mentoring on re-offending: A summary.* London: Home Office. https://www.ojp.gov/ncjrs/virtual-library/abstracts/rapid-evidence-assessment-impact-mentoring-re-offending-summary

McCrae, R. R., & Costa, P. T. (2003). *Personality in adulthood: A five-factor theory perspective* (2nd ed.). New York: The Guilford Press.

Merton, R. K. (1938). Social structure and anomie. *American Sociological Review, 1,* 672–682.

Ministry of Justice. (2021). *Proven reoffending statistics: January to March 2019*. GOV.UK. https://www.gov.uk/government/statistics/proven-reoffending-statistics-january-to-march-2019/proven-reoffending-statistics-january-to-march-2019.

Moffitt, T. E. (1993). Adolescence-limited and life-course-persistent antisocial behavior: A developmental taxonomy. *Psychological Review*, *100*, 674–701.

Montana Department of Corrections. (2021). *Biennial report*. https://cor.mt.gov/

Nagin, D. S. (2013). Deterrence in the twenty-first century. *Crime and Justice*, *42*(1), 199–263.

Olds, D., Henderson Jr, C. R., Cole, R., Eckenrode, J., Kitzman, H., Luckey, D., . . . & Powers, J. (1998). Long-term effects of nurse home visitation on children's criminal and antisocial behavior: 15-year follow-up of a randomized controlled trial. *JAMA*, *280*(14), 1238–1244.

Pratt, T. C., Cullen, F. T., Blevins, K. R., Daigle, L. E., & Madensen, T. D. (2008). The empirical status of deterrence theory: A meta-analysis. In F. T. Cullen, J. P. Wright, & K. R. Blevins (Eds), *Taking stock* (pp. 367–395). London and New York: Routledge.

Raine, A. (1993). *The psychopathology of crime: Criminal behavior as a clinical disorder*. San Diego, CA: Academic Press.

Sampson, R. J., & Laub, J. H. (1993). *Crime in the making: Pathways and turning points through life*. Cambridge, MA: Harvard University Press.

Sampson, R. J., & Raudenbush, S. W. (1999). Systematic social observation of public spaces: A new look at disorder in urban neighborhoods. *American Journal of Sociology*, *105*(3), 603–651.

Schweinhart, L. J., Barnes, H., & Weikart, D. (1993). Significant benefits: The High/Scope Perry Preschool Study through age 27. *Monographs of the High/Scope Educational Research Foundation*, 10.

Shaw, C. R., & McKay, H. D. (1942). *Juvenile delinquency and urban areas*. Chicago, IL: University of Chicago Press.

Sutherland, E. H. (1947). Principles of criminology (4th ed.). Philadelphia, PA: Lippincot.

Tilley, N. (2013). *Analyzing and responding to repeat offending*. Problem-oriented guides for police problem-solving tools Series; No. 11. Washington: U.S. Department of Justice.

Welsh, B. C., & Farrington, D. P. (2010). *The future of crime prevention: Developmental and situational strategies*. Rockville, MD: National Institute of Justice. https://nij.ojp.gov/library/publications/future-crime-prevention-developmental-and-situational-strategies

Wilson, D. B., Gottfredson, D. C., & Najaka, S. S. (2001). School-based prevention of problem behaviors: A meta-analysis. *Journal of Quantitative Criminology*, *17*, 247–272.

Chapter 8
Victimization Prevention

Victimization Prevention

Bradford W. Reyns

Chapter Outline

In this chapter, we will focus on:

Understanding Victimization
- Brief history of victimology
- Identifying victimization risk factors
- Preventing initial victimization

Recurring Victimization as Crime Concentration
- Types of recurring victimization

Theories of Recurring Victimization
- State dependence theory
- Risk heterogeneity theory
- Rational choice theory
- Lifestyle-routine activity theory

Recurring Victimization and Crime Prevention
- Repeat burglaries
- Intimate partner violence
- Sexual victimization

Learning Objectives

After reading this chapter, you should be able to:

8.1 Discuss crime prevention from a victimization perspective

8.2 Define the term recurring victimization

8.3 Identify the different types of recurring victimization

8.4 Explain the primary theories of recurring victimization

8.5 Apply the principles of crime prevention to recurring victimization

Introduction

This chapter draws from the field of victimology to address crime prevention from a victimization perspective. **Victimology** is the scientific study of the victims of crime, including their experiences, behaviors, and needs. Victimology research aims to provide a comprehensive understanding of victimization, including its extent and nature, factors that contribute to victimization, and its consequences. **Victimization**, then, occurs when individuals, households, businesses, or other targets are harmed following a violation of the law. Understanding the extent and nature of victimization is an essential step toward developing effective crime prevention programs and policies oriented toward crime victims. This chapter addresses victimization prevention in two ways. First, understanding how and why targets are initially selected for victimization suggests factors that could be minimized to reduce, discourage, or prevent initial, or first-time victimization. Second, a focus on preventing initial victimization from reoccurring would prevent crime from concentrating within those targets.

Understanding Victimization

Scholars and policy makers have been interested in understanding criminality, criminals, crime, and its aftermath for hundreds of years, and modern criminology takes a scientific approach to these topics that spans many fields of study, such as psychology, sociology, and public policy. Victimology, by contrast, has only been the subject of research attention for the last few decades (Fattah, 2000). Since that time, however, researchers have learned a great deal about crime from the victim's perspective. Victimologists study the extent, nature, causes, consequences, and rights of crime victims with the intention of protecting, supporting, and empowering crime victims.

Brief History of Victimology

Early victimologists viewed crimes as interactive events in which both perpetrators and victims played a role in the criminal event (e.g., von Hentig, 1940). Notable victimologists, such as Hans von Hentig, Beniamin Mendelsohn, and Stephen Schafer each developed typologies of crime victims in an early effort to identify factors that may make individuals vulnerable or susceptible to victimization, such as sex and age (Mendelsohn, 1963; Schafer, 1977; von Hentig, 1940). This era in victimology is associated with explaining victimization as being somehow precipitated by the victim. **Victim precipitation** implies that victims contributed to the criminal event, either by facilitating it or provoking it (e.g., Wolfgang, 1958). Today, this approach to explaining victimization is criticized for blaming the victim.

Later, researchers began to collect empirical data and look for patterns in these data related to victimization. For example, Marvin Wolfgang (1958) collected homicide data in Philadelphia and identified factors related to homicide victimization, such as the presence of alcohol and a prior relationship between the victim and offender. The 1970s saw the advent of victimization surveys, which changed how scholars approached the study of victimization. By surveying individuals about their experiences with crime, researchers were able to move beyond somewhat basic categories of crime victims (e.g., young victims, old victims) and instead begin to develop and test theories of victimization.

The contemporary National Crime Victimization Survey (NCVS), first administered in 1972, led to the development of lifestyle-exposure theory – an opportunity theory that was discussed in Chapter 2. Having analyzed the first administration of the survey, Michael Hindelang and his colleagues (1978) proposed that individuals are vulnerable to criminal victimization, not necessarily because of their personal characteristics (e.g., sex, age, race) but, rather, because of their lifestyles. This approach to understanding victimization introduced the concept of risk and risk factors to the study of crime victims.

The concept of risk was adopted from public health, which views **risk** as the likelihood or probability that an individual or population will be exposed to something that will harm their health. In public health, this may be a risk for heart disease or cancer. Therefore, epidemiologists identify risk factors for diseases and suggest means for prevention and health care. Risk factors, then, are variables that are associated with these unwanted outcomes. By identifying and managing risk factors, epidemiologists look for ways to reduce the risks of developing these diseases. For instance, high blood pressure, smoking, and diabetes are among the risk factors for heart disease. Knowing this, doctors and patients can manage these risk factors through medical treatments and lifestyle changes to help reduce the risk of developing heart disease.

In the context of criminal victimization, **risks factors** for victimization are factors that make individuals more susceptible to being targets of criminal behavior. Just as epidemiologists work toward preventing disease, contemporary victimologists work toward identifying risk factors for victimization that may be used to help prevent crime. And like public health, risk factors will vary depending on the outcome. For instance, the factors that increase individuals' risk for identity theft will necessarily be different from those that make individuals vulnerable to aggravated assault. Overall, identifying victimization risk factors is an important step in developing policies and best practices to mitigate or prevent victimization outcomes by reducing risk.

Identifying Victimization Risk Factors

Perhaps the first step in identifying victimization risk factors is understanding how victimization is patterned. In this context, a pattern is a repeated sequence of events, which help observers to make predictions and identify trends; and, as the rest of this book illustrates, crime prevention strategies are often based on identifying patterns. The work of the early victimologists illustrates this, but so too do modern efforts to measure and estimate the extent of victimization. Knowing the extent of victimization, and patterns in types, victim characteristics, geography, and seasonality of victimization is useful to practitioners, policy makers, and crime prevention scholars. Today, these patterns can be identified from different data sources, such as the National Incident-Based Reporting System or the NCVS in the United States.

Expand Your Understanding – National Crime Victimization Survey

Readers can explore patterns in victimization in the United States using the National Crime Victimization Survey Data Dashboard (N-DASH). From here, it is possible to examine select victim, household, and incident patterns for different types of personal and property crimes.

https://ncvs.bjs.ojp.gov/Home

Early attempts at identifying risk factors for victimization focused on individuals' personal or demographic characteristics. Still today, it is useful to know who is most at risk for experiencing victimization to develop more effective responses or prevention strategies. For example, the NCVS report on criminal victimization in the United States from 2020 indicates that persons 18–24 years old have the highest violent and property victimization rates, as do those who have household incomes less than $25,000 (Morgan & Thompson, 2021). These same principles also apply to other types of crime targets, and so it is useful to identify the characteristics of products, facilities, and places where crime concentrates. Identifying these types of patterns is discussed further elsewhere in the book.

With the introduction of lifestyle-exposure theory, victimology research began to be more theoretically informed (Hindelang et al., 1978). Today, there are many theories that are used to explain victimization and identify factors that place individuals at risk. A major focus of crime prevention experts has been the opportunity perspective, which suggests victimization is more likely when opportunities for crime exist (Felson & Clarke, 1998). These opportunities are usually conceptualized as involving motivated offenders, suitable targets, and facilitating environments lacking guardianship. Victimization research guided by the opportunity perspective is concerned with identifying factors that increase exposure to motivated offenders, make targets (i.e., victims or their property) more attractive, and/or decrease guardianship. Doing so suggests that these are risk factors for victimization. Alternatively, identifying factors related to victimization outcomes may also suggest protective factors. Recall that these concepts were discussed in depth in Chapter 2 as being the building blocks of the routine activity perspective.

The number of empirical research studies devoted to risk factors for victimization makes a comprehensive review here unrealistic (Spano & Freilich, 2009). However, a few classic pieces by crime prevention scholars, and grounded in the opportunity perspective, are discussed to provide representative examples. For instance, in an early test of the opportunity perspective, Robert Sampson and John Wooldredge (1987) used British Crime Survey data to identify risk factors for property victimization. They reported that individual factors, such as the person's age, and contextual dynamics, such as the level of street activity, were significant predictors of personal larceny victimization without contact. Interestingly, they also reported that the percentage of VCR (video-cassette recorder) ownership in the area was significantly related to burglary victimization risk.

In another well-known study of victimization risk factors, Leslie Kennedy and David Forde (1990) utilized data from the Canadian Urban Victimization Survey to study risk factors for several crimes in Canada. They considered nighttime activity variables as predictors of victimization, such the number of times per month going to: a sports bar or pub; a movie theater or restaurant; visiting friends; and walking or driving. Among their findings, they reported that the number of times per month going out to bars, movies, working, and walking/driving were each significantly related to assault victimization risk. Going to bars and walking/driving were, likewise, risk factors for robbery victimization. In another study of victimization risk factors, Janet Lauritsen and colleagues (1991) analyzed data from the National Youth Survey to identify victimization risk factors among adolescents. They reported that adolescents who engaged in deviant or delinquent lifestyles were at greater risks of experiencing victimization, arguing that such activities increased exposure to motivated offenders, while reducing capable guardianship. These three studies provide examples of early efforts to identify victimization risk factors, but readers should also realize that these efforts have been ongoing for decades, with more research being published every day.

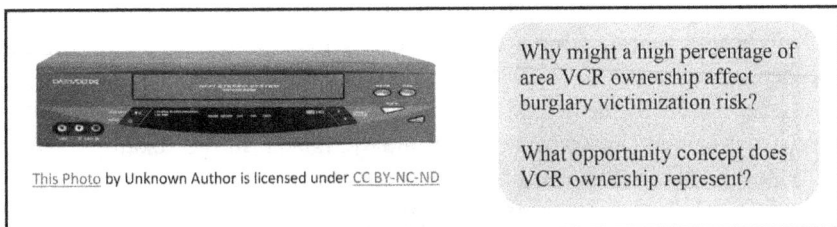

Why might a high percentage of area VCR ownership affect burglary victimization risk?

What opportunity concept does VCR ownership represent?

This Photo by Unknown Author is licensed under CC BY-NC-ND

Figure 8.1 VCR Ownership and Burglary.

It is also noteworthy that there are alternative explanations for victimization, beyond opportunity, that are useful in understanding victimization, such as personality characteristics, low self-control, genetics, and environmental factors (e.g., Kulig et al., 2019; Pratt et al., 2014; Schreck, 1999; Vaske et al., 2012). For example, soon after the general theory of crime was published in 1990 by Michael Gottfredson and Travis Hirschi, it was adapted to explain victimization, and its central concept – low self-control – has since become one of the most robust predictors of victimization (Gottfredson & Hirschi, 1990; Schreck, 1999). According to Chris Schreck (1999), those possessing low self-control are more vulnerable to crime because they engage in higher risk behaviors that expose them to victimization, such as behaviors that increase exposure to motivated offenders. Schreck (1999, p. 637) notes, however, that "[n]ot all victims of crime have low self-control; the theory says only that those who engage in low-self-control behavior risk greater vulnerability to crime." While a substantial body of victimization research has been devoted to exploring these alternative approaches to victimization risk, most victimization prevention remains opportunity-based.

Preventing Initial Victimization

The implicit purpose of identifying risk factors for criminal victimization is to prevent victimization or mitigate risk. Doing so rests on crime prevention policy and education. Victimization research has a wealth of information related to risk factors for different types of victimization that could prove useful to these endeavors. For example, identifying demographic risk factors tells us who is most at risk, and therefore, to whom prevention efforts could be directed. Since young people are the demographic most likely to be associated with bullying – as bullies or victims – anti-bullying messages and campaigns are catered toward that audience. If elders are disproportionately victims of frauds perpetrated by phone, prevention education can be directed toward these potential victims, along with victim resources.

Likewise, understanding opportunity-based risk factors for victimization also suggests ways of preventing victimization. For example, the routine activity perspective proposes that greater exposure and proximity to motivated offenders increases victimization risk, as does greater target attractiveness. Whereas guardianship acts as a protective factor against victimization. Inherent in these propositions is the idea that decreasing exposure/proximity and target attractiveness, and increasing guardianship, will alter opportunity structures and discourage crime and victimization. For example, Kennedy and Forde (1990) identified the number of times per month in which an individual went out to bars as a significant risk factor for assault victimization. Therefore, it appears engaging in this activity less frequently should reduce victimization risk. However, suggesting that certain activities should be avoided also presents us with a problem – constraining our behaviors can limit our quality of life. Individuals should be able to engage in lifestyles and pursuits that make them happy, so there should be a balance between avoiding risk and over-constraining our behaviors to avoid it. At the same time, individuals are responsible for taking reasonable precautions to avoid being victimized.

With regard to individual choices, crime prevention scholars have begun to investigate the factors that influence adoption of crime prevention behaviors. For example, Christopher Schreck and colleagues (2018) analyzed data from Seattle adults and identified factors related to the adoption of crime prevention in the form of defensive precautions (e.g., buying a gun). Notably, they reported that past victimization was a significant predictor of prevention behavior. This suggests that individuals who have experienced victimization will take actions to prevent it from happening again. In a similar study that used data from the Canadian General Social Survey, Bradford Reyns and colleagues (2016) found that online victimization was a significant predictor of online preventative behaviors, but also emphasized that specific types of victimization are related to specific types of preventative behaviors. In another study that also used data from the Canadian General Social Survey, Arelys Madero-Hernandez and colleagues (2022) reported that prior personal victimization, prior property victimization, and perceptions of the police impacted individuals' adoption of crime prevention behavior.

Yet, answering the question of whether these individual adaptations, such as changes to one's routines or adoption of crime prevention behaviors, are ultimately effective in reducing victimization risk remains a challenge. First, much of the research attention in this area has been devoted to assessing the effectiveness of particular crime prevention programs (e.g., campus sexual assault prevention), rather than individual efforts to prevent victimization (e.g., installing alarms). Crime prevention programs and their effectiveness are discussed throughout this book. Second, the existing crime prevention research into "what works," and identifying those factors that might prevent victimization, has almost wholly focused on recurring victimization. Understanding recurring victimization as a form of crime concentration has significant implications for crime prevention, including preventing one-time victims from becoming recurring victims.

Recurring Victimization as Crime Concentration

Just as crime commission concentrates at the individual level in the form of repeat offending and recidivism, as discussed in Chapter 7, so too does victimization concentrate within the targets of criminal behavior. This form of crime concentration is referred to as recurring victimization, and is an important consideration in preventing crime and victimization. **Recurring**

victimization happens when a target is victimized two or more times. The target can be an individual, their property, or another entity such as a business or organization. Recurring victimization takes many forms depending on the type of behavior that has taken place, the target, and the time that has elapsed between incidents. In order to gain a better understanding of this phenomenon, it is helpful to review the types of recurring victimization. Understanding recurring victimization also has important implications for crime prevention.

With respect to repeat offending, research has found that a small group of offenders are responsible for a majority of the crimes that are committed. In the same way, research studies also have reported that a small group of individuals or other targets disproportionately experience the criminal event as the victim, known as recurring victimization. In comparison with repeat offending, recurring victimization has only been the subject of empirical research since the 1980s. However, since that time, a great deal has been learned about recurring victimization, including its prevalence, the different forms that it takes, and the development of theories to explain patterns in recurring victimization. Similar to repeat offending, better understanding the dynamics surrounding recurring victimization is vitally important to crime prevention efforts, because a focus on preventing one-time victims from becoming recurring victims should significantly reduce victimization rates.

Victimization research investigating the prevalence of different types of victimization, particularly those studies that examine recurring victimization, consistently reports three findings related to recurring victimization. First, the majority of persons do not experience criminal victimization. For instance, a report from the U.S. Bureau of Justice Statistics using data from the NCVS estimated a total violent victimization (i.e., rape or sexual assault, robbery, aggravated assault, and simple assault) rate among U.S. residents aged 12 and older of 8.9 per 1,000 persons in 2014 (Oudekerk & Truman, 2017). These estimates suggest that violent victimization is a relatively rare event. Second, among those who are victimized, most are only victimized a single time. This same report using NCVS data estimated a single-time victimization rate of 8.9 per 1,000 persons aged 12 and older. Third, there is a smaller group of victims who were repeatedly victimized. Results from the NCVS indicate that 2.1 per 1,000 individuals aged 12 and older are repeat victims of violence. In other words, this group was violently victimized two or more times within the course of a year (Oudekerk & Truman, 2017).

Just as criminologists have explored patterns in repeat offending, victimologists have investigated patterns in recurring victimization. Identifying these patterns is useful because it helps researchers and practitioners develop strategies for allocating resources to prevent single-time victims from becoming recurring victims. For example, law enforcement may concentrate resources on a street that has experienced motor vehicle break-ins to prevent repeat victimizations. The previously discussed NCVS data suggest some interesting patterns in repeat victimization in the United States. For instance, males and females have similar repeat violent victimization rates. However, a greater percentage of male than female victims experience repeat victimization by a stranger. Additionally, the prevalence and patterns in recurring victimization vary by crime type. As examples, according to the NCVS, 31 percent of victims of rape or sexual assault were repeatedly victimized. For robbery, aggravated assault, and simple assault, these figures are 19 percent, 20 percent, and 23 percent, respectively (Oudekerk & Truman, 2017).

In looking at crime type, it is clear that recurring victims account for a disproportionate share of all victimization incidents of that type. To illustrate, the same NCVS data indicated that 33 percent of victims of intimate partner violence (IPV) who experienced repeat victimization accounted for 68 percent of all IPV victimization incidents (Oudekerk & Truman, 2017). Similar patterns have also been reported outside the United States. For example, Weisel (2005) notes that, according to the International Crime Victimization Survey, 11 percent of repeat victims of assault in the Netherlands suffered 25 percent of all the incidents of assault over a 25-year period. This same pattern is evident when examining other types of crimes, including property crimes. According to the British Crime Survey, 19 percent of victims of burglary accounted for 40 percent of all residential burglary incidents, and 24 percent of victims of vehicle crimes experienced 46 percent of all incidents of vehicle crimes (Weisel, 2005). These statistics speak to the nature of recurring victimization as a form of crime concentration. Just as crimes concentrate geographically to form hotspots of crime, and as particular offenders repeatedly commit crimes, victimization concentrates individually in the form of recurrent victimization.

Types of Recurring Victimization

The number of types, or forms, that recurring victimization takes can at first seem daunting. However, they all share the common characteristic that the victim or other target has been victimized two or more times. From that common starting point, there are variations in 1) crime type and 2) time elapsed between the crime events that distinguish the different types of recurring victimization from each other. Together, there are five distinct types of recurring victimization that have been identified by researchers, each with its own patterns and, to a degree, its own determinants or risk factors. These five types of recurring victimization are outlined in Table 8.1 and include: repeat victimization, revictimization, multiple victimization, series victimization, and polyvictimization.

Table 8.1 Defining Types of Recurring Victimization

Type of Recurring Victimization	Crime Type	Time Elapsed
Repeat Victimization	The same type of crime	Short period of time
Revictimization	Violent crime	Mostly refers to incidents across developmental stages
Multiple Victimization	Different types of crime	Short period of time
Series Victimization	The same type of crime (6 or more incidents)	High frequency within a short period of time
Polyvictimization	Multiple crimes	Short period of time

First, keeping in mind the two primary characteristics that differentiate types of recurring victimization – crime type and time elapsed – **repeat victimization** occurs when the victim experiences the *same* type of victimization two or more times within a short period of time (Pease & Farrell, 2017). For example, if a taxi driver is robbed at the beginning of the month and again robbed at the end of the month, this would be a repeat victimization. Repeat victimizations usually occur in close succession, but not necessarily always, and often there is some sort of connection between the incidents, such as the same offender or similar circumstances (Pease & Farrell, 2017). Typically, repeat victimizations are those that occur within a relatively short time period, such as within one year. The important point is that the incidents occur within the individual's same developmental time period. For instance, if a young adult was assaulted on his way home from school, and experienced assault again in his elder years, this would not be a repeat victimization, as the incidents are not within the same developmental time period and are very likely unrelated to each other in any way. In an analysis of the International Crime Victimization Survey, Farrell and colleagues (2005) found that repeat victimization constitutes 40 percent of all crime across 17 countries.

There are two additional types of repeat victimization for which the incidents are, by definition, related to each other. First, **near repeat victimizations** are those in which the offender purposefully selects a target in close *proximity* to a previously victimized target (Pease & Farrell, 2017). Near repeats have often been studied in the context of burglary, and repeat burglary offenders will frequently choose to burglarize more than one house on a street. Hypothetically, this could be because the homes on the street share similar characteristics that make them attractive targets to the burglar (e.g., expensive décor, high-end appliances, similar floorplans), or because the street or neighborhood itself has characteristics that are suitable to crime (e.g., little guardianship, poor lighting, light traffic). In near repeats, offenders also utilize similar tactics to perpetrate the crime (Pease & Farrell, 2017). Second, **virtual repeat victimizations** are repeat victimizations in which the targets are chosen by offenders because they share *characteristics* similar to previously victimized targets, but not because of their proximity to previously victimized targets (Pease & Farrell, 2017). For example, car thieves might seek out particular vehicle makes and models because they are valuable and/or easy to steal. The stolen cars, then, may come from geographically disparate parts of the city, state, or country. Here, offenders will often adopt the same or similar tactics to commit the crime (Pease & Farrell, 2017).

Revictimization occurs when an individual is violently victimized two or more times across their life course. Here, the distinguishing features of recurring victimization are that it specifically involves violence, and also that the *time* elapsed between the incidents is a longer period of time sufficient to span stages of life (e.g., childhood to adolescence, adolescence to adulthood). Research studies have mostly examined revictimization in the context of rape and sexual assault, IPV, and child abuse, and research suggests that individuals who experience these types of victimization early in their lives are at risk for the same or similar types of victimization later in their lives (i.e., victimizations that span developmental periods). As an example, if an individual is physically abused during their childhood by a parent, and again experiences abuse by an intimate partner as an adult, this would be revictimization. In this example the offenders are different, but there still may be some personal, environmental, or situational factors that increased this victim's risk for victimization, such as depression, anxiety, or disability. In a study on revictimization, Widom and colleagues (2008) reported that abused and neglected children were at greater risk for later revictimization than those who did not experience childhood abuse or neglect.

The next type of recurring victimization, **multiple victimization**, is characterized by the target experiencing *more than one type* of victimization within a relatively short period of time. Similar to repeat victimizations, multiple victimizations happen within a specified time period, such as one year; but unlike repeat victimization, these involve different types of crimes. As an example, if an individual were to be the target of a property crime and a personal crime within the period of one year, they would be classified as a multiple victim. Multiple victimization represents a change in the type of victimization experienced from time 1 to time 2, which is referred to as a crime switch. Reiss (1980) identified the phenomenon of **crime switching** and studied it using data from the National Crime Survey. He concluded that most recurring victimizations involve the same type of victimization (i.e., repeats), but that crime switching does occur (i.e., multiple victimization), although it is comparatively rare. Ultimately, results such as these raise the question of why targets are repetitively victimized, to which Reiss

(1980) suggested some targets may be prone to victimization – an issue addressed by the theories of recurring victimization that are discussed later in this chapter.

While multiple victimization is characterized by the victim experiencing more than one type of victimization, series victimization occurs when the victim experiences similar types of crimes repeatedly. **Series victimization**, then, can be described as *high-frequency* repeat victimization. The NCVS identifies series victimizations as those in which the victim reports experiencing six or more similar crimes during the survey's six-month reference period (Lauritsen et al., 2012). Essentially, in series victimizations, the incidents comprise a chain of events where a single incident may not be distinct from the others in the sequence. Research investigating series victimizations has focused on violent series victimizations, especially those that occur in the home, the workplace, or at school. NCVS findings, for example, report that most series victimizations against men occur at work or on duty and are perpetrated by strangers, while those against women primarily occur at home and are committed by intimate partners (Lauritsen et al., 2012). Common forms of series victimization include IPV, bullying, stalking, and elder abuse.

Polyvictimization can be described as exposure to several different types of victimization. Although the term is frequently used synonymously with any type of recurring victimization, it was originally applied to the study of recurring victimization among children. In applying the term only to children, it is distinguished from multiple victimization and series victimization. Further, polyvictimization occurs within a short time period. Finkelhor, who coined the term, explained that polyvictims experience so many incidents of victimization that "victimization may be better thought of as a condition rather than an event" (Finkelhor et al., 2011, p. 292). In studying polyvictimization, Finkelhor and his colleagues (2011) examined several types of victimization, including physical assault, property crime, maltreatment, bullying, sexual victimization, witnessing family violence, and exposure to community violence. This study found that developmental level was associated with frequency and type of polyvictimization, with younger victims experiencing fewer victimizations, less sexual victimizations, and more victimizations committed by family members. Since Finkelhor and colleagues' (2011) study, however, the term polyvictimization has also been applied to adult victims of recurring crimes, particularly vulnerable populations (e.g., Snyder et al., 2021).

Theories of Recurring Victimization
In addition to identifying types and patterns of recurring victimization, victimologists have also developed theories to explain why some crime victims become recurring victims. The four major theoretical perspectives

on recurring victimization include: state dependence theory, risk heterogeneity theory, rational choice theory, and lifestyle-routine activity theory.

State Dependence Theory

State dependence theory suggests that recurring victimization happens because an initial victimization event creates conditions that makes a subsequent victimization event more likely (Farrell et al., 1995; Grove et al., 2012). Simply put, the first crime "boosts" the chances for a second crime to occur, making one-time victimization a risk factor for future victimization. For example, if during the course of a burglary a door is kicked in, breaking the door frame, the owner may not be able to get it fixed for a few days. In the meantime, this new vulnerability could make the house an attractive target to the same, or other, burglars. There have been several research studies that have reported a link between prior and subsequent victimization (e.g., Clay-Warner et al., 2016; Ousey et al., 2008; Wittebrood & Nieuwbeerta, 2000). For example, a study using national survey data from the Netherlands reported that individuals who have been victimized once are at substantial risk for being victimized again, supporting state dependence as an explanation for recurring victimization (Wittebrood & Nieuwbeerta, 2000). However, researchers have also suggested that the links between first and subsequent victimization events may operate through victim characteristics and behaviors and whether these risk factors change between events (Clay-Warner et al., 2016; Ousey et al., 2008).

Risk Heterogeneity Theory

Like state dependence theory, the risk heterogeneity perspective provides an explanation for why once-victimized individuals or other targets become recurring victims. According to **risk heterogeneity theory**, individuals and other targets are repeatedly victimized because they possess characteristics that make them attractive or susceptible targets to motivated offenders (Farrell et al., 1995; Grove et al., 2012). These characteristics – or "flags" – if left unchanged, continue to increase victimization risk, leading to recurring victimization. For example, a convenience store may be repeatedly targeted because it is open all night and infrequently visited by shoppers or law enforcement. It follows, then, that if the store changed its hours or if law enforcement made more frequent stops or drive-bys, that the store would be a less attractive target to potential robbers because the "flags" would have been removed. The previously mentioned study by Wittebrood and Nieuwbeerta (2000) found that being victimized once increased individuals' chances of being victimized again (a boost explanation), but they also reported that certain characteristics and routines were significant determinants of victimization risk (a flag explanation). Support for this perspective has also been reported in other studies of recurring victimization, including findings that suggest both state dependence and risk heterogeneity influence recurring victimization risk (e.g., Clay-Warner et al., 2016; Lauritsen & Davis Quinet, 1995; Tseloni & Pease, 2003).

Rational Choice Theory

Both state dependence theory and risk heterogeneity theory are informed by rational choice theory. Rational choice was previously discussed in Chapter 2, but in brief, **rational choice** theory asserts that offender decision making is a purposeful decision in which the would-be offender assesses the costs and benefits of criminal behavior. Theoretically, based on a consideration of the information that is available, the individual makes a decision that will maximize benefits while minimizing the costs (Clarke & Cornish, 1985). In thinking about recurring victimization, rational choice theory would suggest that re-victimizing a once-victimized target is often the rational target choice for an offender to make. Farrell and colleagues (1995, p. 386), for example, explain that for an offender, revictimizing the same target is rational because "the repeated offense required less effort, and had fewer risks and more advantages than the available alternatives." In short, the risks and rewards are known from the first crime and can be assumed to be similar. At the same time, some recurring victimizations will involve different offenders across incidents. In these instances, rational choice still plays a role, because the factors that the first rational offender interpreted as creating an attractive crime opportunity will also be interpreted by the second rational offender as presenting an attractive crime opportunity – a flag argument.

Lifestyle-Routine Activity Theory

Lifestyle-routine activity theory was also previously reviewed in Chapter 2, but this perspective, likewise, is informative in understanding recurring victimization. **Lifestyle-routine activity theory** begins with the premise that opportunities are necessary conditions for criminal events (Felson & Clarke, 1998). In other words, without criminal opportunities, crimes are much less likely to occur. Opportunities are generated when motivated offenders and suitable targets meet within environments favorable to crime. These three theoretical concepts – motivated offenders, suitable targets, and facilitating environments lacking capable guardians – are the building blocks of criminal opportunities. Although research has conceptualized the three concepts in differing ways across studies, the theoretical perspective has been supported as a leading explanation for victimization (Spano & Freilich, 2009).

Just as opportunities for victimization are a function of lifestyle and routine activity behaviors, opportunities have also been identified as significant predictors of recurring victimization. The rationale here is that lifestyles and routine activities that generate opportunities for an initial victimization can also create opportunities for recurring victimization, though this hypothesis presumes that these lifestyles and routines do not change between crimes. For example, Turanovic and Pratt (2014) analyzed data from the Gang Resistance Education and Training (GREAT) program and found that engaging in risky lifestyle behaviors was a risk factor for both initial and repeat violent victimization. Presumably, then, if individuals changed these risky behaviors between crimes, they would also decrease their risks for recurring victimization – a hypothesis known as "once bitten twice shy" – which was supported in Turanovic and Pratt's (2014) research. While other studies have supported the notion that some overlap exists for risk factors for both single and repeat victims, there is also research that suggests some factors my differ between victim types (see Snyder et al., 2021, for example).

Recurring Victimization and Crime Prevention
Understanding recurring victimization has significant implications for crime prevention. Since a substantial portion of crimes involve targets that have already been victimized, preventative approaches focused on victims have the potential both to prevent recurring victimization and reduce crime generally. There have been a number of crime prevention initiatives and programs designed to address this issue by focusing prevention efforts on recently victimized targets. However, there are fewer methodologically strong research evaluations that have examined the efficacy of these programs. Further, most evaluations of crime prevention efforts to prevent recurring victimization have focused on repeat burglaries, although a small number of studies have also been designed to address programs involving recurring IPV and sexual victimization (Grove et al., 2012).

Repeat Burglaries
Research has addressed repeat burglary victimization as a form of recurring victimization, and several studies have been published that offer explanations for why repeats occur, often involving boost and flag explanations (Farrell et al., 1995). In a pioneering and now classic study of repeat residential burglary victimization in Canada, Polvi and colleagues (1991) concluded that if a repeat burglary was going to occur, it would happen soon after the first, and that this heightened period for a repeat victimization would gradually dissipate over time. These findings have been replicated in other studies and for different types of victimization – a phenomenon known as the **time course** of repeat victimization (Daigle et al., 2008; Grove

et al., 2012; Polvi et al., 1991). The time course of repeat victimization is illustrated in Figure 8.2 with data from the NCVS.

In addition to understanding the nature of repeat burglary, researchers have evaluated the effectiveness of programs designed to prevent repeat burglary victimization. These programs often involve security assessments by law enforcement, target hardening efforts, such as installing alarms or improving locks, property marking, and Neighborhood Watch (Grove et al., 2012). The characteristics of the time course are also important considerations in developing repeat burglary prevention initiatives, because it may only be necessary to implement additional prevention measures for a short time until the heightened risk for a repeat dissipates.

The Kirkholt Burglary Prevention Project, a well-known program undertaken in Greater Manchester, England, to prevent repeat burglaries, provides an example of the relationship between recurring victimization and crime prevention (Forrester et al., 1990). This initiative was undertaken in the 1980s in response to the high burglary rates against properties in the area, which included repeat burglaries. Based on information collected from several sources, the project team implemented a number of tactics, including security upgrades and a cocoon neighborhood watch. The project was considered a success, with repeat burglaries being entirely prevented (100 percent reduction), and overall crime being reduced by 63 percent (Forrester et al., 1990; Grove et al., 2012). The Kirkholt Burglary Prevention Project is discussed in further depth in Chapter 12.

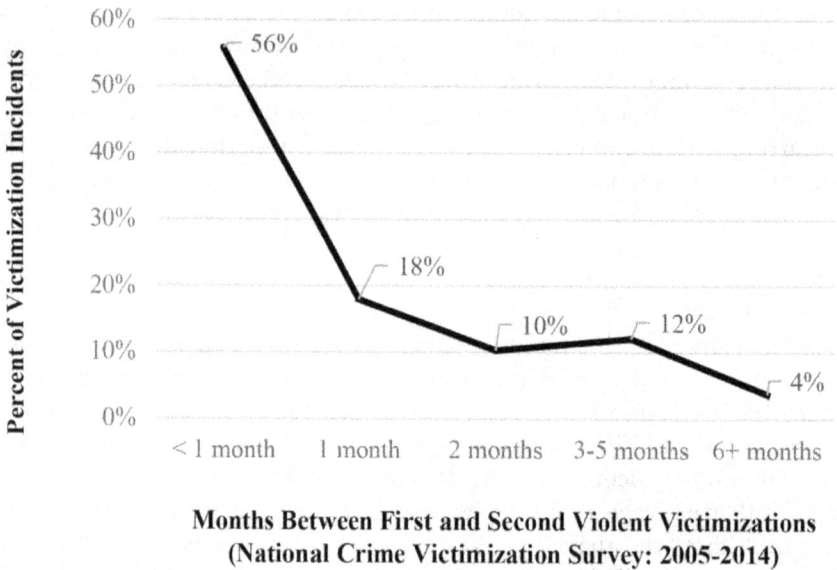

Months Between First and Second Violent Victimizations (National Crime Victimization Survey: 2005-2014)

Figure 8.2 Time Course for Repeat Victimization.
Source: Oudekerk & Truman, 2017.

In assessing the bigger picture, Grove and colleagues (2012) conducted a systematic review of initiatives developed to prevent repeat victimization. As part of their review, they identified 22 evaluations of repeat residential burglary prevention programs. Their assessment of these studies concluded that, overall, there was strong support for the effectiveness of programs designed to prevent repeat residential burglary, which decreased by 17 percent across programs compared with control conditions. They reported similar findings in their analysis of evaluations of repeat commercial burglaries, with crimes decreasing by 20 percent against targets that were the focus of repeat victimization prevention programs compared with control conditions (Grove et al., 2012).

Intimate Partner Violence and Sexual Victimization

Although initiatives have been undertaken to reduce recurring victimization for victims of crimes other than burglary, such as IPV and sexual victimization, there have been few evaluations of the effectiveness of these programs, making general conclusions difficult (Grove et al., 2012). However, the Minneapolis Domestic Violence Experiment provides a well-known example of a prevention effort oriented around IPV (Sherman & Berk, 1984). In this study, an experimental design was utilized whereby police officers in Minneapolis, Minnesota, who were responding to calls for misdemeanor domestic assaults, were randomly assigned one of three responses: 1) arrest the perpetrator; 2) separate the victim from the offender for eight hours; or 3) provide advice to the couple, such as mediation. The results of the study suggested that arresting the perpetrator was an effective response to IPV that reduced the likelihood of recurring victimization (Sherman & Berk, 1984). However, this study has been met with some criticism and subsequent replications have not always found that arrest was an effective deterrent against recurring victimization (Garner et al., 1995). The Minneapolis Domestic Violence Experiment is discussed further in Chapter 12.

With respect to recurring sexual victimization, research has reported that recurring victimization patterns mirror the time course of repeat victimization previously discussed in the context of burglary (Daigle et al., 2008). With respect to sexual prevention programs, though, results are mixed. While there are many programs and evaluations of programs designed to reduce sexual victimization, ranging from education programs to bystander intervention, there are few that specifically address recurring victimization. Of those, results are not encouraging on their effectiveness (Grove et al., 2012). For instance, a study by Breitenbecher and Gidycz (1998) evaluated the effectiveness of a program to reduce recurring sexual victimization against college women with a history of sexual victimization. In this study, participants were assigned to either a treatment or control group, with those in the treatment group participating in a prevention program that focused on education and awareness. The results suggested that the program was not effective at reducing the incidence of sexual assault victimization among participants. In a similar study by Hanson and Gidycz (1993), research findings suggested that a prevention program was effective in reducing incidence of sexual assault for women without a prior history of sexual assault, but not for women with a history of sexual assault victimization. Overall, Grove and colleagues' (2012) review of research into preventing recurring victimization concluded that existing programs designed to prevent repeat sexual victimization have not been effective.

Summary

This chapter emphasized the utility of understanding victimization for the field of crime prevention. A major focus of the study of victimization has been to identify risk factors for victimization so that risk can me lessened or crime and victimization prevented. In addition, an understanding of recurring victimization can aid in crime prevention. There are several types of recurring victimization, each of which has a unique footprint as a form of crime concentration. Repeat victimization, revictimization, multiple victimization, series victimization, and polyvictimization can each be explained to varying degrees by the leading theories of recurring victimization presented in this chapter. Crime prevention programs and initiatives involving the prevention of recurring victimization have produced successful reductions in recurring victimization, and crime generally, but success rates vary by crime type.

Keywords

Victimology, Victimization, Victim Precipitation, Risk, Risk Factors, Recurring Victimization, Repeat Victimization, Near Repeat Victimization, Virtual Repeat Victimization, Revictimization, Multiple Victimization, Crime Switching, Series Victimization, Polyvictimization, State Dependence Theory, Risk Heterogeneity Theory, Rational Choice Theory, Lifestyle-Routine Activity Theory, Time Course

Discussion Questions

1. How might identifying risk factors suggest methods for preventing initial- or recurring-victimization?
2. Why does the rational choice perspective argue that reoffending against the same target is a rational choice?
3. What can happen during the course of a crime that "boosts" the likelihood of another crime against that target?

4. "Flags" for recurring victimization differ from crime to crime. Write a list of crimes and identify some corresponding flags for recurring victimization.

5. What types of lifestyles or routine activities might increase an individual's likelihood of recurring victimization?

6. Why do you think risk for repeat victimization dissipates over time as suggested by the time course?

References

Breitenbecher, K. H., & Gidycz, C. A. (1998). An empirical evaluation of a program designed to reduce the risk of multiple sexual victimization. *Journal of Interpersonal Violence, 13*(4), 472–488.

Clarke, R. V., & Cornish, D. (1985). Modeling offenders' decisions: A framework for research & policy. In M. Tonry & N. Morris (Eds.), *Crime & Justice: An Annual Review of Research*, vol. 6 (pp. 147–185). Chicago, IL: University of Chicago Press.

Clay-Warner, J., Bunch, J. M., & McMahon-Howard, J. (2016). Differential vulnerability: Disentangling the effects of state dependence and population heterogeneity on repeat victimization. *Criminal Justice and Behavior, 43*(10), 1406–1429.

Daigle, L. E., Fisher, B. S., & Cullen, F. T. (2008). The violent and sexual victimization of college women: Is repeat victimization a problem? *Journal of Interpersonal Violence, 23*(9), 1296–1313.

Farrell, G., Phillips, C., & Pease, K. (1995). Like taking candy – why does repeat victimization occur? *British Journal of Criminology, 35*(3), 384–399.

Farrell, G., Tseloni, A., & Pease, K. (2005). Repeat victimization in the ICVS and the NCVS. *Crime Prevention and Community Safety, 7*(3), 7–18.

Fattah, E. A. (2000). Victimology: Past, present and future. *Criminologie, 33,* 17–46.

Felson, M., & Clarke, R. V. (1998). *Opportunity makes the thief: Practical theory for crime prevention*. Police Research Series, Paper 98. London: Home Office.

Finkelhor, D., Shattuck, A., Turner, H. A., Ormrod, R., & Hamby, S. L. (2011). Polyvictimization in developmental context. *Journal of Child & Adolescent Trauma, 4*(4), 291–300.

Forrester, D., Frenz, S., O'Connell, M., & Pease, K. (1990). *The Kirkholt burglary prevention project: Phase II*. London: Home Office.

Garner, J., Fagan, J., & Maxwell, C. (1995). Published findings from the spouse assault replication program: A critical review. *Journal of Quantitative Criminology, 11*(1), 3–28.

Gottfredson, M. R., & Hirschi, T. (1990). *A general theory of crime*. Stanford, CA: Stanford University Press.

Grove, L. E., Farrell, G., Farrington, D. P., & Johnson, S. D. (2012). *Preventing repeat victimization: A systematic review*. Brottsförebyggande rådet/The Swedish National Council for Crime Prevention.

Hanson, K. A., & Gidycz, C. A. (1993). Evaluation of a sexual assault prevention program. *Journal of Consulting and Clinical Psychology, 61*(6), 1046–1052.

Hindelang, M. J., Gottfredson, M. R., & Garofalo, J. (1978). *Victims of personal crime: An empirical foundation for a theory of personal victimization*. Cambridge, MA: Ballinger.

Kennedy, L. W., & Forde, D. R. (1990). Routine activities and crime: An analysis of victimization in Canada. *Criminology, 28*(1), 137–152.

Kulig, T. C., Cullen, F. T., Wilcox, P., & Chouhy, C. (2019). Personality and adolescent school-based victimization: do the big five matter? *Journal of School Violence, 18*(2), 176–199.

Lauritsen, J. L., & Davis Quinet, K. F. (1995). Repeat victimization among adolescents and young adults. *Journal of Quantitative Criminology, 11*(2), 143–166.

Lauritsen, J. L., Sampson, R. J., & Laub, J. H. (1991). The link between offending and victimization among adolescents. *Criminology, 29*(2), 265–292.

Lauritsen, J. L., Owens, J. G., Planty, M., Rand, M. R., & Truman, J. L. (2012). *Methods for counting high-frequency repeat victimizations in the National Crime Victimization Survey*. Washington, DC: Bureau of Justice Statistics.

Madero-Hernandez, A., Lee, Y., Wilcox, P., & Fisher, B. S. (2022). Following their lead: Police perceptions and their effects on crime prevention. *Justice Quarterly, 39*(2), 327–353.

Mendelsohn, B. (1963). The origin of the doctrine of victimology. *Exerpta Criminologica, 3*, 239–245.

Morgan, R. E., & Thompson, A. (2021). *Criminal victimization, 2020* (NCJ 301775). Washington, DC: Bureau of Justice Statistics.

Oudekerk, B. A., & Truman, J. L. (2017). *Repeat violent victimization, 2005–14* (NCJ 250567). Washington, DC: Bureau of Justice Statistics.

Ousey, G. C., Wilcox, P., & Brummel, S. (2008). Déjà vu all over again: Investigating temporal continuity of adolescent victimization. *Journal of Quantitative Criminology, 24*(3), 307–335.

Pease, K., & Farrell, G. (2017). Repeat victimisation. In R. Wortley & M. Townsley (Eds), *Environmental Criminology and Crime Analysis* (pp. 180–198). London and New York: Routledge.

Polvi, N., Looman, T., Humphries, C., & Pease, K. (1991). The time course of repeat burglary victimization. *The British Journal of Criminology, 31*(4), 411–414.

Pratt, T. C., Turanovic, J. J., Fox, K. A., & Wright, K. A. (2014). Self-control and victimization: A meta-analysis. *Criminology, 52*(1), 87–116.

Reiss, A. J. (1980). Victim proneness in repeat victimization by type of crime. In S. E. Fienberg & A. J. Reiss (Eds), *Indicators of crime and criminal justice: Quantitative studies* (pp. 41–53). Washington, DC: U.S. Department of Justice.

Reyns, B. W., Randa, R., & Henson, B. (2016). Preventing crime online: Identifying determinants of online preventive behaviors using structural equation modeling and canonical correlation analysis. *Crime Prevention and Community Safety, 18*, 38–59.

Sampson, R. J., & Wooldredge, J. D. (1987). Linking the micro-and macro-level dimensions of lifestyle-routine activity and opportunity models of predatory victimization. *Journal of Quantitative Criminology, 3*(4), 371–393.

Schafer, S. (1977). *Victimology: The victim and his criminal*. Reston, VA: Reston Publishing Company.

Schreck, C. J. (1999). Criminal victimization and low self-control: An extension and test of a general theory of crime. *Justice Quarterly, 16*(3), 633–654.

Schreck, C. J., Berg, M. T., Fisher, B. S., & Wilcox, P. (2018). That door you just kicked in was locked for your protection, not mine: Developing and testing competing theoretical models of crime prevention behavior. *Journal of Research in Crime and Delinquency, 55*(2), 316–345.

Sherman, L. W., & Berk, R. A. (1984). The specific deterrent effects of arrest for domestic assault. *American Sociological Review*, 49(2), 261–272.

Snyder, J. A., Scherer, H. L., & Fisher, B. S. (2021). Poly-victimization among female college students: Are the risk factors the same as those who experience one type of victimization? *Violence Against Women*, 27(10), 1716–1735.

Spano, R., & Freilich, J. D. (2009). An assessment of the empirical validity and conceptualization of individual level multivariate studies of lifestyle/routine activities theory published from 1995 to 2005. *Journal of Criminal Justice*, 37(3), 305–314.

Tseloni, A., & Pease, K. (2003). Repeat personal victimization. "Boosts" or "Flags"? *British Journal of Criminology*, 43(1), 196–212.

Turanovic, J. J., & Pratt, T. C. (2014). "Can't stop, won't stop": Self-control, risky lifestyles, and repeat victimization. *Journal of Quantitative Criminology*, 30(1), 29–56.

Vaske, J., Boisvert, D., & Wright, J. P. (2012). Genetic and environmental contributions to the relationship between violent victimization and criminal behavior. *Journal of Interpersonal Violence*, 27(16), 3213–3235.

Von Hentig, H. (1940). Remarks on the interaction of perpetrator and victim. *Journal of Criminal Law and Criminology*, 31(3), 303–309.

Weisel, D. L. (2005). *Analyzing repeat victimization*. US Department of Justice, Office of Community Oriented Policing Services. https://popcenter.asu.edu/content/tool-guides-tools-6

Widom, C. S., Czaja, S. J., & Dutton, M. A. (2008). Childhood victimization and lifetime revictimization. *Child Abuse & Neglect*, 32(8), 785–796.

Wittebrood, K., & Nieuwbeerta, P. (2000). Criminal victimization during one's life course: The effects of previous victimization and patterns of routine activities. *Journal of Research in Crime and Delinquency*, 37(1), 91–122.

Wolfgang, M. E. (1958). *Patterns in criminal homicide*. New York: John Wiley & Sons.

Part 3
Crime Prevention Application

Chapter 9
Understanding Crime Problems

Understanding Crime Problems

Heidi Scherer

Chapter Outline

In this chapter, we will focus on:

Crime Prevention Initiatives within Law Enforcement

- Benefits and limitations of police-led crime prevention efforts
- Measuring police effectiveness

Crime Prevention in Modern Policing

- Standard model of policing
- Community-oriented policing
- Problem-oriented policing
- Broken windows policing
- Intelligence-led policing

Police Technologies for Crime Prevention

- Primary technologies that police use to implement crime prevention
- Ethical concerns with police use of technologies

Learning Objectives

After reading this chapter, you should be able to:

9.1 Identify the strengths and weaknesses of police-led crime prevention efforts
9.2 Describe how police effectiveness is assessed
9.3 Compare and contrast crime prevention strategies across the five primary models of policing
9.4 Describe police technologies and evaluate their effectiveness at preventing crime

DOI: 10.4324/9781003401551-12

Introduction

In modern-day society, local law enforcement engages in a wide variety of roles and responsibilities. These roles include activities such as enforcing laws, investigating crimes, apprehending and detaining suspects, and traffic enforcement, in addition to activities related to maintaining order and providing services to the public, such as responding to emergencies and community engagement (Skogan & Frydl, 2004). While the enforcement of laws is often defined as the *primary* role of the police, it is important to recognize that most police officers in the United States also engage in activities focused on the prevention of crime, with crime prevention activities also being viewed as a central aspect of the police role in society. For instance, a study on police from the United States found that approximately 90 percent of police officers perceived being a "protector" as one of their primary roles in society, while almost 70 percent of individuals in the public viewed protection as a central role of the police (Morin et al., 2017). Underscoring this focus on preventing crime, the majority of U.S. police academies report providing new police recruits with training and instruction on components of effective crime prevention, such as problem-solving (75 percent) and community building (77 percent) (Buehler, 2021); while among police departments in jurisdictions of 100,000 or more residents, 95 percent report having designated personnel for crime analysis – a key element for crime prevention activities (Goodison, 2022). Together, these statistics accentuate the fact that both the public and police agencies perceive that the engagement in crime prevention activities is a fundamental expectation of the modern police agency.

Although altering victim crime-reporting practices and the criminological factors that shape crime are beyond the scope of what we can reasonably expect the police to address, as this chapter aims to highlight, if guided by crime prevention theory and armed with an understanding of criminal opportunity, there are many promising ways that police can engage in proactive activities to prevent and reduce crime. To meet this end, this chapter aims to explore crime prevention initiatives within modern law enforcement and the various data sources and measures that are used to evaluate the effectiveness of police. This chapter also examines different models of policing and the types and effectiveness of the crime prevention strategies that are associated with the models, as well as police technologies that are used in the fight against crime.

Crime Prevention Initiatives within Law Enforcement

Benefits and Limitations of Police-Led Crime Prevention Efforts

There are several characteristics of the police that are advantageous for conducting crime prevention-related activities. As the "gatekeepers" of the criminal justice system and the primary responders to crime incidents, local police agencies have access to a wide range of crime data, in their record systems, that can be used to identify crime problems in their jurisdictions and inform potential interventions to reduce and prevent crime. Given their patrol functions in society, police officers also have high visibility to, and frequent interaction with, members of their community, which provide the police with the opportunity to receive feedback from the public on crime concerns and form relationships with community members. This visibility to, and frequent interaction with, the public can play a vital role in devising and implementing effective crime solutions. As a part of the government, the police also have access to a variety of resources (e.g., monetary, equipment, personnel, etc.) and existing inter-agency relationships that can support and facilitate crime prevention efforts. A particularly unique aspect of police that lends itself to crime prevention involves their power to use coercive force and the ability to threaten sanctions and legal actions to encourage compliance with policies and programs focused on reducing crime (Skogan & Frydl, 2004).

While the above features of policework support law enforcements' efforts to engage in crime prevention activities, on the other hand, there are also characteristics of crime itself that pose challenges for police agencies as they work to prevent crime in their communities. Recall from Chapter 1 that the central aspect of crime prevention is that it is **proactive** in nature and involves efforts to stop or reduce crime *before* it occurs. In contrast, policework is highly **reactive** in nature, meaning that the police most frequently respond to criminal incidents either *during or after* the commission of a crime. Typically, police respond to a call for service from a member of the public who has witnessed suspicious or criminal behavior or who has been a crime victim. Or, officers may observe the commission of a crime firsthand such as witnessing a driver suspected to be under the influence of drugs or alcohol. In fact, it is important to note that the majority of crime goes unreported to the police. Also, for certain types of victimizations, if reported, the police may not become immediately aware of the crime incident until some time has passed, once victims are ready to disclose their experiences to others (e.g., sexual violence, domestic violence, child abuse) or become aware that they have been victims of crime (e.g., identity theft). To illustrate, it is estimated that in 2021, only 31 percent of all property and 46 percent of all violent victimizations in the United States were reported to the police by victims (Thompson & Tapp, 2022). Therefore, the very nature of standard policework as a dominantly reactive process poses a notable – but as we will learn in this chapter not insurmountable – challenge for crime prevention carried out by law enforcement.

Just as the nature of policework can present obstacles for law enforcement-led crime prevention practices, so too does the nature of criminal offending. For instance, decades of criminological research provide overwhelming evidence that the factors that shape criminality such as the economy, family and educational characteristics, and antisocial personalities are well beyond the purview of the police (Manning, 1978; Lilly et al., 2018). Therefore, although police have positioned themselves as "crime fighters," Manning (1978) describes this as an "impossible mandate" as police are quite limited in their ability to impact the primary predictors of criminal offending. In fact, even individuals in the general public perceive the main causes of crime outside the control of police (Gabbidon & Boisvert, 2012). Yet, despite this, the public still expresses support for crime prevention actions, such as elevated police spending during times of increased crime rates or crime-related concerns (Parker & Hurst, 2021). These findings underscore the public's belief in the role of police in our society to act as protectors and prevent crime from occurring.

Measuring Police Effectiveness

> To recognize always that the test of police efficiency is the absence of crime and disorder, and not the visible evidence of police action in dealing with them.
>
> – Sir Robert Peel's Policing Principle #9

Since the development of formalized policing, evaluating the effectiveness of the police has been a central focus of consideration. In fact, in his Nine Principles of Policing, Sir Robert Peel specifically addressed the measurement of police effectiveness by asserting that the amount of crime and disorder can be used to assess whether the police were effective at carrying out their role in society (Law Enforcement Action Partnership, 2021). Over 200 years later, official crime statistics still remain the central way by which police agencies are assessed. Specifically, there are four primary measures of **police effectiveness** that are used to gauge police productivity (Alpert & Moore, 1998).

The first of these measures includes crime rates. A **crime rate** is a measure that reflects how much crime is known to the police for a jurisdiction (i.e., the numerator) that is standardized by the total population of the area (i.e., the denominator), typically per 100,000 people (FBI, 2023). Because crime rates are standardized, they can be compared across the same jurisdiction over time or across different jurisdictions (e.g., cities, states, counties) to examine crime trends and patterns. The second primary measure of police effectiveness is **response times**, which pertains to the amount of time it takes for police to respond to the scene after being notified that a crime has occurred or is in progress.

The third primary measure of police effectiveness is **arrest rates**. An arrest rate is a measure that reflects how many arrests were made for offenses in a jurisdiction. Like crime rates, arrest rates are also standardized by the total population of an area, which allows these rates to be compared over time and across locations. **Clearance rates** are the last primary measure of police effectiveness. Clearance rates are measures that reflect the number of offenses that have been closed by law enforcement through either an arrest or by exceptional means (FBI, 2023). A clearance by exceptional means occurs when factors outside of the control of law enforcement prevent them from being able to file charges against the perpetrator (FBI, 2023). Together, these four measures provide law enforcement agencies and communities with metrics that can be used to gauge the effectiveness of police practices and to evaluate how successful the police are at achieving their roles in society, particularly related to the control and prevention of crime. For instance, a police department may be viewed as effective if their jurisdiction has low crime rates, the department has quick response times, and the department has high arrest and clearance rates.

It is important to note that while these four measures are standard in the assessment of police effectiveness, some policing scholars have cautioned against relying too heavily on these measures alone to evaluate the effectiveness of the police. For instance, given that many of the factors that shape crime rates are beyond the control of police, using crime rates as a measure of effectiveness may not provide the most valid means to assess the performance of police (Manning, 1978). To improve how communities evaluate the police, Alpert and Moore (1998) recommend expanding measures of police performance to also include measures of specific activities in which police engage, such as community engagement and problem-solving. Moore and Braga (2003) also suggest evaluating police performance using measures from multiple different dimensions of policework related to the public's expectations for the police, including measures of crime, safety, civility, and offender accountability, but also the appropriate use of resources, force, and authority.

Given that most police departments engage in a variety of activities while carrying out their roles in society, using a diverse array of measures to gauge police performance should provide communities with a varied amount of information that can be used to evaluate the effectiveness of their police departments. This is especially true for the evaluation of police-led crime prevention activities, where measures related to crime and disorder, fear and perceptions of safety, community engagement, proactive operations, and resource allocation may all provide value insights into the effectiveness of police efforts.

Crime Prevention in Modern Policing

As Chapter 1 discussed, the foundations of crime prevention in modern-day policing were being laid in the mid-1700 and 1800s through early forms of policing, such as Henry Fielding's Bow Street Runners and Sir Robert Peel's London Metropolitan Police Department, also known as the "London

Bobbies" (Britannica, 2022). While there have been many advances in policing and changes to society that have occurred over the last 200 years, since the origins of modern policing, key components of these early policing initiatives and Peel's Nine Principles of Policing remain relevant to crime prevention today. These include efforts related to deterring crime through the presence or specific activities of law enforcement officers, responding quickly to crime incidents, and building rapport with the public (Law Enforcement Action Partnership, 2021).

As we will explore further in this section, modern-day crime prevention efforts have been strongly shaped by advances in police technologies, growth in research and data analysis on police effectiveness, and societal changes. Over time, different models of policing have emerged, each with their own specific focuses, goals, and techniques for preventing crime. Below, we will explore these different models of policing, giving particular focus to the types of crime prevention efforts that fall under each model and the empirical evidence related to the effectiveness of these techniques.

Standard Model of Policing

The **standard model of policing,** also called the traditional model of policing, is one of the most recognizable of the policing models, as it involves activities and strategies that have been central to policing for over 90 years (Kelling & Moore, 1988; Telep & Weisburd, 2012). This model aims to prevent and control crime through strategies that rely on allocating police resources or the deterrence of crime through the presence of police and increased enforcement activities (Skogan & Frydl, 2004). Specifically, Weisburd and Eck (2004) have identified five primary strategies that are central to the standard model of policing. These include: 1) increasing the size of law enforcement agencies; 2) community-wide randomized patrol; 3) quick response times to calls for service; 4) criminal investigations; and 5) strict enforcement of laws and application of arrest policies (Weisburd & Eck, 2004). Given that the standard model focuses on the use of these techniques widely across jurisdictions – regardless of the level of crime or specific crime problems – Weisburd and Eck (2004) have labelled this model as a "one-size-fits-all" approach (p. 44). In addition, the standard model has been described as taking a more insular approach to crime control and prevention by relying predominantly on law enforcement to carry out the different strategies with limited input or partnerships with non-police organizations.

While the primary strategies of the standard model have been employed since early modern policing, evidence that demonstrates the effectiveness of this model on the prevention and reduction of crime has been mixed. In one of the most famous criminal justice experiments, Kelling and colleagues (1974) examined the effectiveness of preventive patrol by researching how different police patrol schemes impacted measures of crime and the public's fear of crime in Kansas City, Missouri. From their analysis, they found that there were no significant differences in the levels of crime and citizens' fear of crime or satisfaction with police across beats with standard levels of patrol, increased level of patrols, or no routine patrol. Findings from this landmark study have been used to inform police practices for decades, particularly by providing support for approaches that reallocate police effort from patrol to other, more proactive crime prevention activities (Telep et al., 2016). However, it is important to note that emerging research, including a reanalysis of Kelling et al.'s (1974) data, indicates that preventive patrol may in fact lead to minor impacts on crime rates, yet these impacts are modest in comparison with those observed for targeted patrol strategies such as hotspot policing (Weisburd et al., 2023).

Expand Your Understanding – The Kansas City Preventive Patrol Experiment

In 1974, Kelling, Pate, Dieckman, and Brown published findings from their landmark research experiment that examined the impact that different police patrol schemes had on measures of crime and public perceptions of crime and the police.

Methodology: To examine how the visibility and presence of police may impact crime and public perceptions, the researchers assigned one of three patrol schemes to 15 beats in Kansas City. Using crime and demographic characteristic data for each area, the researchers matched the 15 beats into 5 groups comprising 3 beats to be assigned as reactive, proactive, or control.

- In reactive beats, there were *no patrol activities* and officers only entered the area to respond to calls for service.
- In proactive beats, there was an *increase in patrol activities* with the amount of police patrol in the area two to three times its normal level.
- In control beats, there was *no change in patrol activities* with the amount of police patrol in the area maintained at the normal level.

Analysis and Findings: Before, during, and after the experiment, the researchers collected data from multiple sources to gather information on crime and victimization, police response times, and public attitudes and experiences. This data was analyzed in each of the experimental beats to examine the effectiveness of police patrol. Based on this analysis, Kelling and colleagues (1974) found no significant differences in the rates of crime

Three Patrol Schemes for the Fifteen Experimental Police Beats

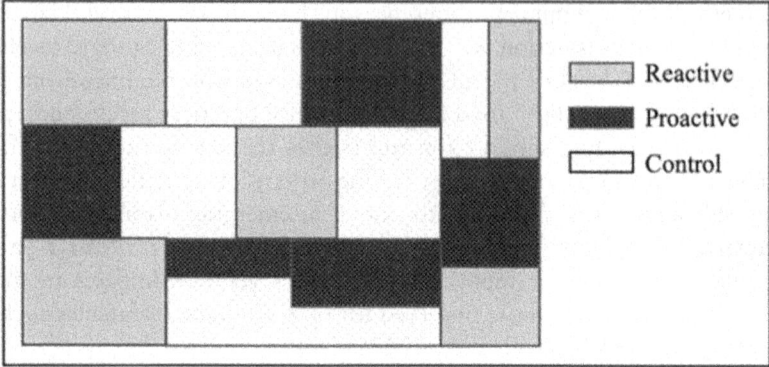

or citizens' fear of crime, satisfaction with police, and attitudes toward the police across the three patrol schemes.

Policy Implications: The results from this landmark study had a substantial impact on the police practices moving forward as it redirected focus on allocating police resources away from the preventive patrol of all areas to more proactive approaches that increase police activities at known crime problems and places with higher concentrations of crime (Telep et al., 2016).

Research examining the crime prevention effects from increasing the size of law enforcement agencies also indicates limited impacts on crime. For instance, comprehensive analyses of prior research examining the relationship between police levels and crime found evidence that the size of the police force had only minor impact on crime, with evidence of only a small inverse relationship (Lee et al., 2016; Carriaga & Worrall, 2015). While rapid response to calls for service is one of the standard model's central strategies, few studies have examined if quick responses to crime produce any reductions in crime, which limits our understanding of whether rapid response may impact crime (Skogan & Frydl, 2004). However, of note, there is evidence that decreasing response times may lead to significant increases in clearance rates as officers are better able to apprehend offenders and interview key witnesses, underscoring that this standard model strategy has the potential to lead to improvements in crime measures (Blanes i Vidal & Kirchmaier, 2018).

Another key strategy of the standard model involves the use of criminal investigations and detective work. In theory, investigation-focused work should lead to the apprehension and arrest of offenders, which in turn should produce both a deterrent and an incapacitation effect on crime

(Eck & Rossmo, 2019). However, a major limitation to this strategy involves national statistics which indicate that just 12 percent of property crimes and 32 percent of violent crimes were cleared through arrest in 2021 (Bureau of Justice Statistics, 2023). Further highlighting some substantial challenges to the effectiveness of this strategy, Eck and Rossmo (2019) report that clearance rates have been decreasing over time, despite technological advances in investigatory tools that should have led to improvements, not declines, in crime resolution. Therefore, while criminal investigation is an important aspect of policework, evidence does not indicate that detective work in and of itself has led to reductions in crime (Eck & Rossmo, 2019).

The final strategy of the standard model involves the enforcement and application of laws and policies. One such policy includes mandatory arrest for domestic violence, which is hypothesized to lead to crime reductions by reducing repeat offending by domestic violence perpetrators. However, contrary to expectations, prior research on these policies does not provide evidence of a deterrent effect of mandatory arrest or a reduction in domestic violence recidivism (Hoppe et al., 2020).

Despite being one of the most common policing models used in the United States, prior research has not shown overwhelming empirical evidence to support that the primary strategies of the standard model have substantial impacts on crime rates. This lack of effectiveness may be due to the generic nature of the standard model where policing strategies are applied similarly across entire jurisdictions, despite the fact that there are variations in rates of crime and disorder in communities (Weisburd & Eck, 2004). In fact, this characteristic has been central to researchers' critiques that the standard model would be more effective if police resources were used to focus on specific crime problems such as the targeted patrol of known hotspots (Weisburd & Eck, 2004) or to provide police with additional skills and knowledge to enhance their investigations and better understand criminogenic factors that shape crime patterns and offending (Eck & Rossmo, 2019).

Community-Oriented Policing

The **community-oriented policing** (COP) model emerged as a dominant philosophy of policing in the mid-1980s. The COP model gained prominence across the United States following a period in society during the 1960s and 1970s characterized by civil unrest, rising crime rates, and wide divides between the police and the public (Kelling & Moore, 1988). Along with societal and political characteristics that contributed to tensions between the police and their communities, during this time there was also criminological research emerging that raised questions about the effectiveness of primary police practices such as the Kansas City Preventive

Patrol Study (Gill et al., 2014). Together, these events propelled police departments to seek a new approach to combatting crime and disorder in their communities, particularly one that moved the police away from the insular methods of the standard model to one that actively seeks input from, and builds partnerships with, the communities they serve (Greene, 2000).

According to Cordner (2014), while the definition of COP often varies across populations, there are four primary dimensions of this model that provide a detailed description of how COP is practiced in police departments and aims to prevent crime. The first dimension is the *philosophical dimension*, which is composed of the three main tenets of COP, including a focus on citizen input, broadening the police role beyond law enforcement activities, and personalized service. The second dimension is the *strategic dimension*, which focuses on the strategies and operations used to carry out COP. These include altering operations to reduce the use of ineffective practices and increase practices that support targeted patrols and in-person interactions, emphasizing the prevention of crime, and focusing operations at the geographic level to build up officer knowledge and bonds to an area. The third dimension, the *tactical dimension*, includes the tactics used to carry out COP strategies such as engaging in activities in the community that promote positive interactions and experiences, developing partnerships with community members and non-police organizations, and engaging in problem-solving activities. The final dimension, the *organizational dimension*, describes the structural characteristics of police departments that support COP activities. These include decentralizing the police organizational and management structure to support greater officer discretion and compiling information from multiple sources (e.g., community surveys, crime data) to inform decision making (Cordner, 2014).

Specific examples of COP strategies employed by police departments with the goals to prevent crime and improve relationships in their community include community newsletters, the use of patrol strategies that increase interaction with citizens – such as foot, bicycle, or horse patrol – permanent assignment of officers to geographic locations, partnerships with businesses, and citizen surveys (Zhao et al., 2001). One of the most longstanding and well-known crime prevention programs implemented under the COP model is the National Neighborhood Watch (NNW) Program, which was developed in 1972 by the National Sheriff's Association with funding assistance from the U.S. Department of Justice (NNW, 2023). Through the NNW program, local law enforcement personnel partner with members of communities to develop and train NNW groups to identify safety concerns in their communities and take an active role in reducing crime. Underscoring the longevity of this program, it is estimated that there are approximately 25,000 active NNW groups working with over 5,000 local police agencies across the United States (NNW, 2023).

A review of past research examining the effectiveness of the COP model provides evidence that efforts to build partnerships and incorporate communities into policing can have beneficial impacts. For instance, Gill and colleagues (2014) conducted a systematic review of 25 COP studies that examined community-policing tactics and found that COP led to improvements in perceptions among the public, such as citizen satisfaction with police and police legitimacy. However, in contrast, the researchers found limited evidence that COP had significant impacts on measures of crime or fear on crime. In contrast, an updated review of 60 studies of COP found evidence that community policing programs led to significant decreases in citizens' fear of crime and measures of crime including burglary, robbery, and gun-related offenses, yet did not appear to impact measures of disorder or drug sales (Ekici et al., 2022). Together, results from these systematic reviews demonstrate that COP's impacts on crime have been mixed but that there is evidence that this model can lead to positive reductions in crime.

There are both strengths and weaknesses of the COP model for the prevention of crime. One of the advantages of COP is that it allows police departments to implement and develop crime prevention strategies that best match the needs and interests of the communities they serve. Therefore, in contrast to the standard model of policing, COP can be less generic and more personalized to a community (Greene, 2000). However, on the other hand, the customizable nature of the COP model can also be a challenge as its implementation can vary quite substantially across locations, making it difficult for police administrators and researchers to identify the specific types and amounts of community policing practices that can lead to a decrease in crime (Gill et al., 2014). Gill and colleagues (2014) assert that the lack of strong empirical evidence for the COP model may be due to the lack of a clear theoretical link between the activities of the COP model – particularly police–citizen partnerships – and measures of crime as this model emerged with the focus on primarily improving relationships between law enforcement and the public.

Problem-Oriented Policing

In 1979, Herman Goldstein introduced the idea for a new model of policing that focused police efforts on identifying and solving crime in communities. This model is referred to as the **problem-oriented policing** (POP) model. Similar to the emergence of community policing, Goldstein's conception of the POP model was also influenced by research surfacing in the late 1970s that indicated a lack of effectiveness for some of the central strategies of the standard model of policing, such as preventive patrol and criminal investigations (1979). In turn, Goldstein aimed to lay the foundation for a new, proactive way for police officers to approach crime prevention, one that focuses on the end result of policing – addressing problems. According to Goldstein (1979), problems comprise the "essence of police work" and refer to "the incredibly broad range of troublesome situations that prompt citizens to turn to police," including different types of crimes, accidents and emergencies, nuisances, and fears of crime or safety concerns (p. 242). In fact, from Goldstein's perspective, the existence of these problems, and the subsequent need for them to be addressed in communities, are why police agencies exist.

A central aspect of POP is that it aims to resolve crime problems by first identifying the underlying social or environmental factors that are contributing to reoccurring crime incidents, and second, attempting to alter those factors to block the opportunity for the crime to reoccur (Braga, 2008). One of the most common methods police use to conduct problem-solving is the SARA model, which provides a systematic process by which to identify and solve crime problems. This process involves *scanning* (S) a community to identify crime problems, *analysis* (A) of a crime problem to identify the underlying causes, creating and implementing a *response* (R) to the crime problem, and *assessment* of the intervention to determine if it was effective (A). (See Chapter 11 for a detailed discussion and application of the SARA model; Eck and Spelman, 1987.) Although building community partnerships is not a specific focus of POP, officer engagement, particularly with stakeholders such as residents, business owners, and other public organizations/agencies, can be extremely valuable for departments involved in POP as it can strengthen the problem-solving process by providing officers direct feedback on the existence, etiology, and potential solutions of crime problems (Braga, 2008). Because POP involves a proactive focus on solving reoccurring crime problems, other proactive policing strategies are often associated with POP, including hotspot policing, situational crime prevention, and focused deterrence strategies, which utilize innovative police approaches to reduce specific crime problems through increasing risk of apprehension for certain offenders.

Another aspect of POP that makes it unique from other policing models is that while the methods for problem-solving (e.g., SARA, situational crime prevention) may be applied similarly both within and across jurisdictions, the actual interventions that police employ to address problems can vary widely. For instance, interventions to reduce open air drug sales will likely involve the use of different crime prevention tools from those used for reducing shoplifting from bodegas. Due to the diversity of interventions that are derived from the POP framework, systematic reviews of POP focus on analyzing the *processes* police used to develop and implement crime prevention interventions and not the specific tactics being employed (Weisburd et al., 2010). From analyses of studies using the SARA model and problem-solving methods a stable finding has emerged – POP-based approaches are effective at reducing crime and disorder (Hinkle et al., 2020; Weisburd et al., 2010).

However, due to inconsistent results from only a small number of studies, it is unclear whether POP is effective at reducing other outcomes such as police legitimacy, fear of crime, and collective efficacy (Hinkle et al., 2020). Underscoring the effectiveness of problem-solving approaches, POP-related police tactics such as hotspot policing (Braga et al., 2019) and focused deterrence strategies (Braga & Weisburd, 2012) have also been found to lead to reductions in crime and disorder.

One of the primary strengths of the POP model is that it provides police departments with the ability to make meaningful changes in their communities to reduce crime and disorder by applying a standard methodology that can be used to devise tailored, problem-specific interventions. In fact, this unique characteristic specifically reflects Goldstein's original intentions in creating POP as a departure from the "one-size-fits-all" approach of the standard model of policing (1979). Another strength of POP is grounded in a strong theoretical foundation and informed by crime prevention theories such as routine activities theory, situational crime prevention, and Crime Prevention through Environmental Design (CPTED) – each of which has been found to be valuable in understanding the extent and nature of crime problems (Braga, 2008).

On the other hand, there are some limitations to the POP model, particularly related to its implementation in police departments. For instance, because detailed training on problem-solving tactics is typically not included in the curriculum of all police academies, departments interested in utilizing POP practices must provide their own training to police administration and officers to provide them with more a more advanced skillset and knowledge on the theories and methodologies that inform POP (Scott, 2000). Further, because POP activities can be perceived by inexperienced officers as requiring more effort and time than traditional police activities such as preventive patrol, officer buy-in may take time to build as they become more experienced and knowledgeable on implementing POP (Scott, 2006).

Broken Windows Policing

In the 1980s, **broken windows policing**, also referred to as order maintenance policing and quality-of-life policing, emerged as a new police approach for crime prevention. The emergence of this model was influenced by the 1982 publication of George L. Kelling and James Q. Wilson's **broken windows theory**, which hypothesized that disorder in a neighborhood has a direct causal relationship to crime by initiating a social process among residents that allows crime to emerge in a community. Specifically, Kelling and Wilson's (1982) theory posits that when social and physical disorder (e.g., graffiti, liter, drug paraphernalia, etc.) appear in a neighborhood it can lead residents to become fearful and to leave the neighborhood or engage in avoidance behaviors to limit their exposure to public spaces. In turn, when law-abiding residents retreat from public spaces, Kelling and Wilson (1982) assert that it can lead to a breakdown of the informal social controls that help to regulate community behavior which, when weakened, attracts crime and offenders in a neighborhood (see Figure 9.1). Therefore, drawing from this theory, and the hypothesis that disorder can provide the context for more serious crime problems to flourish, broken windows policing aims to prevent disorder and disrupt the cycle that permits crime from taking hold in a community.

In practice, broken windows policing typically involves the targeted enforcement of disorder-related crimes and misdemeanor offenses. These activities often include officers visibly enforcing laws and making citations or arrests for minor crimes, such as panhandling, loitering, jaywalking, public alcohol use, and vagrancy. Through the focused enforcement of minor offenses, police aim to send the signal to potential criminals that the neighborhood is being cared for, while also encouraging residents to stay engaged in the community and to not withdrawal into private spaces. In some communities, broken windows policing practices have been implemented by law enforcement in a way that deviates substantially from the original intentions of Kelling and Wilson (1982), by incorporating the strict enforcement of lower-level offenses and/or the frequent use of stop-and-frisks of individuals in a neighborhood to try to identify law violations (Weisburd et al., 2010). These derivations of the broken windows model have been referred to as aggressive order maintenance policing and zero-tolerance policing, as they tend to be strictly enforced with officers applying the law through formal means (e.g., citations, arrest) rather than using their discretion to resolve incidents informally (e.g., warning).

While broken windows policing sets itself apart from the other policing models in its theoretical foundation and specific crime prevention strategies, interventions based on the broken windows model often utilize elements of community-oriented policing and problem-oriented policing, such as partnerships with community members to address disorder or focusing police efforts on reoccurring disorder at hotspots (Braga et al., 2015). From their review of 20 studies that had implemented broken windows-related community and/or problem-solving strategies to address disorder problems,

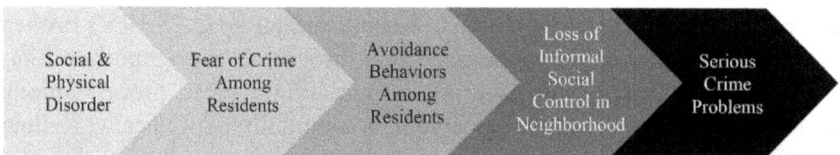

| Social & Physical Disorder | Fear of Crime Among Residents | Avoidance Behaviors Among Residents | Loss of Informal Social Control in Neighborhood | Serious Crime Problems |

Figure 9.1 Broken Windows Theory – The Hypothesized Impact of Disorder on Crime.

Source: Kelling and Wilson, 1982.

Braga and colleagues (2015) found that police-based disorder interventions were quite effective at reducing violent, property, drug, and disorder crimes. On the other hand, not all prior research provides evidence of such promising findings. For instance, from their randomized experiment of a broken windows intervention, Weisburd et al. (2010) observed no significant impacts on central measures from this policing model such as citizens' fear of crime and perceptions of the crime and social and physical disorder in their community, neighborhood collective efficacy, and police legitimacy. Further, variations of broken windows such as aggressive order maintenance and zero-tolerance policing have not been found to produce any meaningful impacts on crime (Braga et al. 2015; Harcourt & Ludwig, 2007).

There are both strengths and weaknesses of the broken windows policing model. As research indicates, when disorder-focused interventions are coupled with established and empirically validated strategies of the COP and POP models, it holds promise of reducing a wide range of crime types and thus can be a valuable tool in the police toolkit for preventing crime. However, police administration should take caution in employing broken windows tactics in aggressive order maintenance or zero-tolerance forms that limit officer discretion as they have not been found to have any notable impacts on crime (Braga et al., 2015). In fact, it has been noted by many scholars that aggressive broken windows tactics can have substantial negative impacts in communities, particularly in communities of color, where disproportionate formal enforcement of minor offenses and/or the frequent use of baseless stop-and-frisk practices can erode police–community relations and lead to a variety of consequences and costs to individuals resulting from a formal arrest for a minor offense (Harcourt & Ludwig, 2007; Howell, 2009). Moreover, Hinkle and Weisburd (2008) note that broken windows policing interventions may lead to varied impacts on citizens' fear of crime and have the potential to both decrease and increase fear of crime as the visibility of police crackdowns may cause some residents to perceive that crime is a problem in their community. In turn, they recommend that police departments implementing broken windows interventions should anticipate this possibility and make efforts to communicate with community members to reduce increasing citizens' fear of crime.

Intelligence-Led Policing

Intelligence-led policing (ILP) is a model of policing that emerged in the 1990s in the United Kingdom and gained increased attention in the United States following the September 11, 2001, terrorist attacks (Carter & Carter, 2009). As its name implies, ILP focuses on gathering crime intelligence to inform decision making, strategic planning, and resource allocation related to the prevention of crime and known or emerging public safety threats

(Carter & Carter, 2009). A central aspect of the ILP model is that it empha-sizes sharing information and crime intelligence across multiple police departments at local, state, and federal levels, and external private and pub-lic agencies to address the multijurisdictional nature of crime and public safety threats, particularly for organized crimes and criminal enterprises such as drug and gun sales, terrorism, human trafficking, and retail theft (Carter & Carter, 2009). According to Ratcliffe (2010), in ILP, patterns in intelligence data are identified and analyzed with the goal of proactivity and the prediction and prevention of future crimes.

Similar to COP, the implementation and adoption of ILP by individual police departments can vary substantially based on their agency mission, resource availability, and community crime patterns and problems (Carter & Phillips, 2015). Yet, despite these differences, there are similarities in crime prevention tactics utilized across agencies with elements of both POP and COP being incorporated into ILP practices. For instance, ILP tactics often involve problem-solving processes such as scanning communities for crime problems and applying theory to understand criminal opportunity. Further, in ILP, partnerships and strong relationships with the public are valuable for two-way communication where police inform the community of public threats and work to reduce fear of crime, and the public inform the police of suspicious activity or crime intelligence (Carter & Carter, 2009; Carter & Phillips, 2015). However, in contrast to the POP and COP models, while line-level officers can be responsible for some intelligence gathering, decision making and strategic planning are largely done by senior police staff and management who are most thoroughly informed on the intelli-gence collected and shared by multiple internal or external units (Ratcliffe, 2010).

Unlike other models of policing, there is a lack of systemic studies or comprehensive reviews that have specifically examined the effectiveness of ILP at preventing crime. However, given that ILP frequently incorporates elements of POP and COP – which have been found to be effective in past empirical research – there are both theoretical and empirical reasons to anticipate that ILP could lead to positive impacts on crime outcomes. In 2008, the Bureau of Justice Assistance (BJA) provided an overview of ten case studies of ILP being used in police departments in the United States to reduce crime in their communities. Across these case studies, agencies reported preliminary evidence of some promising impacts of their ILP programs, including reductions in property and violent crime, increases in information and intelligence sharing across agencies, increases in the disruption, identification, and prosecution of serial offenders and organ-ized crime gangs, increases in conviction rates, increases in weapons sei-zures, and increases in community partnerships (BJA, 2008). On the other hand, based on interviews with 50 police personnel engaged in ILP prac-tices, Ratcliffe (2005) reported that there were challenges in estimating the effectiveness of ILP, as there were variations in the implementation of this model across police units, which precludes the ability to draw firm conclusions on ILP's best practices and its potential to lead to meaningful and sustained reductions in crime.

A primary strength of the ILP model for the prevention of crime includes its incorporation of other established police and/or crime prevention practices such as problem-solving procedures, leveraging community knowledge and relationships, and analyzing crime patterns – which, as Chapters 5 and 6 demonstrated, have a vital role to play in identifying, understanding, and resolving crime problems. In addition to being data-driven, a major strength of ILP is its recognition of the multijurisdictional nature of criminality: that crime problems and threats often extend beyond one jurisdiction and its information systems and thus require cooperation and intelligence sharing with external public and private agencies. However, it is important to note that, in the United States, despite efforts to increase information sharing across agencies post 9/11 and changes in technologies that support inter-agency communications, local law enforcement remains quite fragmented. This poses some challenges to intelligence sharing as police systems that house relevant data and intelligence are often not accessible to outside agencies, and not all agencies have procedures and relationships in place to support information sharing (Carter et al., 2014). Additionally, another weakness of this model is the lack of uniformity in ILP implementation across jurisdictions that makes it difficult to establish standard procedures that can be used to train officers and departments on adopting ILP (Ratcliffe, 2005). Further, it is important to note that the success of ILP on reducing crime can vary substantially across police agencies based on the accuracy of their intelligence data as well as officer access to, and knowledge of, the tools used to gather and analyze intelligence (Burcher & Whelan, 2019).

Police Technologies for Crime Prevention

One could easily make the assertion that **police technologies** play a central role in police efforts related to the prevention and reduction of crime. Since the start of the modern-day police agency, technology has revolutionized how police have identified crime problems, responded to calls for service, patrolled their jurisdictions, and conducted investigations. In fact, in early policing, during the late nineteenth and early twentieth centuries, was the emergence of technologies that to this day remain dominant in the fight against crime. These include the telephone, the radio, the police callbox (similar to the current 9-1-1 system, this served as a direct line from the public to the police), fingerprint systems, and the police car/cruiser (Seaskate, Inc., 1998). In the twenty-first century, the law enforcement field has experienced a boom of even more improved technologies that have further influenced how the police identify and address crime problems (Byrne & Hummer, 2017). In the following section, we aim to provide an overview of some of the key technologies that police employ to prevent and reduce crime. It is important to note that this discussion of police technology is not exhaustive and, due to the rapid growth in this area, new police technologies will likely emerge by the time you finish reading this text.

Primary Technologies that Police Use to Implement Crime Prevention

Since the first police car was introduced in 1899 in Akron, Ohio, the police cruiser has experienced a substantial increase in advancement to support policework. In modern times, most police cruisers are equipped with technologies such as high-resolution, dash-board mounted cameras, license plate readers, and mobile computer stations and laptops that provide officers with real-time access to record management systems (e.g., criminal history, outstanding warrants, etc.) and GPS and map software (Byrne & Hummer, 2017). In particular, license plate readers have been found to be a valuable asset for crime prevention. For instance, studies indicate that the use of license plate readers (e.g., mounted, or fixed, cameras that can read and collect license plate numbers and data) has had positive impacts such as the reduction of drug offenses at hotspots (Koper et al., 2013) and an increased ability to detect stolen vehicles and stolen or lost license plates (Potts, 2018).

Further, when officers step out of their police cruisers to interact directly with the public, their uniforms are also frequently embedded with technologies, such as radios, to communicate with dispatch and police managers, and body-worn cameras that record interactions and observations in the field. While both the public and police appear to support the use of body-worn cameras, past research has not provided consistent evidence of their impact on police or citizen behaviors or crime outcomes (Lum et al., 2019; 2020). However, there is some promising evidence that body-worn cameras may play a valuable role in holding offenders accountable. For instance, Morrow and colleagues (2016) reported that body-worn police cameras increased arrest, prosecution, and conviction rates for intimate partner violence perpetrators.

As this chapter has discussed, crime prevention strategies implemented by the police are most effective when they are informed by crime data in the community. Most police departments utilize several different technologies to assist in crime analyses. Moreover, some of the most valuable technologies that police have at their disposal are their record management and computer-assisted dispatch systems, which contain information on police calls for service and crime data. In turn, these data can be used in geographic information system (GIS) software to identify crime patterns and hotspot analyses. As Chapter 5 discussed, the use of crime data systems and

technologies, such as GIS, to inform police practices such as hotspot policing has been shown to lead to significant reductions in crime (Braga et al.,
2019). Many police departments also utilize the CompStat (computer statistics) performance management process, which involves key police personnel and management meeting at regular intervals to examine crime data to
identify crime problems and inform decision making (BJA, 2013). Research
examining this data-informed performance management system, which has
been widely touted by the New York Police Department as central to their
efforts to decrease crime in the 1990s and 2000s, indicates that CompStat
has led to significant decreases in crime, particularly property rates (Jang
et al., 2010; Mazerolle et al., 2007).

Biometric technologies and those related to the collection and analysis of forensic evidence such as fingerprints, DNA, and facial recognition
analyses also provide police with valuable tools to carry out their roles
in society. Although, to the public, these types of technologies are most
closely associated with the trial stage of the court system, they also can be
informative for police for both the prevention of crime and the apprehension of suspects. For instance, when DNA was collected and processed by
jurisdictions, it was found to significantly increase the percentage of suspects who were identified and arrested (Roman et al., 2009). While many
biometric technologies have a lag in processing time, facial recognition
software can be used in real time to assist the police in crime prevention.
This type of technology allows police to use photographs and/or recorded
and live video feeds to identify individuals using algorithms that match
facial features from two or more photographs, including suspects of crime
or potential threats to public safety (Hill et al., 2022). In fact, if you chose
to travel through one of the over 450 airports in the United States, you may
observe, or even personally experience, Transportation Security Administration (TSA) agents using facial recognition software to assist them in
verifying the identification of travelers at security checkpoints (TSA, 2023).
While it is estimated that a large amount of federal and local police agencies has access to facial recognition software (Cipriano, 2021), there is a
lack of empirical research that sheds light on whether this technology has
led to crime reduction benefits.

Additional technologies that involve analyzing data from video surveillance are also useful tools that police can employ. Closed-circuit television,
most commonly known as CCTV, can be mounted in public spaces and
monitored by police to both identify when crimes occur and provide evidence to support arrests and convictions. In some agencies, CCTV is monitored in real time to provide police with information that can increase
apprehension of the suspect or potentially disrupt the crime from occurring.
As discussed in Chapter 4, mounted cameras also have the potential to serve
as a deterrent to crime as potential offenders may perceive an increased risk
of apprehension due to the presence of surveillance. CCTV has been widely

established as an effective crime prevention tool (Piza et al., 2019) and, specifically, when monitored directly by police, has been associated with significant decreases in property, violent, and social disorder crimes (Caplan et al., 2011; Piza et al., 2019).

Privately owned and operated surveillance has also been used as a crime prevention tool for police. For instance, with the proper warrants or permission by residents, police are able to get access to video surveillance from residential doorbell cameras that they can use to identify if there is footage that can assist in ongoing criminal investigations (Selinger & Durant, 2022). Police agencies can also employ the use of drones, or unmanned aerial vehicles, which can provide them with the ability to have video surveillance that is portable. Drone technologies can be used to support police in many functions including searching for suspects and missing persons, photographic evidence of crime scenes and vehicle accidents, and disaster relief support (Rice, 2019). Drones can also be used during large public events and locations (e.g., festivals, beaches, parks) to allow police to monitor potential safety or security concerns to support a more rapid response (Rice, 2019). As with the use of facial recognition software, while it is known that many police departments utilize technologies like drones and residential surveillance, it remains unknown whether employing these technologies has assisted police in their crime reduction efforts.

A central tenet of the COP model is increasing communication between the police and the community. In modern society, technology plays a key role in this process with police departments relying on department websites and social media platforms such as Facebook and X (formally known as Twitter) to communicate with the public. Information shared by police on social media has been found to be multifaceted, including information on crime and criminals, crime prevention tips, police–public relations, and information on police personnel (Hu et al., 2018). In addition to using social media platforms as a direct communication tool with the public, law enforcement agencies also utilize social media to carry out criminal investigations and gather intelligence (Finklea, 2022). For instance, in social network analysis, investigators can use social media to identify connections between known offenders or suspects by analyzing the content included in individuals' profiles and posts (Radil et al., 2010). The use of social media in criminal investigations has not only been found to be an effective tool for identifying connections between offenders, but also for providing evidence that can be used to support the prosecution of crime (Lane et al., 2018).

Ethical Concerns with Police Use of Technologies

Taken together, it is easy to conclude that technology plays a central role in assisting police in their efforts to prevent crime. As technologies continue to advance, it is likely that police will continue to adopt new technologies to identify crime problems and threats to public safety, communicate with the public, and investigate crimes. However, despite the positive impacts of the police use of technologies, it is it important to recognize that their use is not without limitations or ethical concerns. For instance, emerging research on facial recognition software has found that these technologies can promote racial discrimination due to racial biases such as lower matching accuracy for Black individuals and overrepresentation of minorities in facial databases (Hill et al., 2022). In addition, police use of technologies involving cameras such as residential doorbell cameras, surveillance drones, CCTV, and body-worn cameras has raised concern among the public and interest groups related to the intrusive nature of these technologies, which have the potential to encroach into individuals' rights to privacy (Byrne & Hummer, 2017). These concerns underscore that when police are deciding whether, and to what extent, to adopt certain technologies it is important that they consider how the use of these technologies may not only impact crime but also other outcomes such as privacy concerns, the accuracy of the technology, police–public relationships, and public perceptions of police legitimacy.

Summary

No component of the criminal justice system is more closely associated with the prevention of crime than the police. As this chapter has discussed, characteristics of the police, such as their visibility to the public, their resources, and their authority, can support law enforcement efforts to prevent crime. On the other hand, characteristics of crime and criminal offending can pose challenges to police-led crime prevention efforts as less than half of all crime comes to the attention of the police and the causes of crime are largely outside of the control of law enforcement. However, despite the fact that much policework is reactionary in nature, as this chapter has demonstrated, in the police toolkit there are several proactive strategies that police can employ to effectively prevent and reduce crime and disorder.

Specifically, when guided by knowledge of criminal opportunity and understanding of their community crime problems, evidence-based practices such as community policing (Ekici et al., 2022), problem-oriented policing and the application of the SARA model (Hinkle et al., 2020), hotspot policing (Braga et al., 2019), and focused deterrence strategies (Braga & Weisburd, 2012) have all been found in comprehensive reviews of prior research to have led to meaningful reductions in crime. Further, advances in technology can play a vital role in assisting police in their crime prevention efforts by increasing their ability to communicate with the public, identify crime problems and public safety threats, conduct investigations, and collect evidence to support arrests and convictions. As police technologies continue to advance, future research will be valuable for shedding light on the effectiveness of these technologies and ensuring that their use does not lead to unintended or adverse impacts on the public.

🔍 **Keywords**

Proactive, Reactive, Police Effectiveness, Crime Rates, Response Times, Arrest Rates, Clearance Rates, Standard Model of Policing, Community-Oriented Policing, Problem-Oriented Policing, Broken Windows Policing, Broken Windows Theory, Intelligence-Led Policing, Police Technologies

---

Discussion Questions

1. What are some characteristics of the police that can be an advantage for crime prevention? What are some characteristics of the police that can be a disadvantage for preventing crime?
2. How is police effectiveness evaluated? What are some strengths and weaknesses to using official crime statistics to evaluate police effectiveness?
3. Imagine that you have just been appointed the police chief for a large metropolitan police agency. What crime prevention strategies and models of policing would you employ to identify and address crime problems in your community?
4. How can technology assist the police in carrying out crime prevention? What are some of the pros and cons of the use of technology by police for impacting crime and/or citizen perceptions of, and relationships with, law enforcement?

References

Alpert, G. P., & Moore, M. H. (1998). Measuring police performance in the new paradigm of policing. In G. P. Alpert and A. Piquero (Eds), *Community Policing: Contemporary Readings* (pp. 215–232). Long Grove, IL: Waveland Press.

Blanes i Vidal, J., & Kirchmaier, T. (2018). The effect of police response time on crime clearance rates. *The Review of Economic Studies, 85*(2), 855–891.

Braga, A. A. (2008). *Problem-oriented policing and crime prevention* (2nd ed.). Monsey, NY: Willow Tree Press.

Braga, A. A., & Weisburd, D. L. (2012). The effects of focused deterrence strategies on crime: A systematic review and meta-analysis of the empirical evidence. *Journal of Research in Crime and Delinquency, 49*(3), 323–358.

Braga, A. A., Welsh, B. C., & Schnell, C. (2015). Can policing disorder reduce crime? A systematic review and meta-analysis. *Journal of Research in Crime and Delinquency, 52*(4), 567–588.

Braga, A. A., Turchan, B. S., Papachristos, A. V., & Hureau, D. M. (2019). Hot spots policing and crime reduction: An update of an ongoing systematic review and meta-analysis. *Journal of Experimental Criminology, 15,* 289–311.

Britannica. (2022). *The development of professional policing in England.* Retrieved from https://www.britannica.com/topic/police/English-and-American-policing-in-the-late-19th-century

Buehler, E. D. (2021). *State and local law enforcement training academies, 2018 – Statistical tables.* United States Department of Justice, Bureau of Justice Statistics. Retrieved from https://bjs.ojp.gov/sites/g/files/xyckuh236/files/media/document/slleta18st.pdf.

Burcher, M., & Whelan, C. (2019). Intelligence-led policing in practice: Reflections from intelligence analysts. *Police Quarterly, 22*(2), 139–160.

Bureau of Justice Assistance (BJA) (2008). *Reducing crime through intelligence-led policing.* U.S. Department of Justice, Office of Justice Programs, Retrieved from https://bja.ojp.gov/sites/g/files/xyckuh186/files/Publications/ReducingCrimeThroughILP.pdf

Bureau of Justice Assistance. (2013). *COMPSTAT: Its origins, evolution, and future in law enforcement agencies.* Washington, DC: Police Executive Research Forum. Retrieved from https://bja.ojp.gov/sites/g/files/xyckuh186/files/Publications/PERF-Compstat.pdf

Bureau of Justice Statistics. (2023). *Incident count by clearance status, 2021.* Law Enforcement Agency Reported Crime Analysis Tool. United States Department of Justice, Retrieved from https://learcat.bjs.ojp.gov/IncidentsCrime?Data%20Year=2021&Unit%20of%20Analysis=Count&Crime%20Type=Violent%20Crime

Byrne, J., & Hummer, D. (2017). Technology, innovation and twenty-first-century policing. In M. R. McGuire & T. J. Holt (Eds), *The Routledge handbook of technology, crime and justice* (pp. 375–389). London and New York: Routledge.

Caplan, J. M., Kennedy, L. W., & Petrossian, G. (2011). Police-monitored CCTV cameras in Newark, NJ: A quasi-experimental test of crime deterrence. *Journal of Experimental Criminology, 7,* 255–274.

Carriaga, M. L., & Worrall, J. L. (2015). Police levels and crime: A systematic review and meta-analysis. *The Police Journal, 88*(4), 315–333.

Carter, D. L., & Carter, J. G. (2009). Intelligence-led policing: Conceptual and functional considerations for public policy. *Criminal Justice Policy Review, 20*(3), 310–325.

Carter, J. G., & Phillips, S. W. (2015). Intelligence-led policing and forces of organisational change in the USA. *Policing and Society, 25*(4), 333–357.

Carter, J. G., Phillips, S. W., & Gayadeen, S. M. (2014). Implementing intelligence-led policing: An application of loose-coupling theory. *Journal of Criminal Justice, 42*(6), 433–442.

Cipriano, A. (2021). *Facial recognition now used in over 1,800 police agencies: Report.* The Crime Report. Retrieved from https://thecrimereport.org/2021/04/07/facial-recognition-now-used-in-over-1800-police-agencies-report/

Cordner, G. (2014). Community policing. In M. D. Reisig & R. J. Kane (Eds), *The Oxford handbook of police and policing* (pp. 148–171). Oxford: Oxford University Press.

Eck, J. E., & Rossmo, D. K. (2019). The new detective: Rethinking criminal investigations. *Criminology & Public Policy, 18*(3), 601–622.

Eck, J. E., & Spelman, W. (1987). Who ya gonna call? The police as problem-busters. *Crime & Delinquency, 33*(1), 31–52.

Ekici, N., Akdogan, H., Kelly, R., & Gultekin, S. (2022). A meta-analysis of the impact of community policing on crime reduction. *Journal of Community Safety and Well-being, 7*(3), 111–121.

Federal Bureau of Investigation (FBI) (2023). *Crime data explorer: Glossary.* Retrieved from https://cde.ucr.cjis.gov/

Finklea, K. (2022). *Law enforcement and technology: Using social media.* Congressional Research Service. Retrieved from https://sgp.fas.org/crs/misc/R47 008.pdf

Gabbidon, S. L., & Boisvert, D. (2012). Public opinion on crime causation: An exploratory study of Philadelphia area residents. *Journal of Criminal Justice, 40*(1), 50–59.

Gill, C., Weisburd, D., Telep, C. W., Vitter, Z., & Bennett, T. (2014). Community-oriented policing to reduce crime, disorder and fear and increase satisfaction and legitimacy among citizens: A systematic review. *Journal of Experimental Criminology, 10,* 399–428.

Goldstein, H. (1979). Improving policing: A problem-oriented approach. *Crime & Delinquency, 25*(2), 236–258.

Goodison, S. E. (2022). *Local police departments personnel, 2020* (NCJ 305187). U.S. Department of Justice, Office of Justice Programs, Bureau of Justice Statistics. Retrieved from https://bjs.ojp.gov/sites/g/files/xyckuh236/files/media/docu ment/lpdp20_emb.pdf

Greene, J. R. (2000). Community policing in America: Changing the nature, structure, and function of the police. *Criminal Justice 2000: Policies, Processes, and Decisions of the Criminal Justice System, 3*(3), 299–370.

Harcourt, B. E., & Ludwig, J. (2007). Reefer madness: Broken windows policing and misdemeanor marijuana arrests in New York City, 1989–2000. *Criminology & Public Policy, 6*(1), 165–182.

Hill, D., O'Connor, C. D., & Slane, A. (2022). Police use of facial recognition technology: The potential for engaging the public through co-constructed policy-making. *International Journal of Police Science & Management, 24*(3), 325–335.

Hinkle, J. C., & Weisburd, D. (2008). The irony of broken windows policing: A micro-place study of the relationship between disorder, focused police crack-downs and fear of crime. *Journal of Criminal Justice, 36*(6), 503–512.

Hinkle, J. C., Weisburd, D., Telep, C. W., & Petersen, K. (2020). Problem-oriented policing for reducing crime and disorder: An updated systematic review and meta-analysis. *Campbell Systematic Reviews, 16*(2), 1–86.

Hoppe, S. J., Zhang, Y., Hayes, B. E., & Bills, M. A. (2020). Mandatory arrest for domestic violence and repeat offending: A meta-analysis. *Aggression and Violent Behavior, 53,* 101430.

Howell, B. K. (2009). Broken lives from broken windows: The hidden costs of aggressive order-maintenance policing. *New York University Review of Law and Social Change, 33,* 271–329.

Hu, X., Rodgers, K., & Lovrich, N. P. (2018). "We are more than crime fighters": Social media images of police departments. *Police Quarterly, 21*(4), 544–572.

Jang, H., Hoover, L. T., & Joo, H. J. (2010). An evaluation of Compstat's effect on crime: The Fort Worth experience. *Police Quarterly, 13*(4), 387–412.

Kelling, G. L., & Moore, M. H. (1988). *The evolving strategy of policing* (No. 4). US Department of Justice, Office of Justice Programs, National Institute of Justice. Retrieved from https://www.ojp.gov/pdffiles1/nij/114213.pdf

Kelling, G. L., & Wilson, J. Q. (1982). Broken windows. *Atlantic Monthly, 249*(3), 29–38.

Kelling, G. L., Pate, T., Dieckman, D., & Brown, C. (1974). *The Kansas City Preventive Patrol Experiment: A summary report*. Washington, DC: Police Foundation. Retrieved from https://www.ojp.gov/pdffiles1/Digitization/42537NCJRS.pdf

Koper, C. S., Taylor, B. G., & Woods, D. J. (2013). A randomized test of initial and residual deterrence from directed patrols and use of license plate readers at crime hot spots. *Journal of Experimental Criminology, 9*, 213–244.

Lane, J., Ramirez, F. A., & Pearce, K. E. (2018). Guilty by visible association: Socially mediated visibility in gang prosecutions. *Journal of Computer-Mediated Communication, 23*(6), 354–369.

Law Enforcement Action Partnership. (2021). *Sir Robert Peel's Policing Principles*. Retrieved from https://lawenforcementactionpartnership.org/peel-policing-principles

Lee, Y., Eck, J. E., & Corsaro, N. (2016). Conclusions from the history of research into the effects of police force size on crime – 1968 through 2013: A historical systematic review. *Journal of Experimental Criminology, 12*, 431–451.

Lilly, J. R., Cullen, F. T., & Ball, R. A. (2018). *Criminological theory: Context and consequences*. New York: Sage.

Lum, C., Stoltz, M., Koper, C. S., & Scherer, J. A. (2019). Research on body-worn cameras: What we know, what we need to know. *Criminology & Public Policy, 18*(1), 93–118.

Lum, C., Koper, C. S., Wilson, D. B., Stoltz, M., Goodier, M., Eggins, E., . . . & Mazerolle, L. (2020). Body-worn cameras' effects on police officers and citizen behavior: A systematic review. *Campbell Systematic Reviews, 16*(3), 1–40.

Manning, P. K. (1978). The police: Mandate, strategies, and appearances. In P. K. Manning & J. Van Maanen (Eds), *Policing: A view from the street* (pp. 7–31). New York: Random House.

Mazerolle, L., Rombouts, S., & McBroom, J. (2007). The impact of COMPSTAT on reported crime in Queensland. *Policing: An International Journal, 30*(2), 237–256.

Moore, M. H., & Braga, A. (2003). *The "bottom line" of policing: What citizens should value (and measure!) in police performance*. Police Executive Research Forum.

Morin, R., Parker, K., Stepler, R., and Mercer, A., (2017). *Behind the Badge: Amid protests and calls for reform, how police view their jobs, key issues and recent fatal encounters between blacks and police*. Washington, DC: The Pew Research Center. Retrieved from www.pewsocialtrends.org/2017/01/11/behind-the-badge/

Morrow, W. J., Katz, C. M., & Choate, D. E. (2016). Assessing the impact of police body-worn cameras on arresting, prosecuting, and convicting suspects of intimate partner violence. *Police Quarterly, 19*(3), 303–325.

National Neighborhood Watch (NNW) (2023). *About National Neighborhood Watch*. Retrieved from https://nnw.org/about-national-neigborhood-watch

Parker, K., & Hurst, K. (2021). *Growing share of Americans say they want more spending on police in their area*. Washington, DC: The Pew Research Center.

Retrieved from https://www.pewresearch.org/short-reads/2021/10/26/growing-share-of-americans-say-they-want-more-spending-on-police-in-their-area/

Piza, E. L., Welsh, B. C., Farrington, D. P., & Thomas, A. L. (2019). CCTV surveillance for crime prevention: A 40-year systematic review with meta-analysis. *Criminology & Public Policy*, 18(1), 135–159.

Potts, J. (2018). Research in brief: Assessing the effectiveness of automatic license plate readers. *Police Chief*. Retrieved from http://theiacp.org/sites/default/files/2018-08/March%202018%20RIB.pdf

Radil, S. M., Flint, C., & Tita, G. E. (2010). Spatializing social networks: Using social network analysis to investigate geographies of gang rivalry, territoriality, and violence in Los Angeles. *Annals of the Association of American Geographers*, 100(2), 307–326.

Ratcliffe, J. (2005). The effectiveness of police intelligence management: A New Zealand case study. *Police Practice and Research*, 6(5), 435–451.

Ratcliffe, J. H. (2010). Intelligence-led policing: Anticipating risk and influencing action. *Intelligence*, 1(1), 1–12.

Rice, S. (2019). 10 ways that police use drones to protect and serve. Forbes. Retrieved from https://www.forbes.com/sites/stephenrice1/2019/10/07/10-ways-that-police-use-drones-to-protect-and-serve/?sh=2ccb88fe6580

Roman, J. K., Reid, S. E., Chalfin, A. J., & Knight, C. R. (2009). The DNA field experiment: a randomized trial of the cost-effectiveness of using DNA to solve property crimes. *Journal of Experimental Criminology*, 5, 345–369.

Scott, M. S. (2000). *Problem-oriented policing: Reflections on the first 20 years*. US Department of Justice, Office of Community Oriented Policing Services. Retrieved from https://popcenter.asu.edu/sites/default/files/library/reading/pdfs/Reflections-2.pdf

Scott, M. S. (2006). Implementing crime prevention: Lessons learned from problem-oriented policing projects. *Crime Prevention Studies*, 20, 9–35.

Seaskate Inc. (1998). *Evolution and development of police technology*. U.S. Department of Justice, National Institute of Justice. Retrieved from https://www.ojp.gov/pdffiles1/Digitization/173179NCJRS.pdf

Selinger, E., & Durant, D. (2022). Amazon's ring: Surveillance as a slippery slope service. *Science as Culture*, 31(1), 92–106.

Skogan, W. G., & Frydl, K. (2004). *Fairness and effectiveness in policing: The evidence*. Washington, DC: National Academies Press.

Telep, C. W., & Weisburd, D. (2012). What is known about the effectiveness of police practices in reducing crime and disorder? *Police Quarterly*, 15(4), 331–357.

Telep, C. W., Weisburd, D., Wire, S., & Farrington, D. (2016). Protocol: Increased police patrol presence effects on crime and disorder. *Campbell Systematic Reviews*, 12(1), 1–35.

Thompson A., & Tapp S. N. (2022). *Criminal victimization, 2021* (NCJ 305101). U.S. Department of Justice, Office of Justice Programs, Bureau of Justice Statistics. Retrieved from https://bjs.ojp.gov/content/pub/pdf/cv21.pdf

Transportation Security Administration (TSA) (2023). *Biometrics technology*. U.S. Department of Homeland Security. Retrieved from https://www.tsa.gov/biometrics-technology

Weisburd, D., & Eck, J. E. (2004). What can police do to reduce crime, disorder, and fear? *The Annals of the American Academy of Political and Social Science*, 593(1), 42–65.

Weisburd, D., Telep, C. W., Hinkle, J. C., & Eck, J. E. (2010). Is problem-oriented policing effective in reducing crime and disorder? Findings from a Campbell Systematic Review. *Criminology & Public Policy*, 9(1), 139–172.

Weisburd, D., Wilson, D. B., Petersen, K., & Telep, C. W. (2023). Does police patrol in large areas prevent crime? Revisiting the Kansas City Preventive Patrol Experiment. *Criminology & Public Policy*, 22(3), 543–560.

Zhao, J., Lovrich, N. P., & Robinson, T. H. (2001). Community policing: Is it changing the basic functions of policing?: Findings from a longitudinal study of 200+ municipal police agencies. *Journal of Criminal Justice*, 29(5), 365–377.

Chapter 10
Evaluating Crime Prevention Initiatives

Evaluating Crime Prevention Initiatives

Heidi Scherer

DOI: 10.4324/9781003401551-13

Introduction

The previous chapters have explored a wide range of crime prevention interventions that have been used across the globe to prevent and reduce crime
such as closed-circuit television (CCTV), lighting, and hotspot policing,
among others. Whether these interventions are carried out by community
members or led by the police, the primary goals of implementing crime prevention efforts are to improve people's quality of life by achieving a meaningful change in an outcome such as the reduction of crime, and the fear of
crime and disorder, and to identify programs that can be replicated to reduce
crime problems in other settings and communities. Central to understanding whether crime prevention goals have been achieved is the process that
researchers follow to carry out evaluations of interventions. Through evaluation procedures, researchers have the ability to gain in-depth information
about crime prevention interventions, including specific details about how
the program was implemented (called a process evaluation) and whether the
intervention led to any impacts or changes on behaviors, attitudes, or experiences (called an impact evaluation). The information gained from process
and impact evaluations is vital to the conclusions that researchers can draw
regarding the effectiveness of the intervention. Specifically, the evaluation
allows researchers to understand what worked about the intervention, what
did not work about the intervention, and how the intervention may be
altered to improve its impact.

Given these attributes, it is clear to see that the evaluation stage plays a
crucial role in the crime prevention process. A strong evaluation can give
researchers, criminal justice professionals, and policy makers confidence
in the conclusions drawn from research experiments, which in turn can
increase the application of evidence-based and empirically supported crime
prevention interventions in future settings and communities. The purpose of
this chapter is to provide readers with an understanding of some key considerations and best practices for evaluating crime prevention initiatives. Specifically, this chapter examines different forms of offender adaptation and
how to identify whether crime prevention interventions have led to changes
in offending patterns such as the spread of crime or crime prevention benefits. In addition, this chapter will expand upon the steps of the SARA model
(introduced in Chapter 9) to illustrate its application as an evaluation methodology and tool to be used by researchers and practitioners when identifying and evaluating crime prevention efforts. Finally, this chapter explores
ways to increase the impact of crime prevention interventions through the
development of partnerships with community stakeholders and the incorporation of community members into the crime prevention implementation
and evaluation process.

Defining Offender Adaptation

Displacement

While previous chapters of this book have established that opportunity plays a role in shaping offenders' decision making (see Chapter 2) and is central to developing effective crime prevention, it is important to note that when opportunity-based interventions started to emerge in municipalities' crime prevention toolkits, critics believed that these strategies would not be effective (Reppetto, 1976). Specifically, there was the belief among some experts in the fields of criminology and criminal justice that efforts to reduce crime through altering criminal opportunities would not lead to reductions in crime, but instead would cause offenders to make adaptions around the crime prevention program to continue their offending. Of particular concern among critics was that blocked criminal opportunities would result in a shift or movement of crime to other locations, times, tactics, crime types or targets; a phenomenon referred to as **crime displacement** (Reppetto, 1976). Since the emergence of these concerns, researchers have examined offender adaptation and crime displacement in detail to understand its various forms, how frequently it occurs, and how to anticipate its occurrence (see e.g., Eck, 1993). From this important body of research, some primary findings have emerged: crime displacement is not inevitable; opportunity blocking can lead to meaningful reductions in crime; and, when informed by crime prevention theory and methodologies, researchers can account for offender adaptation when designing and conducting evaluations (Guerette, 2009).

Before we explore the theoretical and methodological factors that shape offender adaptation, it is important to first define the six forms of crime displacement that have been identified from past research on offenders (see Figure 10.1). The first type of displacement is **temporal displacement,** which refers to when offenders alter the time of day that they commit their crimes (Reppetto, 1976; Eck, 1993). For instance, an evening-based community patrol in a neighborhood may lead residential burglars to shift from committing their crimes at nighttime to daytime, when the program is not being implemented. The second type of displacement is **spatial displacement,** also known as territorial or geographical displacement. This form of displacement occurs when crime prevention interventions lead offenders to alter the location where they commit their crimes (Reppetto, 1976; Eck, 1993). An example of spatial displacement is if an increase in surveillance and security at one shopping center would lead offenders to shift their shoplifting offenses to a store in a different location. The third type of crime displacement is **target displacement,** which occurs when offenders alter their crimes from one crime target to another (Reppetto, 1976; Eck, 1993). For instance, measures that banks have made to increase the difficulty of robberies may cause robbers to shift from targeting banks to another target such as convenience stores or gas stations.

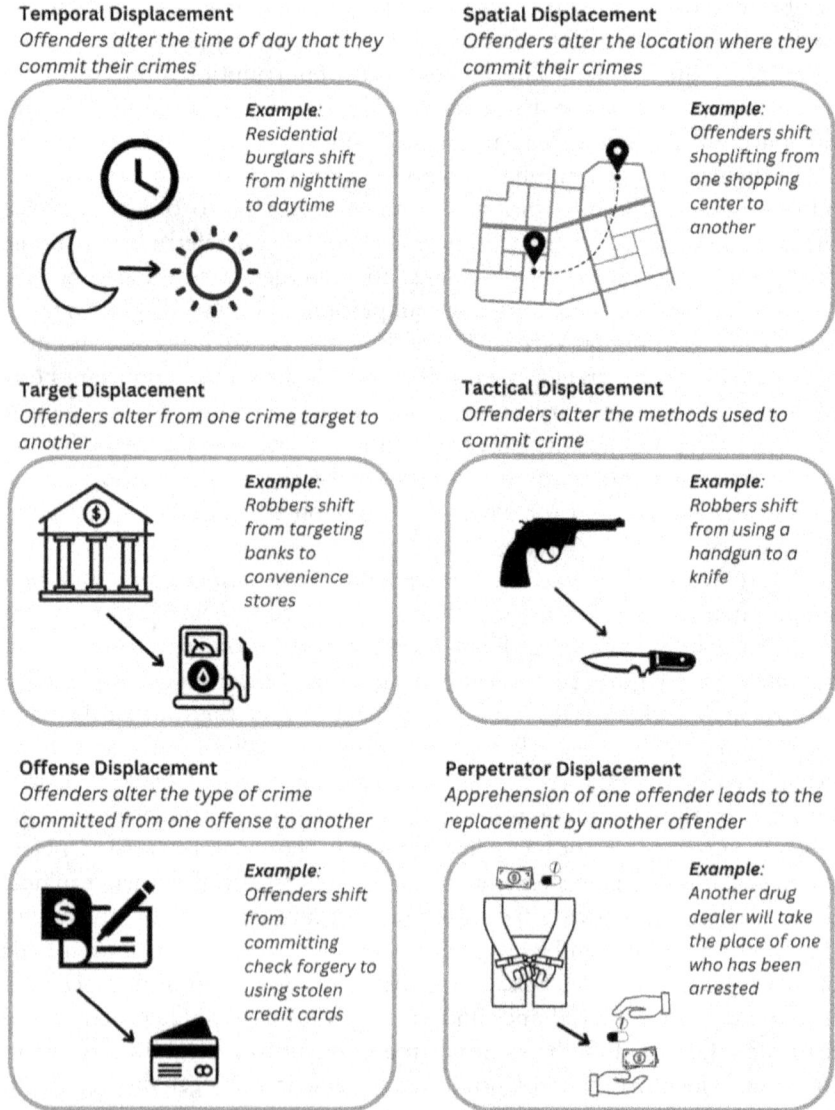

Temporal Displacement
Offenders alter the time of day that they commit their crimes

Example:
Residential burglars shift from nighttime to daytime

Spatial Displacement
Offenders alter the location where they commit their crimes

Example:
Offenders shift shoplifting from one shopping center to another

Target Displacement
Offenders alter from one crime target to another

Example:
Robbers shift from targeting banks to convenience stores

Tactical Displacement
Offenders alter the methods used to commit crime

Example:
Robbers shift from using a handgun to a knife

Offense Displacement
Offenders alter the type of crime committed from one offense to another

Example:
Offenders shift from committing check forgery to using stolen credit cards

Perpetrator Displacement
Apprehension of one offender leads to the replacement by another offender

Example:
Another drug dealer will take the place of one who has been arrested

Figure 10.1 Types of Crime Displacement.

Source: Reppetto, 1976 and Eck, 1993.

Tactical displacement, the fourth type of crime displacement, occurs when offenders alter the methods they use to carry out their offenses as a result of crime prevention efforts (Reppetto, 1976; Eck, 1993). Take, for instance, the introduction of a focused-deterrence strategy that aims to remove firearms off the street and increase sanctions for firearm violations. In turn, offenders may choose to change the methods they use to carry out their offenses, for example shifting from using a handgun during the commission of a robbery to using another weapon such as a knife. Just as offenders may change their crime methods and targets as a result of opportunity blocking techniques, they too may alter the types of crimes that they decide to commit from one offense to another (Reppetto, 1976; Eck, 1993). This fifth type of displacement is referred to as **offense displacement,** or functional displacement, and occurs when offenders alter the types of crime they commit. For instance, target hardening of personal checks may lead an offender to stop committing check forgery and instead commit fraud using stolen credit cards. The final, and sixth, type of crime displacement that has been identified from prior research is **perpetrator displacement** (Barr & Pease, 1990; Eck, 1993). This type of displacement occurs when the apprehension of offenders results in the replacement by other offenders such as the arrest of one street corner drug dealer leading a new drug dealer to take their place.

Together, the six forms of crime displacement illustrate the various ways that offenders can adapt to opportunity reduction strategies to continue their involvement in crime. However, there are two other forms of crime displacement that should be of interest to in the evaluation of crime prevention interventions. These forms of displacement were introduced by Barr and Pease (1990) and are composed of **benign displacement** and **malign displacement.** Although one may conceptualize the occurrence of displacement as an always negative event, Barr and Pease (1990) add some important context to this assumption by highlighting that if displacement shifts from serious crimes to less serious crimes, or redistributes crime more equally across society, then the displacement can be viewed as being benign. For instance, they illustrate the concept of benign displacement with gun control measures that shift offenders from using firearms to less lethal weapons. Although control measures may have led to tactical displacement, the shift from guns to less lethal weapon use (i.e., knives, fists, etc.) should result in less harmful outcomes for society. On the other hand, Barr and Pease (1990) assert that displacement has the potential to occur in ways that are more harmful or desired for society; this form of displacement is referred to as malign displacement. Malign displacement occurs when crime prevention efforts cause offending patterns to change in ways that "have gone from bad to worse" (Barr & Pease, 1990, p. 289). For instance, if crime efforts make it more difficult to burglarize commercial properties during closed hours, leading to robberies of the commercial properties during business hours, malign displacement has occurred.

Diffusion of Benefits

As discussed above, displacement is one possible way that offenders may adapt to crime prevention efforts; however, it is not the only way that offenders may alter their behaviors following the implementation of situational measures. In fact, another form of offender adaptation, called **diffusion of benefits,** has been found to be as common as displacement, yet, as its name implies, is a positive result of crime prevention (Clarke & Weisburd, 1994). Specifically, diffusion of benefits is defined as

> the spread of the beneficial influence of an intervention beyond the places which are directly targeted, the individuals who are the subject of control, the crimes which are the focus of intervention or the time periods in which an intervention is brought.
>
> (Clarke & Weisburd, 1994, p. 169)

Since the process of diffusion involves the unintended distribution of crime prevention benefits rather than crime, it has been described as being the opposite of displacement (Poyner, 1988). For instance, if an intervention implemented in Neighborhood A to reduce burglaries also leads to a decrease in burglaries in Neighborhood B, an adjacent neighborhood that did not receive any intervention, then diffusion of benefits may have occurred.

According to Clarke and Weisburd (1994), diffusion of benefits results from one of two processes. The first is deterrence, where rational offenders are deterred from engaging in crime beyond the areas or times of the intervention out of the belief of an elevated risk of apprehension. Often this process is facilitated by the fact that offenders are not familiar with all the details of an intervention and therefore may only have limited knowledge of the exact crime prevention measures in place to inform their decision making. Thus, in turn, offenders may be deterred from committing crimes within a radius of the intervention as they are not able to identify where the risk of apprehension begins and ends. Therefore, in the example above, under the deterrence process of diffusion, Neighborhood B experiences the benefits of Neighborhood A's intervention as offenders may perceive the intervention to have extended beyond the targeted areas and into the adjacent neighborhood.

The second process is discouragement, which occurs when crime prevention measures discourage offenders from committing crime beyond the intervention sites due to characteristics of the intervention that make rational offenders conclude that the crime is now too difficult, too much effort, or too little reward to complete (Clarke & Weisburd, 1994). For example, situational measures implemented to prevent thefts from vending machines in one area of an entertainment venue may lead to reductions in thefts from unaltered vending machines in other areas due to offenders' beliefs that identifying which vending machines are now suitable targets requires too much effort.

Anticipatory Benefits

Along with diffusion of benefits, **anticipatory benefits** represent another way offenders can adapt to crime prevention interventions that can result in favorable impacts on reducing crime. Anticipatory benefits occur when offenders cease engaging in crime at intervention sites before the crime prevention measures have even formally begun (Smith et al., 2002). Smith and colleagues (2002) describe this phenomenon as one that occurs when offenders observe or become knowledgeable on efforts to implement a crime prevention program that leads them to believe there is already an elevated risk of apprehension, reduced rewards, or increased effort associated with committing a crime even before the crime prevention efforts have been implemented.

There are several different explanations for why anticipatory effects may occur. For instance, offenders may observe the installation of situational measures (e.g., cameras, signage, lighting), see a news story about the upcoming intervention, or observe personnel preparing for the initiative and these actions may influence how offenders make decisions regarding the criminal event. In these instances, rational offenders may not be able to differentiate pre-intervention preparation activities from those involved in the full implementation of the intervention, and therefore may abstain from committing crime at intervention sites as soon as they observe preparation activities under the assumption that crime prevention efforts have already begun. Smith and colleagues (2002) assert that this process can occur accidentally, or researchers could purposefully implement crime prevention in a public way to maximize the possibility of anticipatory benefits.

Understanding the Extent and Nature of Offender Adaptation

Extent of Offender Adaptation

Once opponents of situational crime prevention began to raise concerns of displacement and the belief that crime prevention would just shift crime around (as discussed in Chapter 4), crime prevention scholars and researchers began to prepare their rebuttal by incorporating methods to measure displacement and diffusion of benefits in crime prevention interventions to shed light on how frequently offenders altered their behaviors when being faced with blocked criminal opportunities (Eck, 1993). This line of research, which we will explore in more detail below, has been extremely valuable for providing evidence that while displacement has been observed in some circumstances, complete displacement, that is a 100 percent shift in crime, has *never* been observed (Guerette & Bowers, 2009). In fact, the overwhelming pattern that emerges from evaluations of crime prevention interventions is that opportunity-blocking measures result in a net gain including not only significant reductions in crime at treatment sites but, in many cases, the diffusion of those benefits beyond the intervention's focus (Bowers et al., 2011).

In one of the first systematic evaluations of crime displacement, Eck (1993) reviewed 33 studies that accounted for the possibility of displacement and found that the most common outcome was no observed displacement (55 percent) followed by some displacement (36 percent). In only 9 percent of the reviewed studies was there evidence of much displacement. Although Eck (1993) recommends using caution when interpreting his findings, due to the methodological limitations of the studies, particularly, that many were not designed to account for all forms of displacement, his review provided some of the first evidence that the scope of displacement does not appear to be extensive. Hesseling's (1994) systematic review of the presence of offender adaptation among 55 crime prevention interventions extended upon Eck's (1993) review by also exploring the presence of diffusion and benefits and, again, found evidence that displacement was not an inevitability. Specifically, while 60 percent of the studies did observe some displacement, the amount of displacement was limited, with the most common forms reported being those that required the least amount of effort on the part of the offender. However, among the remaining 40 percent of the studies there was no evidence of displacement, yet in 27 percent of the sample diffusion of benefits was reported.

In 2009, Guerette and Bowers conducted one of the most comprehensive reviews of past research on the extent of offender adaptation, which examined 102 studies for the presence of displacement and diffusion. From their analysis, they reported that displacement and diffusion of benefits were observed at similar rates across the studies; 26 percent and 27 percent respectively. Further, a sub-analysis of studies that examined spatial displacement indicated that when it did occur it was likely to be benign in nature with treatment effects that surpassed any shifts in crime as a result of prevention efforts. Additionally, two more recent meta-analyses examining the presence of offender adaptation also come to similar conclusions of past research – displacement is not a common outcome of crime prevention interventions, and that diffusion of crime prevention benefits occurs more frequently (Bowers et al., 2011; Telep et al., 2014). Of note, it is important to recognize that prior research has also provided evidence of the extent of anticipatory benefits. For instance, from their review of a sample of 52 crime prevention evaluations, Smith and colleagues (2002) reported that approximately 42 percent of the studies indicated changes in measures of crime that were consistent with the concept of anticipatory benefits. Taken together, the findings from past reviews of crime prevention evaluations provide strong and consistent evidence that the belief that situational measures simply shift crime around to other opportunities is not accurate. Instead, the evidence indicates that while some crime displacement occurs, reductions in crime and diffusion of benefits are the more likely outcomes of implementing situational crime prevention measures (Bowers et al., 2011).

Anticipating Offender Adaptation

As discussed above, despite assertions by opponents that opportunity-based crime prevention simply shifts crime around, empirical evidence from decades of research on offender adaptation all converge at the same conclusion – displacement is not inevitable and the presence of diffusion of benefits is often more common as crime displacement. Specifically, this evidence of crime desistance rather than the presence of complete displacement (e.g., 100 percent displacement) provides another layer of evidence in support of the rationality of offenders (Cornish & Clarke, 1987). In fact, just as the rational choice perspective and the various crime prevention theories that fall under its umbrella can provide an understanding of offenders' decision making related to their involvement in crime and how they carry out criminal events, these theories are also informative for helping researchers anticipate the specific ways in which offenders may adapt to situational measures and the extent of displacement that may be anticipated from crime prevention interventions. When examining displacement through a theoretical lens and recognizing the factors that shape offenders' decision making, the findings align with those from empirical studies – crime *desistance*, not crime *displacement* is the most likely outcome of crime prevention interventions (Johnson et al., 2014).

According to Cornish and Clarke (1987), the likelihood of displacement to occur is influenced by the **choice-structuring properties** of individual offenses, which includes the unique offense (e.g., costs, benefits, opportunities) and offender-related (e.g., skill set, experience) characteristics of crimes that offenders take into consideration when making decisions regarding their criminality. They postulate that the threat of displacement should be highest among offenses that share choice-structuring properties where offenders are more likely to displace to different criminal opportunities if the properties are similar enough to align with the skills and interests of offenders. For instance, based on their concept, crime prevention interventions to block the opportunity for burglary would be more likely to result in displacement to an offense such as theft rather than robbery, as violent offenses have choice-structuring properties that vary more substantially from property offenses (e.g., direct interaction with a victim, use of a weapon, different levels of risk, reward, and effort). Building upon the perspective that the likelihood of displacement is influenced by offenders' existing knowledge,

Eck (1993) introduced the concept of **familiarity decay**, which asserts that "displacement is most likely to occur in the direction of familiar places, times, targets, and behaviors" (p. 537). On the other hand, displacement would not be anticipated to move towards unfamiliar directions as rational offenders would have insufficient information needed to identify criminal opportunities and access their perceived risks and benefits. Drawing from this concept, Eck (1993) asserts that displacement can be anticipated and prevented when implementing situational crime prevention measures by also adding prevention in directions familiar to offenders.

According to the Brantingham and Brantingham (2003), offender mobility and knowledge of their awareness spaces also plays an important role in helping researchers and practitioners anticipate how displacement may occur. Based on their crime pattern theory (discussed in Chapter 2), which provides insights into how offenders search for crime targets, they devised several principles of displacement to anticipate how displacement may occur. For instance, they propose that displacement is most likely to shift to areas located within a short distance from intervention sites and toward major activity nodes and paths where offenders are more likely to have spatial awareness. Underscoring the rationality of offenders, they also anticipate that displacement will be most common at locations that share similar social and demographic characteristics (and thus likely similar criminal opportunities and perceived benefits and risks) and during similar time frames (Brantingham & Brantingham, 2003).

Along with offender familiarity and distance to alternative criminal opportunities, Guerette (2009) contends that offender motivation can also impact the likelihood of displacement. For instance, opportunistic offenders and those with violent or destructive motivations should be more likely to desist when presented with blocked opportunities, while those with higher levels of motivation such as career criminals and offenders motivated by addiction and monetary needs should be less likely to desist and more likely to displace and seek out other crime opportunities (Guerette, 2009). However, it is important to note that even individuals who are highly motivated may desist from crime if the alternative methods for carrying out their offenses do not share choice-structuring properties. For instance, Clarke and Mayhew (1988) found that the removal of carbon monoxide from Britain's public gas supply led to a significant decrease in suicides in England and Wales but did not appear to lead to displacement of other methods of suicide (e.g., weapons, medications, etc.) that did not share similar characteristics (e.g., painless, clean, etc.).

Measuring Offender Adaptation

Given the possibility that offenders will adapt when faced with blocked criminal opportunities, evaluations of crime prevention interventions should be designed to account for the measurement of displacement and diffusion of benefits. By building in the capacity to measure offender adaptation, researchers and practitioners will be able to have a greater understanding of the extent of the effectiveness of their interventions and whether they need to make alterations to prevent their efforts from spreading crime beyond the intervention. One of the first steps to this process should involve the application of crime prevention theory to individual interventions to anticipate the ways offenders may adapt. For instance, concepts such as choice-structuring properties (Cornish & Clarke, 1987) and familiarity decay (Eck, 1993) and an understanding of how offender mobility may influence the search for new criminal opportunities (Brantingham & Brantingham, 2003) should help researchers to begin to identify potential directions in which offender adaptation may occur. In turn, those conducting crime prevention evaluations can devise ways to add methods to detect the presence of displacement and diffusion such as collecting and analyzing data from time periods outside of the intervention (i.e., temporal displacement) and gathering data that can be used to identify if offenders shifted their methods, targets, or offenses as a result of opportunity blocking.

One particular method that has been identified as valuable for assessing the presence of spatial displacement is the use of a **buffer zone**. A buffer zone is a geographic area connected to or located near the intervention site that is anticipated to have the greatest likelihood of experiencing spatial displacement (Hamilton-Smith, 2002). The most appropriate size for a buffer zone is one that is large enough to allow researchers to observe if changes in crime patterns have occurred, but not too large to dilute the ability to detect displacement (Weisburd & Green, 1995). Additionally, when selecting a buffer zone, evaluators should also identify which nearby areas share social and physical characteristics of the intervention site and other choice-structuring properties that would increase the likelihood that offenders would displace to the location due to knowledge of criminal opportunities that align with their perceptions of efforts, risks, and benefits (Hamilton-Smith, 2002). By analyzing data at the intervention site, buffer zone, and a control area, evaluators should be able to gain a greater understanding of the effectiveness of their interventions and identify whether crime has shifted into new geographic locations (Bowers & Johnson, 2003).

The SARA Model of Problem-Solving

In Chapter 9, the SARA model was introduced as one of the primary tools used by police to engage in problem-solving activities and was established to be an evidence-based process for reducing crime and disorder (e.g., Hinkle et al., 2020). While the SARA problem-solving framework provides police with a systematic and proactive means to identify and solve crime problems, it is important to acknowledge that the utility of the framework is not limited to the police and in fact can be applied widely by any researcher, practitioner, or community member interested in understanding and addressing problems in their communities, schools, businesses, and/or other major activity nodes. In the following sections, we will explore the SARA model in more detail to illustrate how the framework can be a key device in crime preventers' toolkits to help them fully understand crime problems, devise effective strategies to intervene and block criminal opportunities, and design evaluations to assess the effectiveness of their interventions.

Explaining the SARA Model Process

The SARA model was developed by Eck and Spelman (1987a) to complement the problem-oriented policing movement and provide a structured process that officers could follow to engage in problem-focused crime prevention efforts. Specifically, SARA is composed of four distinct steps that cover the breadth of the problem-solving process, beginning with identifying crime problems in a community and ending with the assessment of the effectiveness of the implemented crime prevention response. Like Goldstein's (1979) POP model, SARA is also focused on identifying and addressing crime problems, which Eck and Spelman (1987a) define as "a group of incidents occurring in a community, that are similar in one or more ways, and that are of concern to the police and the public" (p. 42). Concentrating on reoccurring incidents that share similar characteristics is central to the

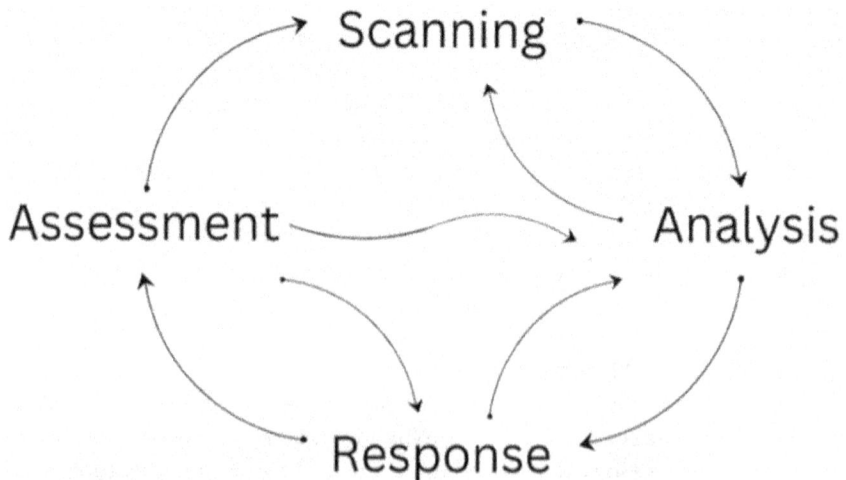

Figure 10.2 The SARA Process.
Source: Adapted from Scott, 2015.

SARA model because it allows for the identification of shared factors among the criminal events, which in turn can inform efforts to devise common prevention solutions (Eck & Spelman, 1987a).

While the SARA model involves four steps that can be completed in sequence, Clarke and Eck (2016) caution against viewing the SARA model as a linear process. In fact, they believe the utility and effectiveness of the SARA model will be maximized when crime preventers approach SARA as an iterative process where, when necessary, problem-solving teams return to previous steps of the process to reevaluate data related to crime problems/patterns, situational characteristics of the crime, planned interventions, identified stakeholders, and/or the evaluation plan (see Figure 10.2). For instance, if crime preventors find at the assessment stage that there was no change in outcomes following the intervention, then they should revisit previous steps of the process to reexamine if they correctly understood the conditions underlying the problem and/or selected a response that aligned with the known opportunity structure for the problem.

The Four Steps of the SARA Process

Scanning

The first step of the SARA model is **scanning,** which involves the identification of crime problems in a community (Eck & Spelman, 1987a). When this process is carried out by law enforcement, patrol officers or community officers assigned to POP duties will scan areas they are assigned to identify if there are criminal events that meet the definition of a crime problem and provide this information to supervisors. Once crime problems have been identified, additional information is collected to facilitate a deeper understanding of the scope of the problems and help inform problem prioritization such as how frequently it occurs, how long it has been occurring, who it impacts, and the types of societal harms caused by the problem (Eck & Spelman, 1987a). As we will explore in more detail later in this chapter, input from community members is central to the scanning process as community members are often the individuals most familiar with the problems in their communities and can bring problems to the awareness of the police and those responsible for prevention, but also can provide insights into the problem that are valuable for future steps of the SARA model. In addition to input from community members, the analysis of local crime data (e.g., arrests, calls for service, COMPSTAT reports) can also be valuable at the scanning stage as it can help problem-solving teams to identify crime problems.

According to Clarke and Eck (2016), the application of crime prevention theory can be particularly valuable at the scanning stage. For instance, examining offender mobility and offenders' journey to crime can help understand how offenders are searching for crime targets and opportunities in the community, which in turn can help problem-solving teams identify and prioritize problems. Further, knowledge of crime concentration at the place- and victim-level can also be an informative resource for identifying hotspots that can be prioritized for intervention (Clarke & Eck, 2016). It is important to note that just as officers can scan for problems in the communities they serve, non-police members of the community can also engage in this process. For instance, administrators at educational institutions and place managers at shopping centers and entertainment districts can scan their activity nodes for problems and engage with other members of the community (e.g., teachers, clerks, parking attendants, etc.) to identify and collect data on crime problems at their facilities.

Analysis

Once the presence of a reoccurring crime problem has been established, the second stage of the SARA model can begin, which is the **analysis** stage. Like the scanning stage, the analysis stage also involves investigating the crime problem, yet now the focus has turned to gaining an understanding of the root causes of the problem and the various social and situational characteristics that may facilitate, proceed, and/or follow its occurrence (Eck & Spelman, 1987a; POP Center, 2023). To help provide the problem-solving team with a roadmap for analyzing crime problems and to prevent the collection of unnecessary data, Clarke and Eck (2016) recommend formulating and testing specific hypotheses on the factors that are believed to be contributing to the crime problem. Similar to the scanning stage, knowledge and application of crime prevention theories can be valuable at the analysis stage for guiding hypothesis formulation and for informing the examination into the causes of crime problems, hotspots, and/or risky facilities identified through the process (Clarke & Eck, 2016).

In addition to exploring the etiology of the crime problem in the specific community, during the analysis stage, crime preventors should also research what is known about that crime problem from prior research as it can inform the identification of the various situational factors that shape the events (POP Center, 2023). This step also includes the collection and analysis of data on any existing strategies for addressing this problem that may be currently implemented in the community and the strengths and weaknesses of these strategies (POP Center, 2023). Once an in-depth understanding of the factors that are shaping the crime such as an understanding of where and when it occurs, who is involved in the crime, and how offenders carried out their offenses is completed, then the problem-solving team can move forward to the next step of the process. This step requires bringing this information together to devise and implement potential solutions.

Response

Once a problem has been established to be reoccurring, and the problem-solving team has undertaken steps to gain an accurate understanding of the root causes of the crime and the opportunity structure facilitating its occurrence, it is time to begin devising solutions that can be implemented to prevent the crime. According to Eck and Spelman (1987a), the **response** step's focus is on alleviating the problem with two main goals: identifying the appropriate solution and implementing it. Like the previous two steps, the response step is also research-intensive and requires crime preventers to engage in activities to research and identify a wide range of potential interventions that align with what was learned about the opportunity structure of the crime problem from the analysis step. Both prior research on crime prevention interventions and crime prevention theory – particularly the situational crime prevention framework – can be incorporated in the response stage to inform the problem-solving team on possible solutions, provide insights into their potential effectiveness, identify potential outcomes of the solutions (e.g., reduction in crime, reduction in fear of crime, increased use of public space, etc.), and help ensure that the responses align with what is known about the specific crime problem and the rational decision making of offenders (Clarke & Eck, 2016).

When identifying potential solutions, the problem-solving team should also identify which individuals in the community will be responsible for, or contribute to, the implementation of the solution. If remedies are selected that extend beyond those that fall under the responsibilities of local police, then relevant community members or government employees (see "Third-party Policing," below) should be involved in the response stage to provide input on solutions and the feasibility of their implementation. In fact, if third parties such as place managers, property managers, or property owners are contributing to the problem in any capacity, it is crucial to "get them to assume responsibility" and take a primary role in alleviating the problem (Clarke & Eck, 2016, p. 87). Further, when selecting the best solution for the problem, it is valuable before the formal program implementation to ensure that the selected solution is cost effective and there are sufficient personnel and monetary resources set aside to support its full implementation (Clarke & Eck, 2016). Once all of the theoretical and practical considerations have been explored, the problem-solving team is ready to complete the final step of the response stage of SARA and launch the crime prevention intervention.

Assessment

Once a solution has been implemented, it is time to engage in the **assessment** step of the SARA process, which involves the monitoring of the intervention and conducting evaluations to determine its effectiveness. At this stage, both process and impact evaluations can provide valuable insights and information to the problem-solving team. Through a process evaluation, data is collected on the actual implementation of the intervention which can provide information on such factors as whether the solution was carried out as intended, if there were any challenges or barriers to implementation, if there were sufficient resources to support implementation, and the experiences and perceptions of key personnel and community members involved with the intervention. On the other hand, for an impact evaluation, quantitative and qualitative data is collected before and after the intervention's implementation, which can be analyzed to draw conclusions on the effectiveness of the intervention and determine whether and in what ways the solution has led to any changes in the study's outcomes (e.g., crime, fear of crime, victimization, etc.). The collection of several different data sources at the assessment stage can be valuable, including official data (e.g., crime rates, calls for service), unofficial data collected via observation of activities at the intervention sites, and/or surveys of those impacted by the crime problem.

The assessment step of the SARA model is particularly important as it will guide decision making regarding how the prevention team moves forward with addressing the crime problem. Therefore, Clarke and Eck (2016) encourage those applying the SARA model to strive for the use of strong methodologies, such as the inclusion of a control group (i.e., a group that did not receive any intervention and can be used to inform researchers of what would happen if no solution had been implemented) and multiple measures of outcomes over time to facilitate examining and understanding trends and changes following implementation. During the evaluation of crime prevention interventions, researchers should also make efforts to measure and account for the different forms of anticipated offender adaptation which can be informed by theoretical and empirical data collected in the previous steps of the model (Clarke & Eck, 2016). If the evaluation data provides evidence that the program was implemented properly and there was significant change in outcome measures in the anticipated direction and zero to limited displacement, then the problem-solving team will likely conclude that the intervention was effective and either cease or continue implementation based on the existing need. However, if evaluation data does not provide evidence of change over time in the crime problem, or the intervention was not implemented properly, then the non-linear nature of the SARA process should be engaged, and the problem-solving team should return to previous stages of the process to reevaluate their knowledge on the problem (*analysis*) and/or effective solutions (*response*).

Through a review of the four steps of the SARA model, the primary strength of the framework emerges. Similar to situational crime prevention, the SARA framework has a broad utility and the ability to be applied to any reoccurring problem in a community including different types of crimes

The Problem:
- *Residents were avoiding the Belmont Community Park due to loitering youth engaged in delinquency*
- *A local POP unit was approached to investigate the problem and conduct the SARA process outlined below*

Scanning:
- *A group of youth were congregating near the park and engaging in drug and alcohol use*
- *Residents were fearful of the youth and avoided the area*

Analysis:
- *The youth had built a shack on a vacant lot next to the park*
- *The owner of the vacant lot was fearful that youth would retaliate if he removed the shack and could not afford costs for demolition*

Response:
- *Other local public agencies acknowledged the problem but did not prioritize taking action*
- *POP officers and county employees decided to demolish the shack and remove debris from property*

Assessment:
- *The youth retreated to private places to engage in drug and alcohol use*
- *Residents reported a decrease in fear near the park*
- *Families and children began using the park for recreation*

Figure 10.3 SARA in Action: The Belmont Treehouse.

Source: Eck and Spelman, 1987b.

(e.g., violent, property, drug, and sexual crimes), different contexts (e.g., along paths, major activity nodes, crime attractors, crime generators), and by individuals both internal and external to local police (see Figure 10.3 for an illustration of the SARA model in action). These unique characteristics, along with SARA's systematic and evidence-based approach to identifying and solving crime problems, make SARA an immensely valuable tool in the problem-solvers' evaluation toolkit.

Extending Crime Prevention Beyond the Police

Community–Police Partnerships for Crime Prevention

As was explored in Chapter 9, the majority of the public and law enforcement community perceive local police as being the individuals in society with the primary responsibility to engage in crime prevention efforts to protect and keep members of the community safe (Morin et al., 2017). The role of the police as crime preventers is also reinforced by empirical evidence illustrating that there are several police practices that have been found to lead to reductions in crime, disorder, and other relevant outcome measures. However, if one takes a closer examination into the police practices that have been found to lead to reductions in crime such as community-oriented policing, problem-oriented policing, focused deterrence strategies, and broken windows policing (see Chapter 9), a common theme can be observed. The most effective police practices involve community members, often who are providing direct input on crime problems and/or cooperating and participating with law enforcement to implement solutions. These findings underscore that while the police may be perceived as the *primary* crime preventers in society, the impact of efforts will always be largest when conducted in collaboration with members of the community.

While establishing strong community–police partnerships can pose a challenge for some agencies, the value of such partnerships cannot be overstated as community members bring instrumental knowledge and value to problem-solving and crime prevention teams. For instance, McCampbell (2014) emphasizes that community partnerships can contribute wide value to police partnerships as they can bring unique insights on the needs of troubled and at-risk community populations, an understanding of the community-specific social factors that are shaping crime, and existing infrastructure to support community needs such as services for youth, families in need, and the unemployed. To form meaningful partnerships, McCampbell (2014) recommends the use of asset mapping that can be used to identify community resources and the various stakeholder groups who share common interests. It is valuable to conceptualize stakeholders broadly and recognize that fruitful problem-solving partnerships can be formed with organizations and individuals from the public sector (e.g., school administrators, elected officials, district attorney's office), the private sector (e.g., business owners, property managers), and the non-profit sector (e.g., faith-based organizations, community organizations, shelters).

Finding common ground can also play a central role in the success and forward progress of partnership (McCampbell, 2014). For instance, if police are interested in addressing a crime problem related to vagrancy, fruitful partnerships may include collaboration with organizations such as food banks, shelters, and faith-based organizations who serve the homeless population and have knowledge, interest, and infrastructure for addressing this population's needs. Other successful approaches to building relationships in the community, which in turn can support crime prevention efforts, include the creation of citizen advisory councils that can provide feedback and awareness to local police on crime problems in the community (Wasserman, 2014). Additionally, activities associated with the community-oriented policing model such as the use of citizen surveys, community newsletters, social media posts, and officer trainings can all be tools police agencies can use to work toward building relationships with the public and opening lines of communication to support problem-solving efforts and the development of stable partnerships (Wasserman, 2014).

Third-Party Policing

Another effective policing practice that involves the use of community partnerships is called **third-party policing**. Third-party policing is a proactive method of policing where police agencies partner with another public or governmental agency (e.g., city attorneys, state liquor bureaus, city code enforcement) to encourage a non-offending person to take responsibility for a crime problem and alter characteristics or behaviors at their property to prevent others from committing crime (Buerger & Mazerolle, 1998). Take for instance an apartment complex that experiences a disproportionately high level of calls for service for drug offenses and crime. Under a third-party policing approach, local police and city attorneys can pursue actions to sue the property owner in a civil court under nuisance laws to pressure them to change their leasing practices to evict drug dealers or improve their blighted properties with the goal to prevent others from committing crime at the apartment. Or, for a nuisance bar or club that experiences overselling of alcohol and/or bar fights, police and state liquor licensing agencies may partner to pressure the bar owners to make changes under the threat of revoking their liquor license. In both examples, the approach taken is unique in that *civil* (e.g., monetary or punitive damages) rather than criminal remedies are being used with the goal of crime prevention and proximate, non-offending individuals, typically place managers, are the target of enforcement rather than the ultimate target, which is the individuals committing the crimes on the property (Buerger & Mazerolle, 1998).

According to Cherney (2008), engaging third parties is ideal for POP- and SARA-based police approaches as it provides police with valuable information to inform the analysis and response steps of SARA, but also an opportunity to actually impact the direct causes of crime, which are often outside their purview. For instance, by applying pressure to the third parties who have direct control over the environments and situational characteristics that are shaping criminal opportunities at the place-level to implement crime prevention techniques, there is a greater chance for crime reduction.

Smith (1998) also asserts that the use of civil remedies like third-party polic-ing can also be a valuable tool for situational crime prevention as third parties have the potential to impact effort, risk, rewards, provocations, and excuses that shape criminal opportunity at their properties.

In addition to aligning with theoretical and methodological crime pre-vention and problem-solving frameworks, third-party policing has been found to be effective and can lead to significant reductions in crime and disorder following implementation. From their analysis of a civil remedies program focused on reducing drug crime in beats in Oakland, California, Mazerolle and colleagues' (2000) observed reductions in drug-related calls for service in the third-party policing sites in comparison with the control sites that utilized patrol actions to address drug problems. Additionally, Manning and colleagues (2016) reported that following the implementation of a third-party policing approach where officers partnered with local bar and club place managers to learn crime prevention skills, place managers reported engaging in more proactive behaviors and had perceptions of less crime and disorder on their properties.

Super Controllers

Sampson and colleagues' (2010) concept of the **super controller** is also related to crime prevention methods that extend beyond the police. Accord-ing to Sampson and colleagues (2010), super controllers refer to the "peo-ple, organizations and institutions that create the incentive for controllers to prevent or facilitate crime" (p. 40). Controllers refer to the individuals from the second layer of the crime triangle who can exhibit control over offend-ers, places, and targets including intimate handlers, place managers, and guardians (see Chapters 1 and 2). In particular, they identify ten different types of super controllers, some of which are formal organizations such as regulatory bodies and the court system; some are diffuse organizations (e.g., collections of individuals) such as the media and local, state, and federal political groups; and some are personal organizations such as families and community groups. Sampson and colleagues (2010) assert that super con-trollers across these domains can be valuable for crime prevention as they have the ability to influence offender decision making and the five categories of situational crime prevention that impact criminal opportunity. Addition-ally, when carrying out the SARA model, police and problem-solving teams may find it beneficial to identity super controllers that may be valuable to partner with for prevention and third-party approaches. Similar to other police practices that involve partnerships with the community, there is also theoretical and empirical evidence to demonstrate that super controllers have the capacity to impact crimes, even ones that extend beyond the typi-cal measures of street crime and disorder such as maritime piracy (Townsley et al., 2016) and fraud (Mui & Mailley, 2015).

Summary

This chapter aimed to explore some central considerations that are valuable for researchers and practitioners to consider when designing and conducting evaluations of crime prevention initiatives. One key aspect of the evaluation process is to gain an understanding of how offenders may respond to crime prevention initiatives that block criminal opportunity and ensure that interventions are leading to positive reductions in crime and not shifting crime around, which is referred to as crime displacement. As this chapter examined, while crime displacement is a possibility, prior research and theory provide convincing evidence that it is not inevitable. In fact, along with reductions in crime at treatment sites, the opposite of displacement – diffusion of benefits and the spread of crime prevention benefits beyond the intervention – appears to be more common than crime displacement, underscoring that there is a net gain of efforts to prevent crime.

Although conceptualized primarily as a tool for law enforcement, this chapter also explored how the SARA model can be applied widely by any teams of problems-solvers to identify and address crime problems in their local communities and spaces (e.g., schools, business establishments, entertainment districts). In particular, SARA provides a reliable and user-friendly framework to support not only the development of crime prevention interventions, but also the creation of a rigorous evaluation that can give crime preventors confidence in the findings from their studies. Finally, this chapter explored the value of community–police partnerships for crime prevention and some best practices for identifying key stakeholders in the community. Specifically, through an exploration of research on third-party policing practices and super controllers, a clear pattern has emerged – when police partner with community members who have knowledge, skills, and infrastructure to contribute to crime prevention, the effectiveness of crime prevention interventions is maximized.

Keywords

Crime Displacement, Temporal Displacement, Spatial Displacement, Target Displacement, Tactical Displacement, Offense Displacement, Perpetrator Displacement, Benign Displacement, Malign Displacement, Diffusion of Benefits, Anticipatory Benefits, Choice-Structuring Properties, Familiarity Decay, Buffer Zone, Scanning, Analysis, Response, Assessment, Third-Party Policing, Super Controller

Discussion Questions

1. How would you respond to the criticism that situational-based crime prevention interventions just shift crime around rather than reduce crime?

2. How can crime prevention theory help researchers, problem-solving teams, and crime prevention evaluators anticipate the extent and type of offender adaptation that may occur following the implementation of a crime prevention intervention?

3. Imagine that you have been hired as a SARA consultant for a local police department interested in expanding officers' use of problem-solving in their communities. One of the officers expressed concerns that they may not have the skills to carry out the SARA model. How would you respond to this officer to appease their concerns?

4. What are some of the unique traits or characteristics that community members and organizations can bring to police partnerships? How can these traits and characteristics lead to improved reductions in crime and disorder from crime prevention interventions?

References

Barr, R., & Pease, K. (1990). Crime placement, displacement, and deflection. *Crime and Justice, 12*, 277–318.

Bowers, K. J., & Johnson, S. D. (2003). Measuring the geographical displacement and diffusion of benefit effects of crime prevention activity. *Journal of Quantitative Criminology, 19*, 275–301.

Bowers, K. J., Johnson, S. D., Guerette, R. T., Summers, L., & Poynton, S. (2011). Spatial displacement and diffusion of benefits among geographically focused policing initiatives: A meta-analytical review. *Journal of Experimental Criminology, 7*, 347–374.

Brantingham, P. J., & Brantingham, P. L. (2003). Anticipating the displacement of crime using the principles of environmental criminology. *Crime Prevention Studies, 16*, 119–148.

Buerger, M. E., & Mazerolle, L. G. (1998). Third-party policing: A theoretical analysis of an emerging trend. *Justice Quarterly, 15*(2), 301–327.

Cherney, A. (2008). Harnessing the crime control capacities of third parties. *Policing: An International Journal of Police Strategies & Management, 31*(4), 631–647.

Clarke, R. V., & Eck, J. E. (2016). *Crime analysis for problem solvers in 60 small steps*. Washington, DC: Office of Community Oriented Policing Services.

Clarke, R. V., & Mayhew, P. M. (1988). The British Gas suicide story and its criminological implications. In M. Tonry & N. Morris (Eds), *Crime and justice: A review of research*, vol. 10, Chicago, IL: University of Chicago Press.

Clarke, R. V., & Weisburd, D. (1994). Diffusion of crime control benefits: Observations on the reverse of displacement. *Crime Prevention Studies, 2*(1), 165–184.

Cornish, D., & Clarke, R. (1987). Understanding crime displacement: An application of Rational Choice Theory. *Criminology, 25*(4), 933–947.

Eck, J. E. (1993). The threat of crime displacement. *Criminal Justice Abstracts*, 25(3), 527–546.

Eck, J. E., & Spelman, W. (1987a). *Problem-solving: Problem-oriented policing in Newport News*. US Department of Justice, National Institute of Justice.

Eck, J. E., & Spelman, W. (1987b). Who ya gonna call? The police as problem-busters. *Crime & Delinquency*, 33(1), 31–52.

Goldstein, H. (1979). Improving policing: A problem-oriented approach. *Crime & Delinquency*, 25(2), 236–258.

Guerette, R. T. (2009). *Analyzing crime displacement and diffusion*. Washington, DC: US Department of Justice, Office of Community Oriented Policing Services.

Guerette, R. T., & Bowers, K. J. (2009). Assessing the extent of crime displacement and diffusion of benefits: A review of situational crime prevention evaluations. *Criminology*, 47(4), 1331–1368.

Hamilton-Smith, N. (2002). Anticipated consequences: Developing a strategy for the targeted measurement of displacement and diffusion of benefits. *Crime Prevention Studies*, 14, 11–52.

Hesseling, R. (1994). Displacement: A review of the empirical literature. *Crime Prevention Studies*, 3(1), 97–230.

Hinkle, J. C., Weisburd, D., Telep, C. W., & Petersen, K. (2020). Problem-oriented policing for reducing crime and disorder: An updated systematic review and meta-analysis. *Campbell Systematic Reviews*, 16(2), 1–86.

Johnson, S. D., Guerette, R. T., & Bowers, K. (2014). Crime displacement: What we know, what we don't know, and what it means for crime reduction. *Journal of Experimental Criminology*, 10, 549–571.

Manning, M., Mazerolle, L., Mazerolle, P., & Collingwood, P. (2016). Place managers in entertainment districts: The role of third party policing in shaping place manager actions. *Policing and Society*, 26(8), 889–906.

Mazerolle, L. G., Price, J. F., & Roehl, J. (2000). Civil remedies and drug control: A randomized field trial in Oakland, California. *Evaluation Review*, 24(2), 212–241.

McCampbell, M. S. (2014). *The collaboration toolkit for community organizations: Effective strategies to partner with law enforcement*. Washington, DC: Office of Community Oriented Policing Services.

Morin, R., Parker, K., Stepler, R., and Mercer, A., (2017). *Behind the Badge: Amid protests and calls for reform, how police view their jobs, key issues and recent fatal encounters between blacks and police*. Washington, DC: The Pew Research Center. Retrieved from www.pewsocialtrends.org/2017/01/11/behind-the-badge/

Mui, G., & Mailley, J. (2015). A tale of two triangles: comparing the Fraud Triangle with criminology's Crime Triangle. *Accounting Research Journal*, 28(1), 45–58.

POP Center (2023). *The SARA Model*. ASU Center for Problem-Oriented Policing. Retrieved from: https://popcenter.asu.edu/content/sara-model-0

Poyner, B. (1988). Video cameras and bus vandalism. *Journal of Security Administration*, 11(2), 44–51.

Reppetto, T. A. (1976). Crime prevention and the displacement phenomenon. *Crime & Delinquency*, 22(2), 166–177.

Sampson, R., Eck, J. E., & Dunham, J. (2010). Super controllers and crime prevention: A routine activity explanation of crime prevention success and failure. *Security Journal*, 23, 37–51.

Scott, M. S. (2015). *Identifying and defining policing problems.* US Department of Justice, Office of Community Oriented Policing Services.

Smith, M. J. (1998). Regulating opportunities: Multiple roles for civil remedies in situational crime prevention. *Crime Prevention Studies, 9,* 67–88.

Smith, M. J., Clarke, R. V., & Pease, K. (2002). Anticipatory benefits in crime prevention. *Crime Prevention Studies, 13,* 71–88.

Telep, C. W., Weisburd, D., Gill, C. E., Vitter, Z., & Teichman, D. (2014). Displacement of crime and diffusion of crime control benefits in large-scale geographic areas: A systematic review. *Journal of Experimental Criminology, 10,* 515–548.

Townsley, M., Leclerc, B., & Tatham, P. H. (2016). How super controllers prevent crimes: Learning from modern maritime piracy. *British Journal of Criminology, 56*(3), 537–557.

Wasserman R. (2014). *Building relationships of trust: Recommended steps for chief executives.* Tallahassee, FL: Institute for Intergovernmental Research.

Weisburd, D., & Green, L. (1995). Measuring immediate spatial displacement: Methodological issues and problems. In J. Eck, & D. Weisburd (Eds), *Crime and Place* (pp. 349–361). Monsey, NY: Criminal Justice Press.

Chapter 11
Domain-Specific Crime Prevention

Domain-Specific Crime Prevention

Jamie A. Snyder

Chapter Outline

In this chapter, we will focus on:

Crime Prevention and Domains
Crime Prevention in Primary and Secondary Schools
- Prevalence of crime in schools
- Student-centered crime prevention programs
- School crime prevention, security measures, and environmental design

Crime Prevention in Higher Education
- Bystander intervention programs

Crime Prevention in Public Spaces
- Crime prevention in bars, night-clubs, and entertainment districts
- Crime prevention in transportation hubs
- Crime prevention in parking lots and garages

Crime Prevention on the Internet
- Prevalence and prevention of Internet crime
- Cyberstalking and online harassment

Learning Objectives

After reading this chapter, you should be able to:

11.1 Identify and describe domains of crime prevention
11.2 Discuss examples of crime prevention in specific domains
11.3 Apply crime prevention techniques in specific domains
11.4 Examine research on crime prevention in specific domains

DOI: 10.4324/9781003401551-14

Introduction

As described throughout this book, crime prevention strategies can be applied to different crimes, offenders, items, and places. This chapter will focus on how crime prevention can be utilized in specific domains and the potential success of these strategies. The first section of this chapter will discuss how crime prevention techniques can be applied in the domain of schools. This section also includes empirical evidence of school crime prevention effectiveness. The second domain that will be explored is public spaces, which include bar and entertainment districts as well as public transit and parking garages. Example crime prevention approaches that can be applied in these areas will be discussed, along with research evidence. The final domain that will be explored in this chapter is the online domain, focusing on crime prevention techniques that can reduce opportunities and their effectiveness for criminal activity over the Internet.

Crime Prevention and Domains

A **domain** is defined as a specific environment or physical/online space that can be altered through crime prevention techniques to reduce or eliminate opportunities for crime. This is sometimes referred to as place-based crime prevention, as discussed in Chapter 6, but in the present context the definition utilized will be broader to include the online/Internet domain. Examples of domains include places like schools, bars, parking garages, and online environments such as the Internet. Research suggests that crime prevention techniques that are more tailored and focused to specific places and crimes are often more effective (Eck & Guerette, 2012). Thus, the efforts in specific domains such as schools or bars should increase the chances of prevention. Additionally, focusing on crime prevention at specific places or domains is likely to be more effective than broad-based crime prevention, given that crime concentrates at specific places, accounting for large proportions of overall crime, across many crime types (Eck & Guerette, 2012). These spaces are sometimes referred to as *crime generators* or *crime attractors* (e.g., shopping and entertainment districts, transit stops, parking areas, schools, bars) (Brantingham & Brantingham, 1995), as was discussed in more detail in Chapter 5, or nodes, as discussed in Chapter 2. It is important to note that there is a wide array of places that could be identified as crime generators or attractors. With that in mind, this chapter will provide an overview of place-based crime prevention strategies by focusing on examples of a few specific domains.

Crime Prevention in Primary and Secondary Schools

Prevalence of Crime in Schools

Due to the nature of the environment, the vulnerability of their populations, and their overall role in society, schools are often seen as domains that necessitate additional protection. As a result, they are often a focal point for crime prevention efforts. Studies suggest that opportunities for crime and deviance within schools can be driven by both environmental design, school surroundings, and individuals within schools. To understand what types of crimes and deviance may need to be targeted, we first present data on what types of offenses are likely to occur in schools in the United States. The School Crime Supplement (SCS) is collected almost every two years by the National Crime Victimization Survey (NCVS). This effort surveys students, aged 12–18, on a wide variety of topics, including crime victimization experiences while in school. The SCS measures both non-fatal and fatal forms of victimization. Non-fatal incidences include theft, as well as several forms of violent victimization (i.e., sexual assault, rape, robbery, simple and aggravated assault). These numbers are typically presented as rates per 1,000 students. For example, in 2019[1] there were 11 non-fatal victimizations per 1,000 students (National Center for Education Statistics [NCES], 2023a). In terms of victimization type, according to the NCES, the most common type of crime within schools is property theft. In 2019, 2 percent of students reported experiencing theft in the last 6 months, or a rate of 9 victimizations per 1,000 students, a decline from 4 percent in 2009 (NCES, 2022; NCES, 2023a). From 2009 to 2019, the SCS also reported decreases in other variables, including fewer students reporting having been in a physical fight on school property (11 percent vs. 8 percent) and fewer students reporting carrying a weapon on school property during the previous 30 days (6 percent vs. 3 percent) (Irwin et al., 2023).

In addition to victimization, the SCS asks several questions about the environment of the school, focusing on gang presence and hate-related experiences. In 2019, 9 percent of students reported the presence of gangs in their schools, while 23 percent of students reported they saw hate-related graffiti on school grounds (Irwin et al., 2023). These numbers have decreased significantly since 2009 (21 percent and 29 percent respectively). Further, students are asked about drug-related behaviors, including their own usage and availability of drugs at school. In 2019: 29 percent of students reported that they had used alcohol on at least one day in the last 30 days, a significant decrease from 42 percent in 2009; 22 percent of students said that they had used marijuana at least once in the last 30 days; while another 22 percent said they were offered, sold, or given an illegal drug at school in the last year. Finally, 7 percent of students said that they were threatened or injured with a weapon on school property in the last year (Irwin et al., 2023).

Bullying in Primary and Secondary Schools

The SCS also contains information about bullying, as a separate experience. **Bullying** can include a wide variety of behaviors, and was measured by the SCS as:

> another student had made fun of them, called them names, or insulted them; spread rumors about them; threatened them with harm; tried to make them do something they did not want to do; excluded them from activities on purpose; destroyed their property on purpose; or pushed, shoved, tripped, or spit on them.
>
> (Irwin et al., 2023, p. 7)

In 2019, 22 percent of children aged 12–18 reported being bullied at school in the last school year (Irwin et al., 2023). Females were more likely to report being bullied (25 percent) than males (19.1 percent), while those who reported they were two or more races had the highest percentage of reported bullying (37 percent).

Student-Centered Crime Prevention Programs

Crime prevention initiatives in schools can vary greatly. They may include broad-based approaches that attempt to reduce all crime and deviance at school or more focused approaches such as bullying or drug-specific programs. In addition, they may include programs that focus on prevention through early interventions, such as the Head Start and Perry programs that were discussed in Chapter 7. To illustrate the design and application of such programs, examples of programs that specifically target school violence and bullying will be outlined below.

Programs to Reduce Violence in Schools

The prevention of violence on school grounds, especially shootings, has become the focus of many school safety programs. Between 2000 and 2021 there were 46 active shooter[2] incidents at primary and secondary schools in the United States, resulting in 108 individuals killed and 168 injured (Irwin et al., 2023). The most common response for most schools, along with enhanced security measures, has been to implement a written plan of action. For example, in 2019, about 96 percent of schools reported they had a written plan for how to manage and respond to an active shooter on school grounds. This is an increase from the number of schools that reported having an active shooter written policy in 2009 (84 percent)

(NCES, 2023a). Further, some schools also utilize active shooter training drills that attempt to provide information on what to do during an active shooter or muti-option programs, which include tactics that are situational (Jonson et al., 2020).

One program that has become increasingly adopted for both prevention and response is **ALICE**, which stands for Alert, Lockdown, Inform, Counter, and Evacuate (ALICE Training Institute, 2018). This program was created in 2001 to provide guidance for students and staff on how to respond to an active school shooter. While not focused on preventing the shooting itself, it does attempt to prevent injury and loss of life using crime prevention tactics. For example, the lockdown tactic builds on access control by locking entrances and classrooms but also by barricading doors and spaces within the building using all available items, such as bookcases, chairs, or desks (Jonson et al., 2020). The other elements of ALICE are intended to provide multiple options for how to respond in a situation. To that end, one study found that in comparison with a simulated lockdown-only option, simulations that used ALICE ended quicker and resulted in less estimated loss of life (Jonson et al., 2020). These results suggest that plans that provide for multiple tactics could be more effective at preventing loss of life, when compared with plans that only include a lockdown option.

While the results seem promising, further research is needed, however, on these programs to draw firmer conclusions on their effectiveness. Additionally, some concerns exist over who ALICE, or active shooter trainings more generally, are most appropriate for, especially younger age groups, and the potential emotional and psychosocial impact these trainings may have on certain demographics (Peterson et al., 2015). Finally, plans and programs, such as ALICE, tend to be reactive in nature, only providing information on what to do if a shooting is occurring and not on how to prevent such incidents. Other preventive measures such as the use of environmental design including Crime Prevention Through Environmental Design (CPTED), Situational Crime Prevention (SCP) metal detectors, law enforcement or resource officers in schools, and other security measures may provide better approaches.

Bullying Prevention Programs

Several programs exist that attempt to reduce or prevent bullying in schools. Often these programs focus on recognizing what behaviors are defined as bullying, what to do if a student thinks they are being bullied or sees someone else being bullied, and steps to prevent it from occurring. Research suggests that these programs can make an impact on the prevalence of bullying, depending on how the program is administered and the topics included. One of the most recognized bullying programs at the primary and secondary level is the Olweus Bullying Prevention Program. The **Olweus Bullying**

Prevention Program (OBPP), started in 1983 by Dan Olweus, is a comprehensive program for K-12 students that incorporates school, class, individual, and community elements, and is designed to improve peer relationships and reduce and prevent bullying (Olweus, 2023). Several studies have evaluated the OBPP, typically finding positive results. A study published in 2021 that investigated the effectiveness of the OBPP in middle schools over an 8-year period found that, after year 3, there were significant declines in both teacher- and student-reported victimization and aggression (Sullivan et al., 2021). These results suggest the significance of examining these programs over multiple years and that impacts may be delayed or take time to emerge, highlighting the importance of longitudinal studies.

Overall, research suggests that prevention programs can be effective at reducing bullying. A meta-analysis that included 100 evaluations of bullying programs concluded that most of the programs were effective, reducing bullying perpetration by 19–20 percent and victimization by 15–16 percent (Gaffney et al., 2019). Additional research has also suggested that programs that contain certain components may be more effective at reducing bullying than others. For example, Ttofi and Farrington (2009) found programs that contained elements such as parental training/involvement, supervision of students, videos, and other hand-on peer activities were most effective at reducing bullying, suggesting that program elements are also important when considering which program to implement. Finally, not all programs may be effective at reducing all types of bullying. Kennedy (2020) reported that most bullying programs implemented in the United States were effective at reducing relational and physical bullying, but were less effective at reducing verbal bullying, providing further evidence of the need to study specific elements of bullying programs.

School Crime Prevention, Security Measures, and Environmental Design

Aside from crime prevention programs that target potential offenders and victims within a school setting, there are also crime prevention initiatives that focus on targeting schools as a whole. Many of these efforts focus on the environmental design of the school, utilizing defensible space, CPTED, and SCP to identify and reduce opportunities for crime. Students may be fearful of specific locations in school, or of being victimized while at school, and thus avoid or engage in other behaviors as a result of this fear. The SCS found that in 2019 about 6 percent of students reported that they avoided either a school activity, a class, or a specific place in school due to a fear of being victimized. About 5 percent reported that they avoided one or more places in school (Irwin et al., 2023). Places that were avoided included specific hallways, the lunchroom, or restrooms suggesting that some places may provide unique opportunities for crime within a school.

Thus, environmental design using defensible space and CPTED, along with situational crime prevention, could help prevent crime within schools. For example, hallway design could include lockers that are set back into the walls, removing hiding spaces and allowing for better surveillance of the area. Improved lighting, large windows, and open spaces also contribute to surveillance opportunities (Schneider et al., 2000). Back stairwells could be closed underneath or surveilled during class changes when large amounts of students are interacting with one another. Open areas in lunchrooms with windows that look out into the hallway allow for surveillance from both ends. Supervision and traffic flow during class changes could be monitored (Schneider et al., 2000). Bathrooms could be designed with maze entries, removing the need for an outside door that could be blocked. Access control could be utilized through the locking of all outside doors during the day and requiring all visitors to check in at the main office and all faculty and staff to have ID badges.

Formal surveillance such as cameras, metal detectors, security, and other forms of technology can add to environmental design features to further reduce opportunities and increase risk perceptions in potential offenders. Many of these techniques have become widespread, with the NCES (2023a) finding that 97 percent of schools reported some access control to buildings, 91 percent used security cameras, and 77 percent required faculty and staff to wear ID badges in 2019.

All of these numbers have increased significantly from 2009 (Table 11.1). Further, 65 percent of schools reported that there were security staff present, such as a School Resource Officer (SRO), at the school at least once a week in 2019 (Irwin et al., 2023). The use of random metal detector checks has remained low, with only about 5 percent of schools reporting they used this tactic in 2018 and about 27 percent of schools reporting that they conducted random contraband checks such as locker or backpack checks (NCES, 2022).

While research is still limited in this area, one study that evaluated the use of these security measures and their impact on school violence, including metal detectors, locker checks, banning book bags, and police presence, found that only the use of metal detectors reduced fear of crime. None of the other security measures significantly impacted violence; however, many

Table 11.1 Common Safety Measures in Schools, 2009 to 2019

Safety Indicator	2009 (% Reporting Use)	2019 (% Reporting Use)
Access Control to Buildings	92%	97%
Security Cameras	61%	91%
Faculty & Staff ID Badges	63%	77%
Security Staff Presence at Least Once a Week	43%	65%

Source: Irwin et al., 2023.

individual-level factors such as involvement in delinquency and delinquent peers were significantly related to violence, suggesting crime prevention efforts should target those who are most at risk of victimization, considering individual-level factors in conjunction with environmental design efforts and security measures (Tillyer et al., 2011). Other studies that have examined the impact of SROs have been mixed, often finding their presence did not meaningfully reduce crime but increased the number of weapons- and drug-related disciplinary actions and reporting of non-serious violence and property crimes (Fisher & Devlin, 2020; Gottfredson et al., 2020). Thus, the presence of resource officers may increase detection, but not decrease crime. More research is needed, however, to fully understand the impact of resource and police officers in schools.

Additionally, the outside spaces around schools can provide opportunities for both crime and disorder, but also for sending strong message of territoriality and image. Landscaping that is kept up, and uses school colors on outside buildings, and clean sidewalks, suggests that the area is cared for and under control of the school, creating barriers against crime. School grounds should be cleaned regularly of any graffiti and all trash should be maintained. The clear marking of school grounds, especially near edge spaces is also important in creating territoriality and maintaining an image of care. Parking lots should be well lit and clearly marked if there are separate parking areas for students and faculty, along with signage designating where there is no parking and arrows to navigate the lot. This helps to assist compliance and remove any excuse individuals may have for breaking rules.

A few studies exist that have attempted to apply CPTED and defensible space techniques to schools, often in addition to traditional security measures such as cameras and metal detectors. These studies have had mixed results, depending on the types of tactics and crimes examined. Studies that include multiple measures of security and CPTED often report more positive outcomes than the utilization of only traditional measures such as security cameras. In fact, a longitudinal study that compared schools that used security cameras with those that did not, reported little differences in overall crime between schools, suggesting the relationship between schools and security is more complex than one tactic (Fisher et al., 2021).

One such study examined a combination of traditional security measures with the addition of other SCP tactics including access control, increasing risks, and reducing provocations (O'Neill & McGloin, 2007). Differences emerged based on crime type with the locking of doors and reducing the number of classroom changes, all associated with lower levels of property crime, while closing campus for lunch increased the risk of property crime. However, only the number of classroom changes was significantly related to violent crime, highlighting the importance of how different tactics may be more effective for different crime types (O'Neill & McGloin, 2007). Further, another study that examined a wide range of SCP tactics and school violence also found no significant effects, except for assisting compliance through the consistent application of policies, again suggesting that SCP tactics may be more effective for property crime than violence in schools (Sevigny & Zhang, 2018). It is also worth noting that Sevigny and Zhang (2018) found that some schools were more successful than others in implementing crime prevention tactics, and this success was hindered in schools that had funding concerns, suggesting that SCP could me more effective if barriers such as funding were lessened. Finally, Vagi and colleagues (2018) examined violence and fear of crime among middle schools using a CPTED School Assessment (CSA). Schools with higher CSA scores had lower violence perpetration and fear suggesting there may be contexts where CPTED could impact violence.

Crime Prevention in Higher Education

While primary and secondary schools are often the focus for crime prevention programs, it is also important to understand opportunities for crime that may be present at the post-secondary or university level. The SCS also collects data for various crimes that occur on college campuses, reporting that the number of on-campus crimes decreased by 15 percent (from 32,100 to 27,200) between 2010 and 2019 (NCES, 2023b). Similar to primary and secondary schools, the most common type of crime experienced on college and university campuses is theft. However, sexual victimization is also an area of concern for college students, with several studies finding high rates of sexual victimization among this population. Perhaps the most commonly cited statistic is that one in five or 20 percent of college women will experience some form of sexual victimization, defined as variety of behaviors, over the course of their college tenure (Krebs et al., 2009). This, and other research finding significant risk among the college population, has led to several efforts to design programming to prevent victimization, with many programs focused specifically on sexual victimization.

Crime prevention programs at this level can employ environmental design and CPTED, as discussed for primary and secondary schools, broad-based prevention, or targeted programming such as bystander intervention. Research on CPTED and environmental design on college and university campuses has found that design features can impact fear, as discussed in Chapter 3 (see Fisher & Nasar, 1992, for example) and overall perceptions of safety (Shariati & Guerette, 2019). However, more research is needed to understand the potential impact of security measures on campus crime, particularly violence.

Bystander Intervention Programs

One type of program that has become commonplace in higher education is Bystander Intervention. **Bystanders** are individuals who observe, or are aware of, potential criminal behavior that is occurring (Banyard et al., 2005). These individuals can make choices as to whether to respond or not in a situation. Thus, **bystander intervention** programs typically involve direct or indirect strategies for intervention during potentially criminal or concerning situations.

Latané and Darley (1970) outlined four major steps to bystander intervention, including: 1) becoming aware of the situation; 2) perceiving the situation as concerning; 3) feeling the need to take action; and 4) having the ability to take some sort of action. For example, someone sees a person who appears to be intoxicated. Another individual is attempting to get the intoxicated person to leave with them. This alone may not be concerning until the bystander realizes it appears the intoxicated person does not know the other person. Now the bystander has a decision to make: do they intervene or do nothing? Bystander intervention then provides tactics for either direct intervention, such as confronting the person, or calling the police if the bystander does not feel comfortable directly intervening (Mainwaring et al., 2023).

Expand Your Understanding – Green Dot Bystander Intervention Program

A popular form of Bystander Intervention is Green Dot. This program was developed in 2007 by Dr. Dorothy J. Edwards. The goal of this program is to provide bystanders with tactics to intervene in situations when sexual victimization may occur reactively, but also to provide proactive information to prevent sexual victimization. More information about this program, including specific techniques for intervention and empirical research can be found at: www.livethegreendot.com

---

Overall, research on bystander intervention programs has been positive. For example, a meta-analysis which included 33 studies that examined several different bystander intervention techniques found the program to be successful. Some elements were more successful than others, with knowledge being the most improved, followed by intention to intervene, efficacy, higher levels of responsibility, actions, greater awareness, and improved knowledge about gender norms and attitudes (Park & Kim, 2023). Other studies have focused on reductions in crime associated with such programs, also finding favorable outcomes. Coker and colleagues (2016) found that compared with two campuses that did not use a bystander intervention program, a campus that had the program had lower rates of interpersonal violence, sexual victimization, and stalking. In addition, a review of bystander intervention programs that evaluated violence reduction found that, of the four that did measure violence reduction, all of them reported reductions in either dating violence, sexual victimization, or harassment. This suggests that, while more studies are needed in this area, the current empirical evidence supports that bystander intervention can be effective at reducing multiple forms of violence on college and university campuses (Bell et al., 2019).

Crime Prevention in Public Spaces

The second major domain described in this chapter is that of public spaces, specifically bars and entertainment districts, transit locations, and parking lots or garages. Opportunities for crime vary by public space, with some public spaces having higher levels of certain types of crime. For example, transit stops and parking garages may be targeted for robbery or auto theft, while bars and clubs may experience higher rates of physical assault. Thus, the types of prevention techniques often differ depending on the place being examined. To illustrate this, we will provide an overview of crime prevention tactics for several public space domains.

Crime Prevention in Bars, Nightclubs, and Entertainment Districts

Entertainment districts that contain bars and nightclubs have long been found to provide opportunities for crime. The interaction of large numbers of potential victims and perpetrators, along with alcohol use, serves as a good example of a crime generator, as well as an attractor, as discussed in Chapter 5. Both SCP and CPTED have been applied to bars and clubs in entertainment districts, suggesting both physical design and situational factors can influence opportunities. Eck and Guerette (2012) summarized several studies specifically focused on reducing opportunities for crime in bars and clubs, suggesting crime prevention tactics have been effective. The effective SCP techniques included utilizing server training and intervention, specific regulations and limitations on alcohol consumption, and the removal of large amounts of available cash. Programs targeting place managers such as the "Safer Bars" program in Toronto, Canada has also been found to be successful, reducing aggression and violence in the targeted bars significantly compared with bars that did not implement the program (Graham et al., 2004). Other programs have focused on reducing the interaction of patrons entering and exiting these establishments, increasing lighting in surrounding areas, and using "lockouts" to reduce issues outside of these venues (Fraser, 2018). All of these techniques attempt to reduce provocations and remove excuses, as discussed in Chapter 4.

> **Expand Your Understanding – Be Safe Late Program**
>
> The "Be Safe Late Program" was implemented in Ballarat, Victoria, Australia as an approach to reduce crime and disorder related to alcohol in the city's bar and entertainment district. The Program consisted of three main components: 1) the use of a 2 a.m. lockout of all businesses in the district (preventing individuals from entering the bar after this time and limiting "barhopping"); 2) improved lighting in the area; and 3) targeted police patrol. Several types of crime decreased significantly during the 12-month program, such as assaults (about a 40 percent decrease) and property damage (about a 17 percent decrease) (University of Ballarat Centre for Health Research and Practice, 2004).

Research on the application of environmental design has also been positive, with studies suggesting the physical design of bars and nightclubs can have an impact on crime within this space. Macintyre and Homel (1997) examined several bar features such as the location of the dance floor, restrooms, main bar, entrances and exits, along with their relationship to density and violence. The design of the bar influenced density, which, in turn, influenced levels of violence, with the highest levels of density also being associated with high levels of violence (Macintyre & Homel, 1997). This suggests that the physical design of a bar can lead to crowding, thus creating greater opportunities for violence. To address this, bars can be designed with separate entrance and exit points, and flow patterns that reduce crowding such as not having people cross the dance floor to get to the bathrooms or main bar.

Another example is provided by Marselle and colleagues (2012) in a study that focused on reducing crime outside of bars after they closed. The area under examination had experienced larger levels of crime, particularly assault and conflict, in the surrounding streets once the bars closed for the evening. The sidewalks outside of the bars were particularly narrow, forcing patrons to walk very closely to one another or in the street, increasing the chances of provocations and conflict. Thus, the solution was to close the streets to vehicle traffic directly outside the bars during specific periods of time, providing a much larger lane for pedestrian traffic. Results suggested a small decrease in violence in these areas, overwhelming support from individuals surveyed about the change, and significant reductions in fear (Marselle et al., 2012). Overall, the available research suggests that many of the design principles of CPTED can be utilized in this type of space, with further research needed to fully understand the impact of these techniques on different types of crime opportunity.

Crime Prevention in Transportation Hubs

Transit stops and other spaces, such as parking lots and garages, have been the focus of numerous prevention efforts. These spaces are often seen as providing ample opportunities for crime, due to the large amount of people that use these spaces and favorable conditions for crime, such as lack of surveillance or low territoriality. For example, Liu and colleagues (2020) found that the addition of a bus stop in a specific location increased the instances of robbery around the added bus stop. Prevention in these spaces often focuses on environmental design and CPTED, although SCP has also been applied in this domain. Below, some examples will be provided for crime prevention in the locations.

Transit hubs such as bus stops, metro stations, and train stations are often seen as crime generators or attractors, given the large numbers of people who move through these locations each day. These areas are sometimes identified as "hotspots," as discussed in Chapter 5, further highlighting the importance of examining these areas for potential crime prevention interventions. For example, several studies have focused on bus stops as hotspots, often finding that crime clusters near and around certain stops, at certain times of day, and disproportionally impacts certain riders (Adams et al., 2015; Block & Davis, 1996; Loukaitou-Sideris, 1999). Hart and Miethe (2015) found that half of robberies in their study were clustered at nine different activity nodes, with bus stops having the highest occurrence of robbery. Thus, many crime prevention efforts have attempted to address these opportunities through the use of CPTED and SCP.

One study that examined the ten most "dangerous" bus stops in Los Angeles, California found that these bus stops often lacked surveillance and defensible space/CPTED characteristics (Loukaitou-Sideris, 1999). The author then makes several recommendations for increasing safety and blocking opportunities in these spaces. These recommendations include: 1) placing bus stops strategically in front of businesses that are thriving, and can provide surveillance, instead of abandoned or empty buildings; 2) increasing lighting; 3) the removal of walls, bushes, and other features that may block surveillance and provide hiding spaces; 4) upkeep of the area including removing graffiti and trash; and 5) gating or blocking off alleyways near bus stops that allow for hiding or escape of the potential offender (Loukaitou-Sideris, 1999).

Research on metro stops, such as subway stations, finds that some of these locations may act as hotspots for crime, similar to bus stops. In particular, certain subway stations may provide opportunities for robbery. Herrmann and colleagues (2021) examined the relationship between subway stations and robbery, finding that the strategic closing of some stops reduced robbery significantly, with impacts extending from directly next to the bus stop to as far away as a 5-minute walking distance. Additional research has explored how hotspot policing may be utilized. Ariel and Partridge (2017) found that hotspot policing at specific bus stops reduced driver-reported incidents significantly; however, other crimes increased nearby, suggesting displacement once offenders recognized patrol parameters. These results suggest hotspot policing could have some impact, though displacement should be anticipated and considered.

Another study illustrates how transit locations may vary in their opportunities for crime and how these opportunities may vary over situational factors such as location, time of day, and crime type. Irvin-Erickson and La Vigne (2015) found that several factors contributed to higher crime levels at certain transit stations, including higher levels of foot traffic, greater access, and greater connectedness to other stations. From a routine activities' perspective, these stations would have a higher likelihood of potential offenders coming into contact with potential victims, suggesting increased surveillance or guardianship may reduce opportunities for crime. In these situations, there is some evidence that hotspot policing may be helpful. Finally, in a rare study that used both a treatment and control group, Ariel and colleagues (2020), randomized hotspot policing at London underground railway stations, adding patrol where none had existed before. The findings illustrate how deterrence may function in these situations beyond expectations. Specifically, crime significantly decreased in the policed stations, but mostly when patrol was not present, suggesting residual deterrence effects (Ariel et al., 2020).

Expand Your Understanding – Crime Prevention in National Parks

Parks are public spaces that may act as crime attractors or generators, with some National Parks servicing millions of visitors per year. Thus, some attention has been paid to possible prevention strategies in this domain. Strategies for this domain include environmental design, CPTED, and SCP. For example, Snyder and Freng (2023) reported that within National Parks, being verbally assaulted, followed by theft were the most common types of victimization experienced. Parking lots were the most common location for crime, followed by hiking trails, and park campgrounds. In terms of prevention, suggestions include the use of SCP through access control on the number of visitors to limit conflict over parking spaces, trails, and other popular locations, increased surveillance by park rangers and highlighting less used areas in parks to reduce provocations that may arise in highly trafficked areas (Snyder & Freng, 2023).

Crime Prevention in Parking Lots and Garages

While not the same domain, parking garages and lots are often located near major transit locations like bus stops or metro stations and share many of the same opportunities for crime. Thus, the recommendations are similar for these spaces with added lighting, especially for surface parking lots that are expansive, but also include on-site security, cameras, or parking attendants to further enhance surveillance opportunities. Smith (1996) argues that parking garages in particular can be rife with opportunities for crime. They are often under-surveilled, have inadequate lighting, may contain ample hiding spaces, and may not be well kept up in terms of image. Similar to those for bus stops, several recommendations are made for parking garages. Smith (1996) suggests that parking garages should maximize flat and open spaces to increase surveillance, stairwells and elevators should be transparent glass or open to the outside, unnecessary walls or barriers should be removed, access control measures such as gates, bars, or IDs to enter and exit the facility should be utilized, and spaces under stairwells should blocked along with avoiding nooks and crannies. Further, parking attendants should be utilized, when possible, along with cameras and other target-hardening measures (Smith, 1996). Fennelly and Perry (2018) also suggest that cameras could be mobile, moving up and down parking rows to maximize surveillance along with limiting pedestrian entry, high ceilings, and white painted walls to reflect light.

Existing research suggests that when these tactics are implemented in parking garages, they can be successful at reducing crime. One study that used CPTED in a parking garage on the Ohio State University campus reported that two years after the changes were made, crime had decreased by half in that parking garage compared with prior to the changes (Tseng et al., 2004). Other studies have found that elements of CPTED such as increased surveillance in the form of patrol (Barclay et al., 1996) can reduce auto theft, the use of CCTV (Tilley, 1993), and that lighting can also be effective at crime reduction (Poyner, 1991).

Crime Prevention on the Internet

The final domain that will be examined in this chapter is that of the Internet or online domain. **Internet crime** or cybercrime includes actions that use a computer and the Internet to facilitate illegal activities (FBI, 2023). These actions can look similar to traditional crimes, such as stalking, but require the use of a computer or other Internet-capable device to facilitate the action. For example, instead of repeatedly calling a person on the phone to harass them, a potential offender sends them repeated harassing emails or online messages. Internet crime costs the United States billions of dollars each year, and in 2022 the FBI's Internet Crime Report (ICR) noted there were over 800,000 complaints to the FBI's Internet Complaint Center (IC3) (FBI, 2023). The IC3 was launched in 2000 to provide potential victims of cybercrimes a place to submit complaints. These complaints serve both as data collection and as a way to assist victims, through partnership with law enforcement. Case in point, the IC3's Recovery Asset Team (RAT) has successfully frozen over 433 million dollars in fraudulent transfers since its inception in 2018 (FBI, 2023). This information can also be used to identify the most common complaints and provide data for prevention efforts.

Prevalence and Prevention of Internet Crime

Internet crime can take many forms, from identity theft to phishing, and each type of crime may have a different opportunity structure. Table 11.2 outlines some of the most common forms of Internet crime and their definitions from the FBI IC3. The most common crime reported to the IC3 in 2022 was phishing, followed by personal data breaches (FBI, 2023).

Table 11.2 Common Types of Internet Crime, as Defined by the FBI

Crime Type	Description
Identity Theft	Someone steals and uses personal identifying information without permission to commit fraud or other crimes and/or (account takeover) a fraudster obtains account information to perpetrate fraud on existing accounts.
Advanced Fee	An individual pays money to someone in anticipation of receiving something of greater value in return, but instead, receives significantly less than expected or nothing.
Credit Card Fraud	A wide-ranging term for theft and fraud committed using a credit card or any similar payment mechanism as a fraudulent source of funds in a transaction.
Phishing	The use of unsolicited email, text messages, and telephone calls purportedly from a legitimate company requesting personal, financial, and/or login credentials.
Data Breach	The use of a computer intrusion to acquire confidential or secured information (not personal computers).
Employment Fraud	An individual believes they are legitimately employed and loses money, or launders money/items during the course of their employment.
Government Impersonation	A government official is impersonated in an attempt to collect money.
Cyberstalking/ Harassment	Repeated words, conduct, or action that serve no legitimate purpose and are directed at a specific person to annoy, alarm, or distress that person. Engaging in a course of conduct directed at a specific person that would cause a reasonable person to fear for their safety or the safety of others or suffer substantial emotional distress.

(Continued)

Table 11.2 (Continued)

Crime Type	Description
Investment Fraud	Deceptive practice that induces investors to make purchases based on false information. These scams usually offer the victims large returns with minimal risk.
Lottery/Inheritance	An individual is contacted about winning a lottery or sweepstakes they never entered, or to collect on an inheritance from an unknown relative.
Malware	Software or code intended to damage or disable, or capable of copying itself onto a computer and/or computer systems to have a detrimental effect or destroy data.
Ransomware	A type of malicious software designed to block access to a computer system until money is paid.
Botnet	A group of two or more computers controlled and updated remotely for an illegal purchase such as a Distributed Denial of Service or Telephony Denial of Service attack or other nefarious activity.
Romance	An individual believes they are in a relationship (family, friendly, or romantic) and is tricked into sending money, personal and financial information, or items of value to the perpetrator or to launder money or items to assist the perpetrator.
Real Estate	Loss of funds from a real estate investment or fraud involving rental or timeshare property.
Tech Support	Subject posing as technical or customer support/service.

Source: Adapted from: FBI IC3 pp. 29–31 https://www.ic3.gov/Media/PDF/AnnualReport/2022_IC3Report.pdf

While efforts to understand the types of Internet crimes that are being committed have made strides, empirical research on Internet crime prevention is still lagging in comparison with crime prevention in other domains. Further, due to the wide variety of Internet crimes that can be carried out, some areas have received more attention than others. For instance, several studies have focused on identity theft and its prevention. Nearly 24 million Americans were estimated to be victims of some form of identity theft in 2021, with credit card misuse reported as the most frequent type experienced (Harrell & Thompson, 2023). Common suggestions for prevention in this area include strong passwords, frequent changing of passwords, never providing sensitive information such as personal identification numbers (PINs) or social security numbers to "access" a locked account from a suspicious email and how to spot scams that may target identifying information. A study of individuals working in identify theft prevention asserted that prevention should take advantages of biometrics, such as facial recognition or fingerprints, two-factor authentication, and the use of chips in credit cards (Piquero et al., 2022). Many of these suggestions were echoed by White and Fisher (2008), who also advocated for the use of biometrics among other tactics such as increased security when opening new accounts, education, and the use of a uniform definition for identity theft. These prevention techniques can be viewed from a Situational Crime Prevention (SCP) lens, through target hardening, increasing effort, increasing risks, and reducing rewards, as discussed in Chapter 4.

Additional prevention efforts have focused on providing awareness and knowledge to consumers about the prevalence and harm associated more generally with Internet crimes. Drew (2020) found that individuals who perceived a greater prevalence of cybercrime and associated harms were more likely to take target hardening protective actions, suggesting that awareness and education may be helpful in encouraging prevention. Similarly, in a study that focused on phishing, researchers found that certain types of factors were related to phishing, and they recommended the use of Machine Learning and text mining to better detect phishing scams, along with awareness and alerting users to links or emails that could be potential phishing scams (Aleroud & Zhou, 2017).

Finally, in a review of research studies across Internet crimes, Ho and colleagues (2022) examined the usefulness of SCP in this context. They concluded that while not many articles existed that applied SCP to specific cybercrimes, it could be useful, especially with increasing offender effort and risk. Examples of each of the 25 techniques and how they can be applied to SCP are provided, including virus scanning, the use of place managers to supervise, and education (Ho et al., 2022). Overall, the existing literature points to the potential usefulness of several prevention tactics, especially SCP, however little empirical research has been conducted to examine if these tactics actually prevent Internet crimes. Ho and colleagues (2022) assert that this is a point forward in the area, with empirical studies being critical to understanding what SCP tactics might work best for specific crimes.

Cyberstalking and Online Harassment

While many people think of identity theft when they imagine cybercrime, the Internet also provides unique opportunities for harassment and stalking. Estimates on the prevalence of cyberstalking vary widely, often due to the lack of standardization in definitions (Fissel et al., 2020), with some studies finding lower levels (Kraft & Wang, 2009) and others finding as high as almost 41 percent of people experiencing cyberstalking in their lifetime (Reyns et al., 2012). A few studies have also attempted to understand who may be at highest risk for cyberstalking and harassment, providing recommendations for prevention. One study that focused on the use of the lifestyle-routine activities framework (LRAT) provided support for the framework's use in understanding cyberstalking. Reyns and colleagues (2011) found that behaviors associated with exposure (having a higher number of social networks), proximity (being more likely to add strangers), and guardianship (having deviant peers and using a profile tracker) were significantly associated with

Table 11.3 Situational Crime Prevention and Cyberstalking Examples

Increasing Effort	Increasing Risk	Reducing Rewards	Reducing Provocations	Removing Excuses
Blocking Messages	Easier Reporting Site Monitoring	Not Accepting Messages from Strangers	Never Replying to Stalkers	Codes of Conduct on Sites/Safety Reminders
Privacy Restrictions	Personal Email Identifiers	Not Posting Identifying Photos	Less Frequent Page Updates	Acknowledgment of Rules

Source: Adapted from Reyns (2010).

experiencing cyberstalking. SCP has also been applied to cyberstalking and harassment. Reyns (2010) makes several suggestions for how SCP tactics could be applied to cyberstalking including increasing effort through access control and target-hardening measures, among others. Table 11.3 provides some examples of these tactics in a cyberstalking context. Collectively, the available studies demonstrate the potential that crime prevention techniques may have in this area, but additional research is needed on specific types of cybercrimes to fully understand what prevention may work best.

Summary

The main goal of this chapter was to explore crime prevention in specific domains that are often identified as crime generators or attractors. Considering crime opportunities vary by place, it is important to examine prevention in specific spaces. First, the domain of schools was explored with both programming, environmental design, and SCP discussed as prevention strategies. Next, the domain of public spaces, including places of entertainment and transit, was discussed. The final domain in this chapter was that of the Internet. This emerging domain was discussed in terms of current and future prevention opportunities.

Keywords

Domain, Bullying, ALICE, Olweus Bullying Prevention, Bystanders, Bystander Intervention, Internet Crime, Identity Theft, Advanced Fee, Credit Card Fraud, Phishing, Data Breach, Employment Fraud, Government Impersonation, Cyberstalking/Harassment, Investment fraud, Lottery/inheritance fraud, Malware, Ransomware, Botnet, Romance Scams, Real Estate Fraud, Tech Support Fraud

Discussion Questions

1. Why do you think it is important to consider domain when implementing a crime prevention program? Why might the opportunities for crime be different in a school compared with a bar?

2. Discuss three ways we can use environmental design in primary and secondary schools to reduce opportunities for crime and delinquency.

3. Public transit locations such as train stops and parking lots/garages often present opportunities for crime. Why might these locations experience higher levels of crime compared with other locations?

4. Online crime is a growing area for crime prevention. Discuss three ways we can utilize crime prevention techniques in an online environment.

Notes

1. Data collection efforts in 2020 and 2021 for the SCS were interrupted by the COVID-19 pandemic, therefore numbers from 2019 are utilized throughout this section unless otherwise noted.
2. Defined by the Federal Bureau of Investigation (FBI) as "one or more individuals actively engaged in killing or attempting to kill people in a populated area." See: https://www.fbi.gov/file-repository/active-shooter-incidents-20-year-review-2000-2019-060121.pdf/view

References

Adams, W., Herrmann, C. R., & Felson, M. (2015). Crime, transportation and malignant mixes. In V. Ceccato, & A. Newton (Eds), *Safety and security in transit environments: an interdisciplinary approach* (pp. 181–19). New York: Palgrave Macmillan.

Aleroud, A., & Zhou, L. (2017). Phishing environments, techniques, and countermeasures: A survey. *Computers & Security, 68*, 160–196.

ALICE Training Institute. (2018). *ALICE: An easy to remember acronym*. Retrieved from https://www.alicetraining.com/our-program/alice-training/

Ariel, B., & Partridge, H. (2017). Predictable policing: Measuring the crime control benefits of hotspots policing at bus stops. *Journal of Quantitative Criminology, 33*, 809–833.

Ariel, B., Sherman, L. W., & Newton, M. (2020). Testing hot-spots police patrols against no-treatment controls: Temporal and spatial deterrence effects in the London Underground experiment. *Criminology, 58*(1), 101–128.

Banyard V. L., Plante E. G., & Moynihan M. M. (2005). *Rape prevention through bystander education: Bringing a broader community perspective to sexual violence prevention*. U.S. Department of Justice. https://nij.ojp.gov/library/publications/rape-prevention-through-bystander-education-bringing-broader-community

Barclay, P., Buckley, J., Brantingham, P. J., Brantingham, P. L., & Whinn-Yates, T. (1996). Preventing auto theft in suburban Vancouver commuter lots: Effects of a bike patrol. *Preventing Mass Transit Crime. Crime Prevention Studies, 6*, 133–161.

Bell, S. C., Coker, A. L., & Clear, E. R. (2019). Bystander program effectiveness: A review of the evidence in educational settings (2007–2018). In W. T.

O'Donohue & P. A. Schewe (Eds), *Handbook of sexual assault and sexual assault prevention* (pp. 433–450). New York: Springer.

Block, R., & Davis, S. (1996). The environs of rapid transit stations: A focus for street crime or just another risky place. *Preventing Mass Transit Crime. Crime Prevention Studies*, 6, 237–257.

Brantingham, P., & Brantingham, P. (1995). Criminality of place: Crime generators and crime attractors. *European Journal on Criminal Policy and Research*, 3, 5–26.

Coker, A. L., Bush, H. M., Fisher, B. S., Swan, S. C., Williams, C. M., Clear, E. R., & DeGue, S. (2016). Multi-college bystander intervention evaluation for violence prevention. *American Journal of Preventive Medicine*, 50(3), 295–302.

Drew, J. M. (2020). A study of cybercrime victimisation and prevention: Exploring the use of online crime prevention behaviours and strategies. *Journal of Criminological Research, Policy and Practice*, 6(1), 17–33.

Eck, J. E. & Guerette, R. T. (2012). Place-based crime prevention: Theory, evidence, and policy. In B. C. Welsh & D. P. Farrington (Eds), *The Oxford handbook of crime prevention* (pp. 354–383). New York: Oxford University Press.

Federal Bureau of Investigation (FBI) (2023). FBI Internet Crime Report 2022. https://www.ic3.gov/Media/PDF/AnnualReport/2022_IC3Report.pdf

Fennelly, L., & Perry, M. (2018). *CPTED and traditional security countermeasures: 150 things you should know*. London and New York: CRC Press.

Fisher, B. S., & Nasar, J. L. (1992). Fear of crime in relation to three exterior site features: Prospect, refuge, and escape. *Environment and Behavior*, 24(1), 35–65. doi:10.1177/0013916592241002

Fisher, B. W., & Devlin, D. N. (2020). School crime and the patterns of roles of school resource officers: Evidence from a national longitudinal study. *Crime & Delinquency*, 66(11), 1606–1629.

Fisher, B. W., Higgins, E. M., & Homer, E. M. (2021). School crime and punishment and the implementation of security cameras: Findings from a national longitudinal study. *Justice Quarterly*, 38(1), 22–46.

Fissel, E. R., Reyns, B. W., & Fisher, B. S. (2020). Stalking and cyberstalking victimization research: Taking stock of key conceptual, definitional, prevalence, and theoretical issues. *Psycho-criminological approaches to stalking behavior: The international perspective*, 11–36.

Fraser, H. (2018). *Best practices in the prevention of crime within entertainment districts*. Crime Prevention Ottawa. https://www.crimepreventionottawa.ca/wp-content/uploads/2019/02/Best-Practices-in-the-Prevention-of-Crime-within-Entertainment-Districts-EN.pdf

Gaffney, H., Ttofi, M. M., & Farrington, D. P. (2019). Evaluating the effectiveness of school-bullying prevention programs: An updated meta-analytical review. *Aggression and Violent Behavior*, 45, 111–133.

Gottfredson, D. C., Crosse, S., Tang, Z., Bauer, E. L., Harmon, M. A., Hagen, C. A., & Greene, A. D. (2020). Effects of school resource officers on school crime and responses to school crime. *Criminology & Public Policy*, 19(3), 905–940.

Graham, K., Osgood, D. W., Zibrowski, E., Purcell, J., Gliksman, L., Leonard, K., ... & Toomey, T. L. (2004). The effect of the Safer Bars programme on physical aggression in bars: results of a randomized controlled trial. *Drug and Alcohol Review*, 23(1), 31–41.

Harrell, E., & Thompson, A. (2023). *Victims of identity theft, 2021, Bulletin.* United States Department of Justice, Office of Justice Programs, Bureau of Justice Statistics. https://bjs.ojp.gov/document/vit21.pdf

Hart, T. C., & Miethe, T. D. (2015). Public bus stops and the meso environment: Understanding the situational context of street robberies. In V. Ceccato & A. Newton (Eds), *Safety and security in transit environments: An interdisciplinary approach* (pp. 196–212). New York: Springer.

Herrmann, C. R., Maroko, A. R., & Taniguchi, T. A. (2021). Subway station closures and robbery hot spots in New York City – Understanding mobility factors and crime reduction. *European Journal on Criminal Policy and Research*, 27, 415–432.

Ho, H., Ko, R., & Mazerolle, L. (2022). Situational Crime Prevention (SCP) techniques to prevent and control cybercrimes: A focused systematic review. *Computers & Security*, 115, 102611.

Irwin, V., Wang, K., Cui, J., & Thompson, A. (2023). *Report on indicators of school crime and safety: 2022*. National Center for Education Statistics (NCES), U.S. https://bjs.ojp.gov/document/iscs22.pdf

Irvin-Erickson, Y., & La Vigne, N. (2015). A spatio-temporal analysis of crime at Washington, DC metro rail: Stations' crime-generating and crime-attracting characteristics as transportation nodes and places. *Crime Science*, 4(1), doi:10.1186/s40163-015-0026-5

Jonson, C. L., Moon, M. M., & Hendry, J. A. (2020). One size does not fit all: Traditional lockdown versus multioption responses to school shootings. *Journal of School Violence*, 19(2), 154–166.

Kennedy, R. S. (2020). A meta-analysis of the outcomes of bullying prevention programs on subtypes of traditional bullying victimization: Verbal, relational, and physical. *Aggression and Violent Behavior*, 55, 101485.

Kraft, E. M., & Wang, J. (2009). Effectiveness of cyber bullying prevention strategies: A study on students' perspectives. *International Journal of Cyber Criminology*, 3(2), 513.

Krebs, C. P., Lindquist, C. H., Warner, T. D., Fisher, B. S., & Martin, S. L. (2009). College women's experiences with physically forced, alcohol-or other drug-enabled, and drug-facilitated sexual assault before and since entering college. *Journal of American College Health*, 57(6), 639–649.

Latané, B., & Darley, J. M. (1970). *The unresponsive bystander: Why doesn't he help?* Saddle River, NJ: Prentice-Hall.

Liu, L., Lan, M., Eck, J. E., & Kang, E. L. (2020). Assessing the effects of bus stop relocation on street robbery. *Computers, Environment and Urban Systems*, 80, 101455.

Loukaitou-Sideris, A. (1999). Hot spots of bus stop crime: The importance of environmental attributes. *Journal of the American Planning Association*, 65(4), 395–411.

Macintyre, S., & Homel, R. (1997). Danger on the dance floor: A study of interior design, crowding and aggression in nightclubs. *Policing for Prevention: Reducing Crime, Public Intoxication and Injury*, 7(1), 91–113.

Mainwaring, C., Gabbert, F., & Scott, A. J. (2023). A systematic review exploring variables related to bystander intervention in sexual violence contexts. *Trauma, Violence, & Abuse*, 24(3), 1727–1742.

Marselle, M., Wootton, A. B., & Hamilton, M. G. (2012). A design against crime intervention to reduce violence in the night-time economy. *Security Journal*, 25, 116–133.

National Center for Education Statistics (NCES) (2022). *Prevalence of criminal victimization at school. Condition of education*. U.S. Department of Education,

Institute of Education Sciences. Retrieved December 10, 2023, from https://nces.ed.gov/programs/coe/indicator/a03

National Center for Education Statistics (NCES) (2023a). *Incidence of nonfatal victimization at school and away from school. Condition of education.* U.S. Department of Education, Institute of Education Sciences. Retrieved December 10, 2023, from https://nces.ed.gov/programs/coe/indicator/a02

National Center for Education Statistics (NCES) (2023b). *Criminal incidents at postsecondary institutions. Condition of education.* U.S. Department of Education, Institute of Education Sciences. Retrieved December 9, 2023, from https://nces.ed.gov/programs/coe/indicator/a21

O'Neill, L., & McGloin, J. M. (2007). Considering the efficacy of situational crime prevention in schools. *Journal of Criminal Justice, 35*(5), 511–523.

Olweus (2023). *About the OBPP.* Retrieved from https://olweus.sites.clemson.edu/about.php

Park, S., & Kim, S. H. (2023). A systematic review and meta-analysis of bystander intervention programs for intimate partner violence and sexual assault. *Psychology of Violence, 13*(2), 93–106. doi:10.1037/vio0000456

Peterson, J., Sackrison, E., & Polland, A. (2015). Training students to respond to shootings on campus: Is it worth it? *Journal of Threat Assessment and Management, 2*(2), 127.

Piquero, N. L., Piquero, A. R., Gies, S., Green, B., Bobnis, A., & Velasquez, E. (2022). Preventing identity theft: Perspectives on technological solutions from industry insiders. In D. Rebovich & J. M. Byrne (Eds), *The New Technology of Financial Crime* (pp. 163–182). London and New York: Routledge.

Poyner, B. (1991) Situational crime prevention in two parking facilities. *Security Journal, 2,* 96–101.

Reyns, B. W. (2010). A situational crime prevention approach to cyberstalking victimization: Preventive tactics for Internet users and online place managers. *Crime Prevention and Community Safety, 12,* 99–118.

Reyns, B. W., Henson, B., & Fisher, B. S. (2011). Being pursued online: Applying cyberlifestyle–routine activities theory to cyberstalking victimization. *Criminal Justice and Behavior, 38*(11), 1149–1169.

Reyns, B. W., Henson, B., & Fisher, B. S. (2012). Stalking in the twilight zone: Extent of cyberstalking victimization and offending among college students. *Deviant Behavior, 33*(1), 1–25.

Schneider, T., Walker, H., & Sprague, J. (2000). *Safe school design: A handbook for educational leaders applying the principles of crime prevention through environmental design.* ERIC Clearinghouse on Educational Management, 5207 University of Oregon, Eugene, OR 97403-5207.

Sevigny, E. L., & Zhang, G. (2018). Do barriers to crime prevention moderate the effects of situational crime prevention policies on violent crime in high schools? *Journal of School Violence, 17*(2), 164–179.

Shariati, A., & Guerette, R. T. (2019). Resident students' perception of safety in on-campus residential facilities: Does crime prevention through environmental design (CPTED) make a difference? *Journal of School Violence, 18*(4), 570–584.

Smith, M. S. (1996). *Crime prevention through environmental design in parking facilities.* US Department of Justice, Office of Justice Programs, National Institute of Justice. https://www.ojp.gov/pdffiles/cptedpkg.pdf

Snyder, J. A., & Freng, A. (2023). Victimization and fear in national parks: That's my parking spot! *Victims & Offenders*, 1–18. doi:10.1080/15564886.2023.220 8108

Sullivan, T. N., Farrell, A. D., Sutherland, K. S., Behrhorst, K. L., Garthe, R. C., & Greene, A. (2021). Evaluation of the Olweus Bullying Prevention Program in US urban middle schools using a multiple baseline experimental design. *Prevention Science*, 22(8), 1134–1146.

Tilley, N. (1993) Understanding car parks, crime and CCTV: Evaluation lessons from safer cities. *Crime Prevention Unit Series Paper 42*. London: HMSO.

Tillyer, M. S., Fisher, B. S., & Wilcox, P. (2011). The effects of school crime prevention on students' violent victimization, risk perception, and fear of crime: A multilevel opportunity perspective. *Justice Quarterly*, 28(2), 249–277.

Tseng, C. H., Duane, J., & Hadipriono, F. (2004). Performance of campus parking garages in preventing crime. *Journal of Performance of Constructed Facilities*, 18(1), 21–28.

Ttofi, M. M., & Farrington, D. P. (2009). What works in preventing bullying: Effective elements of anti-bullying programmes. *Journal of Aggression, Conflict and Peace Research*, 1, 13–24.

University of Ballarat Center for Health Research and Practice (2004). *Operation Link: Be Safe Late Program: A partnership approach to responsible patrol management at nightclubs to reduce the occurrence of alcohol related crime, disorder, and nuisance within the Central Business District of the City of Ballarat.* Mt. Helen, Victoria (Australia): University of Ballarat.

Vagi, K. J., Stevens, M. R., Simon, T. R., Basile, K. C., Carter, S. P., & Carter, S. L. (2018). Crime Prevention Through Environmental Design (CPTED) characteristics associated with violence and safety in middle schools. *Journal of School Health*, 88(4), 296–305.

White, M. D., & Fisher, C. (2008). Assessing our knowledge of identity theft: The challenges to effective prevention and control efforts. *Criminal Justice Policy Review*, 19(1), 3–24.

Chapter 12
Crime Prevention in Action

Crime Prevention in Action

Heidi Scherer

<table>
<tr><td>

Chapter Outline

In this chapter, we will focus on:

Crime Prevention Research Methods
- Elements of effective research methods
- Limitations of experimental designs in crime prevention

Examining Crime Prevention Experiments
- Police-led crime prevention experiments
- Neighborhood crime prevention experiments
- Judicial and correctional crime prevention experiments

Future Trends in Crime Prevention
- The continued role of law enforcement
- The developing role of technology
- The importance of community

</td><td>

Learning Objectives

After reading this chapter, you should be able to:

12.1 Explain methodological approaches and challenges related to conducting crime prevention strategies

12.2 Compare and contrast approaches to designing and evaluating crime prevention strategies

12.3 Describe the methodologies and results from well-known crime prevention experiments

12.4 Discuss some future trends in crime prevention

</td></tr>
</table>

DOI: 10.4324/9781003401551-15

Introduction

In previous chapters, we examined some of the most influential crime prevention studies that have been conducted, such as the Minneapolis Hot Spot Experiment (Sherman & Weisburd, 1995), the Kansas City Preventive Patrol Study (Kelling et al., 1974), and the Redesign of the Port Authority Bus Terminal (Felson et al., 1996), among others. Exploring the methodology and findings from previous crime prevention studies is valuable as they can serve as a guidepost for future research and provide insights into the effectiveness of crime prevention strategies and the validity of crime prevention theories and concepts. In this final chapter, we aim to highlight additional well-known and influential studies in crime prevention and criminal justice that have impacted the field of crime prevention and inspired crime prevention scholars and students.

First, the chapter begins with a brief exploration of some primary social science research methods that are used to evaluate interventions and carry out experiments in crime prevention, with a focus on highlighting some best practices for devising experiments as well as methodological limitations and challenges that can emerge when engaging in research in real-world settings. Next, this chapter explores some additional well-known crime prevention studies that have been carried out in policing, neighborhoods, and the judicial and correctional systems. This text closes with some final reflections on future trends in crime prevention.

Crime Prevention Research Methods

Before examining the design and outcomes of crime prevention experiments, it is valuable to first understand some primary research methods and approaches used in crime prevention research. To be clear, as with much other social science research, the general purpose of crime prevention experiments is to establish a cause-and-effect relationship between two variables (e.g., the crime prevention intervention and an increase, stabilization, or reduction in crime). When researchers and crime prevention practitioners follow standard research method practices, they can increase the rigor of their studies, which can lead to greater confidence in the study's analyses, results, and conclusions.

Elements of Effective Research Methods

There are several key elements and processes that can help make research more effective. Specifically, a strong research design should include measures of the primary outcome variables from both before, called **pretest data**, and after, called **posttest data**, the crime prevention intervention was implemented. In fact, multiple measures of pretest and posttest data over time (e.g., monthly or weekly rates of crime/calls for service) can be particularly informative as these data allow researchers to evaluate trends in behavior over time and establish **temporal order,** indicating that the crime prevention intervention occurred before any change in the outcomes measures.

While multiple measures of data points at the intervention site are critical to examine the presence of change over time, the use of a **control group,** also called the comparison group, can also strengthen the rigor of a study's research design. The control group, which can be a group of individuals or single or multiple locations (e.g., neighborhood, store, street segment), varies from the intervention site, also called the **treatment group,** because it is the group that does not receive any of the implemented crime prevention tactics. The use of a control group is a vital component of a strong research design because when its pretest and posttest data are compared with data from the treatment group, it provides researchers with an estimate of what would have been observed at the treatment site if the intervention had never been implemented. It is important to note that in order for treatment and control groups to be meaningfully compared, the two groups should be as similar as possible in all respects. In some cases, researchers utilize a form of non-random criteria to select treatment and control groups and verify their similarities, such as selecting a control group that shares similar environmental or demographic-related characteristics to the treatment group. When researchers examine pretest and posttest data from multiple groups but use some form of non-random criteria to select the treatment and control groups, this is called **non-equivalent control group design,** which is a quasi-experimental design.

Table 12.1 Types of Experimental Research Designs

Type of Experiment	Elements	Strength
Randomized or True Experiment	• Treatment & Control Groups • Randomized Assignment to Groups • Pretest & Posttest Analysis • Independent Variable Manipulated	Strongest Form of Experimental Research
Quasi-Experiment or Non-Equivalent Control Group Experiment	• Treatment & Control Groups • Pretest & Posttest Analysis • Independent Variable Manipulated	Moderately Strong Form of Experimental Research
Pre-Experimental or Non-Experiment	• Pretest & Posttest Analysis • Independent Variable Manipulated • May Involve Multiple Groups	Weakest Form of Experimental Research

On the other hand, when designing research studies, researchers can also choose to utilize some form of **random selection** to obtain equivalence across treatment and control groups such as randomly assigning participants or sites to intervention or comparison groups. When researchers compare pretest and posttest measures before and after implementation of an intervention and use random assignment to select treatment and control groups, this is called a true or **randomized experiment**, which is an experimental research design. Randomized experiments are often referred to as the gold standard in science and, according to Weisburd and Hinkle (2012), "offer the most persuasive evidence on the true impacts of crime-prevention policies and interventions" (p. 447). This is because, through the use of randomization, equivalence between control and treatment groups should be obtained, which allows researchers to account for and rule out the possible impact of confounding variables that are often difficult to fully identify in criminological research (Weisburd & Hinkle, 2012). Given its superiority to make causal inferences, many prominent criminology scholars assert that crime prevention evaluators should strive to increase their use of the randomized experiment above all other designs (Farrington & Welsh, 2006; Weisburd & Hinkle, 2012).

Limitations of Experimental Designs in Crime Prevention

While both quasi-experimental and experimental designs are strong research designs, it is important to note that both have some limitations and/or challenges associated with their use. Among a quasi-experimental design like the non-equivalent control group with non-random assignment of the control and treatment groups, one of the greatest limitations involves concerns over the equivalency of the two groups and whether there is a threat of selection bias. **Selection bias** can occur when there are differences between the treatment and control group and comparisons across the groups could lead to invalid conclusions due to these differences. Because crime prevention research occurs in real-world settings and not laboratories, selection bias concerns are a legitimate threat for crime prevention researchers to consider as no two neighborhoods, police departments, classrooms, or street segments are identical. Although randomization into control and treatment groups would control for the occurrence of selection bias, as randomization should produce two equivalent groups, randomized experiments also have challenges when carried out in real-world settings. For instance, criminal justice practitioners and public officials partnering with researchers to implement crime prevention may be leery of utilizing randomization if it influences discretion or determines the action of criminal justice professionals (Weisburd & Hinkle, 2012). Additionally, because randomized experiments can be more complex to implement, they often require more planning, skills, and resources than other research designs, which may limit their feasibility for some research teams (Eck, 2006).

Despite their respective limitations, quasi-experiments like the non-equivalent control group and randomized experiments are strong research designs that contribute important knowledge on the effectiveness of crime prevention interventions (Eck, 2006). In situations where random assignment is not possible or appropriate, based on characteristics of the intervention or research team, non-random designs can still provide valuable insights. When coupled with **replication** (e.g., repetition of experiments using similar methodologies), these insights can give crime prevention scholars and practitioners a clearer understanding of the validity of crime prevention theories and the effectiveness of crime prevention interventions.

Examining Crime Prevention Experiments

In the sections below, we explore some of the most well-known and influential crime prevention and criminal justice experiments, focusing on the methodology, results, and implications for each study. These experiments make important contributions to the field of crime prevention not only by producing findings that inform practice, but also by providing examples of how to conduct rigorous and strong research studies in the field, which can be used to inspire future experiments and the use of replication and verification. First, we explore crime prevention experiments that predominately involved police interventions (e.g., foot patrol, third-party policing, hotspot policing), followed by those implemented within neighborhoods (e.g., crime prevention through environmental design (CPTED), burglary prevention), and the judicial (e.g., drug treatment) and correctional systems (e.g., intensive supervision probation/parole).

Police-Led Crime Prevention Experiments

The Newark Foot Patrol Study

Along with the Kansas City Preventive Patrol Study (Kelling et al., 1974) that was explored in detail in Chapter 9, the Newark Foot Patrol Study (The Police Foundation, 1981) is another significant policing study that played a role in influencing modern policing policies and practices. In the 1970s, as part of the Safe and Clean Neighborhood Program, the Newark Police Department implemented a foot patrol scheme in Newark, New Jersey, where officers would patrol beats and respond to calls for service on foot. This would allow officers to become more familiar with the characteristics of the communities that they were assigned and with the community members who resided and worked in the beats. To examine whether, and to what extent, foot patrol influenced measures of crime, evaluators identified 12 beats in the city where the level of foot patrol could be manipulated for this quasi-experiment. First, eight beats in Newark were identified that had consistently utilized foot patrol as a police practice over the course of the

Safe and Clean Neighborhood Program. These eight beats were next split into matched pairs, where foot patrol would continue in half of the beats (n = 4) but would be discontinued in the other half (n = 4). Next, four additional beats that had no previous foot patrol schemes were selected to receive foot patrol during the experiment. Multiple measures of crime and perceptions of residents were analyzed from both before and after implementation of the practice to examine the impact of foot patrol in Newark. Overall, no evidence emerged that foot patrol led to significant changes in crimes reported to police, arrests, or victimization. From the analyses of collected residential data, some positive impacts of foot patrol were observed with some residents perceiving the presence of foot patrol as leading to a reduction in the severity of the neighborhoods' crime problems.

The findings from the Newark Foot Patrol Study led to two major impacts on the field of policing, each of which was influenced by how the findings were interpreted by policing scholars and practitioners at the time of its release. First, similar to the Kansas City Preventive Patrol Study (see Chapter 9), the non-significant findings related to foot patrol's impact on crime bolstered the belief that traditional police strategies were not as effective as more tailored responses that emerged during the community- and problem-oriented policing eras. On the other hand, the study's findings on citizen perceptions informed Kelling and Wilson's (1982) broken windows thesis and provided some foundational support that police activities that impact order and disorder can provide the basis for effective police practice. This study also inspired future experiments on foot patrol such as the Philadelphia Foot Patrol Experiment, which utilized a randomized control trial to examine if foot patrol would be effective at reducing violent crime at hotspots (Ratcliffe et al., 2011). When foot patrol was randomly assigned to violent hotspots, significant reductions in violent crime were observed in the treatment areas, underscoring that foot patrol has the potential to be an even more effective police practice when targeted at known crime attractors and hotspots.

The San Diego Nuisance Abatement Experiment

Eck and Wartell's (1998) San Diego Nuisance Abatement Experiment provides an excellent illustration of the use of randomizing interventions to evaluate and understand the effectiveness of crime prevention strategies. This study focused on the use of a third-party policing strategy to target property managers who operated rental properties (N = 121) that were identified as nuisances due to their extensive record of police actions at the properties related to drug dealing and crime. Once problem sites were identified, the research team devised the experiment to take place. First, screening data were collected by the San Diego Police Department on each of the sites to gain relevant information on ownership practices and physical characteristics of the sites. Next, the sites were randomly assigned to three groups. The first group served as the control group and received no further intervention (Group 1 n = 42). The second group was assigned to receive letters from the Drug Abatement Response Team (DART) specialized unit, which informed owners that the police would provide them with assistance to remove drug dealers from their property, but also notified owners that punitive legal action through the city would be taken (e.g., a large fine and/or property closed for up to one year) if they did not take the appropriate steps to resolve the drug problems at their property. No further action was carried out for this second group beyond the letter in the mail (Group 2 n = 42). In the third group, the owners received a letter from DART notifying them of the punitive legal actions that the city could enforce against them, but also requiring a meeting between the owner and a member of the DART team and the city's Code Compliance Department. During the meeting, the public employees worked with the owner to identify solutions to address the drug problem and then followed up to ensure that the actions were taken (Group 3 n = 37).

To evaluate the effectiveness of the intervention, analyses were conducted to examine changes in crime rates at the sites for a period before and after the experiment was implemented. Based on these analyses, significant differences emerged across the three groups. Specifically, notable crime reductions were observed in the meeting group in comparison with the control group with 60 percent less crime in the sites that were randomly assigned the meeting with the DART and city employees. While the findings were less conclusive, there was also some promising evidence of crime reductions in the latter group for some, but not all, of the time periods examined. This study made two primary contributions. First, it contributed empirically strong additional support on the effectiveness of third-party policing and the use of civil remedies to address nuisance properties. Second, it underscored the role of place managers in the second level of the crime triangle as key players in influencing crime at places.

The Jersey City POP in Violent Crime Places Experiment

Another experiment that has been influential to the field of policing is Braga and colleagues' (1999) randomized experiment of problem-oriented policing (POP) at violent crime places in Jersey City, New Jersey. Prior to this study, there was limited research on whether POP strategies would be effective on more serious crime problems such as violent street crimes or at violent hotspots. To shed light on the extent of POP's effectiveness, Braga and his research team of academics and police personnel from Jersey City used crime-mapping technology to identify 56 violent places in the city that met inclusion criteria of high and stable crime rates over time. These 56 places were then matched based on environmental or situational characteristics into 28 pairs that each consisted of one potential control and one potential treatment site. From the sample of 28 pairs, the research team identified

12 pairs that would be appropriate to be randomly allocated to receive the POP intervention (e.g., were not located spatially adjacent to each other and would not overwhelm officer caseload). For each pair, a coin flip was used to determine which site would receive the treatment and which site would serve as the control. At the control sites only traditional police enforcement was utilized, while at the treatment sites officers engaged in the POP/SARA process to analyze the violence problems at the location and devise and implement solutions to address them. A wide range of POP strategies were identified including aggressive responses to social and physical disorder, drug enforcement, third-party policing, and situational crime prevention, among others. Following the implementation of these strategies, officers engaged in the last step of the SARA model – assessment – to identify if the interventions were successful or if they needed to revisit a previous stage to better understand and respond to the problem.

To examine the overall effectiveness of the POP process at the violent locations, the research team collected and analyzed pretest and posttest data on official measures of crime and observations of social and physical disorder at the sites. These analyses provided strong support for the effectiveness of POP as there were observed decreases in crime at the treatment groups in comparison with the control groups, and evidence that POP helped to address the amount of social and physical incivilities at the sites. Further, there was little evidence of any meaningful displacement, indicating that the POP interventions were not just shifting crime around to other locations. Taken together, the findings from this study were valuable for establishing POP as a policing practice that has the capacity to address serious crime problems and not just minor crime problems that emerge in communities.

The Minneapolis and Milwaukee Domestic Violence Experiments
In 1984, Sherman and Berk published the results from their randomized experiment on mandatory arrest for domestic violence that had a very significant impact on how police departments directed their officers to respond to instances of intimate partner violence. For their Minneapolis domestic violence experiment, Sherman and Berk were interested in identifying which response to a domestic violence incident was most effective at reducing future domestic violence experiences and recidivism. In order to examine their research question, Sherman and Berk partnered with the Minneapolis Police Department to design an experiment in which officers would use random assignment to select one of three responses to a misdemeanor domestic violence incident, including: 1) arrest; 2) separation; and 3) advice or mediation by an officer. Misdemeanor domestic violence incidents were selected as the officers would have greater discretion in how to respond versus a felony assault where one party may have experienced an injury that would dictate arrest, and not a randomly assigned response. At the start of the experiment,

during eligible domestic violence incidents, officers would select the top sheet of the randomly ordered report pad to determine how to respond (i.e., arrest, separation, advice/mediation). The experiment ran from March 1981 to August 1982, which resulted in approximately 300 cases of randomly selected police responses to domestic violence.

In order to examine which response was most effective, the research team analyzed data on police-recorded failure (e.g., no rearrest or report to police for domestic violence) and victim interviews (e.g., no repeated incident with the same suspect) for six months following the close of the experiment. From these analyses, Sherman and Berk (1984) reported that individuals from the arrest group had lower domestic violence recidivism in comparison with the individuals who were separated by police (observed with official data) and those who were advised or who received mediation (observed with victim data). Given their findings, the authors asserted that the primary implication from the study was one that supported deterrence theory and the recommended use of arrest for domestic violence. These findings also provided support for the expansion of mandatory arrest policies across the United States. However, it is important to note that these findings would be reevaluated in a different light following the results of the Milwaukee Domestic Violence Experiment (Sherman et al., 1992). The Milwaukee Domestic Violence Experiment utilized a similar methodology with randomized selection of responses to examine the impact of arrest on domestic violence incidents, yet altered the treatment conditions to align with the mandatory arrest policy that was already implemented in the state. In this updated experiment, officers would randomly select one of the following three response options: 1) arrest and release on bail/cash; 2) arrest and release on own recognizance; and 3) make no arrest but provide a warning of arrest if police returned. Based on their analyses, Sherman and colleagues (1992) found no evidence of a deterrent effect of arrest for domestic violence but did find that the impact of arrest on domestic violence recidivism was more nuanced than originally recognized and that it varied based on the characteristics of perpetrators. For instance, they found that among perpetrators who were unemployed, unmarried, and high school dropouts, they appeared to be more likely to continue engaging in domestic violence after arrest in contrast to their employed, married, and educated counterparts. These findings indicate that, for some perpetrators, arrest can escalate or increase their perpetration and put their victims at increased risk of harm.

The Boston Gun Project: Operation Ceasefire

In 1996, a strong partnership between academics at Harvard University and professionals from local, state, and federal law enforcement, district attorneys' offices, and community organizations led to the development and implementation of the first focused deterrence strategy, the Boston Gun Project, also known as Operation Ceasefire (Kennedy et al., 1996). "Focused deterrence strategies combine law enforcement, community mobilization, and social services in an attempt to reduce offending behavior for specific crime types" (Braga et al., 2019, p. 1). Operation Ceasefire utilized both supply- and demand-side strategies with the goal to reduce youth gun violence and disrupt illegal gun sales. Demand-side approaches included pulling legal enforcement levers and enforcing all available laws, restrictions, and warrants on gangs, a communications campaign where law enforcement notified gangs that they were being targeted directly due to their engagement in violence, and gang mediation specialists. Supply-side approaches included activities related to disrupting the illegal gun market, such as tracing data on illegal guns and examining patterns of gun acquisition among youth. Based on an evaluation of crime data from before and after the implementation of Operation Ceasefire, Braga et al. (2001) reported meaningful violence reduction impacts. Specifically, they found that there were significant reductions in youth homicides, citywide shots-fired calls, citywide all-age gun assault incidents, and youth gun assault incidents following the start of the program in 1996.

The Boston Gun Project was particularly impactful to the field of policing and crime prevention as it established focused deterrence strategies, which have been found to be one of the most effective tools in the law enforcement toolkit for addressing gang and gun violence. For instance, following in Operation Ceasefire's footsteps were several effective and influential focused deterrence strategies, including the Cincinnati Initiative to Reduce Violence (CIRV), Lowell, Massachusetts' Project Safe Neighborhoods, Chicago's Group Violence Reduction Strategy, among others (Braga et al., 2018). Findings from recent meta-analyses also underscore the legacy of Boston Ceasefire and find that focused deterrence strategies can lead to significant reductions in crime (Braga et al., 2018; 2019).

The Kansas City Gun Experiment

The Kansas City Gun Experiment is another policing experiment focused on reducing gun violence (Sherman & Rogan, 1995). Funded through the U.S. Bureau of Justice Assistance's Weed and Seed program, the Kansas City Missouri Police Department and researchers at the University of Maryland partnered to implement and evaluate the city's effort to reduce gun crime in the city. The intervention selected for this experiment involved three components aimed at increasing gun seizures including: 1) soliciting door-to-door for anonymous tips related to gun crime; 2) police training to recognize body language that would indicate gun carrying; and 3) field interrogations and increased police patrol at gun crime hotspots. To carry out their experiment, the researchers selected a target beat that would receive the treatment and a control beat, that received no additional patrol time, that would be used as a comparison. From July 1992 to January

1993, extra patrol activities at gun crime hotspots were carried out in the target beat and guns were predominately removed from the street through safety frisks during traffic stops, plain view searches, and searches incident to a lawful arrest on other charges.

To determine the effectiveness of the intervention activities, particularly the increased police activity at the gun hotspots, Sherman and Rogan examined gun-related crimes before and after the intervention at both the treatment and control beats. Based on this analysis, the Kansas City Gun Experiment was found to be effective and led to increased gun seizures and less gun crime in the treatment beat in comparison with the control beat. Additionally, drive-by shootings and homicides were found to be significantly reduced in the treatment beat during the intervention. Further, no displacement was observed in any of the seven beats connected to the treatment beat, and some evidence of diffusion of benefits was observed. While the authors note that rates increased following the cessation of the program, its effectiveness was again established when gun crime decreased at the treatment beat following a reinstatement of the intervention. This study makes an important contribution to the area of crime prevention and policing by illustrating that straightforward directed patrol activities can lead to meaningful reductions of crime.

The Illinois DARE Longitudinal Evaluation

With funding support from the Illinois State Police, researchers from the University of Illinois at Chicago and the Research Triangle Institute conducted a longitudinal analysis of the Drug Abuse Resistance Education (DARE) Program (Ennett et al., 1994; Rosenbaum et al., 1994; Rosenbaum & Hanson, 1998). DARE is a drug prevention program created in the early 1980s with an anti-drug abuse curriculum taught by local police officers across a 17-week period inside elementary school classrooms. By the 1990s the DARE program experienced rapid growth and was implemented in all 50 states across the United States. Yet, despite its extensive implementation, much remained unknown about the program's effectiveness. To address this gap in knowledge, Rosenbaum and colleagues conducted a randomized experiment of 36 schools in Illinois that were matched into 18 pairs based on location and socio-demographic characteristics of the school populations. Next, randomization and selection procedures were used to select which school in each pair would receive the DARE program. For six years, students and teachers would complete surveys to provide the research team with information on the program's impact on students' drug-related attitudes and behaviors and any additional exposure students may have had to other anti-drug prevention programs in the school.

At different waves of the study, the research team examined the longitudinal impacts of the DARE program. Studies examining the program

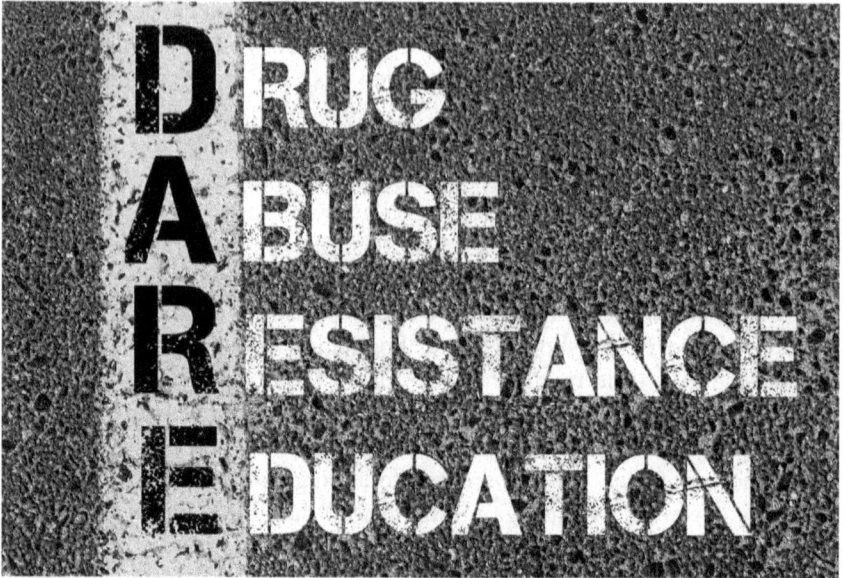

Image 12.1 The DARE Program Logo.

within the first two years of exposure reported little evidence of the positive effects of DARE, with no significant improvement on measures of drug, alcohol, and/or tobacco use and no significant impact on students' school performance (Ennett et al., 1994; Rosenbaum et al., 1994). Further, after the close of the study, the research team analyzed the six years of follow-up data to examine if long-term impacts on participants had emerged since the previous analyses (Rosenbaum & Hanson, 1998). Unfortunately, this analysis produced findings consistent with the results from previous waves of the data – that there were no observed longitudinal impacts on students' drug use or attitudes toward drugs. Overall, the research team found no significant differences across the treatment and control groups in their drug use over the course of the study. Together, the findings from these longitudinal evaluations had important implications as they raised valuable questions about the effectiveness of the DARE curriculum and whether there was the need to reevaluate the "one size fits all" nature of the program curriculum.

Neighborhood Crime Prevention Experiments

The Bronx and Palo Alto Car Vandalism Experiment

In 1969, psychologist Philip Zimbardo was interested in systematically studying vandalism to gain a greater understanding of the characteristics of offenders and the conditions that shape its occurrence. To study these questions, Zimbardo conducted a field experiment where two cars were left on a street, one in the Bronx, New York and one in Palo Alto, California. To call attention to the vehicles, Zimbardo removed their license plates and opened their hoods. Next, he observed the cars for 64 continuous hours to examine whether they would be viewed by offenders as suitable targets for vandalism and if so what types of acts would be carried out on the vehicles and by whom. During the 64-hour period, Zimbardo made several notable observations. First, in New York, within the first ten minutes of the experiment, vandals began to search through the vehicle for valuables and remove parts of the car that had some monetary value. For the rest of the first day of observation, other vandals removed most, if not all, of the valuable parts of the vehicle. Once the valuable parts were removed, Zimbardo reported that the vandalism became more destructive with children and teenagers smashing or throwing objects at the car. Other relevant observations from New York were that the vandalism was most frequently carried out during the day and was observed by other passersby in the neighborhood.

On the other hand, the car parked in Palo Alto experienced no episodes of vandalism during the 64-hour window and was even protected by a resident who closed the hood of the car when it began to rain. In order to further prompt vandalism on the Palo Alto vehicle, Zimbardo and his students vandalized the car while it was parked on the street in sight of other individuals. In turn, this opened the door for additional vandalism on the vehicle, which was observed that evening when young men began to smash up the car. This study had important implications for crime prevention as it illustrated that neighborhood characteristics may influence participation in crime and the acceptability of disorder in the community. Along with the Newark Foot Patrol Study, this experiment was also impactful as it influenced Kelling and Wilson's (1982) broken windows theory by underscoring how untended property may create the stage for more serious disorder to flourish in a neighborhood.

The Kirkholt Burglary Prevention Project

The Kirkholt Burglary Prevention Project is one of the most well-known crime prevention experiments to be conducted at the neighborhood level. It also provides one of the most effective blueprints for reducing repeat burglary victimization of residential properties. Kirkholt is a residential public housing neighborhood in the UK that was selected as a location in need of intervention after data from the 1984 British Crime Survey identified the neighborhood as having a substantial and disproportionally high rate of domestic burglaries. The first stage of the project involved data collection procedures to gain an understanding of the crime problem from burglars, residents, and victims (Forrester et al., 1988). Based on this data collection process, the Home Office Police Department research team determined that the best course of action to impact burglary rates in the community would be to focus on reducing repeat burglaries given their predictability, which lends well to the implementation of situational and community-based interventions. The Kirkholt project involved several different components. The first crime prevention initiative undertaken was to remove and replace pre-payment gas and electric meters that housed tokens or payments as they were often the primary, and sometimes only, target of burglars. The next initiative involved security advisement to prior burglary victims by a local police officer to address the home's access vulnerability and identify ways to prevent burglars from being able to re-access the home through similar methods as the first burglary. The third component of the project involved the implementation of mini cocoon Neighborhood Watch schemes of approximately six homes near prior burglarized properties that would observe and report any suspicious activities. The final initiative was the inclusion of support from project workers who provided residents with updates on any new and emerging burglary prevention techniques.

To assess the effectiveness of the intervention, the research team evaluated monthly burglary rates before and after the implementation for Kirkholt and a local area that served as a control group and a buffer zone for displacement. Analysis of the data indicated success for the Kirkholt initiative with significant reductions in burglary and repeat burglary victimization following the project's implementation that was not observed at the control location. Further, there was no evidence of burglary displacement as a result of the intervention. Given the initial success of the program on burglary victimization rates, a second phase was launched soon after. This phase focused on trying to learn more about offender motivations and social factors that shape offending, which could inform crime prevention and criminal justice responses to burglars (Forrester et al., 1990). This study made valuable contributions to the field of crime prevention by providing insights into effectively reducing repeat burglary victimization. It also served as an example of how other organizations and agencies can implement successful crime prevention programs neighborhood wide.

The Mini-Neighborhoods of the Five Oaks Project

In the early 1990s, Five Oaks, a large neighborhood located in downtown Dayton, Ohio, was experiencing traffic, disorder, and serious crime problems that were negatively impacting the quality of life for the approximately 5,000 people living in community. Contributing to the emergence and stability of physical and social incivilities and crime in the community were the environmental design and location of the neighborhood to the downtown area. For instance, the streets of Five Oaks were regularly used as main paths for offenders as they traveled to criminal opportunities and crime attractors, some of which were inside the neighborhood at drug and prostitution houses. They were also used by outside individuals, who entered the community solely to cut through to avoid downtown traffic overwhelming legitimate use of the space by residents. The increase in crime also led to social tension in the neighborhood between homeowners and renters and led prosocial residents to move out of the community, leaving behind more properties to fall into disrepair or under the control of slumlords. Given these issues in the community, officials from Dayton sought the assistance of Oscar Newman's Institute for Community Design Analysis to assist in creating a plan to redesign Five Oaks into a defensible space (see Chapter 3 for a detailed discussion of defensible space theory).

Based on his review of the neighborhood, Newman (1996) recommended dividing Five Oaks into mini-neighborhoods through the use of street barriers and gates in order to increase the defensibility of the space by the residents. In theory, the creation of the mini-neighborhoods would increase risk for drug buyers who would have to turn around in cul-de-sacs to exit the neighborhood after purchasing drugs, while also preventing others from using the community as a cut-through to downtown Dayton. With support of the residents, Five Oaks was transformed into ten similarly sized mini-neighborhoods with only one entrance and exit through the closure of 35 streets and 25 alleys. To increase territoriality over the new mini-neighborhoods, each was given a new name based on the largest street in the new mini-neighborhood. In addition to the neighborhood redesign, police and code enforcement was also increased in Five Oaks to help stabilize the area. Several sources of data were analyzed to examine the effectiveness of the neighborhood redesign which indicated positive impacts from the intervention. For instance, city data indicated a decrease in overall traffic and noise, while police data provided evidence of a decrease in robbery, burglary, assault, and auto theft following the redesign, with no evidence of displacement. Of note, data from a survey of residents provided evidence of some notable social changes as a result of the intervention, including many residents reporting perceptions that the community is a safer place to live and more involvement by community members in community activities. Following the implementation of these changes, the Five Oaks Project has received much attention from other communities interested in increasing defensible space through similar redesign strategies.

Judicial and Correctional Crime Prevention Experiments

The Baltimore Drug Treatment Court Randomized Study

Over the last several decades, there has been an increase in the use of specialized courts, particularly those that target drug users. As these courts have grown in their popularity and use, researchers' interests in understanding the effectiveness and best practices of implementing these courts have also grown. To meet these needs, Gottfredson and Exum (2002) partnered with the Baltimore City Drug Treatment Court (BDTC) to conduct a randomized experiment to determine if the BDTC program was effective at reducing drug use/recidivism. For this experiment, the research team would identify participants who met the criteria for inclusion in the study and notify the eligible clients that they could participate in the study. They would then be randomly assigned to either the BDTC treatment group or the control group, which would receive standard drug treatment procedures. This process resulted in a total of 235 clients in the study who were assigned into the treatment or control group. Next, for each of the clients, data were collected on demographic characteristics and risk factors, including drug use history from before the study, and recidivism data for 12 months after the study.

Following completion of the study, the outcomes were compared across the two groups to assess the effectiveness of the program. Based on these analyses, there was evidence of effectiveness of the drug court program, with a smaller percent of drug treatment clients (48 percent) arrested for new offenses compared with the controls (64 percent). Additionally, among the felony cases, there was also evidence of significant differences across the two groups, with 32 percent of treatment participants being arrested within 12 months versus 57 percent of the control group. To further explore the long-term effects of the BDTC program and examine if the impact on recidivism persisted after active treatment had stopped, Gottfredson and colleagues (2003; 2006) conducted follow-up studies on the 235 drug offenders. Findings from both follow-up analyses provide support that participation in the drug court program led to positive impacts in the clients' lives over time, which lends support for the value of specialized courts to prevent or reduce crime and drug use.

The Nationwide Intensive Supervision Probation/Parole Experiment

In the 1980s and 1990s there was an increased interest in the use of intermediate sanctions, such as intensive supervision probation/parole (ISP), that could serve as a deterrent to criminal involvement for offenders while holding them accountable and keeping them out of prison. Given growth in the interest to expand the use of ISPs across the United States, the National Institute of Justice and Bureau of Justice Assistance worked with researchers from the RAND Corporation to conduct a rigorous evaluation of the effectiveness of ISP at 14 sites across 9 states. With funding to support the projects, these 14 sites were asked to develop an ISP program that met the needs of their communities, with the only required parameter being that the ISP programs must target adult offenders with no violent convictions. Prior to the ISP implementation, at each of the 14 sites, eligible offenders were identified for participation in the study and then randomly assigned to a treatment or control group. In total, about 2,000 adult offenders participated in the experiment; data on demographics, risk factors, and recidivism were collected for each participant.

At the close of the implementation of the 14 programs, data were analyzed to provide insights into the ISPs' impact on recidivism and other relevant outcomes. Overall, in comparison with control sites, ISP sites involved greater levels of contacts and monitoring and more features that restricted participant freedoms. Regarding recidivism outcomes, the experiment did not find evidence of less recidivism among the treatment group and in fact, in some instances, the treatment participants recidivated at non-significantly higher rates than the control group. However, it is important to note that only official measures of recidivism were utilized and self-report data may have produced different results. Additionally, the ISP participants also experienced higher rates of technical violations, and subsequent commitments to jail/prison, than the control group, which was likely due to the increased monitoring that accompanied the ISP conditions. In turn, the impacts of technical violations also likely resulted in the ISP sites being more costly than the control group sites where participants only received routine supervision. On a positive note, there was evidence that the ISP participants received more access to treatments (e.g., drug/alcohol counseling, employment assistance) than the control group. The results from this experiment were particularly impactful on the field of corrections by highlighting that ISP programs are multifaceted and that many factors can shape their effectiveness, underscoring the need for more research on the topic before wide-scale adoption of the programs.

Expand Your Understanding – Evaluating Crime Prevention Programs

Interested readers can explore more examples of crime prevention experiments and evaluations at the following sites:

- The National Institute of Justice's Crime Solutions (Crimesolutions.gov): This database compiles and synthesizes evaluations on criminal justice-related programs and uses a standardized rating system.
- The Arizona State University's Center for Problem-Oriented Policing (Popcenter.ASU.edu): The situational crime prevention evaluation database compiles and provides summaries for a wide range of crime prevention evaluations focusing on opportunity blocking techniques.

Future Trends in Crime Prevention

Since the emergence of modern-day crime prevention, there have been some crime prevention strategies and techniques that have stood the test of time to become staples in the crime prevention toolkit, such as police/community partnerships, the use of technology to monitor areas for security threats, and connectiveness among community members. Given their stability in the crime prevention landscape, there is reason to anticipate that these strategies will remain dominant as we move into the future. Yet, one may anticipate that they begin to take some different shapes as we move toward a future with quickly growing technologies that link us together in unique ways to prevent crime.

The Continued Role of Law Enforcement

As previous chapters have explored in more detail, partnerships between the police and community have been central to police-led crime prevention since the community-policing model gained momentum. In the future, it is anticipated that police partnerships will continue to grow and strengthen in the private sector domain in industries such as loss prevention, private security, and cybersecurity as both the public and private sectors bring unique and valuable resources, knowledge, and skills to the table. In fact, given growing trends of violence in organized retail crime, leaders in the retail sector have specifically expressed the need for partnerships with law enforcement to devise solutions (Poe, 2023). One example of such is the Georgia Retailers Organized Crime Alliance (2023), which is a coalition of over 600 professionals working in retail loss prevention and law enforcement across the state who network together to share intelligence and coordinate investigations and arrests. Given that these types of partnerships can be quite beneficial for each partner and the general public, it is anticipated that they will continue to grow and be central to crime prevention efforts in the future.

The Developing Role of Technology

The future of crime prevention may also be shaped by the continued emergence and growth of artificial intelligence (AI), which is becoming increasingly more affordable and accessible to everyone, including law enforcement agencies. As Chapter 9 explored, aspects of artificial intelligence are already in use by law enforcement, such as facial recognition software in CCTV or drones, and will likely continue to play an important role in the monitoring of public spaces and investigations. However, with the emergence of generative AI (GenAI), which can produce content, in the future, law enforcement and crime preventers may begin utilizing AI in more creative and proactive ways such as using it to predict trends in crime, generate COMPSTAT reports, or analyze police data (Mohindroo, 2023). Additionally, in the future, police may find GenAI informative for problem-solving activities, particularly related to the SARA model. For instance, police may prompt GenAI to analyze the social media of residents to scan for crime problems or request that GenAI summarize findings from past crime prevention research on a crime problem, which could be used to inform the problem-solving process. It is important to note that AI should be viewed as just one of the many unique tools in the crime preventer's toolkit and information produced by it should always be reviewed by key law enforcement personnel who can verify its accuracy.

The Importance of Community

One of the most important criminological concepts related to crime in neighborhoods is the strength of informal social control among community members. These informal bonds bring members of the community together and signal to outsiders that the residents are invested in the safety and security of the neighborhood. Over time, changes in society have impacted the nature of how community members communicate among each other, but the overall importance of this communication has not shifted and will continue to play an important role in crime prevention in the future. For instance, increased use of technological devices aimed at home security such as Amazon's Ring doorbell and camera systems, and social apps to increase sharing of information among residents located in a geographic area such as Nextdoor, Neighbors, and Citizen, provide new ways for community members to share information on crime with each other for the purposes of protection and prevention. In fact, these apps can lead to almost immediate sharing of information following the crime and safety threat, often before law enforcement are able to warn or respond to the public, which underscores these technologies' likelihood to remain at the forefront of neighborhood crime prevention efforts in the future.

Summary

As this book has illustrated, the field of crime prevention encompasses a diverse amount of theories, methodologies, practices, and techniques that come together to inform scholars' and practitioners' work to understand offender decision making and apply and evaluate situational crime prevention to reduce crime and disorder in communities across the globe. In this last chapter of the textbook, we have explored several well-known crime prevention experiments illustrating concepts addressed across the book which provide evidence that, when opportunities for crime are blocked, rational offenders will assess the situational characteristics of environments to make decisions regarding their engagement in crime. In many instances, these decisions will involve people desisting from crime rather than displacing their offending elsewhere. While crime prevention may continue to shift in the future due to technological or societal changes and trends, the primary strengths of the field are its theories (e.g., rational choice theory) and methodologies (e.g., situational crime prevention, SARA model), which have wide-scale generalizability and adaptability to different crime problems, crime types, and crime settings. These characteristics solidify crime prevention as its own subfield of criminal justice and criminology, particularly one that can withstand and produce strong rebuttals against attacks on the value of opportunity blocking techniques from critics and opponents.

Keywords

Pretest Data, Posttest Data, Temporal Order, Control Group, Treatment Group, Non-Equivalent Control Group Design, Random Selection, Randomized Experiment, Selection Bias, Replication

Discussion Questions

1. Congratulations! You have been hired by your local police department to help design a rigorous crime prevention experiment to evaluate the effectiveness of a new patrol scheme to reduce traffic infractions. Describe how you would design the study using research methods terms discussed in this chapter.
2. Replication of scientific studies is an important way that a scientific community evaluates the validity of research studies. How do the Minneapolis and Milwaukee Domestic Violence Experiments illustrate the importance of replication?
3. What do you perceive are some of the advantages of the use of artificial intelligence (AI) in efforts to prevent and reduce crime? What do you perceive are some of the disadvantages to using AI for crime prevention?
4. Beyond the ones discussed in this chapter, what do you believe are some future trends in crime prevention? How do you think the field may change in the future?
5. What are some of the methodological challenges that researchers may face when designing an experiment and deciding whether to use random or non-random selection methods to assign treatment and control groups?

References

Braga, A. A., Kennedy, D. M., Piehl, A. M., & Waring, E. J. (2001). *Reducing gun violence: The Boston Gun Project's Operation Ceasefire.* US Department of Justice Office of Justice Programs.

Braga, A. A., Weisburd, D., & Turchan, B. (2018). Focused deterrence strategies and crime control: An updated systematic review and meta-analysis of the empirical evidence. *Criminology & Public Policy, 17*(1), 205–250.

Braga, A. A., Weisburd, D., & Turchan, B. (2019). Focused deterrence strategies effects on crime: A systematic review. *Campbell Systematic Reviews, 15*(3), 1–65.

Braga, A. A., Weisburd, D. L., Waring, E. J., Mazerolle, L. G., Spelman, W., & Gajewski, F. (1999). Problem-oriented policing in violent crime places: A randomized controlled experiment. *Criminology, 37*(3), 541–580.

Eck, J. E. (2006). When is a bologna sandwich better than sex? A defense of small-n case study evaluations. *Journal of Experimental Criminology, 2,* 345–362.

Eck, J. E., & Wartell, J. (1998). Improving the management of rental properties with drug problems: A randomized experiment. *Crime Prevention Studies, 9*(16), 1–185.

Ennett, S. T., Rosenbaum, D. P., Flewelling, R. L., Bieler, G. S., Ringwalt, C. L., & Bailey, S. L. (1994). Long-term evaluation of drug abuse resistance education. *Addictive Behaviors, 19*(2), 113–125.

Farrington, D. P., & Welsh, B. C. (2006). A half century of randomized experiments on crime and justice. *Crime and Justice, 34*(1), 55–132.

Felson, M., Belanger, M. E., Bichler, G. M., Bruzinski, C. D., Campbell, G. S., Fried, C. L., . . . & Williams, L. M. (1996). Redesigning hell: Preventing crime and disorder at the port authority bus terminal. *Preventing Mass Transit Crime, 6,* 5–92.

Forrester, D., Chatterton, M., Pease, K., & Brown, R. (1988). *The Kirkholt Burglary Prevention Project, Rochdale.* London: Home Office.

Forrester, D., Frenz, S., O'Connell, M., & Pease, K. (1990). *The Kirkholt Burglary Prevention Project: Phase II.* London: Home Office.

Georgia Retailers Organized Crime Alliance. (2023). History of the Georgia Retailers Loss Prevention Council (GRLPC) and the Georgia Retailers Organized Crime Alliance (GROC). Retrieved from: https://www.georgiaroc.org/index.php/about-groc.

Gottfredson, D. C., & Exum, M. L. (2002). The Baltimore City drug treatment court: One-year results from a randomized study. *Journal of Research in Crime and Delinquency, 39*(3), 337–356.

Gottfredson, D. C., Najaka, S. S., & Kearley, B. (2003). Effectiveness of drug treatment courts: Evidence from a randomized trial. *Criminology & Public Policy, 2*(2), 171–196.

Gottfredson, D. C., Najaka, S. S., Kearley, B. W., & Rocha, C. M. (2006). Long-term effects of participation in the Baltimore City drug treatment court: Results from an experimental study. *Journal of Experimental Criminology, 2,* 67–98.

Kelling, G. L., & Wilson, J. Q. (1982). Broken windows. *Atlantic Monthly, 249*(3), 29–38.

Kelling, G. L., Pate, T., Dieckman, D., & Brown, C. (1974). *The Kansas City Preventive Patrol Experiment: A summary report.* Washington, DC: Police Foundation. Retrieved from https://www.ojp.gov/pdffiles1/Digitization/42537NCJRS.pdf

Kennedy, D. M., Piehl, A. M., & Braga, A. A. (1996). Youth violence in Boston: Gun markets, serious youth offenders, and a use-reduction strategy. *Law and Contemporary Problems, 59*(1), 147–196.

Mohindroo, S. K. (2023). Harnessing generative AI in law enforcement: A vision for smarter, safer communities. *Medium*. Retrieved from: https://medium.com/@sanjay.mohindroo66/harnessing-generative-ai-in-law-enforcement-a-vision-for-smarter-safer-communities-13adb6082823/

Newman, O. (1996). *Creating defensible space*. Washington, DC: U.S. Department of Housing and Urban Development.

Poe, S. (2023). Retail leaders call for collaboration, partnerships on retail security issues. *National Retail Federation*. Retrieved from: https://nrf.com/blog/retail-leaders-call-collaboration-partnerships-retail-security-issues

Ratcliffe, J. H., Taniguchi, T., Groff, E. R., & Wood, J. D. (2011). The Philadelphia foot patrol experiment: A randomized controlled trial of police patrol effectiveness in violent crime hotspots. *Criminology*, 49(3), 795–831.

Rosenbaum, D. P., Flewelling, R. L., Bailey, S. L., Ringwalt, C. L., & Wilkinson, D. L. (1994). Cops in the classroom: A longitudinal evaluation of Drug Abuse Resistance Education (DARE). *Journal of Research in Crime and Delinquency*, 31(1), 3–31.

Rosenbaum, D. P., & Hanson, G. S. (1998). Assessing the effects of school-based drug education: A six-year multilevel analysis of project DARE. *Journal of Research in Crime and Delinquency*, 35(4), 381–412.

Sherman, L. W., & Berk, R. A. (1984). The specific deterrent effects of arrest for domestic assault. *American Sociological Review*, 49, 261–272.

Sherman, L. W., & Rogan, D. P. (1995). Effects of gun seizures on gun violence: "Hot spots" patrol in Kansas City. *Justice Quarterly*, 12(4), 673–693.

Sherman, L. W., & Weisburd, D. A. (1995). General deterrent effects of police patrol in crime "hot spots": A randomized, controlled trial. *Justice Quarterly*, 12(4), 625–648.

Sherman, L. W., Schmidt, J. D., Rogan, D. P., & Smith, D. A. (1992). The variable effects of arrest on criminal careers: The Milwaukee domestic violence experiment. *Journal of Criminal Law & Criminology*, 83, 137–169.

The Police Foundation. (1981). *The Newark Foot Patrol Experiment*. Washington, DC: Police Foundation.

Weisburd, D., & Hinkle, J. C. (2012). The importance of randomized experiments in evaluating crime prevention. In D. P. Farrington & B. C. Welsh (Eds), *The Oxford handbook of crime prevention* (pp. 446–465). Oxford: Oxford University Press.

Zimbardo, P. G. (1969). The human choice: Individuation, reason, and order versus deindividuation, impulse, and chaos. *Nebraska Symposium on Motivation*, 17, 237–307.

Index

For Product Safety Concerns and Information please contact our EU
representative GPSR@taylorandfrancis.com
Taylor & Francis Verlag GmbH, Kaufingerstraße 24, 80331 München, Germany

www.ingramcontent.com/pod-product-compliance
Lightning Source LLC
Chambersburg PA
CBHW050332270326
41926CB00016B/3426

9 781032 512815